THE HANDBOOK OF
THE BOND
AND MONEY
MARKETS

By the Author

The Complete Bond Book (1975); 2d rev. ed. (forthcoming)
McGraw-Hill

David M. Darst

THE HANDBOOK OF
THE BOND
AND MONEY
MARKETS

McGraw-Hill Book Company

New York   St. Louis   San Francisco   Auckland   Bogotá
Hamburg   Johannesburg   London   Madrid   Mexico
Montreal   New Delhi   Panama   Paris   São Paulo   Singapore
Sydney   Tokyo   Toronto

Library of Congress Cataloging in Publication Data

Darst, David M, date.
  The handbook of the bond and money markets.
  Includes index.
  1. Bonds—Handbooks, manuals, etc. 2. Investments—
Handbooks, manuals, etc. 3. Money market—Handbooks,
manuals, etc.
  I. Title.
HG4527.D37   332.63'23   80-36816
ISBN 0-07-015401-5

3 4 5 6 7 8 9 O D O D O 8 9 8 7 6 5 4 3 2

The editors for this book were Kiril Sokoloff and Tobia L.
Worth, the designer was Elliot Epstein, and the production
supervisor was Paul A. Malchow. It was set in Garamond by
ComCom.

Printed and bound by R. R. Donnelley & Sons.

With love and gratitude to C.D.E.W.D.
and E.M.D.

Contents

Preface

This book contains a great deal of practical information to aid the reader in the difficult task of investing in fixed-income securities. It furnishes a comprehensive range of tools and concepts specifically designed to (1) provide historical perspective and new insights into the bond and money markets, (2) develop an understanding of the manifold influences acting upon fixed-income issues, (3) analyze the investment behavior and preferences of every significant investor group in bonds and money market instruments, and (4) organize and implement sound and profitable investment strategies.

Rapidly changing developments in the fixed-income securities markets during the past few years have created the need for a book which integrates essential and complete investment information for the practical use of all types of investors. A significant number of new fixed-income securities and investor groups have exerted a meaningful influence on the securities markets, while at the same time the overall volume of extant and newly issued securities has reached new cyclical and secular peaks. Wide fluctuations have occurred in yields, prices, and real rates of return in both the bond and the money markets. The fixed-income securities arena has become much more international in scope and subject to a higher degree of influence by international economic and political conditions. New participants, new investment procedures and tactics, new technological aids, and new regulatory, legal, and tax parameters have vastly increased the range, complexity, and even the character of the fixed-income securities markets. *The Handbook of the Bond and Money Markets* has been written and expressly organized to help the investor become informed about all these new developments.

Numerous important events in 1980 demonstrated the pace, variety, and extent of the changes which fixed-income investors have had to face. These far-reaching occurrences have included: (1) completely revised definitions and release dates by the Federal Reserve System for basic measures of the U.S. money supply; (2) tumultuous market conditions and a virtual cessation of bond-trading activity for several days during the first quarter; (3) the imposition and subsequent relaxation of severe restrictions on borrowing and lending activity throughout the economy; (4) extremely sharp rises and equally dramatic declines in short-term interest rates in the first half of 1980; (5) the highest coupons placed on U.S. government securities since the founding of the American nation; and (6) passage of the Depository Institution Deregulation and Monetary Control Act of 1980, arguably one of the most profound reforms of the American financial system since the 1930s.

The value of *The Handbook of the Bond and Money Markets* derives from its detailed treatment of a broad range of subjects including the analysis of debt statistics and the Flow of Funds Accounts of the Federal Reserve System, the causes and effects of inflation and deflation, the history and calculation methods of major economic and price level indicators, the yield and price relationships of fixed-income securities of various coupons and maturities, the effects of currency changes on realized returns from fixed-income securities, and a wide variety of bond-swapping tactics. In addition, the book describes the following topics:

Investors' ownership of and
trading activities in the
following types of securities

U.S. government securities
Federally sponsored agency issues
Mortgage pool securities
State and local government securities
Corporate and foreign bonds
Mortgages
Consumer credit
Bank loans
Commercial paper
Bankers' acceptances
Federal funds and security repurchase
agreements

Factors determining the investment practices of
the following investor groups

Households	Commercial banks
Trust companies	Savings and loan associations
Foundations	Mutual savings banks
Endowment funds	Credit unions
Union retirement funds	Life insurance companies
Businesses	Property-casualty insurance companies

Closed-end investment companies
State and local governments
Foreign official and
   private investors
United States government
Federally sponsored credit agencies
Federal Reserve System

Private pension funds
State and local government
   employee retirement funds
Finance companies
Real estate investment trusts
Open-end investment companies
Security brokers and dealers

A large number of special analytical features have been brought to bear on each of the areas listed above. Matrices, decision trees, charts, guidelines, graphs, tables, questionnaires, simplified formulas, detailed pragmatic examples, and worksheets are all designed to enhance the usefulness of this book over a long period of time and in any investment climate. In many cases, this book provides the first-known application of such techniques to the current and anticipated problems of fixed-income securities investors. Throughout the book emphasis has been placed on the synthesis of new methods, on explicitness, usefulness, and thoroughness, and on a full description of the risks and disadvantages of each subject under discussion.

The Handbook of the Bond and Money Markets helps the investor solve a number of commonly encountered problems in a detailed, flexible, and efficient manner. With its aid the investor can (1) establish a systematic framework for organizing and critically analyzing economic and investment data from a large number of sources; (2) analyze the relative attractiveness of debt securities within the social, political, and financial environment of the United States or any other nation; (3) identify parallel or contrasting relationships between current inflationary or deflationary market conditions and historical patterns; (4) review and anticipate the effect of external and internal influences on the investment behavior of any investor group in the financial markets; (5) set specific standards of safety in the management of a fixed-income securities portfolio; (6) formulate criteria to scrutinize specific issues on a comparative basis; (7) graphically plot, locate, and project the points of maximum and minimum risk and return for any given maturity, coupon, and interest rate environment; (8) investigate the key components and relative merits of many types of securities swaps; and (9) construct and execute sound and perspicacious strategies over both the short and the long term.

The Handbook of the Bond and Money Markets is intended for a wide audience. It should appeal to all individual and professional investors who desire a comprehensive analysis of fixed-income securities markets, participants, and investment techniques. Individuals who supervise their own funds will have a special interest in this book because of the insights it provides into the activities and actions of all types of investors. Money managers at investment-counseling firms, endowment funds, trust companies, foundations, public and private pension funds, insurance companies, commercial and investment banks, thrift institutions, credit unions, mutual funds, and money market funds will find much detailed information in this book which has application for them.

Securities brokers and dealers, as well as supervisory and regulatory agencies such as the Federal Reserve System, the Securities and Exchange Commission, the Federal Deposit Insurance Corporation, and the Comptroller of the Currency, should appreciate the value of this book in training newly hired personnel and in advancing the knowledge of their professional staffs. Corporate and governmental financial officers will have a dual interest in this book because of their activities both as borrowers of funds through the issuance of bonds, notes, and other securities and as investors of temporarily excess cash in short-term money market instruments of all types. Public and private investors from overseas who place or plan to place funds in the United States, as well as American investors who may invest funds abroad, will have a particular interest in the description of the currency-related aspects of international fixed-income securities. Finally, students in undergraduate and graduate courses dealing with capital markets, corporate finance, business administration, investment banking, commercial banking, insurance, institutional investing, personal financial planning, international finance, and economics will have a keen interest in the ideas, data, and methodology of this book.

It should be pointed out that in the past 10 years the above-mentioned investors and educational groups have become more diversified, more sophisticated, more catholic, and much more discerning in the sources of investment information which they use. Five unifying features of this book should make it appeal to such a diverse group of readers as described here. First, the book has comprehensive and clear coverage of the investment behavior of the participants in the bond and money markets on both an introductory and an advanced level. Second, its primary orientation is toward practicality, with many worksheets and other analytical tools designed for frequent and repeated use by the investor. Third, it takes a broad and historical point of view in examining the range of economic factors which bear upon the course of interest rates and fixed-income securities prices. Fourth, it assembles, for the first time in one place, data and commentary on an extremely broad range of fixed-income–related topics. Fifth, it guides the reader toward the development of reasoned intelligence for operating in the bond and money markets on an ongoing basis. No other book in print incorporates all these features.

The Handbook of the Bond and Money Markets is offered to the user with the conviction that long-term success in investing is impossible without good judgment. Good judgment is an extremely elusive characteristic to define, much less to impart merely through words, numbers, graphs, and tables. Timing, sensitivity to the components of true value in a security and in the market as a whole, a blend of flexibility and conviction, and a keen awareness of the origin, nature, and range of forces which affect the components of the fixed-income universe—these are a few of the components of good investment judgment.

My gratitude cannot be adequately expressed to the many organizations and individuals who have supported and encouraged me in this work. I am much indebted to the research departments and libraries of the Federal Reserve System in Washington, D.C., and in the 12 Federal Reserve District Banks in Atlanta, Boston, Chicago, Cleveland, Dallas, Kansas City, Minneapolis, New York, Philadelphia, Richmond, St. Louis, and San Francisco. I am also pleased to acknowledge the assistance of the editors of *The Money Manager* and *Euromoney* magazines; they have kindly granted me permission to edit substantially and to lengthen considerably articles which I have written for their publications. This material is included in revised form as part of Chapters 12, 14, and 15.

A great number of my business colleagues and superiors have contributed to my learning about the financial markets. Among them are John L. Weinberg, John C. Whitehead, Henry H. Fowler, Howard R. Young, George E. Doty, James P. Gorter, Thomas B. Walker, Jr., Michael H. Coles, Richard L. Menschel, H. Corbin Day, Robert E. Rubin, Eric P. Sheinberg, George M. Van Cleave, Leon G. Cooperman, Roy C. Smith, Roy J. Zuckerberg, Frank P. Smeal, James C. Kautz, and Gary M. Wenglowski. I could not have had more stimulating associates than my fellow team members in Zurich, London, Tokyo, and New York. They have been helpful, engaging, and sensitive.

I would like to remember and thank my family, my professional counterparts, and my friends who have so profoundly inspired and sustained me in the research and writing of this book. I am deeply thankful for their counsel. Especially important have been Nathaniel de Rothschild, Robert L. Louis-Dreyfus, Thierry J. Lovenbach, the Viscount Bridport, E. Robert Wassman, Martin J. Pring, William Hodson Mogan, Mark B. Dayton, Jeremy Soames, and Kiril Sokoloff.

This book is intended to fortify the investment skills of a wide audience over the course of many market cycles. I wish the reader much success in investing with the aid of *The Handbook of the Bond and Money Markets.*

DAVID M. DARST

*Introduction to the
Bond and Money Markets*

1

Introduction

Purpose and Scope of This Book

This guide is intended to provide detailed information on the wide array of short-term and long-term fixed-income issues and the principal groups of investors in these securities. *The Handbook of the Bond and Money Markets* also aims to help the reader form a flexible, objective, and discerning framework for analyzing both the historical developments and the new trends which affect the marketplace.

Such a system should permit a balanced perspective on (1) both short-term and long-term trends, (2) both domestic and international forces, (3) all sectors of the fixed-income securities markets, and (4) all participants in the fixed-income arena. A key objective of this book is to help the investor isolate and recognize both recurring and previously unencountered patterns and factors which are expected to wield significant influence on the yields and prices of fixed-income securities. The book should strengthen the ability of the investor to deal with and profit from a great variety of rapidly shifting market conditions, while at the same time remaining aware of the risks inherent in any chosen course of portfolio strategy.

There are four sections. Section 1 contains an introduction to the bond and money markets and gives a broad overview of the size, growth rate, and segmentation of the fixed-income securities universe. Methods of analyzing data about the debt markets also are included.

Section 2 describes the forces affecting the bond and money markets. Particular emphasis is placed on the role of inflation and deflation in (*a*) moving the overall level of interest rates upward or downward and (*b*) influencing the real rates of return derived from fixed-income securities investments. In addition, Section 2 analyzes the configurations of financial intermediation which have evolved in the domestic and international financial system as well as the patterns of investment which have shaped the markets for each major type of fixed-income security.

Section 3 reviews in detail the participants in the bond and money markets. Following the classification format used in the Flow of Funds Accounts of the Federal Reserve System, this section examines each of the significant external and internal factors which determine the investment behavior of households, businesses, governmental bodies, international entities, commercial banks, savings institutions, credit unions, insurance companies, pension funds, finance companies, Real Estate Investment Trusts, mutual funds, money market funds, and security brokers and dealers. Whenever one of these categories encompasses more than one principal type of investor (for example, the insurance companies category includes both life insurance companies and property-casualty insurance companies), each classification is treated separately.

Section 4 describes a large number of fundamental and sophisticated techniques for investing in the bond and money markets. Yield and price relationships are thoroughly examined and charted for several hundred types of fixed-income securities. Bond-swapping procedures, the effects of currency changes, and international bond markets are explored in depth by both conventional forms of analysis and many new analytical methods such as bond matrices and decision trees. This section concludes with a detailed review of the process of developing and implementing successful fixed-income investment strategies under varying market conditions. The final chapter of the book contains a carefully selected compendium of more than 150 official and private sources of further information on the topics contained in *The Handbook of the Bond and Money Markets.* It includes periodicals, books, articles, special studies, and many other sources of pragmatic knowledge and advice on fixed-income securities and markets.

Special Features of This Book

As mentioned earlier, this book contains a large number of special features that are of particular value to the investor because of their originality, practicality, comprehensiveness, and application to a broad range of market circumstances. A representative but by no means all-encompassing sample of these features and their location in the book are shown in Table 1-1. This list of 22 special features is meant merely to indicate the range of topics covered in individual chapters. Numerous other guidelines, concepts, and teaching aids are located throughout the book.

TABLE 1-1

Representative List of Special Features Contained in the Guide to the Bond and Money Markets

Chapter number	Description of special feature
2	A worksheet lists 26 factors for strategically analyzing the degree of favorableness in the environment for investing in fixed-income securities. Such factors include (1) federal, state, and local government policies, (2) international conditions, (3) the social and political background, and (4) economic and financial circumstances.
2	Interest rate charts show the historical development of yield levels on four series of long-term bonds and three series of short-term instruments since the 1930s.
3	Tables and charts show the amount of debt outstanding in the United States since 1900, both on an aggregate basis and by major groups of borrowers.
3	A worksheet provides comments on seven broad analytical paths for evaluating and organizing debt statistics.
4	Charts and tables display the course of price level changes in the United States since 1800 and in the United Kingdom and other countries over longer and shorter time periods.
4	A detailed description outlines the methods of construction of the consumer and producer price indices, the implicit price deflator of the gross national product, various measures of the unemployment rate, and the labor force participation rate.
4, 5	Matrices provide a comparison of (1) price level changes with purchasing-power changes and (2) the effects of various rates of inflation and deflation on the realized purchasing power of financial instruments over various lengths of time.
5	More than 20 causes and effects of inflation and deflation are investigated from the viewpoint of the investor in fixed-income securities.
6	A statistical analysis surveys the largest and most rapidly growing investor groups during various time periods in the post-World War II era.
6	More than 25 factors covering such areas as taxation, regulatory constraints, liquidity preferences, and legal structure are analyzed to determine their impact on any specific investor group.
7	Matrices and charts display the classification conventions and methodology of the Flow of Funds Accounts and the largest and most rapidly growing categories of credit market instruments during various time periods since World War II.

TABLE 1-1

Representative List of Special Features Contained in the Guide to the Bond and Money Markets *(Continued)*

Chapter number	Description of special feature
8, 9, 10, 11	More than 60 charts and tables portray the principal earning assets and funds flows of each of the 20 major public and private, domestic and international investor groups contained in the Flow of Funds Accounts during various time periods of the post-World War II era.
12	Actual and percentage bond price changes for more than 550 combinations of beginning yield level, coupons, maturities, and interest rate shifts have been calculated and exhibited in several different tables for ease of reference by the investor.
12	Decision trees have been constructed to show the degree of relative influence which various configurations of coupon, maturity, and beginning yield level have on bond price changes.
13	More than 55 examples of incremental bond price shifts have been calculated to show the interactive effects and ratios of changed yield levels, maturities, and coupons.
14	A bond matrix shows the yield, maturity, issuer, and relative valuation of 64 bonds; several case examples have been included to demonstrate practical applications of the matrix.
14	A worksheet lists and analyzes 30 income, capital position, safety, quality, maturity, market condition and currency outlook, and special and technical factors which determine the objectives of a fixed-income investor.
14	A worksheet reviews 25 critical criteria for evaluating the differentials between the securities involved in a specific swap transaction.
14	Several tables show (1) the effects of transactions costs on yield to maturity, (2) semiannual yield equivalents compared with annual yield equivalents, and (3) the effects of exchange rate movements on yields to maturity for more than 400 combinations of coupon, maturity, and magnitude and timing of a given currency change.
15	Three separate tables list (1) 46 factors that influence the choice of a fixed-income security, (2) 40 features which determine the value of a specific fixed-income issue, and (3) 36 factors which affect overall yield levels and/or sectoral yield levels.
15	A table with 12 factors shows an actual example of the process of forecasting the direction and level of interest rates.
15	A matrix demonstrates in detail how to translate an expected interest rate scenario into (1) a portfolio strategy response and (2) specific percentage breakdowns of a fixed-income securities portfolio at the end of selected future time periods.

Recent Developments Which Underscore the Relevance of This Book to the Bond and Money Markets

Many developments during the past few years have intensified the need for a book such as this handbook. A few of these trends are grouped together under the same headings as the four sections of this book and described in the following paragraphs.

Introduction to the Bond and Money Markets

In recent years, economic and financial news have received much greater prominence than in immediately preceding periods. Today much wider attention is focused on the effects of inflation and deflation, currency changes, economic growth, corporate profitability, interest rates, and monetary and fiscal policies. Political debates have been conducted over such questions as interest rate ceilings, usury laws, the proper rates of growth of the public sector versus the private sector, and the appropriateness of incentives to savings and investment. All these issues influence or are influenced by the functioning of the bond and money markets; yet the problems and solutions are complex and far-reaching. This book helps the investor to establish a system for analyzing and reacting to these changes.

The last half of the 1970s witnessed an acceleration in the growth rates of borrowing by corporations, individuals, governments, and foreign entities. Such debt issuance very often followed new channels of intermediation and forced investors and creditors to reexamine the regularly released data from the Federal Reserve Board as well as the very processes of statistical collection, reporting, and analysis for fixed-income securities. This task was further complicated by the blurring of distinctions between various forms of credit instruments, between certain sectors of the domestic and international financial markets, and between categories of investors. The issuance in the late 1970s of U.S. Treasury bonds denominated in foreign currencies (also known as Carter bonds), the appearance of Yankee bonds, and the spread of the Eurocurrency and Eurocapital markets frequently contributed to this growth and indefinability. This guide dwells on the problems and means of obtaining and correctly defining debt statistics before making investment decisions.

Forces Affecting the Bond and Money Markets

Under generally more volatile market conditions, new cyclical and secular peaks in yields have been attained in recent years. At the same time, the risks and effects of high inflation and/or severe deflationary forces have received much greater consideration from all groups of investors and borrowers. On November 1, 1978, and again on October 6, 1979, the Federal Reserve Board adopted strong monetary measures (and in the latter case new operating-policy targets) which were in large part motivated by international considerations. This book devotes particular attention to the effects of inflation, deflation, and international influences on fixed-income securities markets.

Among the most notable of the forces affecting the bond and money markets has been the proliferation of new types of credit market instruments. Such securities include floating-rate notes and certificates of deposit, variable-interest-rate mortgages, Eurobonds and Yankee bonds, mortgage-backed bonds, conventional mortgage pass-through certificates, tax-exempt housing bonds, money market certificates, and loan participation certificates. In addition, a much greater variety of terms has appeared on many individual issues, permitting contractable or extendable maturities and new features relating to callability, purchase funds (which allow bonds to be purchased for sinking-fund purposes up to a specified amount and generally only if they are trading below par), sinking funds, coupons, and even currency repayment and indexation options. Such a wide variety of novel terms and security characteristics has created many profitable swap opportunities, but at the same time it has complicated the task of properly comparing one issue with another. Swapping guidelines and evaluation worksheets have been included in this book to assist the investor in such activity on an ongoing basis.

Participants in the Bond and Money Markets

New groups of financial intermediaries, including money market funds, tax-exempt bond funds, and captive insurance companies, have been formed or have risen to significant size in the past decade. Other financial intermediaries have greatly altered the relative mix of their funding sources to include such avenues as the federal funds market, security repurchase agreements, large certificates of deposit, the Eurocurrency markets, the sale of loans, and special borrowings from other institutions. An increasing ability and willingness to pass on incremental interest rate costs to ultimate borrowers, greater employment of arbitraging and hedging activities, and changes in the tax, legal, and regulatory environment have led to new attitudes and new patterns in the behavior of many groups of investors. This book dissects and interprets the course of these movements since the early 1950s.

Investing in the Bond and Money Markets

Many new developments must be taken into account before investing. The reach of these occurrences ranges from the constraints imposed by the Employee Retirement Income Security Act of 1974 (ERISA) to the widely publicized financial difficulties of some major borrowers in the 1970s and to the new operating policies of the Federal Reserve Board in place at the beginning of the 1980s. These factors are important not only because of their influence on the investor's own portfolio strategy but also because of their anticipated impact on the portfolio movements of many other investor groups and on the likely direction which official policies may take to counteract or reinforce such events.

The advent of a wide variety of interest rate futures on both short-term and long-term fixed-income securities has also opened up new side effects in the marketplace and new investment techniques. Increased emphasis on such analytical concepts as duration and immunization is also bringing about new investment methods and market conduct. Finally, technological advances for the use of the investor (such as pocket yield calculators and minicomputers) and for the benefit of the marketplace (such as instantaneous dissemination of prices, relative valuations, and other information over video communications systems) have helped identify swap opportunities. These new parameters and many other influences can all be analyzed within the structured approach of this book to (1) evaluate the investment environment, (2) set portfolio strategy, and (3) select specific securities.

2

Perspective on Debt Markets

Overview

In recent years, investors have faced a complex array of developments in virtually every sector of the securities markets, the domestic and international economy, and society itself. Powerful inflationary and deflationary forces have often seemed to operate in rapid succession or even simultaneously, vastly complicating the task of the investor: to preserve and augment portfolio capital.

Not many market participants have been prescient about or prepared for the changes which have taken place. Even fewer have fully appreciated the extent of the differences between a given period of years and the span of time immediately preceding or succeeding it. In the United States, the 1950s were characterized by relatively low levels of outstanding debt and a strong growth in the demand for goods and services. The economic upswing of the early 1960s gave way to times of recession and credit stringency, in 1966, again in 1970, and in 1974–1975, the last-named period exhibiting the longest and steepest decline in economic activity in the postwar era to that point. Early 1980 also witnessed the onset of recessionary conditions.

Other sorts of financial problems began to surface in the 1970s. Financing difficulties of Real Estate Investment Trusts (REITs) in 1974–1975 were followed by the municipal finance problems of New York in late 1975 and in 1976. Cyclical pressures also manifested themselves in the marketplace during the 1970s. A cyclical high of 13.75 percent for the federal funds rate was reached in 1974, but even this level was substantially surpassed in early 1980, when federal funds traded at a rate of more than 19.2 percent.

Such unprecedentedly high interest rates, amid conditions of greatly increased price volatility and reduced trading liquidity for a substantial percentage of fixed-income securities, were stimulated by several major policy changes initiated by the Federal Reserve Board to curb credit expansion more directly. In addition, differences in yield between bonds of differing creditworthiness widened considerably in the wake of Federal Reserve Board actions in 1979, recalling the difficult market conditions of 1975. In 1975 the yield spread between high-quality and low-quality issues reached the widest levels since the early 1930s. Figure 2-1 below shows the yield spread between corporate bonds with Aaa ratings and corporate bonds with Baa ratings for the period from the late 1920s to the early 1980s.

The events of these alternating periods of growth and retrenchment, of relative calm and relative strain, have displayed many previously unwitnessed patterns of economic behavior. Even during the three recessionary periods of the 1965–1975 decade, the inflation rate dropped only moderately, with the result that the United States gross national product (GNP) as measured in current dollars did not slow nearly so much as the real GNP, and in some cases it kept rising right through the recessionary phase of the business cycle.

In a number of industrial countries, an even lengthier period than in the United States was required to rein in inflation on a cyclical basis after the worldwide boom of the early and middle 1970s. In some nations, governments were able to dampen price rises only through wage-price controls and/or the maintenance of an overvalued currency exchange rate.

Beginning in the early 1970s, extremely large transfers of wealth took place from oil-consuming nations to oil-producing countries. This process continued throughout the decade. The burgeoning Eurocurrency markets served as intermediaries in financing the balance-of-payments deficits of many oil-importing nations as their total indebtedness mounted dramatically. The 1960s and 1970s also saw an increasing percentage of total United States government outlays represented by transfers, in the form of social security payments, revenue sharing, and health, education, and welfare spending. Dislocations such as periodically recurring financial crises, as well as the coexistence of high unemployment and high inflation, changed the attitude of the public about the efficacy of corrective economic efforts by government.

Remedial forces of varying strength and duration have often followed such periods of economic excess or structural weakness. For example, between early 1975 and early 1977 greater conservatism on the part of both borrowers and investors led to greater emphasis on improved credit standing and more attainable and cautious investment performance objectives. Some of the shifts which counterbalance more fundamentally rooted and longer-term conditions have taken effect more gradually. The late 1970s witnessed the beginnings of movements (if not more substantive actions) in favor of more realistic economic and social expectations and stronger investor and taxpayer demands for greater accountability by all levels of government for moneys under public stewardship.

Market participants now have many computer-assisted analytical techniques and other tools at their disposal to evaluate all types of fixed-income securities and to help predict the future level of interest rates. Such scrutiny was not brought to bear on the investment process 10 or 20 years ago. Partly because of low absolute interest levels and the relatively small variability of long-term interest rates, investors paid little close attention to interest movements. More recently, in part because of higher interest levels and greater volatility in interest patterns, investors, corporate executives, union officials, central bankers, government leaders, economists, and others have carefully observed the fluctuations of interest rates. In addition, a large part of these investors' increased attention to predicting the course of interest rates stems from the potentially large profits or losses associated with declining or rising yield levels.

Yet many investors have not made similar progress in their ability to relate investment decisions to the large-scale intermediate- and long-term influences on their portfolios. For the fixed-income securities investor, it is vitally important to recognize structural changes and their degree of influence in the political, social, financial, and international spheres. It is equally crucial to develop an understanding of how the current market environment and investor dispositions toward fixed-income securities fit into cyclical and secular phases of economic and investment activity. Only after an awareness of historical relationships and long-term influences has been cultivated can the investor properly focus on the detailed analysis of specific securities.

It is difficult to predict the changes which the 1980s and the 1990s will bring to investor psychology and the financial markets. One unanticipated development which occurred with increasing force and frequency during the 1970s was a tendency for financial markets to react with greater and greater speed to domestic and international developments. At the same time, investors began to discount the effects not only of these developments but also of the countervailing policy actions which were expected to follow in their train. For example, recessionary economic signals (which in earlier decades had often implied higher fixed-income securities prices because of lower interest rates) came to be viewed *negatively* rather than positively by bond and money market participants because of fears that the monetary and fiscal stimulus applied to *counteract* the expected recession would lead to higher inflation rates, higher interest rates, and thus *lower* fixed-income securities prices.

As an aid to the investor in analyzing the investment environment, an investment worksheet (Table 2-1) with examples of some of the questions which the investor should consider is included at the end of the chapter. Depending upon the circumstances at the time when the analysis is undertaken, certain areas can be given greater or lesser emphasis. The investor is encouraged to use the worksheet merely as a starting point for the inclusion of additional topics and question areas.

Recent Developments

Changes in the Investment Community

The changing economic background has led to a variety of new and some-times-interrelated developments among investors, issuers, governmental bodies, securities brokerage firms, dealers, and commercial banks. For example, passage of the Employee Retirement Income Security Act of 1974 (ERISA) has heightened awareness of the role and potential liabilities of fiduciary institutions in the management of pension and retirement funds. In turn, this has brought about an emphasis on prudence, conservatism, and predictability in investment selection. A related effect has led to a more professional analysis of the fixed-income securities markets, larger flows of capital into bonds and other fixed-income securities, and, in some cases, more active management and higher levels of turnover for the fixed-income sector of investors' portfolios.

Other groups of investors have stepped up their involvement in fixed-income securities. For instance, foreign and international investors expanded their total ownership of U.S. Treasury issues from $11 billion at the beginning of 1970 to more than $120 billion at the end of the decade. Individual investors purchased an estimated $30 billion worth of U.S. government issues in 1978, or almost 3 times the level of their 1977 purchases. Individuals invested roughly 16 percent of total disposable household savings in all classes of marketable fixed-income securities in 1976, 23 percent in 1977, and close to 30 percent in 1978.

Participants in the fixed-income markets have become more diversified, more sophisticated, and more demanding in the services they require from the securities brokerage firms and commercial banks through which they transact business. At a time when the total roster of securities firms has been declining, a small number of new firms have been founded to specialize in independent research, analysis of monetary policy, and other fixed-income investment services. Whereas only one firm was trading Government National Mortgage Association (GNMA; "Ginnie Mae") securities in 1970, more than 20 firms were thus engaged by 1980.

Similarly, the number of recognized primary government bond dealers reporting to the Federal Reserve Bank of New York rose from 20 firms in the late 1960s to almost 40 dealers by the late 1970s. This expansion has aided and accompanied higher levels of overall trading activity. Among primary government bond dealers alone, average daily turnover in U.S. government securities rose from more than $2.5 billion in 1970 to $13.2 billion in 1979. Beginning in the mid-1970s, favorable trading conditions in the bond markets led to higher salaries for and enlargements of fixed-income securities sales and trading staffs.

The greater number of participating firms in the fixed-income securities business then began to create more intense competition and lower trading spreads. When periods of declining fixed-income securities prices were encountered, profit margins became even narrower and some losses occurred. Many firms instituted tighter controls on the capital commitment process and limited the size of positions which their traders were allowed to carry. In addition, growing use was made of the newly developed interest rate futures markets to hedge positions and control risk. The whole process of upgrading administrative and position management procedures, together with advances in settlement and transfer operations, has continued to improve the structure and functioning of the secondary trading markets in fixed-income securities during recent years.

A new but important element in the gradual restructuring of the marketplace has been the rapid development of financial centers in the Far East and Europe and their greater degree of interconnection with New York and other principal financial centers in the United States. In spite of the increased degree of international technological and financial interchange, signs of greater emphasis on national concerns at the expense of international cooperation had begun to appear by the early 1980s. This trend was caused in part by widely differing inflation rates, governmental policies, economic growth patterns, and energy dependence.

Changes among Borrowers

While transitions and innovations have been taking place in the domestic and international investment community, numerous changes have also occurred among the borrowers of money in the economy. New types of securities and borrowing arrangements have been created to meet the needs of issuers and investors, to finance extremely large capital projects, to take advantage of changing tax laws or other regulatory legislation, or to adapt to prevailing market conditions. Among other instruments, negotiable certificates of deposit, GNMA pass-through issues (which brought the mortgage markets and debt securities markets closer together), and various types of Eurocurrency securities were developed in the 1960s. In the 1970s, some of the new fixed-income instruments which appeared included floating-rate notes and certificates of deposit, variable-interest-rate mortgages, Yankee bonds, tax-exempt housing bonds, mortgage-backed bonds, conventional mortgage pass-through securities, money market certificates, and loan participation certificates.

On October 1, 1979, the Bankruptcy Reform Act of 1978 went into effect, with extensive ramifications for both borrowers and lenders of funds. This bankruptcy legislation had several main elements including (1) consolidation of the previous Roman-numeral–designated bankruptcy law Chapters X, XI, and XII into a more streamlined Chapter 11 (designated by Arabic numerals), (2) provision of several new protective tools to assist creditors to the business sector, and (3) establishment of new federal exemptions (subject to official actions at the state level) which allow consumer debtors to retain greater amounts of personal property after declaring bankruptcy.

Other market changes have involved financing strategy. During the past 30 years, corporations have demonstrated an increasing reliance on debt of shorter maturities, with cyclical reversals in this trend after periods of significant economic and financial difficulty. For example, after the credit deterioration in 1974 and 1975, in which debt maturity structures were shortened further, debt-equity ratios declined, and debt maintenance capacity (the margin of revenues and income levels over scheduled repayments of principal and interest) was impaired, corporations took measures over the next couple of years to restructure their balance sheets. Beginning in 1975 and throughout 1976, businesses issued large amounts of long-term debt and equity securities and significantly reduced or repaid portions of their short-term debt such as commercial bank loans. While the secular trend since the early 1950s toward short-term–financing sources was thus shifted briefly, the total amount of corporate external financing moved from $40 billion in 1975 to $61 billion in 1976, $87 billion in 1977, $98 billion in 1978, and $124 billion in 1979.

The fulfillment of social needs has also stimulated new financing forms and the issuance of greater amounts of debt securities. From the mid-1950s to the mid-1970s, state and local expenditures (exclusive of federal aid) grew more rapidly than any other sector of the economy, at a compound annual growth rate of 7.4 percent in the first 10 years and 11.6 percent in the second 10 years. By 1975 state and local government spending represented 15 percent of total GNP, a postwar peak. This rise in municipal outlays was accompanied by newly formulated securities offerings for municipal bond banks, education and health care facilities, industrial revenue and pollution control projects, and a multitude of housing, transportation, and other public needs.

In the middle and late 1970s, owing to higher income levels and to a perceived expectation of continued price appreciation for the property being purchased, households altered some of their borrowing practices. Individuals and families expanded the amount and, in some cases without selling their existing homes, extended the maturity of their mortgage loans (which represent approximately three-quarters of total consumer indebtedness). A portion of such mortgage debt extensions was often diverted into consumer spending, and this phenomenon contributed to the consistently stronger-than-expected expansion in economic activity during the period from 1975 to 1979.

A large percentage of loan maturities on new automobiles was lengthened from 24 to 48 months. Other lending institutions facilitated the process of consumer credit extension through such mechanisms as revolving-credit agreements and overdraft facilities in checking accounts. The ratio of total consumer credit outstanding to total annual personal income moved from 3.3 percent in 1947 to 8.9 percent in 1955, 10.6 percent in 1960, 12.4 percent in 1965, 12.1 percent in 1970, 12.2 percent in 1975, and 20.2 percent in 1979. Total new household borrowing in the mortgage and consumer credit markets rose from $49 billion in 1975 to $88 billion in 1976, $135 billion in 1977, $155 billion in 1978, and $159 billion in 1979.

Along with the increasing amounts of debt liabilities due to changes in corporate, governmental, and individual financing behavior during the 1970s, the servicing costs of this debt also rose owing to the gradual dismantling of many types of controls over interest rates. Relaxation of interest rate ceilings on many types of savings deposits, upward modification of many mortgage rate ceilings, and legalized circumvention of coupon ceilings on large amounts of U.S. Treasury issues led to yield levels which more accurately mirrored actual and expected inflation rates than had yield levels in earlier periods. In somewhat of a vicious circle, the removal or vitiation of these interest rate ceilings, coupled with a vastly more efficient capital market mechanism, helped finance and maintain higher levels of inflation than would have been possible otherwise.

The Role of Debt and Capital Adequacy

The substantial growth of debt, particularly in the 1960s and throughout most of the 1970s, has raised questions concerning the proper amounts and uses of debt as well as the availability of enough debt and equity funds to meet the future capital requirements of the national economy. Borrowing in any form represents a commitment to future repayment of the debt incurred. With the capital thus raised from the investing and saving sectors of the economy, the borrower can consume and/or produce more than would otherwise have been possible.

Provided that excessive amounts of debt are not assumed, with resultant impairment of liquidity and financial safety, and provided that an appropriate and salubrious mix of debt is maintained in the economy for the purposes of greater *future production* (and thus the ability to service and repay debt) as against greater *current consumption,* debt can powerfully assist the development of higher overall living standards and wealth levels.

Investors and borrowers alike should keep in mind the substantial risks, as well as the benefits, which can result from an overreliance on debt. Ability to withstand periods of financial stress, at any level and in any sector of an economic system, is thus lessened. All market participants should set and periodically evaluate standards of safety in the management of their investment and financial affairs.

Future credit requirements, capital needs, and debt growth depend upon the willingness of borrowers to assume greater debt burdens and on lenders' perceptions of borrowers' ability to meet repayments of principal, interest, and other debt covenants in a timely fashion. The degree of inflation or deflation, the outlook for overall economic activity, the tax treatment of debt, confidence levels, psychological considerations, and a number of other fundamental factors also have an important influence on the supply and demand for debt funds.

The ability of the United States economy to generate enough investment capital to meet realistic future growth and employment goals will be determined by several considerations. During periods of sustained high rates of inflation, there is little incentive for households to save but much incentive to consume. Decisions also have to be made concerning the degree and rate of desired expansion of the public sector relative to the private sector. When the government runs large budget deficits at the same time that the economy approaches full employment, savings and capital are shifted away from the private sector.

Voters and lawmakers have to target proper levels of short-term consumption which permit higher investment and economic growth rates over the longer term. Tax policies must be structured so as to induce greater savings and investment by investors and to promote higher rates of capital formation by the productive borrowing sectors. While there is little that the investor can do to influence these decisions in the short run, it is worthwhile to ponder these issues and their secular effects upon the fixed-income securities markets.

Interest Rates

Function and Influence

Interest rates play a pivotal role in the bond and money markets. For the investor or lender, interest rates constitute a return on capital advanced to securities issuers and borrowers. The level of interest rates thus has a crucial impact on how much capital is provided to which seekers of funds. For example, in the late 1970s a number of state legislatures repealed or substantially raised interest rate ceilings (also known as usury ceilings). These changes were enacted in response to voter pressure, because market interest rates on certain types of consumer loans had risen above the stated ceilings and many finance companies and commercial banks therefore had sharply curtailed their consumer lending. By stipulating a preference for the availability of funds at market interest rates rather than substantially reduced funds under interest rate ceilings, consumers confirmed the important position which interest rates occupy in the capital allocation process and in many phases of economic and financial activity.

Changes in interest rates also exert an important influence on the equity markets. Interest levels are a major determinant of stock price-earnings ratios through the discount rate used to value an expected dividend stream. In addition, interest expenses affect corporate profits and thus to some degree the absolute level of stock prices. The costs of purchasing stock on margin also rise and fall with upward and downward swings in interest rates. Finally, interest returns from competing financial instruments influence the relative attractiveness of holding common stocks.

When adjusted to comparable computation bases, interest rates provide an effective measure for comparing a wide range of investments. For the debt issuer or borrower, interest rates constitute an expense which helps determine whether it is economically worthwhile to make direct or portfolio investments or to purchase such items as a house or an automobile. In general, low levels of interest rates usually tend to stimulate economic activity by reducing the propensity of capital suppliers to save more and capital users to spend less. In periods of very rapid inflation, however, these conditions do not hold true. This latter topic is discussed at greater length in Chapter 5.

A number of other factors determine the degree of influence which higher or lower interest rates can have on economic activity. These include but are not limited to (1) interest rates outside the United States, (2) conditions in the equity and mortgage markets, (3) the current status and trend in liquidity positions of corporations and other major borrowers, (4) the structure of interest rates (also known as the yield curve), (5) the degree of disintermediation or reintermediation in the economy, (6) the availability of funds for borrowers and investors, (7) the pace of innovation in payments technology and other parts of the financial system, and (8) the liberalization or tightening of credit terms at financial institutions which supply funds.

An important characteristic of interest rates is their interrelatedness. Even though they do not always move in tandem, short-term rates influence long-term rates, and vice versa. Each sector of the credit markets can affect or be affected by the other sectors. For example, interest rates on corporate bonds can be moved upward or downward by interest rate levels and financing pressures in the government bond market, the mortgage market, the municipal bond market, and other parts of the long-term credit markets such as the private-placement market or the Eurobond market. The last-named sector became a more important influence beginning in the mid-1960s and continuing through the late 1970s. The greater degree of internationalization of American credit and capital markets has added numerous external and often incompletely understood forces to the workings of the domestic financial system.

Interest Rate Movements

For the 100 years prior to the mid-1960s, the American economy experienced a period of relatively stable long-term interest rates for high-quality securities. Prior to the large secular rises in interest rates which began in the 1970s, the major exceptions to this record of stability occurred in 1920 and again in the early 1930s, particularly on lower-rated bonds. As shown in Figure 2-1, which depicts long-term bond yields for four groups of securities, in 1930 and 1931 Baa-rated corporate bonds experienced a sharp upward movement in yields while Aaa-rated corporate bonds exhibited a much more modest rate rise, followed by a continuation of the interest rate decline which had begun in 1920.

Although analysis of short-term yield patterns often presents problems because of the influence of various legislative and policy actions on short-term interest rates and financing patterns, it is nevertheless useful to observe short-term interest rates at the same time that long-term rates are being examined. Figure 2-2 portrays short-term interest rates from the late 1920s to the early 1980s.

Even though short-term interest rates occasionally moved to very high levels during periods of financial duress, high-quality long-term interest rates generally fluctuated between 3.5 and 4.5 percent in the 100-year span of time beginning in the mid-1860s, with the highest level for a high-quality long-term bond in this period being reached in 1920.

The interest rate experience from the beginning of the twentieth century until the early 1980s can be divided into three principal phases. From 1900 to 1920 highest-quality corporate bond yields exhibited a generally rising trend, from 3.25 percent upward to 5.56 percent. From 1920 to 1946 highest-quality corporate bond yields demonstrated a generally falling trend, moving downward from 5.56 to 2.37 percent, with the much lower average yields for this period traceable to the depressed economic conditions of the 1930s and the artificially low interest rates achieved to help finance American involvement in the Second World War. Since 1947 there have been substantial rises in interest rates interrupted by relatively small cyclical declines. The yields of highest-quality corporate bonds have generally moved upward, from 2.37 percent in 1947 to well over 12 percent on highest-quality long-term securities in 1980, when the 3-month Treasury bill rate (an indicator of highest-quality short-term interest levels) also reached 15.6 percent.

From observation of the history of interest rates in the United States in the twentieth century, it can *generally* be stated that interest rates have been at low levels and trending downward in periods of economic retrenchment. During periods of economic growth, interest rates tend to be at high levels and trending upward. Notable exceptions include (1) the relatively high interest rates during the first 12 months of the 1920–1921 recession, (2) the

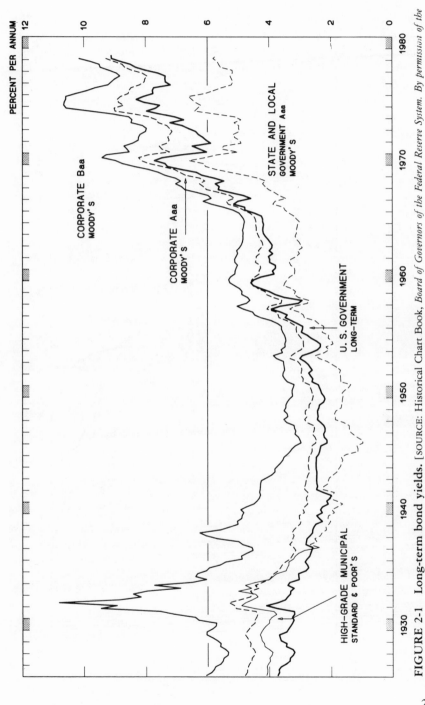

FIGURE 2-1 Long-term bond yields. [SOURCE: Historical Chart Book, *Board of Governors of the Federal Reserve System. By permission of the Board of Governors of the Federal Reserve System.*]

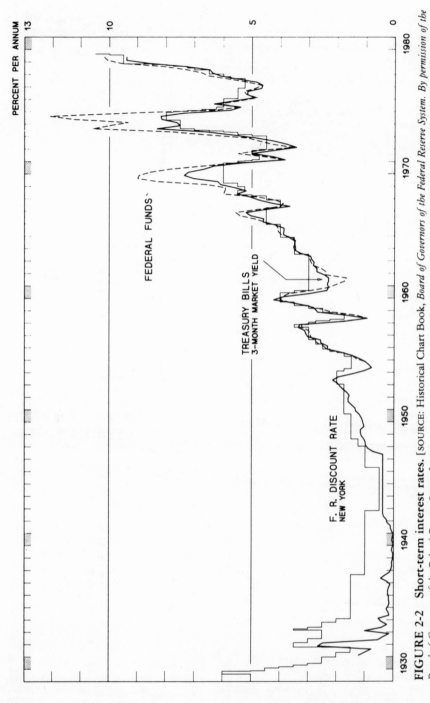

FIGURE 2-2 Short-term interest rates. [SOURCE: Historical Chart Book, *Board of Governors of the Federal Reserve System. By permission of the Board of Governors of the Federal Reserve System.*]

interest rate uptrend during the severe 1931 economic decline (particularly on medium- and lower-quality securities), and (3) the relatively low interest rates during the period of strong economic growth after the Second World War.

By a period varying from several weeks to many months, major changes in the direction of interest rates tend to precede or follow actual upward or downward economic turning points. This has been particularly evident in recent years. For example, for quite a number of months after the officially agreed-upon starting point of the 1974–1975 recession, municipal and corporate bond yields continued to move upward.

TABLE 2-1
Strategic Analysis of the Investment Environment

WORKSHEET

For each of the categories listed in this worksheet, factors which influence a given investment environment have been included. The investor should investigate whether each factor tends to cause an improvement or a deterioration in the investment environment for financial assets in general and for fixed-income securities in particular. Of special importance is the need to recognize that certain factors can act either in concert, producing an even stronger influence on the investment climate, or in counterbalanced fashion, producing a substantially mitigated or even neutral effect upon the investment environment.

In applying this worksheet to practical investment problems, it is often difficult to measure precisely the absolute condition and trend of many factors. A high degree of subjectivity and a large number of diverse sources of information (from court rulings to public opinion surveys) can frequently affect the investor's judgment of how some of these factors influence the secular attractiveness or unattractiveness of fixed-income securities.

Category	Likely degree of influence
FEDERAL, STATE, AND LOCAL GOVERNMENT ACTIONS	
1. Degree of actual and perceived success and degree of reliance on the public versus the private sector in solving economic problems and in meeting the socioeconomic needs of the population	_____
2. Absolute level of taxes and government expenditures and the degree of equity and incentive in the tax structure	_____
3. Confidence in leadership of major governmental institutions and agencies	_____

TABLE 2-1
Strategic Analysis of the Investment Environment *(Continued)*

Category	Likely degree of influence
4. Degree of legislative, administrative, and regulatory involvement in investment, savings, production, consumption, wages, and prices	_____
5. Responsiveness and appropriateness of monetary, fiscal, and currency exchange rate policies during various stages of the economic cycle	_____
INTERNATIONAL ELEMENTS	
1. Economic, military, and financial position of the country relative to other nations or blocs of countries in the world	_____
2. Degree of dependence on other countries for security, raw materials, finished products, access to geographic areas, or other critical resources	_____
3. Amount of protectionist sentiment within country or in other countries restricting the cross-border flow of goods and capital	_____
SOCIAL ELEMENTS	
1. Attitude of the population toward work versus leisure, savings versus consumption, and stability versus change	_____
2. Degree of reliance on group effort versus individual effort to accomplish societal goals	_____
3. Position of capital formation and wealth accumulation in public opinion	_____
4. Degree of enforcement of ethical standards	_____
5. Direction of change in norms of behavior in relationships between the individual and government, business, other groups, and other individuals	_____
6. Form and availability of aftertax stimuli to reward energy, ingenuity, and technological advances	_____

TABLE 2-1
Strategic Analysis of the Investment Environment *(Continued)*

Category	Likely degree of influence
POLITICAL ELEMENTS	
1. Forms and degree of competition between rival political groups	_____
2. Stability of political institutions and means of effecting political change	_____
3. Appropriateness and responsiveness of political structure to personal characteristics, historical legacy, and demographics of the population	_____
4. Ability of any individual sector of society to impose its will upon other sectors	_____
ECONOMIC ELEMENTS	
1. Attitude toward risk taking by portfolio and direct investors	_____
2. Return on investment and profitability of business	_____
3. Ability of business and investors to balance long-term goals with short-term objectives	_____
4. Amount of capital being raised by all types of borrowers for purposes of production versus consumption	_____
FINANCIAL ELEMENTS	
1. Robustness of the financial system and soundness of all types of borrowers' financial structures	_____
2. Degree of trust on the part of debtors and creditors that their counterparts will uphold their respective contractual duties	_____
3. Realism in investors' performance objectives	_____
4. Strength of investor confidence and state of investor psychology	_____

3

The Analysis of Debt Statistics

Overview

When analyzing aggregate-debt statistics, it is easy to become overinvolved in the numbers themselves and to lose sight of what they imply. The average investor often experiences difficulty in comprehending the magnitudes involved in a discussion of debt totals. An additional complication is created by the profusion of international and domestic governmental and private bodies which release figures relating to debt. Some agencies have different data collection methods and standards of required accuracy than others. Many use differing interpretations of words or terms to classify reported amounts. For example, short-term securities or loans might be defined by one statistical agency as those securities having an original maturity of under 1 year, whereas a second bureau might use a demarcation line of under 2 years or some other standard. The investor should find out how the statistical source defines each of the important terms used to delineate the data being released.

Before reviewing historical debt statistics, the investor needs to develop a system for organizing the many types of data which will be encountered. Three broad categories may be used to separate debt statistics. The first category encompasses the total amount of debt outstanding. These figures are usually expressed in amounts as of a certain date. An economist might refer to them as stock figures. The second category includes the volume of debt issued during a given time period. These numbers are generally stated in amounts covering a specific time interval, such as a year, a quarter, or some multiple thereof. An economist might refer to them as flow figures. A closely related set of debt statistics combines total net amounts of funds raised by various broad categories of issuers and borrowers with total net amounts of funds supplied by various broad classes of investors and lenders. This so-called flow-of-funds analysis is described in Chapter 6. A third and less commonly encountered category of debt statistics covers secondary-market trading volume in fixed-income securities. These figures are also expressed in amounts (usually averages) per time interval, such as per day, per week, per month, or per year. Each of these three categories may be subdivided in numerous ways, some of which are set forth in Table 3-1.

Many statistical sources have created even finer subclassifications for some of the categories in Table 3-1. For example, under the heading "Instrument," "corporate obligations" may be split according to credit rating, industry group (such as utility or railroad issues), method of offering (such as private placement or public underwriting), or other rubrics.

Such a broad diversity of sources and nomenclature makes it imperative for the investor to develop a method of organizing and checking debt statistics of all types. While difficult to develop, a sense of relative magnitudes can help the investor judge whether a single number or set of figures sounds correct. Debt statistics should stand the test of consistency with other orders of magnitude and, if possible, with other numbers in which the investor has a high degree of confidence. Particularly when large sums of money are involved, it can be risky to base investment conclusions and actions on data (or arguments supported by data) which have not been carefully scrutinized and which are not understood in their proper context. A list of sample questions and comments for use in analyzing debt statistics is contained in the worksheet (Table 3-8) at the end of the chapter.

Debt Aggregates

To give a broad overview of the total debt picture in the United States, a variety of figures, tables, time periods, and sources have been selected for a description in the following paragraphs of (1) total debt outstanding, (2) total annual volume of debt issued, and (3) total trading volume. Because of lags between the gathering and issuance of data on the one hand and the normal passage of time involved in book publishing on the other, some of the figures cover more recent periods than others. Nevertheless, the investor should be able to identify trends, compare various methods of presentation, and obtain updated statistics from the sources listed in the figures and tables. While the analytical procedure described in the worksheet (Table 3-8) has not been applied in every case to these figures and tables, the investor is encouraged to keep the questions and comments in mind as the exhibits are being reviewed.

TABLE 3-1
Selected Classifications for Aggregate Debt Statistics

Category	Means of classification
Extent	Gross Net
Market- ability	Marketable Nonmarketable
Ownership	Publicly held Privately held
Nationality	Domestic International
Maturity	Short-term Intermediate-term (occasionally used) Long-term

Borrowing
sector
	Public
	  United States government
	  Federal agency
	Private
	  Nonfinancial
	    State and local government
	    Households
	    Farm
	    Nonfarm noncorporate
	    Corporate
	    Foreign
	  Financial
	    Commercial banks
	    Bank affiliates
	    Foreign banking agencies
	    Savings and loan associations
	    Life insurance companies
	    Other insurance companies
	    Finance companies
	    Real Estate Investment Trusts
	    Open-end investment companies
	    Money market funds

Instrument	U.S. government and federal agency securities State and local obligations Corporate obligations Foreign obligations Mortgages Consumer credit Bank loans Open-market paper and repurchase agreements

Total Debt Outstanding

Figure 3-1 shows the growth in total debt outstanding in the United States since the beginning of this century. From approximately $30 billion in 1900, total public and private debt grew to well over $3000 billion ($3 trillion) by mid-1980. As of that date, the amount of debt greatly exceeded the total market value of publicly traded equities in the United States.

It is interesting to witness the shifting patterns represented by the issuers of total outstanding debt. Figure 3-2 displays the mix between federal and nonfederal debt. From a relatively low level in the early 1920s, federal debt

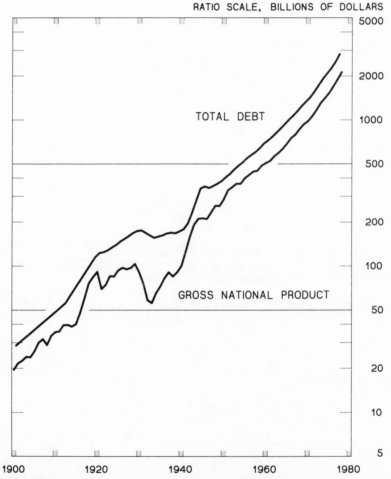

RATIO SCALE, BILLIONS OF DOLLARS

TOTAL DEBT

GROSS NATIONAL PRODUCT

FIGURE 3-1   Debt in the United States. [SOURCE: Historical Chart Book, *Board of Governors of the Federal Reserve System. By permission of the Board of Governors of the Federal Reserve System.*]

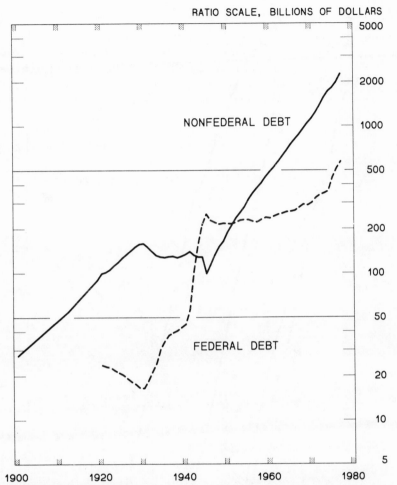

RATIO SCALE, BILLIONS OF DOLLARS

NONFEDERAL DEBT

FEDERAL DEBT

FIGURE 3-2 Federal debt versus nonfederal debt. [SOURCE: Historical Chart Book, *Board of Governors of the Federal Reserve System. By permission of the Board of Governors of the Federal Reserve System.*]

expanded dramatically during and immediately after the Second World War. Since the early 1950s the growth in nonfederal debt has far outstripped gains in federal debt, so that the former exceeded the latter by more than $1 trillion in the early 1980s.

The growth of certain sectors of the nonfederal debt outstanding since 1947 is presented in Figure 3-3. While the growth rates of farm, state and local government, business, and household debt have tracked roughly similar paths, by the early 1980s households and businesses each had the largest absolute amount of debt outstanding, followed far behind by state and local governments and even farther behind by farm debt.

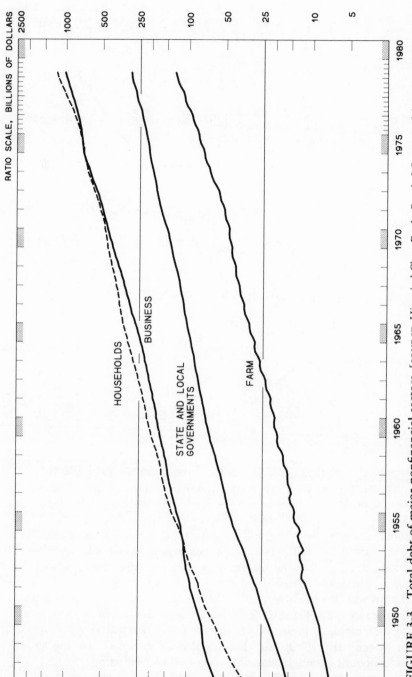

FIGURE 3-3 **Total debt of major nonfinancial sectors.** [SOURCE: Historical Chart Book, *Board of Governors of the Federal Reserve System.* By permission of the Board of Governors of the Federal Reserve System.]

32

TABLE 3-2
Net Public and Private Debt, End of Selected Calendar Years, 1929-1975
(*In billions of dollars*)

Year	Public			Private							Total public and private debt
	Federal	State and local	Total	Corporate		Individual and noncorporate				Total	
				Long-term	Short-term	Mortgage		Nonmortgage			
						Farm	Nonfarm	Farm	Nonfarm		
1975	$525.1	$216.1	$741.2	$611.0	$695.2	$51.9	$566.1	$46.1	$285.5	$2255.9	$2997.1
1974*	437.2	206.4	643.7	557.6	681.4	46.3	523.7	42.9	273.0	2124.9	2768.6
1973*	408.9	189.5	598.4	491.8	615.0	41.3	482.7	37.7	265.3	1933.7	2532.1
1972*	382.6	176.9	559.5	443.6	531.7	35.8	426.2	32.4	246.8	1716.5	2275.9
1971*	365.8	162.8	528.6	400.0	471.3	32.2	372.7	30.3	215.7	1522.1	2050.7
1970*	339.9	144.8	484.7	360.2	437.1	30.3	332.4	27.5	197.4	1384.9	1869.6
1969*	319.9	133.3	453.2	323.5	410.7	29.2	303.9	26.0	191.1	1284.4	1737.6
1968*	313.4	122.7	436.0	283.6	347.9	27.4	284.9	24.3	179.3	1147.4	1583.4
1967*	295.4	112.8	408.1	255.6	298.1	25.1	266.9	22.8	163.0	1031.5	1439.6
1966*	283.0	104.7	387.8	231.3	275.3	23.1	251.6	19.1	151.6	952.1	1339.9
1965*	275.3	98.3	373.6	209.4	244.9	21.2	236.8	18.1	141.0	871.4	1245.0
1964	271.5	90.4	361.9	192.5	217.1	18.9	218.9	17.1	125.3	789.7	1151.6
1963	264.7	83.9	348.6	174.8	201.7	16.8	198.6	16.4	114.0	722.3	1070.9
1962	258.9	77.0	335.9	161.2	187.0	15.2	180.3	15.0	101.4	660.1	996.0
1961	250.7	70.5	321.2	149.3	174.9	13.9	164.5	13.6	92.8	609.1	930.3
1960	243.3	64.9	308.1	139.1	163.7	12.8	151.3	12.3	86.9	566.1	874.2
1959	245.1	59.6	304.7	129.3	154.0	12.1	141.0	11.7	80.2	528.3	833.0
1958	233.5	53.7	287.2	121.2	138.4	11.1	128.1	12.1	71.6	482.4	769.6
1957	225.4	48.6	274.0	112.1	134.6	10.4	118.1	9.8	69.3	454.3	728.3
1956	226.7	44.5	271.2	100.1	131.7	9.8	109.4	9.6	66.7	427.2	698.4
1955	232.5	41.1	273.6	90.0	122.2	9.0	98.7	9.7	62.8	392.2	665.8
1954	230.4	35.5	265.9	82.9	100.0	8.2	86.4	9.3	53.3	340.0	605.9

TABLE 3-2
Net Public and Private Debt, End of Selected Calendar Years, 1929–1975 *(Continued)*
(In billions of dollars)

Year	Public			Corporate		Private					Total public and private debt
	Federal	State and local	Total	Long-term	Short-term	Individual and noncorporate				Total	
						Mortgage		Nonmortgage			
						Farm	Nonfarm	Farm	Nonfarm		
1953	228.2	30.7	258.9	78.3	101.2	7.7	76.7	9.1	49.8	322.7	581.6
1952	222.8	27.0	249.8	73.3	97.7	7.2	68.9	8.0	45.3	300.4	550.2
1951	218.2	24.2	242.4	66.6	95.9	6.7	61.7	7.0	38.9	276.8	519.2
1950	218.1	21.7	239.8	60.1	81.9	6.1	54.8	6.2	37.3	246.4	486.2
1949	218.3	19.1	237.4	56.5	61.4	5.6	47.1	6.4	31.3	208.4	445.8
1948	215.9	17.0	232.9	52.5	65.3	5.3	42.4	5.5	27.3	198.4	431.3
1947	222.4	15.0	237.4	46.1	62.8	5.1	37.2	3.5	23.5	178.3	415.7
1946	229.5	13.7	243.2	41.3	52.2	4.9	31.8	2.7	20.5	153.4	396.6
1945	252.5	13.4	265.9	38.3	47.0	4.8	27.0	2.5	20.4	140.0	405.9
1944	211.9	13.9	225.8	39.8	54.3	4.9	26.0	2.8	16.9	144.8	370.6
1942	101.7	15.4	117.1	42.7	49.0	6.0	26.8	3.0	14.1	141.5	258.6
1940	44.8	16.4	61.2	43.7	31.9	6.5	26.1	2.6	17.8	128.6	189.8
1939	42.6	16.4	59.0	44.4	29.2	6.6	25.0	2.2	17.0	124.3	183.3
1933	24.3	16.3	40.6	47.9	29.0	7.7	26.3	1.4	15.6	127.9	168.5
1929	16.5	13.6	30.1	47.3	41.6	9.6	31.2	2.6	29.5	161.8	191.9

SOURCE: *Statistics on State and Local Government Finance*, published by the Bond Buyer.

NOTE: Net debt is equal to gross debt less certain types of duplicating governmental and corporate debt. State and local government securities held by state and local governments are eliminated. In the corporate sector, the consolidation applies only to affiliated corporate systems. Net federal debt is equal to gross debt outstanding less federal securities held by the federal government, its agencies, and trust funds. It thus equals federal government and agency debt held by the public.

*Data in the years 1965–1974 revised by the Department of Commerce; compiled by the Bond Buyer from figures prepared by the Department of Commerce.

Table 3-2 comes from a different source and presents net public and private debt for a large number of selected years in the five-decade period beginning in 1929. It can be seen that total public and private debt grew by 516 percent, from $486.2 billion to $2997.1 billion, over the 1950–1975 time period. The largest absolute gain was represented by corporate short-term debt, which grew by $613.3 billion, from $81.9 billion to $695.2 billion. The largest percentage gain was displayed by private nonfarm mortgage debt, which rose by 933 percent, from $54.8 billion to $566.1 billion. Table 15-1 in Chapter 15 contains data on aggregate debt outstanding as of a single fixed point in time rather than over a period of years, as shown in Table 3-2.

Table 3-3 shows the size and growth rate of American credit market instruments outstanding and the holders of these instruments through the 1970s. Because of definitional differences and certain other factors discussed in the worksheet (Table 3-8), many of the numbers in Table 3-3 do not match exactly those in Table 3-2, but much useful additional information is provided through the exposition of holders of the specific credit market instruments in Table 3-3 as well as the calculation of the compound annual rate of increase in both credit market instruments outstanding and the ownership of those instruments.

A number of trends can be identified in Table 3-3. As of the end of 1978, mortgages accounted for the largest share (31.1 percent) of total credit market debt instruments outstanding, followed by U.S. government and federal agency issues (21.9 percent). In the 1967–1978 period, open-market paper showed the fastest rate of growth in outstandings (16.6 percent), followed by the categories of other loans (11.7 percent) and bank loans not classified elsewhere (11 percent). At the end of 1978, the largest holders of total American credit market instruments were commercial banks (with 27.2 percent of the total), followed by savings institutions (18.1 percent). The two classes of institutions which showed the largest compound annual rates of increase in holdings of credit market instruments, either through loans or through purchases of debt securities, were mortgage pools (41.1 percent annually) and international entities (23.7 percent annually).

By omitting the large amounts of nonmarketable credit in the form of loans and a major part of mortgages, Table 3-4 concentrates on selected segments of the *marketable* portion of debt outstanding for selected years from 1950 through 1979. As of the end of 1975, the volume of the selected marketable debt instruments shown in the table amounted to $1.2 trillion, which represented a 6.1 percent compound annual rate of growth from the $283 billion outstanding at the end of 1950. The largest share of the $1.2 trillion total was accounted for by United States government debt (35.5 percent), followed by corporate and foreign bonds (25.3 percent). During the 1965–1975 period, particularly rapid rates of growth in total outstand-

TABLE 3-3
Size and Growth Rate of American Credit Markets

Category	Billions of dollars as of year-end			Percentage of 1978 total	Compound annual rate of growth, 1967–1978 (percent)
	1967	1978	1979		
CREDIT MARKET DEBT INSTRUMENTS OUTSTANDING					
U.S. government and federal agency issues	297.7	825.3	916.7	21.9	9.7
State and local government obligations	113.7	291.4	312.7	7.7	8.9
Corporate and foreign bonds	149.7	422.0	455.7	11.2	9.9
Mortgages	382.9	1172.5	1333.7	31.1	10.7
Consumer credit	115.4	340.0	382.3	9.1	10.3
Bank loans not classified elsewhere	112.9	358.2	406.8	9.5	11.0
Open-market paper	21.4	115.9	156.4	3.1	16.6
Other loans	71.6	242.5	281.6	6.4	11.7
Total for all credit market instruments	1265.3	3767.8	4246.0	100.0	100.0
HOLDERS OF CREDIT MARKET DEBT					
Households	197.8	486.0	552.5	12.9	8.5
Nonfarm noncorporate businesses	9.0	16.9	18.8	0.4	5.9

Nonfinancial corporate businesses	32.2	60.8	77.2	1.6	5.9
State and local governments	25.5	82.5	97.6	2.2	11.3
International entities (rest of the world)	16.5	171.8	164.6	4.6	23.7
United States government	47.1	129.5	152.4	3.4	9.6
Federally sponsored credit agencies	23.3	127.0	156.6	3.4	16.7
Mortgage pools	2.0	88.6	118.0	2.4	41.1
Federal Reserve System	49.3	119.2	126.9	3.2	8.4
Commercial banking	354.3	1025.0	1144.8	27.2	10.1
Savings institutions*	207.3	682.0	736.4	18.1	11.4
Insurance companies and pension funds	247.9	608.9	685.4	16.1	8.5
Other financial entities†	53.2	169.6	214.9	4.5	11.1
Total holders of credit market debt	1265.3	3767.8	4246.0	100.0	100.0

SOURCE: Board of Governors of the Federal Reserve System, *Flow of Funds Accounts: Assets and Liabilities Outstanding, 1968–1978*. September 1979; *Flow of Funds Accounts: Assets and Liabilities Outstanding, 1969–1979*. February 1980.

*Includes savings and loan associations, mutual savings banks, and credit unions.

†Includes finance companies, Real Estate Investment Trusts, open-end investment companies, money market funds, and security brokers and dealers.

TABLE 3-4
Volume of Selected Marketable Debt Instruments Outstanding, 1950–1979
(In billions of dollars)

Debt instrument category	1950	1955	1960	1965	1970	1975	1979
U.S. government securities*†	216.5	230.0	235.0	260.6	299.3	445.2	662.9
Federally sponsored credit agencies and mortgage pools†	1.9	3.1	8.1	14.7	43.6	112.9	253.8
Short-term state and local government securities	1.3	2.1	3.5	5.5	13.3	16.7	12.6
Other state and local government issues	23.1	43.8	67.3	94.8	131.1	207.1	281.0
State and local government pollution control issues	0.0	0.0	0.0	0.0	0.0	6.8	19.2
Corporate and foreign bonds	39.2	60.1	90.0	123.0	201.6	317.2	455.7
Commercial paper	0.9	2.1	4.5	9.3	33.1	47.7	106.5
Bankers' acceptances	0.4	0.6	2.0	3.4	7.1	18.7	49.9
Large negotiable certificates of deposit	0.0	0.0	1.1	16.3	26.1	82.9	97.8
Total	283.3	341.8	411.5	527.6	755.2	1255.2	1939.4
Memorandum:							
Corporate equities‡	146.0	317.0	451.0	749.0	907.0	854.7	1198.3

SOURCE: *Flow of Funds Accounts*, Board of Governors of the Federal Reserve System. Data for all periods through 1975 are taken from the *Flow of Funds Accounts, 1946–1975*, issued in December 1976; data for periods subsequent to 1975 are taken from the *Flow of Funds Accounts, 1969–1979*, issued in February 1980. Because of occasional revisions in the Flow of Funds Accounts data, certain statistics from the latter source and subsequent releases may vary somewhat from those contained in the *Flow of Funds Accounts, 1946–1975*.

*Includes nonmarketable U.S. savings bonds and certain other nonmarketable debt issues.

†Includes both short-term and long-term securities.

‡Includes both convertible and nonconvertible preferred stock as well as common stock.

ings were exhibited by federally sponsored credit agencies and mortgage pools as well as by certain short-term debt instruments, including commercial paper, bankers' acceptances, and large negotiable certificates of deposit.

Total Debt Issuance

Figure 3-4 shows the total volume of new long-term debt issued by the private domestic nonfinancial sectors each year from 1947 to the mid-1970s. Particularly evident is the growth in total long-term borrowing, from approximately $15 billion per year in 1950 to more than $90 billion annually by 1975. Also striking is the large rise in total long-term borrowing accounted for by mortgages. This trend has been assisted in part by various governmental insurance, subsidy, and guarantee programs as well as by the development of federal agencies to raise money in the capital markets for the purchase of mortgages.

Figure 3-5 presents for the 1947–mid-1970s period the total level of new short-term debt assumed in the form of securities issuance and direct borrowing each year by private domestic nonfinancial sectors. Negotiable certificates of deposit, bankers' acceptances, and commercial paper issued by finance companies (a large part of the total commercial-paper market) have been excluded from the figure because they are issued by financial enterprises. Of interest are (1) the volatility of short-term credit usage; (2) the significance of business bank loans and consumer credit as the two most important sources of short-term borrowing; and (3) the decline in all forms of short-term borrowing (even to the extent of paying down total bank loans, shown as a move of the line of business bank loans into negative territory) in the aftermath of the 1974–1975 financial stresses described in Chapter 2.

Table 3-5 displays data on the total credit market funds raised each year by both the financial and the nonfinancial sectors of the economy for the period from 1969 through 1979. A number of interesting conclusions can be drawn about the growth of the credit and capital markets from a careful review of this table. First, the 1970s witnessed a large expansion in the annual amounts of credit market funds raised. From $116.4 billion in 1969, total annual credit market funds raised grew at a 17 percent compound rate through 1978, when $478.0 billion was raised in the credit and capital markets. Second, this period of rapid growth was interrupted by declines of 6.9 percent in 1971, 5.2 percent in 1974, and 6.1 percent in 1975. Third, total credit market funds raised grew dramatically in the late 1970s, rising by 33.4 percent in 1976, 36.7 percent in 1977, and 23 percent in 1978.

The funds raised varied quite a bit in some credit market categories during the 1970s. Yearly borrowings by the U.S. Treasury and federal agency sector exhibited a large growth in 1970 and 1971 and again from 1975 through 1978. In 1978 U.S. Treasury and federal agency borrowings represented

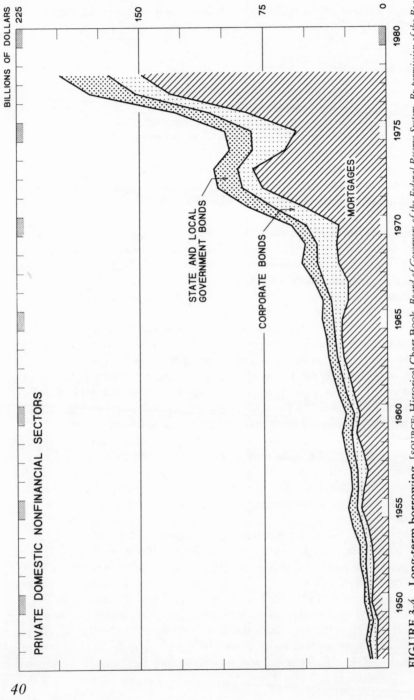

FIGURE 3-4 Long-term borrowing. [SOURCE: Historical Chart Book, *Board of Governors of the Federal Reserve System. By permission of the Board of Governors of the Federal Reserve System.*]

PRIVATE DOMESTIC NONFINANCIAL SECTORS

BILLIONS OF DOLLARS

225

150

75

0

1950   1955   1960   1965   1970   1975   1980

STATE AND LOCAL
GOVERNMENT BONDS

CORPORATE BONDS

MORTGAGES

40

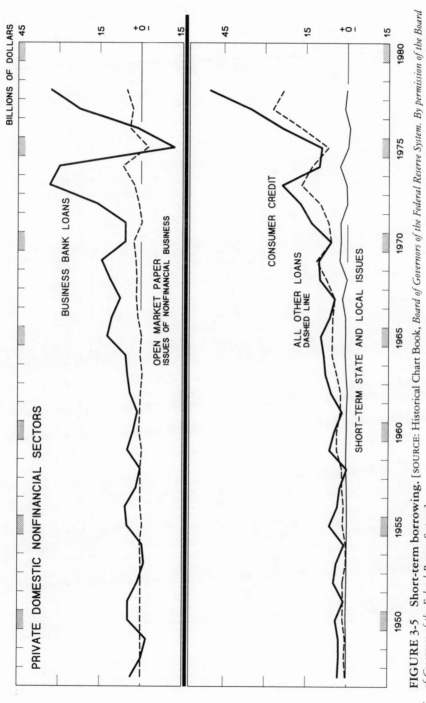

FIGURE 3-5 Short-term borrowing. [SOURCE: Historical Chart Book, *Board of Governors of the Federal Reserve System. By permission of the Board of Governors of the Federal Reserve System.*]

41

TABLE 3-5
Total Credit Market Funds Raised, 1969–1979
(In billions of dollars)

Credit market instrument	1969	1970	1971	1972	1973	1974	1975	1976	1977	1978	1979
U.S. Treasury and federal agency securities	6.2	21.7	30.9	23.6	28.3	34.3	98.2	88.1	84.3	95.2	89.9
State and local government obligations	9.9	11.2	17.4	14.7	14.7	16.5	16.1	15.7	23.7	28.3	21.3
Corporate and foreign bonds	13.8	23.3	23.5	18.4	13.6	23.9	36.4	37.2	36.1	31.6	33.7
Mortgages	30.7	29.9	52.5	76.8	79.9	60.6	57.2	87.1	134.0	149.0	159.5
Consumer credit	10.8	5.4	14.7	19.8	26.0	9.9	9.7	25.6	40.6	50.6	42.3
Bank loans not classified elsewhere	16.8	7.3	11.0	26.1	48.8	41.0	−12.2	7.0	29.8	58.4	49.5
Open-market paper	12.5	2.1	−0.1	1.6	8.3	17.7	−1.2	8.1	15.0	26.4	40.5
Other loans	15.8	7.5	3.5	8.4	19.1	22.7	8.7	15.3	25.2	38.6	39.2
Total for all instruments	116.4	108.4	153.4	189.3	238.8	226.4	212.8	284.1	388.5	478.0	475.8
Memorandum: Corporate equities	5.2	7.7	13.7	13.8	10.4	4.8	10.8	12.9	4.9	4.7	6.6

SOURCE: *Flow of Funds Accounts*, Board of Governors of the Federal Reserve System. Data for all periods through 1975 are taken from the *Flow of Funds Accounts, 1946–1975*, issued in December 1976; data for periods subsequent to 1975 are taken from the *Flow of Funds Accounts, 1969–1979*, issued in February 1980. Because of occasional revisions in the Flow of Funds Accounts data, certain statistics from the latter source and subsequent releases may vary somewhat from those contained in the *Flow of Funds Accounts, 1946–1975.*

19.9 percent of total credit market funds raised, up from 5.3 percent in 1969.

Yearly borrowings by state and local governments showed large gains in 1971, 1977, and 1978 and accounted for 5.9 percent of total credit market funds raised in 1978, a decline from 8.5 percent of the total in 1969. The issuance of corporate and foreign bonds rose considerably in 1970, declined in 1972 and 1973, and then demonstrated modest declines in 1977 and 1978 from a relatively high level in 1976. In 1978 corporate and foreign bonds represented 6.6 percent of total credit market funds raised, down from 11.9 percent in 1969. With extremely large increases in annual borrowing volume in 1973, 1974, 1976, 1977, and 1978, mortgages rose from 26.4 percent of total credit market funds raised in 1969 to 31.1 percent of the total in 1978.

Consumer borrowings declined in 1970 from 1969 levels and exhibited similar declines in 1974 and 1975. However, these retrenchments were offset by large increases in annual amounts of consumer borrowing in 1976, 1977, and 1978. Because of a cyclical movement toward financial conservatism in 1974 (discussed in Chapter 2), both open-market paper and bank loans not elsewhere classified exhibited net repayments in 1975. Each of these two credit market instruments showed strong expansion in the years 1976 through 1978, as did the category of other loans.

The long-term pattern of annual credit market borrowings and their aggregate size relative to the annual issuance of common and preferred stocks are placed in perspective in Table 3-6. Particularly notable is the 10.9 percent compound annual rate of growth in total credit market funds raised over the 1950–1978 period, from $26.6 billion in 1950 to $478.0 billion in 1978. Equally interesting is the relationship between total debt funds raised and total equity funds raised. Equity funds raised as a percentage of total credit market funds raised ranged from 4.4 to 10.3 percent during the 1950s, from 0.1 to 6.1 percent during the 1960s, and from 1 to 8.9 percent in the 1970s.

Total Trading Volume

Many otherwise-prolific statistical sources on debt do not commonly gather or issue figures on the total secondary-market turnover in fixed-income securities. An additional inhibiting factor is that the preponderance of total debt trading volume takes place in a diversified, and to some degree dispersed, over-the-counter (OTC) marketplace, among broker-dealer firms of all types, the Federal Reserve System Open-Market Trading Desk, all categories of institutional investors, and individuals.

When analyzing aggregate trading volume statistics, it is worthwhile to keep in mind that gross turnover totals may overstate the actual level of trading. This tends to happen because dealers most often buy and sell securities into and from their own inventories and because each dealer includes

TABLE 3-6
Total Credit Market Funds Raised by All Sectors, 1950–1979
(In billions of dollars)

Year	Credit market funds raised by financial and nonfinancial sectors	Funds raised through common and preferred stock
1950	26.6	1.4
1951	23.3	2.4
1952	32.3	2.6
1953	29.5	1.9
1954	25.9	2.2
1955	41.3	1.9
1956	28.7	2.7
1957	30.5	2.8
1958	39.7	2.5
1959	56.8	2.5
1960	40.4	1.7
1961	47.6	2.9
1962	59.6	0.6
1963	67.0	0.1
1964	73.5	1.5
1965	80.4	0.3
1966	76.6	1.1
1967	80.4	2.5
1968	109.0	0.6
1969	116.4	5.2
1970	108.4	7.7
1971	153.4	13.7
1972	189.3	13.8
1973	238.8	10.4
1974	226.4	4.8
1975	212.8	10.8
1976	284.1	12.9
1977	388.5	4.9
1978	478.0	4.7
1979	475.8	6.6

SOURCE: *Flow of Funds Accounts,* Board of Governors of the Federal Reserve System. Data for all periods through 1975 are taken from the *Flow of Funds Accounts, 1946–1975,* issued in December 1976; data for periods subsequent to 1975 are taken from the *Flow of Funds Accounts, 1969–1979,* issued in February 1980. Because of occasional revisions in the Flow of Funds Accounts data, certain statistics from the latter source and subsequent releases may vary somewhat from those contained in the *Flow of Funds Accounts, 1946–1975.*

both the initial buy or sell side of a transaction and its later offset in the dealer's own reported figures, rather than combining the purchase and the sale and dividing by 2 to reflect the fact that only one "trade" (comprising two "transactions") has produced separate buy and sell tickets for the dealer involved. If several dealers happen to trade the same lot of securities repeatedly among themselves, these transactions may also inflate the overall volume totals since such a turnover does not involve "final" investors. Final investors, also known as "retail" investors, encompass in this context both individuals and institutions. Purchasing demand from final investors is also known as "final" or "going away" demand, as distinguished from "street" demand (named for Wall Street), which involves trading with another dealer or dealers.

If these caveats are borne in mind, Table 3-7 shows the par value of U.S. government securities dealers' average daily trading volume in U.S. government and federal agency securities for the years 1969 through 1979. Of note are (1) the 323 percent increase in U.S. government securities daily trading volume from 1969 through 1978; (2) the 425 percent increase in federal agency securities daily trading volume; (3) the high percentage of combined U.S. government and federal agency securities trading volume accounted for by U.S. Treasury bills—74 percent of the total in 1969 and 51 percent of the total in 1978; and (4) the range in the ratio of federal agency securities trading volume to U.S. government securities trading volume, from a low of 14.8 percent in 1969 to a high of 27 percent in 1974.

The paramount trading position of U.S. Treasury and federal agency securities underscores the need for market participants to understand how various forces exert their influence on the government sector of the fixed-income securities markets. Not only because of quality considerations but also because of trading practices, major price moves in short-term and long-term Treasury issues tend in varying degrees to influence virtually all the other segments of the debt marketplace.

TABLE 3-7

Average Daily Trading Volume of U.S. Government Securities Dealers, 1969–1979

(In millions of dollars)

Item	1969	1970	1971	1972	1973	1974	1975	1976	1977	1978	1979
U.S. government securities	2,434	2,513	2,700	2,930	3,439	3,579	6,027	10,449	10,838	10,285	13,182
By maturity											
Bills	2,078	2,032	1,988	2,259	2,643	2,550	3,889	6,676	6,746	6,173	7,914
Other within 1 year*	...	...	...	...	...	250	223	210	237	392	455
1–5 years	231	311	431	422	471	465	1,414	2,317	2,318	1,889	2,416
5–10 years	87	136	240	189	243	256	363	1,019	1,148	965	1,121
Over 10 years	39	34	41	63	83	58	138	229	388	866	1,276
By type of customer:											
U.S. government securities dealers	946	977	940]	726	665	652	885	1,360	1,267	1,135	1,448
U.S. government securities brokers				411	795	965	1,750	3,407	3,709	3,838	5,171
Commercial banks	880	929	963	998	1,092	998	1,451	2,426	2,295	1,804	1,905
All others†	511	510	664	796	886	964	1,941	3,257	3,567	3,508	4,658
Federal agency securities	361	463	636	527	743	965	1,043	1,548	1,729	1,894	2,724

SOURCE: *Federal Reserve Bulletin*, Board of Governors of the Federal Reserve System.

NOTE: Averages for transactions are based on the number of trading days in the period. Transactions include market purchases and sales of U.S. government securities dealers reporting to the Federal Reserve Bank of New York. All totals exclude allotments of and exchanges for new U.S. government securities, redemptions of called or matured securities, purchases or sales of securities under repurchase agreements, reverse repurchase (resale) agreements, or similar contracts.

*Not provided separately in statistics published prior to 1974.

†Among others, includes foreign banking agencies, the Federal Reserve System, and all other brokers and dealers in commodities and securities.

TABLE 3-8

Methods for Organizing and Evaluating Debt Statistics

WORKSHEET	
Question area	Comment
1. Are the statistics correctly and completely titled? What does the title signify?	The title may indicate that important items have been included or excluded. For example, the heading "Total bank loans" may or may not count lending to the household sector as well as to the business sector, and it may or may not include intermediate-maturity lending as well as short-term loans.
2. How are the statistics collected and derived? Are they ever revised, and if so, why and how frequently?	If the statistics cover recently elapsed time periods and/or are being gathered from original sources, such as groups of financial institutions or corporations, revisions may have to be made to reflect errors, omissions, and other adjustments in the data base. The investor should investigate to what degree past revisions have altered originally issued statistics. Sometimes, the statistics may rely completely on another statistical source without expressly stating the fact. If the statistics have been gathered in this manner from secondary sources, the same standards should be applied as for the original sources in the evaluation of collection methods, revisions, and other changes.
3. What do the statistics encompass?	Some sources include the securities of certain independent or quasi-independent agencies of the United States government under the category called "Federal government issues." Similarly, "State and local spending" might or might not include federal aid or transfer payments. The investor should ascertain whether the statistics under review are being counted twice. If so, other categories may have to be adjusted to reflect this fact. The "gross" figures for debt issuance do not subtract (as do "net" figures) debt repayments in the form of interest, bond redemptions or calls, sinking funds, and maturing debt issues.
4. What body is the source of the statistics? To what audience are the statistics usually directed, and what is the purpose of the statistical source in collecting and disseminating these data?	Because of the interests of its primary constituency, a private or governmental source of data may include, for example, both convertible and nonconvertible debt under the heading "Corporate bonds," whereas another source with a different audience may decide to include only nonconvertible debt. Depending upon such factors as regulatory direction, tradition, and definitional differences, another common statistical divergence may arise when the statistical source decides whether to include notes (for example, municipal, corporate, or U.S. Treasury notes) under the heading "Bonds."

TABLE 3-8
Methods for Organizing and Evaluating Debt Statistics *(Continued)*

WORKSHEET

Question area	Comment
5. How do the statistics relate to other statistics?	If the data refer to a specific category of debt issuance (e.g., "Bankers' acceptances"), depending upon the investor's purposes they may become much more meaningful when compared with (1) related data for the same category, such as the total amount of bankers' acceptances outstanding or traded in a given year; (2) data for similar categories such as "Commercial paper" or "Treasury bills"; (3) other amounts for earlier or for projected future time periods, both in absolute and in percentage terms; (4) aggregate-debt figures, such as total debt outstanding as of a certain date or issued during a certain time period; (5) the size of selected macroeconomic figures, such as total bank loans, aggregate personal income, consumer balance-sheet totals, and the gross national product for the United States; and (6) selected items from categories 1 through 5 for other major industrial nations.
6. Is anything unusual present in or absent from the statistics?	Depending upon financing conditions and other factors at work in the capital markets, discussions of a commonly employed set of debt data may overlook significant influences on the total market. For example, many analysts employ total long-term funds raised by *nonfinancial* corporations as a proxy for aggregate corporate debt issuance. At certain times, however, these data may neglect large volumes of debt issued by some or all of the *financial* corporations listed in Table 2-1. If loan demand is strong, particularly at the money center banks, commercial banks and bank affiliates may issue large quantities of debt securities. Similarly, the level of mortgage loan commitments, coupled with absolute amounts of savings flows, determines the degree to which savings and loan institutions may have to tap the capital markets through the issuance of long-term–debt securities. Finance companies' long-term–debt capital needs are influenced in part by their desired mix of short-term and long-term liabilities on their balance sheets and partly by corporate and consumer borrowing through finance companies.
7. Have the statistics been seasonally adjusted?	Seasonal adjustments to data, because of known seasonal influences such as holidays, the weather, or tax payment deadlines, may obscure or delay the recognition of true underlying trends. Errors may enter into seasonal adjustments owing to gradual shifts over time of assumed stable seasonal patterns and the interactive effects of seasonal

TABLE 3-8
Methods for Organizing and Evaluating Debt Statistics *(Continued)*

WORKSHEET	
Question area	Comment
7. Have the statistics been seasonally adjusted? *(Continued)*	patterns with any past policy actions taken to offset such influences. Also, significant changes can transpire between preliminary and final seasonal adjustments, to such an extent that revisions for seasonal factors can often have a larger impact on seasonally adjusted statistics than all revisions of the underlying data, including benchmark revisions.
8. What real-life story are the statistics depicting?	It is often helpful to step back and think about the financial, tax, economic, regulatory, and other reasons why certain flows of funds are being borrowed or lent. For various liquidity reasons and other considerations, the funds being raised may in fact be reinvested in deposits at another financial institution or in another type of security being issued by a different type of borrower. For example, if the proceeds from a large percentage of municipal bond issues are reinvested in U.S. Treasury issues (which happened in 1977, as described more fully in Chapter 8), such actions may have a vastly different effect on the economy and on the financial markets than if these funds were borrowed for capital spending projects or to cover budget deficits. The investor should always consider the other side of a debt issuance transaction and whether this can have offsetting influences in the debt markets. The financial situation of the investor as well as that of the issuer should be kept in mind. Many sectors of the economy act both as borrowers and investors, either simultaneously or at different time periods. Awareness of whether and where the money is spent or deposited by the issuer and whence all types of investors receive funds for investment can be of valuable assistance in gaining a deeper understanding of the forces and pressures at work in fixed-income securities markets. Recent years' flow-of-funds statistics, described further in Chapter 6, can help to provide this knowledge.

Forces Affecting the Bond and Money Markets

4

The History and Mechanics of Price Level Changes

Overview

Price level changes can have an extremely important bearing upon virtually every aspect of fixed-income securities investing. Over a period of years, money managers need to understand, allow for, and protect against the effects of inflation (a rising general level of prices) and deflation (a falling general level of prices) as well as their numerous variants. Among these variants are stagflation (a combination of inflation and no growth or recession), disinflation (a movement toward slower rates of inflation), and hyperinflation (prodigiously high rates of inflation).

Price level changes directly influence many critical sectors within the economy, including employment, consumer outlays for goods and services, business spending, income levels and distributions of wealth, and international trade and capital flows. In addition, reported price level changes can greatly influence economic policy actions and currency movements. Just as importantly, price level changes can affect debtor-creditor relationships by increasing or decreasing the real value of the funds which pass from lender to borrower and eventually back again. The purchasing power of savings and defined flows of income such as rents, royalties, and retirement benefits all depend on movements in the level of prices.

For example, $1 at the end of 1977 would buy 68.4 percent of $1's purchasing power at the end of 1972 and 57 percent of its buying ability at the end of 1967. Inflation can erode or even eliminate the real returns from fixed-income investing. On the other hand, periods of *declining* prices can *augment* the real returns provided by bonds and other fixed-income securities. If price level changes become amplified in strength and duration, they can profoundly alter patterns of behavior by investors, as each seeks to avoid the possibly deleterious effects of inflation or deflation.

Economic history shows that the direction of price trends, as well as the absolute level of prices, is prone to change. Investors should remember that prices can move on both an upward and a downward path over the short term and the long term. For this reason, this chapter looks at conditions of rising and descending price levels. While numerous analysts compare current economic and price circumstances with a series of changes in industrial production, real gross national product (GNP), payroll employment, and price indices for both the recessionary and the recovery phases of several recent economic *cycles,* the *secular* ebb and flow of price levels are no less significant.

Historical Comments

Modern societies are not the only ones which have grappled with the problems of inflation and deflation. For example, ancient civilizations such as the fifth Egyptian dynasty responded to rapidly increasing price levels by mandatory controls. Similar controls were imposed by governmental bodies in ancient Greece and in Rome, where in the late third century A.D. the emperor Diocletian imposed wage controls on more than 125 classifications of labor and price controls on more than 900 commodities. In most cases, price controls led to shortages of goods, since consumers wanted to obtain more of the articles whose prices were frozen than producers were willing to supply at the artificially depressed price levels.

Price Levels in Europe and Asia

Thanks to many of the colonial powers of the fifteenth century and afterward, price records which provide data over several hundred years have been preserved. It is thus possible, for example, to trace in detail the price inflation which resulted in Europe in the sixteenth century from the discovery and subsequent importation of gold and silver from the New World.

Observation of price levels through the centuries does not yield a steady pattern of results. Price changes could be so modest as to appear practically invariable. Exhibiting a compound average rate of increase of just 0.5 percent annually, prices doubled in the United Kingdom between 1585 and 1718. As is shown in Figure 4-1, prices in the United Kingdom in 1931 were at approximately the same level as in 1688, with many variations in the intervening years.

Yet periods of excessive price changes have also occurred, as in France between 1790 and 1800. The twentieth century provides several examples of very high inflation rates, ranging from 50 percent to several hundred percent per year in a number of developing countries during the 1970s.

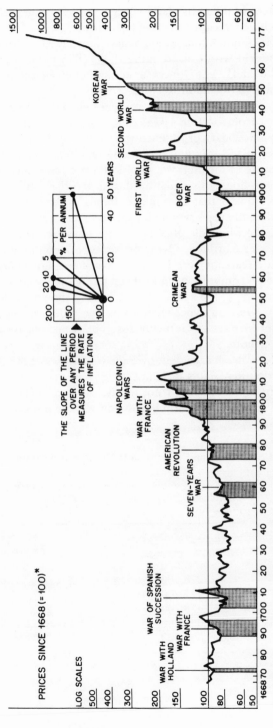

FIGURE 4-1 Price level changes in the United Kingdom, 1668–1977. [SOURCE: The Economist, June 10, 1978. Reprinted by permission of The Economist Newspaper Ltd., London.]

*Linked index. Main sources: Mitchell and Deane, Abstract of British Historical Statistics; Department of Employment, British Labour Statistics, Historical Abstract 1886–1953. Basic series: Schumpeter-Gilboy price index 1661–1697 (1697=100) and 1697–1823 (1701=100); Rousseaux price indices 1800–1923 (1865–1885=100): Sauerbuck-Statist price indices 1864–1938 (1867–1877=100); DE index of internal purchasing power of the pound 1914–1977 (1963=100).

More famous instances of the particularly virulent strain of inflation known as hyperinflation include the experiences of Japan in the 1939–1948 period, when prices rose 116 times; China in the years immediately following the end of the Second World War; Poland in the 1921–1923 period; and Hungary during World War II, when one Hungarian pengö depreciated by a factor of 827 octillion (an octillion is 1 plus 27 zeros).

Perhaps the most widely cited period of hyperinflation in this century occurred in Germany from 1920 to 1923. Among contemporary industrial nations, Germany's inflationary experience was unprecedented. As a guide to the swift progression and spiraling magnitude of a hyperinflation, Table 4-1 sets forth the course of the German wholesale price index and the total amount of Reichsbank notes in circulation during the hyperinflation. It is interesting and tragic to note that from the beginning of January 1920 until November 1923, when the mark was no longer accepted in payment by the German population, the wholesale price index rose by more than 58 billion times, from 1260 to 72.6 trillion. Over the same period, the amount of Reichsbank notes in circulation rose by more than 2.6 billion times, from 35.7 billion marks to 180 quintillion marks. Even though the nominal supply of money rose dramatically, the real supply of money showed little or no expansion during the German hyperinflation. At one point during this period, short-term interest rates in Germany rose to 28 percent *per day,* or 10,000 percent per annum.

While there has been much argument over the true causes of the German hyperinflation, contributing factors included (1) governmental financing of German involvement in World War I not through higher taxes and long-term borrowing but through short-term borrowing; (2) the post-World War

TABLE 4-1
German Wholesale Price Index and Reichsbank Notes in Circulation, 1920–1923

Date	Wholesale price index*	Reichsbank notes in circulation
Jan. 1, 1920	1,260	35,700,000,000
Jan. 1, 1921	1,440	68,800,000,000
Jan. 1, 1922	3,670	113,600,000,000
Jan. 1, 1923	278,500	1,984,500,000,000
Apr. 1, 1923	521,200	5,517,900,000,000
July 1, 1923	7,478,700	17,291,100,000,000
Sept. 1, 1923	2,390,000,000	3,183,681,200,000,000
Nov. 20, 1923	72,600,000,000,000	180,000,000,000,000,000,000

SOURCE: Deutsche Bundesbank.
*July 1, 1914 = 100.

I loss of much productive land and equipment; (3) large external demands for reparations payments by Germany; and (4) expansion in the supply of money, coupled with a prodigious rise in the velocity of money.

In its accelerating final stages, particularly in 1923, the hyperinflation wrought serious and lasting social damage in a great number of ways. Stabilization of prices was finally achieved by a new head of the German central bank, Hjalmar Schacht, who abruptly truncated the flow of new credit to the German government and to the market. Even though the new currency unit (known as the Rentenmark, equal to 1 trillion Reichsmarks) had no special reserve backing, Schacht was able to persuade the German public that its issuance would be tightly limited. This limitation was achieved in spite of enormous pressures by many entities that had expected further inflation and had taken actions which proved costly when the hyperinflation was suddenly brought to a halt.

Price Levels in the United States

Although the United States has witnessed a number of inflationary and deflationary periods of varying duration, it has been fortunate not to have experienced extremes of price inflation or deflation during the period from 1800 to 1980. Figure 4-2 shows the evolution of the producer price index (known as the wholesale price index prior to 1978) in the United States from 1800 until the early 1980s.

In almost all cases, the major inflations sustained by the United States have accompanied or followed a period of wartime activity, whereas the country's principal deflationary experiences are difficult to correlate with a major phase of social or national movement. Some of these occurrences are briefly reviewed in the following paragraphs. In addition to the major moves in the price indices which are discussed here, numerous short-lived and sometimes intense swings in price levels were experienced in periods later referred to by historians and economists as times of prosperity, panic, boom, or bust.

The large quantities of continental dollars issued by Congress to wage the Revolutionary War, together with limited supplies of goods and services in the 13 former colonies, contributed to an extremely severe inflation. By 1781 the continental money had depreciated to one-thousandth of its original value. This sharp depreciation gave rise to the expression "Not worth a continental." Many of the direct social side effects of such rampant inflation were avoided because a large portion of the American population was engaged in agriculture. The primary impact of the hyperinflation thus fell upon financiers and tradespeople in the cities along the Eastern seaboard of the United States. The inflation subsided when the First Bank of the United States gradually withdrew currency from circulation. For the first time since the founding of the nation, severe deflationary forces prevailed during the

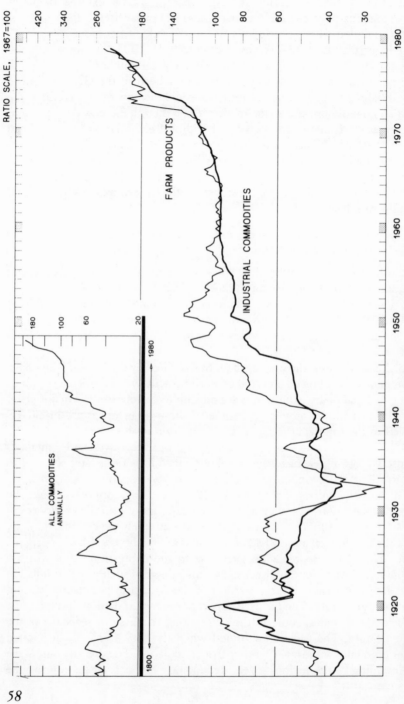

FIGURE 4-2 Producer (wholesale) prices in the United States. [SOURCE: Historical Chart Book, *Board of Governors of the Federal Reserve System. By permission of the Board of Governors of the Federal Reserve System.*]

late 1780s, with falling demand and price levels for key commodities and finished goods.

In the period of the War of 1812, strong inflationary pressures erupted again, with the sustained rise in the general price level partially originating from the large amounts of money issued by the United States government in response to a fall in tariff income caused by the sudden contraction in trade with the British.

From 1837 until the mid-1840s, the United States suffered a period of particularly acute deflation in prices, partly caused and partly accompanied by difficulties in the agricultural sector, bank insolvencies, and shrinkage in the money supply. During the Civil War, prices doubled, stimulated by the vigorous issuance of greenback notes by the U.S. Treasury to supply the Union Army. Through a systematic withdrawal of paper currency in the Reconstruction years, the Treasury was able to restore price stability to the economy.

The two harshest deflationary experiences in the first two centuries of American history occurred from 1873 to 1879 and during most of the 1930s. Both periods witnessed prolonged declines in price levels as well as mass unemployment, corporate bankruptcies, liquidation of debt, and extremely depressed economic conditions. Aided in part by an expansion in the money supply due to large Federal Reserve purchases of U.S. government debt, prices rose by 60 percent during and after the Second World War, at an average rate of 7.1 percent per year from 1940 to 1948.

To some degree, the postwar emphasis on full employment and the gradual relegation of price stability to the status of a secondary economic objective may be traced to a national desire to avoid the harsh conditions of the 1930s. Following the conflict in Southeast Asia, a conscious policy to foster and maintain economic growth was chosen, even though it entailed risks of inflation. This was deemed preferable to the stop-go strategies of alternating restraint and stimulus which had characterized the 1950s.

A large growth of the money supply, federal government deficits, and a number of other factors described in Chapter 5 led to a singularly extended period of high inflation during peacetime, lasting more than 15 years, from the mid-1960s through the end of the 1970s. The extent of this phenomenon in a historical context can be noted by reference once again to Figure 4-2. Even though producer prices exhibited large fluctuations in the first 160 years of United States history, by the 1930s and again in 1940 the producer price index stood near the levels experienced at the beginning of the 1800s. From 1940 to the late 1970s producer prices rose more than 4.5 times, with a doubling of the producer price index in the latter half of this period.

Figure 4-3, covering a considerably shorter time span than Figure 4-2, shows the path of the consumer price index from 1913 to 1980. With the exception of 2 years, from the late 1940s through the late 1970s the index

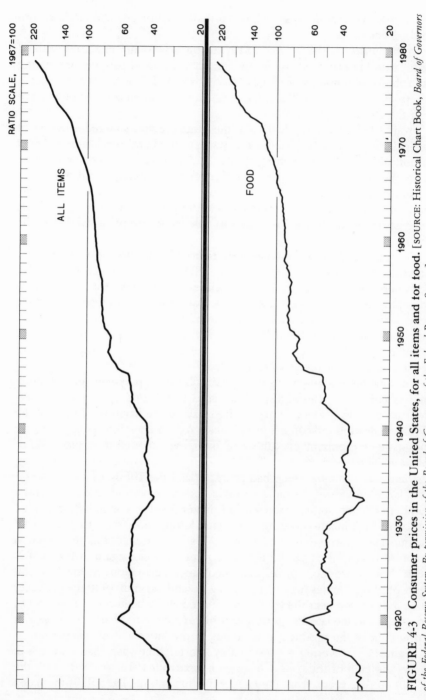

RATIO SCALE, 1967=100

ALL ITEMS

FOOD

FIGURE 4-3 Consumer prices in the United States, for all items and for food. [SOURCE: Historical Chart Book, *Board of Governors of the Federal Reserve System. By permission of the Board of Governors of the Federal Reserve System.*]

60

rose steadily. This upward progression is also delineated by the data in Table 4-2.

Table 4-2 and, particularly, Figure 4-3 show that since 1913 the consumer price index has risen meaningfully in about 45 percent of the years, risen by an insignificant amount in 15 percent of the years, and remained even or

TABLE 4-2
Consumer Price Index in the United
States

Year	Percentage change in the index
1948	2.7
1949	− 1.8
1950	5.8
1951	5.9
1952	0.9
1953	0.6
1954	− 0.5
1955	0.4
1956	2.9
1957	3.0
1958	1.8
1959	1.5
1960	1.5
1961	0.7
1962	1.2
1963	1.6
1964	1.2
1965	1.9
1966	3.4
1967	3.0
1968	4.7
1969	6.1
1970	5.5
1971	3.4
1972	3.4
1973	8.8
1974	12.2
1975	7.0
1976	4.8
1977	6.5
1978	7.7
1979	11.3
1980	15.5

SOURCE: U.S. Department of Labor, Bureau of Labor Statistics.

declined in about 40 percent of the years. The two periods of sharpest sustained consumer price rises occurred from 1915 to 1920, when the consumer price index doubled, and from 1967 to 1980, when it rose by more than 150 percent.

The Mechanics of Price Indices

Especially when large inflationary or deflationary movements cause concern about substantial price changes, national scrutiny usually focuses intensely on a few regularly issued price indices. The investor should analyze the construction, uses, and limitations of the major publicly and privately produced indices, including the producer price index and the consumer price index, whose historical records are displayed in Figures 4-2 and 4-3. In examining the makeup of price indices or in comparing the performance of a price index in one country with that of another country, the investor should keep several caveats in mind.

First, the price index may incompletely measure the economic sector under investigation because goods and/or services which figure importantly in current consumption preferences have been omitted. Other inaccuracies may arise from an overemphasis of one or more articles or commodities through multiple counting of their prices in various stages of production, distribution, and consumption. The sampling techniques used to derive a given price index are crucial to its quality. The sample must achieve appropriate levels of frequency, geographic and product scope, accuracy, and completeness, especially in reflecting the mainstream of spending patterns.

Second, spending patterns may shift over time, in part because of the substitution of lower-priced items for higher-priced ones (owing to price elasticities in the demand for such items), in part because of changes in the tastes and preferences of buyers, and in part because of the introduction of new products. The dynamics of rapid inflation or deflation often bring about shifts in economic behavior that vastly complicate the task of correctly measuring the speed of price changes. For these reasons, it is important to make sure that (1) the relative weights of the components in the price index are realistic and (2) an appropriate base period of time has been selected and maintained long enough to allow the comparison of subsequent time periods not only with the base period but with each other. The most commonly used price indices, including both the producer price index and the consumer price index, employ a fixed base period and fixed weights of components (weights are updated from time to time to maintain the representativeness of the index) in a so-called weighted-average-of-relatives index. This method of calculation is a modification of that developed by Etienne Laspeyres in 1864.

Third, the index may imprecisely measure and adjust for changes in quality among its components.

Fourth, a large portion of the transactions in a particular article may take place at unofficial prices quite different from the prices which are recorded in the price index. When economic conditions are sluggish, many firms may offer discounts or special terms which amount to discounts from list prices. In some countries, governmentally imposed price controls may lead to shortages and black-market dealings at prices substantially exceeding official quotations.

Fifth, the data base for a particular price index may have been revised to include more representative prices of selected goods and services, limiting the comparability of current figures with those of prior years.

Sixth, owing to variations in the rate of price change for the subcategories of a given index, its aggregate performance may obscure the actual incidence of price increases or decreases for selected goods or services.

Seventh and finally, the annual average of monthly changes in a price index may differ significantly from changes in the index from year-end to year-end, especially during periods of rapidly accelerating or decelerating price changes. To gauge the actual amount of price change which has taken place during a given 12-month period, year-over-year calculations provide a more accurate reading than an annual average of monthly price changes.

Producer Price Index

The producer price index (PPI) was started in 1913 as the wholesale price index and received its present name in 1978. The index for each month is produced by the Bureau of Labor Statistics (BLS), which releases it shortly after the beginning of the following month.[1]

The BLS collects data for the PPI by mailing questionnaires to several thousand producing business firms. Price quotations are taken on more than 10,000 items in a few thousand categories of commodities, including raw materials, fuels, food products, and manufactured goods. Beginning in 1967, respondents to the questionnaire have been requested to report the prices in effect on the Tuesday of the week in which the thirteenth of the month falls. The survey is voluntary, and it is not always possible to ascertain all price levels precisely owing to (1) the tendency of producers to delay publication of price reductions, (2) divergences between list prices and transaction prices caused by discounts and add-ons, and (3) the unwillingness of some firms to supply price quotations on certain goods.

Separate price indices are constructed and combined into weighted averages according to the net value of quantities shipped, using *Census of Manufac-*

---

[1] A free monthly copy of the *Producer Price Index News Release* is available from the Bureau of Labor Statistics, 200 Constitution Ave. N.W., Washington, D.C. 20212.

tures: 1972 data as a guide. The 1972 weights (and the 1963 weights for comparison purposes), showing the relative importance of commodities included in the PPI (updated by changes in relative prices as of December 1975 but not by changes in weightings), are spelled out by industry and by stage of processing in Table 4-3.

Over time the BLS has sought and is continuing to improve the PPI in a number of ways. More extensive and scientifically rigorous samples of prices are under development, with more frequent updating of category weightings, coverage of a greater number of industries, inclusion of price quotations of small as well as large firms in the data base, and improved disclosure of actual transaction prices as opposed to list prices. Whenever possible, the BLS has reduced the double counting of price increases as a given commodity moves from the raw-material stage to become a semifinished good and, later, a finished product. It has accomplished this objective through greater emphasis on separate reporting of the three components of the PPI as shown in the bottom half of Table 4-3: the raw goods index (11.33 percent of the overall PPI), the intermediate goods index (47.11 percent of the overall PPI), and, particularly, the finished goods index (41.56 percent of the overall PPI). The finished goods index is an improved indicator of eventual price changes at the retail level.

The PPI is employed in numerous price escalation clauses on long-term contracts covering raw materials and other goods supplied and consumed by the business sector. In addition, it is used to revalue corporate assets in the replacement-cost accounting regulations of the Securities and Exchange Commission. A great number of analysts regard the PPI as a reasonably accurate harbinger of changes in the consumer price index.

In actual fact, the value of the PPI as a forecaster of consumer prices is somewhat limited. Consumers do not directly purchase a substantial majority of the items in the PPI, such as machinery, raw materials, and semifinished goods. The PPI does not include numerous items which are contained in the consumer price index, for example, the cost of mortgage interest, rental payments, or any services such as medical care. To the extent that prices for these goods and services rise or fall at rates different from those for PPI commodities, rates of change in the consumer price index will diverge from those exhibited by the PPI.

Consumer Price Index

The consumer price index (CPI) was begun in the 1917–1919 period. It also is produced by the Bureau of Labor Statistics, which releases the index for each month around the third week of the following month.[2]

[2] A free monthly copy of the *Consumer Price Index News Release* is available from the Bureau of Labor Statistics, 200 Constitution Ave. N.W., Washington, D.C. 20212.

TABLE 4-3
Relative Weightings of Commodities Included in Producer Price Index,
December 1975

Commodity	Relative weighting	
	1963	1972
BY INDUSTRY		
Farm products	11.28	8.40
Processed foods and feeds	16.55	14.37
Textile products and apparel	5.76	5.78
Hides, skins, leather, and related products	1.08	.76
Fuels, related products, and power	10.39	10.34
Chemicals and allied products	6.55	7.17
Rubber and plastic products	2.02	2.80
Lumber and wood products	2.54	2.23
Pulp, paper, and allied products	4.75	5.28
Metals and metal products	13.45	13.00
Machinery and equipment	11.32	11.84
Furniture and household durables	2.86	3.44
Nonmetallic mineral products	3.05	2.82
Transportation equipment	6.26	8.61
Miscellaneous products	2.14	3.19
BY STAGE OF PROCESSING		
Crude materials for further processing	12.31	11.33
Foodstuffs and feedstuffs	7.84	6.97
Nonfood materials except fuel	3.18	3.15
Crude fuel	1.29	1.21
Intermediate materials, supplies, and components	47.28	47.11
Materials and components for manufacturing	25.62	25.59
Materials and components for construction	8.45	7.94
Processed fuels and lubricants	4.53	4.85
Containers	1.58	1.39
Supplies	7.09	7.35
Finished goods (including raw foods and fuel)	40.41	41.56
Consumer goods	31.47	29.71
Producer finished goods	8.94	11.85

SOURCE: U.S. Department of Labor, Bureau of Labor Statistics.

The BLS collects data on the best-selling items among approximately 400 categories of goods through several hundred BLS agents who visit a representative sample of more than 20,000 retail stores and service establishments in 85 major metropolitan areas. Private research firms and governmental agencies supply prices for used automobiles, housing expenses, educational fees, and numerous other items. Dwelling rental rates are provided by a group of more than 40,000 tenants. Mailed questionnaires collect information on such outlays as public transportation fares and utility rates. The price changes for various categories of goods and services are weighted according to their estimated importance in consumer budgets as of a certain base time period.

Relative weights for the principal spending categories in the so-called market basket used in constructing the CPI are based upon an extensive consumer expenditure survey conducted every several years. The relative weights of the items in the market basket can change between major surveys owing to changes in *relative prices* of the various items since the most recent bench-mark revision even though the *quantities* of such items are kept constant until the next consumer expenditure survey is carried out. In Table 4-4 the relative weights for several earlier survey periods are compared with the weights derived from the 1972–1973 consumer expenditure survey.

In 1978 the CPI underwent substantial revisions, resulting in the creation of two separate indices: (1) the CPI for urban wage earners and clerical workers (known as the CPI-W), which covers the spending patterns of middle-class city dwellers, who account for about 40 percent of the United States population; and (2) the CPI for all urban residents (known as the CPI-U), which encompasses the spending patterns of 80 percent of the population, including not only wage earners and clerical workers living in the city but also urban professionals, corporate executives, retirees, salaried workers, self-employed persons, and individuals who are unemployed or are receiving welfare. The spending patterns of Armed Forces personnel, farm families, and others who live outside major metropolitan areas are excluded from the CPI-U. As of the beginning of the 1980s, most attention was directed to the CPI-U as the preferred measure of changes in the CPI.

As with the PPI, the BLS has remedied a great many of the shortcomings of the price indices for consumer goods. To reflect more accurately changes in consumer life-styles and buying patterns, new products, and quality improvements, both the market basket of goods and services and consumer budget-spending patterns are updated more frequently. More attention has been paid to the problems of monitoring changes in housing costs (a particularly difficult area to measure accurately and equitably), income taxes, social security taxes, and medical insurance, each of which represents an important portion of an average consumer's budget.

These changes are important because the CPI is such a widely quoted

TABLE 4-4
Relative Weights of Principal Components of Consumer Price Index

Major group	Wage earners and clerical workers					All urban consumers, 1972–1974§	All urban consumers, December 1977¶
	1935–1939*	1952†	1963‡	1972–1973§	December 1977¶		
Food and alcoholic beverages	35.4	32.2	25.2	20.4	20.5	18.8	18.8
Housing	33.7	33.5	34.9	39.8	40.7	42.9	43.9
Apparel	11.0	9.4	10.6	7.0	5.8	7.0	5.8
Transportation	8.1	11.3	14.0	19.8	20.2	17.7	18.0
Medical care	4.1	4.8	5.7	4.2	4.5	4.6	5.0
Entertainment	2.8	4.0	3.9	4.3	3.9	4.5	4.1
Personal care	2.5	2.1	2.8	1.8	1.8	1.7	1.8
Other goods and services	2.4	2.7	2.9	2.7	2.6	2.8	2.6

SOURCE: U.S. Department of Labor, Bureau of Labor Statistics.
*Relative importance for the survey period 1934–1936 (updated for price change).
†Relative importance for the survey period 1947–1949 (updated for price change).
‡Relative importance for the survey period 1960–1961 (updated for price change).
§Relative importance for the survey period 1972–1973.
¶Relative importance for the survey period 1972–1973 (updated for price change).

indicator of changes in the cost of living for the average individual. As such, it is used to deflate other economic indicators, such as wage rates and retail sales figures, in order to calculate real gains or losses. The CPI governs escalation clauses in union contracts as well as in social security, military, civil service, and certain private benefit plans covering millions of American citizens. Each of these groups thus assumes a major interest in any proposed changes in calculation methods which would tend to increase or decrease the rate of change in the CPI. Numerous government transfer payments such as food stamps and school lunches, as well as worker-training and related welfare programs, are linked to changes in the CPI. Many other contractual obligations, such as royalty agreements, leases, and charters of transportation equipment, are also attached in some way to the rate of change in the CPI.

Implicit Price Deflator for the Gross National Product

The implicit price deflator for the gross national product, more commonly known as the GNP deflator, is produced by the Bureau of Economic Analysis in the U.S. Department of Commerce. Its chief virtue as an indicator of price change is its broad coverage of the economy. The GNP deflator is calculated by dividing the various subcategories of the GNP by the related price indices in order to convert the current-dollar GNP total into a real, or constant-dollar, GNP which is adjusted for inflation or deflation. The PPI is used as the deflator for numerous classes of capital goods, while the CPI index is employed to deflate various classifications of consumer outlays. Private industry supplies some specific price indices which are used to deflate specific components of the GNP such as construction outlays and imports. The deflated figures are then combined to arrive at a single total for the real GNP. This real GNP number is then divided into the current-dollar GNP to produce the GNP deflator. The GNP deflator from 1947 to 1979 is presented in Table 4-5.

Since services account for more than 45 percent of the United States GNP, the GNP deflator suffers somewhat from an inability to calibrate changes in the quality, as opposed to strict price changes, of services consumed. Another weakness of the GNP deflator is that it incorporates the shortcomings of the calculation methodology for both the CPI and the PPI, to the degree that these two price indices are relied upon to deflate the current-dollar components of the GNP.

Because of the way in which it is computed, the GNP deflator mirrors changes in the *composition* of national output as well as pure *price movements.* Therefore, changes in the reading of the GNP deflator could in theory take place even in the absence of price changes. The GNP deflator is released together with preliminary GNP data about 3 weeks after the end of each

TABLE 4-5
Implicit Price Deflator, Gross National Product

Year	Percentage change
1947	13.3
1948	6.9
1949	−1.0
1950	2.0
1951	6.8
1952	1.3
1953	1.5
1954	1.4
1955	2.2
1956	3.2
1957	3.4
1958	1.6
1959	2.2
1960	1.7
1961	0.9
1962	1.8
1963	1.5
1964	1.6
1965	2.2
1966	3.3
1967	2.9
1968	4.5
1969	5.0
1970	5.4
1971	5.1
1972	4.1
1973	5.8
1974	9.7
1975	9.6
1976	5.3
1977	5.5
1978	7.3
1979	8.9

SOURCE: U.S. Department of Commerce, Bureau of Economic Analysis.

quarter. It often happens that the GNP deflator is revised as many as three or four times in subsequent reporting periods, thus limiting its utility for the analysis of short-term fluctuations.

In November 19__ the Department of Commerce also began issuing a personal consumption expenditure (PCE) deflator on a monthly basis. In contrast to the _____ approach of the CPI, the PCE deflator takes into account _____ in consumption patterns. It also uses an imputed-rent _____ costs of homeownership, rather than following the C_____ certain percentage of the population buys and finance_____.

Privately Produced

Several private _____ various price indices which track price changes for a _____ than those covered by the governmentally issued _____ Moody's daily (spot) commodity price index. _____ index is composed of 15 actively traded items _____ daily price changes that directly influence co_____ The wide swings from 1973 to 1978 are du_____ price movements for such commodities as _____ place heavy reliance on privately produced price _____ published data covering major subcategories o_____ and the PPI. When using such specialized price _____ investor should keep in mind the general warning _____ construction of price indices set forth above.

Trends in _____ often foreshadowed by commodity price indices _____ Moody's, and by the raw industrial materials price _____ the BLS. The latter traces the spot prices of 13 _____ tallow, and burlap which are freely traded _____ processing, and are especially sensitive to _____ The raw industrial materials price index usually _____ or decreases in the broader price indices.

Another _____ the Livingston survey, has been published _____ Livingston, now associated with The Philadelphia _____ represents a relatively small group of business _____ levels of the PPI and CPI indices for _____ following year. In June it presents forecasts for _____ June. The survey is usually conducted in _____ the most recent observations available _____ generally those in force 2 months before publication.

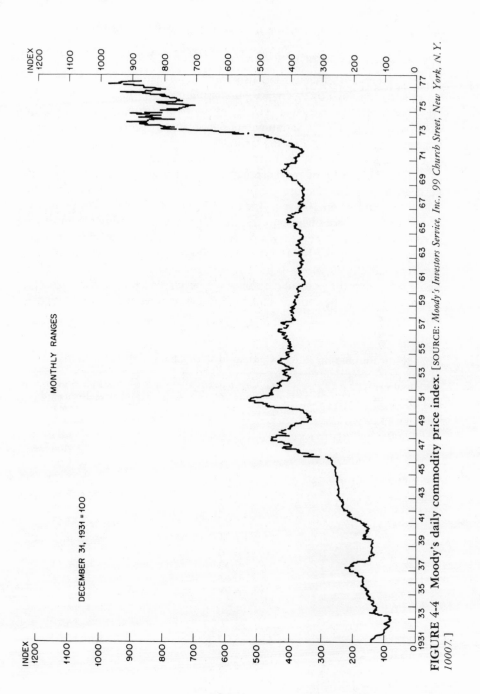

FIGURE 4-4 Moody's daily commodity price index. [SOURCE: *Moody's Investors Service, Inc., 99 Church Street, New York, N.Y. 10007.*]

Price Changes Compared with Purchasing-Power Changes

Price changes are often erroneously cited interchangeably with gains or losses in purchasing power. In fact, purchasing-power changes are the *reciprocal* of changes in the particular price index under discussion, with the assumption that the consumer is planning to purchase goods or services whose prices are being measured by a particular index.

For example, if the CPI declines at an annual rate of 5 percent, the increase in purchasing power of the currency is not precisely 5 percent but 5.26 percent. This is true because the price index has moved, for instance, from 100 to 95, and when 100 is divided by 95, the result is 1.0526. Similarly, if the price index rises by 6 percent, the decline in purchasing power of the currency equals not 6 percent but 5.66 percent, which is derived by dividing 100 by 106, to produce 0.9434, which represents an effective decline of 5.66 percent ($1.0000 - 0.9434 = 0.0566$) from the original level of the index. Table 4-6 shows the percentage change in purchasing power of a currency, given an absolute percentage change upward or downward in a particular price index.

TABLE 4-6
Changes in Purchasing Power Compared with Changes in Price Indices

Absolute price index change (percent)	If price index moves upward (+ percent)	If price index moves downward (− percent)
1.00	− 0.99	+ 1.01
2.00	− 1.96	+ 2.04
3.00	− 2.91	+ 3.09
4.00	− 3.85	+ 4.17
5.00	− 4.76	+ 5.26
6.00	− 5.66	+ 6.38
7.00	− 6.54	+ 7.53
8.00	− 7.41	+ 8.70
9.00	− 8.26	+ 9.89
10.00	− 9.09	+ 11.11
11.00	− 9.91	+ 12.36
12.00	− 10.71	+ 13.64
13.00	− 11.50	+ 14.94
14.00	− 12.28	+ 16.28
15.00	− 13.04	+ 17.65
16.00	− 13.79	+ 19.05
17.00	− 14.53	+ 20.48
18.00	− 15.25	+ 21.95
19.00	− 15.97	+ 23.46
20.00	− 16.67	+ 25.00

It is important to note that when the price index moves *upward* by a specified amount, the absolute value of the percentage *decline* in the purchasing power of the currency is *less* than the absolute value of the upward price change. Conversely, when the price index *falls* by a specified amount, the absolute value of the percentage *increase* in the purchasing power of the currency is *greater* than the absolute value of the downward price movement. The investor should keep these concepts in mind when stripping current-dollar results of the effects of price changes. For example, if a company's retail sales volume increased by 20 percent, from $100 million to $120 million, and if the average price inflation for the goods it sold during the period amounted to 5 percent, its real sales gain would not be precisely 15 percent but, instead, $120 million divided by $100 million, in turn divided by 1.05 ($\dfrac{\$120 \text{ million}}{\$100 \text{ million}} \div 1.05$), which equals 1.1429, or a real volume gain of 14.29 percent.

The following formula can be used to convert percentage changes in the price index to percentage increases or decreases in the purchasing power of the currency:

Percentage change in purchasing power (expressed as a decimal)=

$$\frac{1}{1 \pm \text{percentage price change (expressed as a decimal)}} - 1$$

For example, if the CPI declines by 4.5 percent, the percentage increase in purchasing power equals

$$\frac{1}{1 - 0.045} - 1 = \frac{1}{0.955} - 1 = 1.0471 - 1 = 0.0471, \text{ or } 4.71 \text{ percent}$$

In the autumn of each year the *Monthly Economic Letter*[3] contains a survey of purchasing-power changes in approximately 50 industrialized and developing countries. In addition, the International Monetary Fund each month issues detailed consumer price data for more than 75 countries.[4] More technical background on the use and construction of price indices is contained in *Inflation Accounting*[5] as well as in the text and bibliography of *Measuring Price Changes.*[6]

[3]Published by the Economics Department of Citibank, N.A., 399 Park Ave., New York, N.Y. 10022.
[4]Further information on this series can be obtained from the International Monetary Fund, Washington, D.C. 20431.
[5]Sidney Davidson, Claude P. Stickney, and Roman L. Weil, *Inflation Accounting,* McGraw-Hill Book Company, New York, 1976, pp. 91–100.
[6]Published by the Federal Reserve Bank of Richmond.

Unemployment Rate

The unemployment rate measures the percentage of the civilian labor force that is seeking work but does not have jobs. It gauges the unutilized or excess supply of labor in the market at existing wage rates. Although the unemployment rate is not an indicator of price changes in the economy, it is useful for investors to understand the construction, limitations, and extensions of this index because of its manifold relevance to prices as a reflection of job market pressures, consumer income and spending trends, and consumer psychology.

The coverage of the unemployment index varies widely from country to country. Furthermore, it does not reflect the number of foreign workers who may have been sent back to their own countries, the number of laborers who may be working on substantially reduced workweeks so that layoffs may be avoided, or the proportion of unemployed individuals who have just entered the job market or have voluntarily quit their jobs. In addition, the unemployment rate does not take account of the possible effects which minimum wage laws and state unemployment compensation practices may have on changing the total amount of labor demanded or supplied. Nevertheless, the unemployment rate is popularly accepted as a sign of the economic health or suffering of a nation. As such, it has often been regarded as a precursor to stimulative or restrictive monetary or fiscal actions which could directly affect interest rates and thus fixed-income securities prices.

For a number of years, many economists subscribed to the theory that a stable trade-off exists between price inflation and unemployment. This hypothesis is illustrated by the Phillips curve, named after A. W. Phillips, an economist who published a major article in 1958 on the connection between inflation and unemployment. The Phillips theory and much subsequent related work predict that an economy can obtain low levels of unemployment by allowing more inflation while striving for high economic growth rates. On the other hand, an economy can maintain a high degree of price stability if it is prepared to accept restrictive policies which may entail a higher unemployment rate. The events of the late 1960s and many years of the 1970s demonstrated that in numerous countries inflation rates and unemployment levels rose at the same time. Investors witnessed a simultaneous deterioration in the discomfort index, composed of the percentage unemployment rate added to the percentage change in the most commonly utilized price change index.

On the basis of the experience of the late 1960s and the decade of the 1970s, many economists concluded that while there may be a Phillips-curve type of trade-off between inflation and unemployment over the *short run*, no such trade-off is operative in the longer run since inflation raises the average level of unemployment. In fact, during the 1970s a number of major industrialized nations witnessed the following ... declining unemployment and declining inflation, (2) declining un... coupled with slightly rising inflation, (3) rising unemployment ... tion, and (4) rising unemployment and declining inflation. ... red to center on successively higher unemployment and ... in the 1970s. The application of monetary stimuli was found ... ingly less effect on reducing unemployment and increasingly ... raising the inflation rate. Some possible reasons for this phen... ation causing higher unemployment levels are discussed in C...

The unemployment rate is calcula... the BLS through a survey to find the employed and unem... of 56,000 American families. The data are released in the ... each month for the index of the previous month. Any out-... over a certain age who is exerting a nominal effort to ... d as unemployed. This number, divided by the total ... rce, produces the unemployment rate. In 1967 the mini... in calculating the index was raised from 14 to 16; since 90... 16- and 17-year-old population attends school, considera... o raising the minimum age to 18.

A number of different unemployme... mputed and identified by subscripts similar to those em... ns of the money supply. Seven of the most commonly ... es of unemployment are listed in Table 4-7. Addition... es are calculated for specific portions of the population ... o sex, age, race, skill level, geographical region, and ... nt that a particular group represents only a small percent... rican population

TABLE 4-7
Measures of Unemployment

Category symbol		
U_1	Unem...	...er
U_2	Indi...	...t jobs
U_3	Unem...	...old
U_4	Un...	...full-time jobs
U_5	O...	
U_6	W...	...U_4 as well
		...ing for
		...workers
		...ment
U_7	M...	...discouraged
		...of force

SOURCE: U.S. Department of Labor, Bureau of ...

and thus a small percentage of the survey sample, its unemployment rate can shift substantially up or down in response to small changes in the absolute number of workers or labor force participants from that group.

Many economists take issue with the minimum age requirement as well as with a number of other aspects of the calculation methodology for the unemployment rate. The legal requirement that recipients of welfare payments or food stamp assistance be counted as looking for work adds an estimated 0.5 to 2 percentage points to the unemployment rate. Certain seasonal adjustments, which even out the statistical series by removing changes caused by regularly recurring factors such as layoffs due to the start of winter weather, do not accurately reflect the realities of employer or employee behavior, particularly during recessions. For these and other reasons, it is useful to look at two additional labor force statistics as well as the employment rate.

The employment ratio is that proportion of the working-age civilian population that is employed. It measures the degree of utilization of potential labor resources whose services have been purchased in the labor market. The employment ratio takes into account shifts into and out of the labor force (those employed or looking for jobs). For example, when more persons move into the labor force, it is possible to have a high unemployment rate simultaneously with a high employment rate. This may mean that the labor market is tighter than is indicated by the unemployment rate.

The labor force participation rate is that proportion of the working-age population which is working or looking for work. Natural population growth affects the labor force participation rate, as does the entry of nontraditional labor participants into the labor force. The *percentage* composition of the labor force as of 1950 and 1977 is set forth in Table 4-8. The entry of greater numbers of adult females into the workforce between 1950 and 1977 led to an expansion of both the total labor force and adult females' representation in it.

A clearer comprehension of the actual economic conditions suggested by

TABLE 4-8
Percentage Composition of the United
States Labor Force

Category	1950	1977
Adult males	66	54
Adult females	27	37
Teen-agers	7	9
Total	100	100

SOURCE: U.S. Department of Labor, Bureau of Labor Statistics.

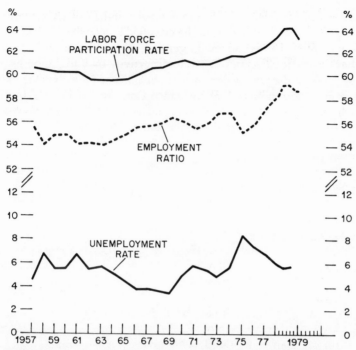

FIGURE 4-5   Labor force data. [SOURCE: *U.S. Department of Labor, Bureau of Labor Statistics; and Moody's Investors Service, Inc., 99 Church Street, New York, N.Y. 10007.*]

a given unemployment rate can be derived from an awareness of how the labor force participation rate can move upward or downward as (1) individuals decide to look for a job or not to seek employment and (2) demographic and social changes add or subtract certain groups to or from working-age population totals. For example, pursuit of such a line of analysis reveals that a majority of the unemployed persons in 1978 were living in families in which the head of household was working. Figure 4-5 shows the labor force participation rate, the employment ratio, and the unemployment rate for the period 1957–1979. The formulas for each of the three data series in the figure are as follows:

$$\text{Unemployment ratio} = \frac{\text{number of individuals without work seeking jobs}}{\text{total working-age civilian labor force}}$$

$$\text{Employment ratio} = \frac{\text{number of employed individuals}}{\text{total population over working age}}$$

$$\text{Labor force participation ratio} = \frac{\text{number of individuals working or looking for work}}{\text{total population over working age}}$$

A fairly reliable precursor of employment and business activity is the help-wanted index, compiled from the classified sections of a broad group of newspapers in the United States. In general, downturns in the help-wanted index have preceded declines in economic activity by 3 to 7 months during business cycles of the post-World War II period. The index was begun in the 1920s by the Metropolitan Life Insurance Company of New York; in the 1960s the Conference Board, a nonprofit economic information service, became responsible for its maintenance and publication.

5

The Causes and Effects of Inflation and Deflation

Overview

The causes and effects of inflation and deflation exert a powerful influence on investments in general and on fixed-income securities in particular. Although a number of nations have exhibited price stability for rather lengthy time spans, such behavior has not often been the norm. Throughout recorded history, inflations and deflations have followed one another with inexorable regularity. Each period of increase or decrease in the general price level has had its own unique duration and degree of severity, yet a close analysis of the events of prior eras can help the investor identify certain common trends and factors which can greatly reduce the risk of major losses as the cycles of inflation and deflation run their course.

One very significant but often ignored conclusion which can be drawn from a study of price level changes is the fact that many of the causes of inflation originate in the effects of or antidotes to the previous period of deflation, and vice versa. Another important observation concerns the difficulty of separating causes and effects for any given interval of inflation or deflation. Thus causes and effects are treated together in this chapter. Among economists, politicians, and the public at large there is very little agreement on the causes of the major inflations and deflations of the twentieth century. It is interesting to note the cyclicality even of certain economic theories, which flourish for a time, become discredited, and then are revitalized.

Some of the principal theories of business cycles, which seek to explain income, employment, and price changes, can be generally classified into two groups: (1) *demand*-oriented theories, which may be further divided into the monetarist school and the Keynesian school; and (2) *supply*-oriented theories. Some key tenets of these theories, as they apply to inflation and deflation, are described in the following paragraphs.

Monetarist School

Monetarists hold that the growth rate of the money supply is an independent *determinant* of price changes and other economic conditions rather than a passive and dependent *reflection* of economic fluctuations. Demand is managed by central bank actions on bank reserves to inject money into the economy or to withdraw it. Additional beliefs of the monetarist persuasion are (1) that changes in the behavior of the money supply are closely associated with changes in economic activity, money income, and prices and (2) that the interrelation between money and economic change has been highly stable in spite of significant changes in the economic and financial infrastructure.

The *adaptive-expectations branch* of monetarism holds that price changes are caused by aggregate demand and price expectations. Price expectations are said to be determined by past price history and hence by previous aggregate demand. Previous aggregate demand is derived from monetary growth rates. A less widely accepted hypothesis, the *rational-expectations branch* of monetarism, assumes that the public as a whole fully and swiftly discounts all the predictable elements which influence price changes. Accordingly, because they have already been correctly anticipated, systematic official policies which attempt to influence the rate of change in prices will not be successful and may actually be counterproductive. Only *unpredictable,* random disturbances are thought to produce monetary changes and thus variations in the behavior of prices.

Keynesian School

The economists who place primary emphasis on nonmonetary factors in explaining cyclical patterns in income, employment, and prices are often referred to as Keynesians. The Keynesian school is named after the British economist John Maynard Keynes (1883–1946) even though many of the nonmonetarists' views may not always coincide with those of Keynes. Keynesians hold that several economic variables other than money have systematic and pervasive effects on price changes. The variables include fiscal policy, the level of interest rates (which is importantly influenced by the real money supply), and investment spending (including both households' purchases of durable goods and businesses' investment outlays). Relatively small changes in investment spending, acting through a so-called multiplier effect, are felt to exert a major impact on prices, aggregate income, and employment.

Demand may be managed through changes in government spending, borrowing, and tax policies to distribute greater or lesser amounts of purchasing power to various sectors of the economy. Inflation or deflation can result from important upward or downward shifts in investment spending, which gives rise to increased or decreased levels of consumption expenditure.

Supply-Side School

The supply-oriented theory of income, employment, and prices concentrates on the role of suppliers in the marketplace. According to theories promulgated by the French economist Jean-Baptiste Say (1767–1832), changes in supply create changes in demand. Surpluses or deficits in the supply of goods and services can raise or lower demand, costs, and hence prices. Monetary and fiscal policies are relegated to a secondary role of accommodating price increases or decreases in order to maintain employment and production at a desired level. Commodity surpluses or deficits, the actions of unions and cartels, and other autonomous international occurrences which influence the supply side of the economy are deemed to have an important bearing on inflationary or deflationary trends.

Both the demand-oriented and the supply-oriented explanations of inflation and deflation have many convincing and useful elements. In the interests of completeness, parts of the models of each school are discussed in this chapter. The remainder of the chapter reviews (1) the causes and effects of inflation, (2) the causes and effects of deflation, and (3) the effects of inflation and deflation on capital value.

The Causes and Effects of Inflation

Definitions of Inflation

Inflation has numerous shades of meaning, but an essential feature of any definition of inflation is the condition of a substantial and continuing rise in the *general* level of prices. This condition should be distinguished from a rise in the price of a *specific* good or service because of a relatively transitory and self-correcting imbalance between supply and demand. Some economists distinguish between demand-pull inflation, when the flow of total expenditures exceeds the available flow of goods and services in the markets, and cost-push inflation, when the available flow of goods and services in the markets falls short of the flow of total expenditures. Further ambiguities in precisely describing inflation derive from the use of one term to describe many different rates of price increase, ranging from a rate as low as 1 percent or less annually to one as high as 100 percent or more annually. In addition, the rate of inflation has rarely proved to be constant. Over a period of years, inflation tends to accelerate or decelerate. Although the fact is not included in most textbook definitions of inflation, it should always be remembered that money loses value during inflationary periods. If the general price level doubles, the investor with the same amount of funds before and after such a price rise loses purchasing power to the same degree as if prices had remained stable and one-half of the investor's total funds had been completely lost.

Social and Demographic Origins of Inflation

In many societies, rising expectations of the public, group pressures, and competing, difficult-to-arbitrate claims on finite national output lie at the root of governmental policies and/or central bank actions that lead to inflation. Although many commentators and special-interest factions may attempt to do so, in pluralistic nations it is virtually impossible to fix the *ultimate* responsibility for the creation and furtherance of inflationary conditions. In a number of major industrial countries, narrowly elected legislative majorities have accommodated a popular desire for high employment, high income levels, and as high a degree of income and job security as possible even at the cost of inflation. In the United States, avoidance of the severe deflationary conditions of the 1930s was one of the key motivations behind the Employment Act of 1946, which directed the federal government to put primary emphasis on the promotion of maximum employment, followed by production and purchasing power.

Governments at the federal, state, and local levels may consciously decide to pursue inflationary policies and financing strategies because of a belief that such actions will help economic growth and/or assist officials and legislators in gaining reelection. Another major but often unrecognized source of support for increasing government expenditures (even if these are inflationary) is the large proportion of the American people who depend upon spending by one or more levels of government for a significant portion of their income. Table 5-1 shows the percentages of the population that consisted of government beneficiaries as of 1960 and 1977.

Of the 11.2 percentage-point gain between 1960 and 1977 in the share of the American population that depends on government for a major portion of its income, 9.2 percentage points were concentrated in the social security and welfare categories. It is noteworthy that the benefits transferred by the government to these two groups are generally indexed to inflation and incur relatively low rates of tax.

Part of the reason for the higher social security outlays stems from the greater absolute and relative numbers of individuals who receive disability

TABLE 5-1
Government and Nongovernment Beneficiaries, 1960 and 1977

Category	1960 (percent)	1977 (percent)
Not dependent on government		
Private sector employees and proprietors	26.4	26.5
Dependents of private sector workers	31.3	20.0
Subtotal, not dependent on government	57.7	46.5
Dependent on government		
Government employees and dependents		
Federal military	3.0	1.6
Federal civilian employees	2.8	1.9
State and local government employees	7.2	9.4
Private employment due to government		
spending, including dependents	10.2	8.3
Transfers and pensions		
Government pensions	0.8	2.2
Veterans' pensions	1.7	2.1
Social security	9.7	16.5
Welfare	1.9	5.3
Unemployment insurance	1.0	1.1
Dependents of transfer beneficiaries	3.3	3.2
Other recipients of government benefits	0.7	1.9
Subtotal, dependent on government	42.3	53.5
Total	100.0	100.0

SOURCE: A. Gary Shilling & Company, Inc., Economic Consultants, New York, N.Y.

payments, retirement benefits, or survivor benefits, and part derives from the voting power and cohesiveness of individuals over 55 years of age. Because they have higher voting percentages than those of younger age groups, citizens over 55 hold more than 40 percent of the voting power in most of the developed countries. The ratio of adult workers to individuals over 65 years of age was 3 to 1 in early 1980, compared with 11 to 1 when the social security program was established in 1935.

Another source of popular support for policies which allow inflation to continue is the group of citizens who have built up large amounts of mortgage debt and consumer installment debt. Along with corporate debtors, individual borrowers are able to repay depreciated dollars as long as inflation persists. In addition, under American tax laws most interest payments are deductible from taxable income.

*Domestic and International Monetary Growth as Key
Determinants of and Accompaniments to Inflation*

In virtually every period of inflation, one common condition has been an increase in the money supply, possibly coupled with a rise in the rate of turnover, or velocity, of the money supply. This holds true because the general price level is established by the quantity of money in circulation relative to the total amount of goods and services being supplied. Provided there are no large changes in the velocity of money and no lasting changes in the supply of goods and services, with some degree of lag the general price level will rise over time if the money supply is increased and the general price level will decline over time if the money supply is reduced.

If a country's monetary velocity rises (or falls), a given supply of money is able to finance an increased (or decreased) volume of economic transactions. Many analysts consider the effects of an expansion in monetary velocity to be as important as similar percentage increases in the money supply in raising inflationary tendencies. Although influenced by several variables, monetary velocity is greatly affected by *expectations* of inflation. When the general price level is steady or declining, the public appears to accept higher bank balances for a given level of economic activity, leading to a lower velocity of money. When the price level is increasing, individuals and businesses avoid holding excess money, which causes a rise in monetary velocity.

In general, changes in velocity move in the same direction as changes in the money supply. As inflation reaches sufficiently high levels, large increases in the velocity of money can take on a life of their own and cause prices to continue rising even though the real money supply may have ceased to expand and may in fact be in a declining phase. Sustained monetary growth can be initiated and augmented by a variety of nonmonetary forces and events, and such growth can take any of a variety of forms.

First, the money supply can be increased by means of an increase in the volume of bank reserves and thus in bank credit. This often happens as a result of various central bank actions which increase the reserve positions and lending ability of member commercial banks. Since this has been the primary means of increasing the money supply in the United States in recent decades, it is discussed at greater length below. Second, the money supply can be increased through rapid gains in the physical printing and circulation of paper currency. This happened in the United States after the Revolutionary War and during the Civil War and twice in France during the eighteenth century. Third, the money supply can be increased through debasement of the coinage. By clipping the edges off coins and/or melting down coins with a specific weight of precious metal and reissuing them with certain amounts of substituted metals of lesser value, governments have been able to make a given supply of precious metal go further. Fourth, the money supply can be increased through the rapid influx of new amounts of the principal standard of value in usage at the time. The most prominent example was the inflation in the sixteenth century which resulted after the Spanish discovery of gold in the New World and its importation into Europe. There have been other instances of inflations caused by a sudden surge in the supply of gold, owing to important new discoveries or to the conquest of one country by another, without a corresponding rise in the supply of goods and services.

It should be stressed that actions of the Federal Reserve System which increase the money supply often are taken not unilaterally but in response to real and perceived pressures from the administration and Congress to (1) assist in financing federal budget deficits (in the years from 1950 through 1980, the federal government experienced 25 years of budget deficits and 5 years of budget surpluses), (2) stimulate economic growth and employment, and (3) maintain interest rates at reasonable levels. The Federal Reserve Board can utilize several means of influencing the money supply through member bank reserves. The most direct method involves changes in the reserve levels against various types of customer deposits which member banks are required to maintain and not lend to borrowers.

A much more frequently used means of influencing banks' reserve positions and thus the growth of the money supply consists of Federal Reserve purchases of U.S. government securities which are paid for by creating a credit in favor of the seller's bank at the Federal Reserve. Such a process is known as the *monetization* of government debt. Monetization immediately augments the monetary base and adds to the growth of the money supply in its narrow and/or its more inclusive definition. The specific pattern of increase in the money supply depends on (1) the speed and strength of borrowers' reactions and (2) the extent of credit expansion caused by commercial banks' increased lending activities resulting from their higher reserve positions.

Specific measures of the money supply and their velocities can often exhibit varying rates of growth owing to changes in asset preferences, such as the increased tendency of many investors to place a portion of their temporarily excess cash balances in an environment of high interest rates in money market funds, whose assets amounted to $79.2 billion as of July 1980. Other factors which influence growth rates and velocities for various monetary aggregates include the more intensive use of cash management practices by individuals and businesses, as well as the introduction of new investment instruments and new technology for the transfer of demand and time deposits.

Behavioral changes in the financial sector of the economy can also have a significant though not immediately noticeable effect on the degree to which central bank policies and/or money supply increases influence inflationary trends. For example, to the extent that greater amounts of assets are controlled by commercial banks which are not members of the Federal Reserve System, commercial banks' liability management practices, lending policies, and other activities become less subject to the direct and immediate thrust of Federal Reserve restrictionary or expansionary policies. Banks and several other groups of financial institutions have developed techniques for obtaining funds and for avoiding or minimizing any deleterious results of rising interest rates. These new developments have tended to reduce the discipline which the central bank and the absolute level of interest rates once may have imposed on the financial system.

Another difficult-to-predict influence on currency balances and money supply growth is the so-called subterranean economy. The subterranean economy includes economic activity and income that is not reported to the tax authorities, sometimes for illegal reasons. Several sources estimated that the subterranean economy accounted for more than $225 billion in 1980, or an additional one-tenth of the American gross national product. Such activity appears to have been a factor behind the 10 percent compound annual rate of growth between 1965 and 1980 in currency in circulation, to more than $100 billion.

Monetization of government debt was further facilitated by two legislative acts of the 1960s which severed links between the United States currency and its gold stock. In March 1965, the gold reserve requirement was removed for Federal Reserve deposit liabilities. Prior to this measure, the Federal Reserve System had been required to hold a minimum of gold certificates (which represented the gold held by the U.S. Treasury) equal to 25 percent of the reserve deposits held on behalf of member banks and to 25 percent of all outstanding Federal Reserve notes. In March 1968, the 25 percent gold coverage requirement behind Federal Reserve notes was also removed.

Two other less powerful and less immediate contributors to money supply growth are bank lending to the private sector (including businesses and individuals) and the net foreign position of the banking system. The latter responds to outflows and inflows of funds caused by interest rate differentials, leads and lags in corporate money transfers, and other changes in the various current and capital accounts of a country's balance of payments.

Because of their effects not only on inflation but also on interest rates, changes in the money supply have extremely important implications for investors in fixed-income securities. Central bank measures to speed up monetary growth may often result in a *temporary downward* pressure on interest rates. Until inflationary expectations are affected, expansionary monetary policies generally stimulate output and employment. However, over the longer term, in part because of the public's rational expectations (described at the beginning of this chapter), an increased rate of monetary expansion can lead to higher actual and expected rates of inflation than otherwise would have been incurred. Such conditions usually result in *higher* interest rates, reduced output, and lower employment. On the other hand, low interest rates do not usually reflect forceful expansion of a country's money supply but, instead, a relatively restrictive monetary stance.

This seeming contradiction (as far as money is concerned) of the normal laws of supply and demand for most goods has been resolved through theories developed by the economist Irving Fisher (1867–1947). Fisher hypothesized that nominal interest rates comprise (1) a real interest rate component, defined as the nominal interest rate minus the anticipated rate of price change, and (2) an interest rate premium component, which is influenced by borrowers' and lenders' expectations about future price level changes.

Thus market participants do not act under so-called *money illusion,* which is behavior based on nominal values rather than on real values that have been adjusted for inflation or deflation. If inflation is expected to increase, borrowers acquiesce to higher nominal rates of interest since they anticipate that their debts will be repaid in reduced real terms. In like fashion, under inflationary conditions investors demand a higher nominal rate of interest to compensate for the lessened purchasing power of the interest and principal payments which they will receive. Although it was originally believed that the real rate of interest hovered around a relatively constant level over long periods of time, in practice both the real and the nominal rates of interest can fluctuate. Each is subject in varying degrees to economic forces, to the total supply of and demand for capital, and to other financial conditions.

To the degree that money can be easily moved across national boundaries, global trends in money supply growth can reinforce or vitiate the effects of a given rate of increase in a country's domestic money supply. When measuring total money supply growth in the world or in a large sample of major countries, investors should take into account (1) the domestic money supplies of the investor's home country and the other countries under review, (2) the effect of exchange rate changes when converting a country's money supply figures into the currency which the investor has chosen for analysis (*weaker* currencies than the investor's base currency will tend to *decrease* the money supply totals contributed by their respective countries to the world total, while *stronger* currencies will have the opposite effect of *increasing* the money supply when measured in terms of the base currency), and (3) the total Eurocurrency market. The Eurocurrency market is based upon the acceptance of deposits and the making of loans in currencies other than that of the country in which the bank is located. For the most part, Eurocurrency deposits are not included in countries' domestic monetary statistics.

Economists do not agree on whether the rapid growth of the Eurocurrency market in the 1970s actively contributed to or merely accompanied the acceleration of inflation in industrial countries. Resolution of this issue depends in part on the degree to which Eurocurrency deposits substitute for money balances or for other near-money instruments instead. If Eurocurrency deposits have in fact served as a substitute for *money balances*, the growth of the Eurocurrency market would tend to generate an increase in the total supply of credit unless it was counteracted by policies of central banks to reduce their respective national money supplies. On the other hand, if Eurocurrency deposits have served as a substitute for *near-money instruments*, the growth of the Eurocurrency market would tend merely to direct credit flows to new sources without expanding the world supply of credit (except for the freed-up reserves which otherwise would have to have been held against certain domestic time deposits). In any case, the psychological effects of the rapid expansion of the Eurocurrency markets during the 1970s very possibly influenced international investors' perceptions of credit expansion and potential currency movements in the key currencies which comprise the Euromarkets.

To determine whether the aggregate internal and external credit demands of a particular country are excessive compared with those of other nations, many analysts employ a measure known as Domestic Credit Expansion. This indicator includes (1) foreign financing granted to the government sector (for example, in the form of foreign central banks' purchases of domestic government debt), (2) bank credit to the domestic nonbank private sector, and (3) bank credit directly to the domestic public sector. If a country's total domestic spending and borrowing demands exceed aggregate domestic production and savings, the resulting monetary expansion and balance-of-payments deficit can lead to (1) an accumulation of the domestic country's currency by foreign central banks, (2) relending of this currency back to the domestic country's government sector through foreign central banks' purchases of domestic government debt, and (3) expansion of the foreign countries' money supply in response to a shortfall in the supply of savings to meet their internal credit demands. If a reduction in a country's balance-of-payments deficit is not accompanied by a diminution in its total public and private credit demands relative to the supply of savings, pressures can build up for higher rates of money supply growth and/or higher interest rate levels.

The actual level of Domestic Credit Expansion increases more rapidly than the growth rate in a country's broadly defined money supply, such as M_2, when the country is running a balance-of-payments deficit on private account. Conversely, when a nation experiences a balance-of-payments surplus on private account, Domestic Credit Expansion rises less rapidly than its broadly defined money supply growth rate. Since a given country's domestic money supply aggregates may be moving in a different direction or at a growth rate substantially different from that of its Domestic Credit Expansion index, close examination of this variable can often provide greater insight into the total monetary pressures likely to be operating on its own price indices and/or its currency exchange rates.

If monetization activities or other measures are used to hold interest rates at an artificially low level, inflationary trends are likely to continue. In addition, such low interest rates relative to investors' expectations may stimulate flows of investment funds into other countries. This can occur either because of possible higher nominal returns outside the investor's home country or because of a judgment that real returns may be higher in another country after adjustment for a relatively more favorable course of inflation and its eventually positive relative impact on that country's currency.

As the rate of inflation fluctuates, the rate of growth in the nominal and the real money supply often demonstrates a changing pattern. It was mentioned earlier in this section that the growth rate of the *nominal* money supply is an important determinant of *price changes*. The growth rate of the *real* money supply, which importantly influences *economic activity,* generally remains positive in the early stages of an inflation, as the money supply is rising faster than the rate of price increase. When the growth rate of the real money supply turns downward, inflation outstrips gains in the nominal money supply. Depending on the level of inflation and the velocity of money, it is possible to experience high rates of inflation even as economic activity and the real money supply are demonstrating significant declines.

The following paragraphs review a number of other influences which contribute to inflation. Many factors are actually the reactions of a particular sector of society to a rising general price level, while other factors manifest the social tensions, shifts in relative prices, and other policies which augment price increases.

Governmental Actions

Past a certain point, many actions of governmental bodies (at the federal level and also at the state and local levels) can directly or indirectly augment inflationary pressures. A partial listing of governmental policies which may contribute to inflation is included as Table 5-2.

At this point, it may be worth repeating that a great many of the root causes of inflation cannot be ascribed solely to "government." Most of the policies of government have been enacted by legislative and executive bodies that usually are reflecting the priorities of public sentiment, which may hold other goals (for example, avoidance of unemployment or recession) as higher objectives than combating inflation. In addition, governmental actions may have been taken in response to pressures from well-organized special-interest groups wishing to recapture lost purchasing power or to avoid or transfer to another social group the costs of certain programs while reaping their benefits.

Recent years have often witnessed an emphasis by government officials, and frequently by a large segment of the voting public, on the apparent short-term resolution of problems with little regard for possible deleterious

TABLE 5-2
Some Means by Which Governmental Policies May Contribute to Inflation

1. Excessive government spending policies	Government spending can influence inflationary pressures, depending on *(a)* its timing relative to the economic cycle, capacity utilization levels, recent inflationary experience, and inflationary expectations; *(b)* the type of government outlays and the sectors of the economy that are most severely affected; *(c)* its size and growth rate relative to the overall size and growth rate of the gross national product; *(d)* the balance-of-payments situation and other international factors; and *(e)* the combination of taxes and/or government borrowing through which the spending and deficit, if any, are financed.
2. Taxation policies which effectively increase the demand for goods and services and/or reduce the supply of goods and services	Misdirected taxation policies may *(a)* channel funds into inefficient uses, *(b)* encourage consumption at the expense of saving, *(c)* discourage capital formation, and *(d)* hinder research and development outlays and investment in more productive plant and equipment.
3. Excessive use of large-scale government guarantees, direct and indirect subsidies, and income transfers (U.S. federal government transfer payments totaled $250 billion in fiscal year 1980, up from $80 billion in fiscal year 1970)	Subsidized financing programs, transfer payments, and many other forms of government redistributions of income (often away from productive economic sectors) may enable increasingly large segments of the economy to receive and/or spend funds which market forces would not otherwise have allowed.
4. Excessive involvement in the pricing mechanism in certain sectors of the economy through such devices as rate-setting agreements, minimum wage levels, agricultural or industrial market price support programs, tariffs, import barriers, price controls, or restrictions on output	Demand for the good or service in question may be overly stimulated and/or supplies may be withheld from the market if prices are held below equilibrium levels. Alternatively, if prices are held above equilibrium levels for certain goods or services, costs and price structures may be maintained at higher levels than could be otherwise achieved, and lesser amounts of the good or service will be consumed.

TABLE 5-2
Some Means by Which Government Policies May Contribute to Inflation
(Continued)

5. Excessively perfectionist regulation of industry standards in such areas as safety, employment and retirement practices, and the environment	Such measures may cause the diversion of economic resources toward the provision of regulatory services by the public sector and compliance with regulatory measures by the private sector. In the process, costs may be pushed upward and economic efficiency reduced.

consequences in the longer run. This emphasis has been frequently compounded by the necessity of swiftly reacting to events or policies which influence the United States economy but which have been initiated outside the country. Finally, many advanced democratic societies exhibit some measure of difficulty in developing a national understanding of economic issues and a consensus on policy actions.

A further difficulty may arise when one branch of government takes overstimulative measures to counter what it considers to be restrictive policies by another branch or level of government. Even the threat of such action can limit the range and effectiveness of proposed disinflationary programs.

In the government sector, inflation thus tends to produce an expansion of state, local, and federal involvement, both in response to political demands for assistance and as a result of the higher level of nominal tax receipts usually generated under inflationary conditions. Because of the real income redistribution caused by inflation and the erosion of all forms of fixed dollar payments, such as principal and interest, rent, salaries, annuities, insurance policies, and other types of unindexed money flows, inflation creates demands on the government to structure mechanisms which will protect the recipients of fixed money payments against the declining purchasing power of the currency. Such devices include indexation and price escalation clauses. Although wage-price controls are well known for the dislocations and shortages which they bring about, continued inflation often leads to temporary support for such programs as well as for rationing schemes.

Other Inflationary Influences

Besides the social, monetary, and governmental factors which have already been reviewed in this chapter, numerous other factors can add to the inflation rate. In many cases, these factors may be able to impart lasting effects only because of underlying inflationary conditions in the social, monetary, and governmental spheres. In many other cases, these factors may act on the prices of specific goods and services rather than on the general price level. Nevertheless, owing to existing rigidities in the marketplace, a rise in the price of a specific good or service does not always lead immediately to a reduction in demand for the good or service in question and/or a downward adjustment in prices for other goods and services.

In such special cases, a *specific* price rise may in fact contribute to a rise in the *general* price level. This was the case with petroleum and several other forms of energy for certain periods during the 1970s and the beginning of the 1980s. It should also be mentioned that the degree of sensitivity of prices to changes in demand can vary greatly for individual goods and services. Factors which determine the degree of sensitivity of prices for a given good or service to changes in demand include (1) the number, market dominance, and pricing power of individual producers, (2) the extent of internationalization of production and trade, (3) the amount of actual and perceived product inventory levels and the degree of speculative or hedge buying of the good or service in question, and (4) the existence of statutory price support programs.

At a specified level of *demand,* external factors such as harvest conditions in general tend to influence price levels by changing the *supply* of goods and services. On the other hand, at a specified level of *supply* macroeconomic policies such as the amount of government spending and other factors tend in general to affect price levels by influencing the *demand* for goods and services. As mentioned earlier, any actions or events which tend to increase demand relative to supply or to reduce supply relative to demand will tend to raise prices for the good or service in question. The degree of influence of a specific external factor or policy action on the inflation rate also depends on the lead time necessary for it to take effect and the cyclical and secular stage of expansion or contraction in the domestic and international economy.

The growth rate of consumption relative to the productive capacity of various branches of the economy, such as housing, automobiles, or basic industry goods, can greatly influence price levels over the short and intermediate runs. Once a certain capacity utilization figure for a given industry has been surpassed (usually in the middle to high 80 percent range), incremental output gains are achieved at the expense of rising prices and higher marginal costs because the least efficient factors of production are usually employed in the later stages of an economic cycle. Similarly, the most efficient plant and equipment are generally the last to be idled in the trough of an economic downturn and the first to be reemployed when the economy turns up again. This process accounts for the relatively small productivity gains which occur late in an economic cycle and the large productivity advances which may be attained early in an economic cycle.

Capacity limits relate not only to capital equipment but also to the supply of labor. When labor unions as well as the nonunionized workforce negotiate higher wages, in part to maintain or recoup real purchasing power, businesses may institute price increases in order to restore profit margins and increase the flow of internally generated funds. Some labor contracts have cost-of-living escalator clauses which link wage gains to increases in a specified price index. The actual effect of wages on prices depends on (1) the rate of gain in employee productivity, (2) the domestic and international competitive situation in a particular industry, and (3) whether profit margins and rates of return are sufficiently high to reduce the perceived necessity of businesses to increase selling prices.

In the case of oil, significantly higher prices in the decade of the 1970s contributed to inflationary trends in several ways. First, energy costs were raised in the United States and in many other countries. As mentioned earlier, consumption patterns were often slow in reacting to these price increases because of certain structural rigidities. Second, higher revenue flows to oil-producing countries were often followed by increased demand and higher domestic prices for goods and services imported by the oil-producing nations. Third, higher oil prices generally exacerbated the deficits in the American balance of trade and balance of payments. This phenomenon was one factor in lowering the external value of the United States dollar and in causing the oil-producing countries to raise their prices still further.

Currency Exchange Rates

The system of currency exchange rates can have a pronounced influence on inflationary tendencies. Under the classic gold standard system, which the U.S. Congress adopted in 1879 and abandoned on June 5, 1933, nations defined their currency in terms of gold and allowed their currency to be exchanged for gold. The importation and exportation of gold was also permitted under the gold standard. When excessive inflation and a balance-of-payments deficit built up in a particular country, its government was forced by the system to implement restrictive economic policies. This process of demand restraint and falling prices eventually restored the balance of payments to equilibrium and helped the deficit country maintain the exchange parity and gold convertibility of its currency. Such an institutionalized brake on inflation carried the offsetting disadvantages of occasionally high unemployment levels and severe deflation.

The gold exchange standard, maintained from 1944 until 1971, pegged currencies to the United States dollar rather than to gold itself. The dollar was made convertible into gold on demand at a price of $35 per ounce. The gold exchange standard sought to avoid the competitive devaluations and the resultant harsh economic adjustments of the 1930s (under the gold standard) through putatively more modern mechanisms such as the adjustable-peg exchange rate system and stabilization funds established by the International Monetary Fund. This system of relatively fixed exchange rates tended to reduce wide disparities in inflation rates among major nations as balance-of-payments deficits transferred purchasing power from domestic citizens to foreigners in surplus countries. Such transfers tended to balance out the monetary pressures acting upon the inflation rate in various countries.

The United States dollar's convertibility into gold was suspended in August 1971, and the dollar was devalued in late 1971 and in early 1973, signaling the advent of freely floating exchange rates. Under such a system, currency rates are determined by foreign exchange market forces, supplemented to varying degrees by central bank intervention.

Aside from the higher costs associated with wider spreads on foreign exchange markets under conditions of floating currency rates, it has not been proved that floating exchange rates are more inflationary than fixed exchange rates. Nevertheless, floating exchange rates have produced a much wider range of inflation rates than obtained under the fixed-parity system. Under floating exchange rates, each country has greater independence in determining or combating its inflationary experience, since nations showing a balance-of-payments surplus are no longer obligated to support the United States dollar, as they were under the gold exchange standard.

Support measures for the United States dollar have the effect of increasing a country's domestic money supply and allowing inflationary pressures to build up. However, in the 1975–1979 period some surplus countries chose to keep their domestic inflation rates on a downward path, even at the expense of lower real economic growth, higher exchange rates, and a less competitive export position (which was due to the fact that such nations' currencies were rising).

Exchange rate movements can contribute to inflation as well as reflect inflationary trends relative to those experienced in other nations. If a country encourages or experiences devaluation of its currency while domestic inflation continues, goods imported from abroad become more expensive and domestic producers of similar goods may raise their prices rather than seek a competitive price advantage compared with the foreign producers. As mentioned earlier, foreign purchases of lower-priced domestic goods and services may increase under conditions of a depreciating currency in a given country, adding to inflationary demand pressures.

Under certain circumstances, once a country has demonstrated a trend and an attitude toward its domestic inflation, floating exchange rates can exacerbate currency movements and thereby affect a country's domestic inflation rate. Balance-of-payments *surplus* countries with relatively lower inflation rates and stronger currencies may attract additional inflows of funds in settlement of their balance of payments or in expectation of continued currency appreciation. This puts upward pressure on the value of the currency, lowering the local price of imported goods and hastening the anticipated slowdown in the domestic inflation rate.

Conversely, balance-of-payments *deficit* countries with relatively higher inflation rates and weaker currencies may experience outflows of funds which put downward pressure on the currency. This augments the domestic inflation rate by increasing the domestic currency price of imported goods. Similarly, when a country's authorities consciously seek to depreciate the external value of their currency, they may actually aggravate domestic inflation to a point which results in a currency level lower than that intended. This phenomenon, known as "overshooting," can also take place in reverse for a country whose currency is appreciating. Continued inflation may give rise to an eventual loss of international confidence in the inflating country's currency. In extreme cases, inflation may bring about an insistence upon exchange by barter, which causes economic inefficiencies and lower production levels. Regardless of the form of exchange rate system, when wide divergences in inflation rates persist in various countries over long periods of time, any high levels of unemployment may lead to trade barriers, capital controls, and other protectionist measures.

Indexation

Indexation is the regular adjustment of wages, interest payments, rents, pensions, and other forms of income to the inflation rate. Rather than slowing the inflation rate in a given country, indexation can actually cause it to rise. This may occur because of the immediate and automatic feedback of higher wage costs into higher prices, leading in turn to higher wage costs. Such a wage-price spiral adds to pressures by competing groups to redistribute the national income in order to maintain their purchasing power. Finally, indexation may divert efforts away from the central task of reining in inflation.

Effects of Inflation

The effects of inflation are many and varied. They range from purely economic effects to far-reaching social changes, depending on the duration and the severity of the inflation. Many of the effects of inflation are inextricably bound up with their causes and have been mentioned earlier in this chapter.

The effects which inflation has on varying sectors of the economy depend upon (1) whether the annual rate of price change is low, moderate, high, or in the double-digit category, (2) whether the rate of price change is accelerating or decelerating, and (3) whether corrective actions are expected to be instituted to reverse or slow down the price trend. The investor should keep in mind that there is no such thing as a set of average inflationary or deflationary conditions, just as there is no constant rate of price increase or decline. A number of the most significant effects of inflation cannot be precisely measured. These include extremes of optimism or pessimism, a deterioration in life-style for many segments of the population, greater conflict among societal groups, strains between them and official institutions, and heightened tensions between nations themselves.

Although inflationary periods are often permitted to endure because of a public aversion to the costs of ending inflation, ultimately the *failure* to control high rates of inflation has usually proved to have an even higher social cost. Over time, the behavior of various sectors of an economy in an inflationary phase usually is altered by increasing sophistication, technological change, and the effects of the inflation itself.

As discussed earlier, when inflationary pressures mount, public opinion often swings in favor of various forms of economic guidelines and controls. Such controls may be imposed on wages, prices, dividends, extensions of credit, and international capital flows. As a means of trying to contain inflation, controls have frequently been discredited since they are often adopted as an alternative to acceptance of stringent disinflationary monetary and fiscal initiatives. In addition, certain groups may be able to obtain exemption from controls because of their political power and/or control of the production of vital necessities. Controls tend to cause the misallocation of economic resources, and they may also lead to serious imbalances in sectors which are not controlled.

For example, controls on wages may lead to excessive job changing so that employees can obtain higher compensation that their existing employers are not allowed to grant. Controls on prices may lead to a diversion of productive capacity to uncontrolled products or to international markets offering higher prices. Owing to a resultant contraction in profit margins, businesses may reduce their investment in new domestic production capacity and eventually may close facilities. Credit controls may lead to fierce competition between various public and private users of capital.

As long as it is freely allowed, inflation generally encourages borrowing. This is often due to the borrower's expectations that (1) the debt can eventually be repaid in devalued currency in real terms, (2) the inflation-adjusted, aftertax cost of servicing the debt will be low, and (3) the price gain in assets purchased will outstrip debt charges. The resultant rush to purchase real assets and concomitant high absolute interest costs can vastly increase the financial risk and reduce the liquidity of borrowers. The additional debt is taken on because of increased money needs arising from higher costs of operating and of capital outlays, a reliance on loans and bonds rather than equity financing owing to the lower aftertax costs of capital, and the downward pressure on stock prices engendered by sustained inflation. Contrary to popular belief, even under hyperinflationary conditions broad stock market averages have not exhibited sharp price rises except for certain brief periods.

Over time, inflation-induced borrowing impairs the liquidity and solvency of many business enterprises and thus restricts the use of capital to expand production facilities. These supply constraints come about in inflationary periods because of (1) a need to restructure corporate balance sheets, (2) depressed current rates of return compared with the cost of capital, and (3) low expected profitability levels of new investment due to heightened uncertainties about sales prices, production costs, and production factor availability.

Investment moneys, possibly supplemented with borrowed funds, are often diverted by individuals and other corporate and institutional investors away from sound undertakings into liquid assets or into more speculative ventures which promise faster and larger rewards. In such times, speculative skills in business are often more highly rewarded than productive skills, and the public's opinion of the business sector suffers accordingly. Funds are channeled away from financial assets into real assets such as art, precious metals and other commodities, real estate, and even more esoteric investment media. This excessive demand usually drives up the prices of such goods beyond reasonable levels, increasing these goods' attractiveness to speculators and refueling the upward price spiral.

Inflation wreaks a great deal of damage in financial markets, particularly on fixed-income securities prices because of rising interest rates. It has been shown that long-term interest rates have tended to move up and down in fairly close correlation with the long-range momentum of commodity price trends. This has almost always been the case except during periods of capital rationing, when inflation rates may be high for a brief period of time. At such times, investors usually have not demanded appropriately high interest rates because they have correctly judged that the high inflation rate would not persist.

After an extreme hyperinflation, such as that which occurred in Germany in the early 1920s, bonds were wiped out and several years later were revalued by law to 25 percent of their original face value. In the difficult economic times in Germany immediately after World War II, bonds were devalued to 6.5 percent of their original face value. More recently, in the high-inflation period of 1974–1975 in Great Britain, the British 2.5 percent consol bonds (with a perpetual maturity) sold down to a market price (below 15 percent of par value) which was lower than their yield (17 percent). In large part owing to very high inflation rates, fixed-income yields in the United States also reached record high levels in 1980.

In addition to the effect of high interest rates, even a comparatively modest rate of inflation can destroy the purchasing power of a financial asset over a period of years. This is demonstrated in Table 5-4 below. Inflation can also disrupt the trading mechanism of the securities markets, causing less active and less liquid market-making activity by broker-dealer firms, reduced dealer positions, and generally wider trading spreads for a given class of securities.

Because lenders and investors tend to experience losses in real terms during inflation, they may seek securities with asset protection as well as earnings capacity. Significant interest rate concessions and other special inducements are often required for borrowers to market their debt. It becomes increasingly difficult for lower-rated issuers to raise funds in the securities markets, and these issuers are usually compelled to rely upon sources of short-term finance for capital. Financial intermediaries which borrow at short-term interest rates and lend at fixed long-term interest rates may face a severe liquidity or profit margin squeeze if inflation causes short-term interest rates to rise significantly above long-term interest rates.

Some lenders and investors choose not to provide long-term funds during an inflationary environment, causing a reduction in the average length of fixed-income securities' maturities for newly issued bonds, particularly those of medium- and lower-rated issuers. Commercial banks may sustain increased risk or actually realize losses when inflation causes their borrowing clients to add increasing amounts of debt to their financial structure. Because continued inflation eventually erodes the real worth of *all* financial assets, pension funds and other institutional and individual investors may find that their total investment assets fall far short of future actuarial needs and other requirements.

At *moderately* rising levels of inflation, experience has shown that in a number of countries consumers may step up their rate of savings because of expectations that future expenses will cost more and because of precautionary motivations related to uncertainties about prospective income and job security. However, as actual and expected inflation rates move higher, a substantial reduction takes place in the personal savings rate in favor of the acquisition of numerous forms of tangible assets.

In the private sector, high inflation encourages business and individual consumption patterns which outstrip rates of growth in supply. Such practices lead to hoarding and scarcities as producers withhold sales while consumers attempt to purchase more than their current needs on account of anticipated price rises. While this process produces large inventory profits for business, the profits are illusory since the inventories must be replaced at higher costs. An additional source of overstated corporate earnings in inflationary periods is the practice of basing depreciation charges on the original (lower) costs of plant and equipment rather than on the much higher replacement costs.

It should be emphasized that (1) not all inflations follow the same course and (2) some of the effects of inflation take place with a high degree of variability according to the severity of the inflation rate. If a society has the misfortune to pass through very high rates of inflation (and perhaps hyperinflation), it becomes increasingly difficult for businesses and consumers to find protection against inflation. As this occurs, the value of the savings and currency holdings of large numbers of people is severely impaired if not destroyed altogether.

The lack of capital formation, the increasingly speculative orientation and yet illiquid financial positions of businesses, and the depreciation of the internal and external value of the currency all contribute to declining production rates, higher levels of unemployment, greater divisiveness among various societal groups, and a growing distrust of government and most forms of economic statutes. On many occasions in the history of nations, extremely high inflation has precipitated radical social change. Eventually such high inflation sows the seeds of its own collapse and of a subsequent severe deflation.

In view of the dire consequences of allowing high inflation to run its course, much debate has been focused on the means and costs of reducing and eventually eradicating inflation. As inflation accelerates, it becomes increasingly difficult to combat high rates of price increase through conventional monetary and fiscal policy initiatives. It is generally agreed that absent an unexpected event in the economic or political sphere to slow inflation, it can be brought under control only when the costs of inflation to a large majority of the voting population vastly outweigh the perceived benefits of inflation or the not insignificant costs of eliminating inflation.

When the political climate favors a broad-scale reduction of inflation, a number of measures may be taken. Most of these actions are oriented toward increasing production and/or restricting demand. Some of the measures proposed to decrease the inflation rate include (1) a reordering of government spending priorities and a greater degree of restraint on the relative growth of the public sector; (2) balanced governmental budgets; (3) greater emphasis on productivity gains and supply-side expansion (through the dismantling of controls where necessary) in the private sector; (4) restoration of incentives to save, work, and invest; (5) significantly slower or negative rates of monetary expansion, credit growth, and debt monetization; and (6) the firm linkage of the monetary system to some form of widely accepted, relatively inelastically supplied, freely convertible medium of exchange and store of value such as gold.

The Causes and Effects of Deflation

Definitions of Deflation

The term "deflation" refers to a declining trend in the general price level. Since deflations often accompany periods of declining economic activity (usually known as recessions or, in their more severe form, as depressions), the terms "deflation" and "depression" are often erroneously confused with each other. The years of the early 1930s in the United States, widely known as the Great Depression, have been extensively analyzed by both economists and historians for insight into the major causes and effects of deflation. Because of this and because the Great Depression era was so severe and lasted so long, this period is referred to extensively in this chapter.

In the trough of the Depression, industrial production had declined by 53 percent from its earlier peak levels in the United States and by close to 20 percent in the United Kingdom. Unemployment reached a high of 25 percent of the labor force in the United States, 13 percent in the United Kingdom, and 30 percent in Germany. Some additional statistics comparing the Great Depression with the eight major business slowdowns in the United States since the Depression are shown in Table 5-3.

Two Major Schools of Thought on the Causes of Deflation

Disagreement persists over the underlying reasons for deflations in general and for the deflationary experience of the Great Depression in particular. As with inflation, it is difficult if not impossible to isolate and identify a *single* cause of deflation. Deflationary forces and events, like inflationary ones, are often not immediately recognizable as such since their impact may seem slight until it is combined with or reinforced by other deflationary factors. In general, the main schools of opinion are grouped in one way or another around (1) the *monetary* explanation, which holds that the economic decline of the 1930s was caused by negative growth in the money supply and the collapse of the banking system, and (2) the *spending* explanation, which holds that a massive decline in spending by both consumers and businesses played a key role in causing the economic falloff of the 1930s.

The monetarists point to the decline in the narrowly defined money supply (M_1) from \$28.2 billion in September 1929 to \$13.5 billion in March 1933, a decline of 52 percent. In part, such a decline in the money supply was allowed because of the prevalence of the "liquidationist" theory among several members of the Federal Reserve Board. This line of thought held that

TABLE 5-3
Comparative Statistics for Nine Periods of Declining Economic Activity

Official onset of economic decline	Official end of economic decline	Length in months of economic decline	Percentage decline in industrial production	Peak unemployment rate experienced during decline (percent)
August 1929	March 1933	43	53.4	24.9
May 1937	June 1938	13	32.4	20.0
February 1945	October 1945	8	38.3	4.3
November 1948	October 1949	11	9.9	7.9
July 1953	May 1954	10	10.0	6.1
August 1957	April 1958	8	14.3	7.5
April 1960	February 1961	10	7.2	7.1
December 1969	November 1970	11	8.1	6.1
Nobember 1973	March 1975	16	14.7	9.1

SOURCE: National Bureau of Economic Research.

money should be created only to meet the actual needs of the business sector. It was felt that "liquidation" would eventually stimulate business loan demand. Therefore, the Federal Reserve Board decided against expansion of the money supply through open-market purchases of U.S. Treasury securities.

Conscious actions to reduce price levels have often been associated with declining or even negative rates of monetary growth. A decrease in the money supply produces contractionary effects on the total volume of spending as well as on debt levels. For example, in response to a very high rate of price inflation in 1920 the Federal Reserve Board sharply decreased the money supply. This action played a major role in lowering the consumer price index in 1921 by 11 percent and in reducing the nominal GNP in 1921 by 24 percent, while unemployment rose from 600,000 to 4,800,000 workers.

During the 52 percent decline in the money supply in the 1929–1933 period, the United States GNP fell from $103.1 billion in 1929 to $55.6 billion in 1933. Meanwhile, unemployment rose from 1,600,000 workers to 12,800,000 workers. Commercial bank failures (which in many cases encouraged withdrawals by depositors and the hoarding of assets in liquid form), the liquidation of securities margin debt, and Federal Reserve policies all contributed to the reduction in the money supply.

Just as rising debt creation, the widespread use of leverage, and excessive borrowing activity add to inflationary tendencies, the liquidation of debt through bankruptcies or other means such as accelerated debt repayment or debt renegotiation can sharply reduce the total amount of money seeking to purchase goods. Such conditions generally put downward pressure on prices. Almost 10,000 banks (out of 25,000 banks then existing in the United States) with total deposits of $7 billion suspended operations through merger, failure, or liquidation in the 1930–1938 period. Total *losses* to depositors amounted to $1.3 billion during this period.

When individuals and business enterprises use their income or capital to pay down debt, by definition they are diverting resources which otherwise could have have been spent on the consumption of goods and services. Particularly when the economy is starting from high levels of mortgage debt, installment debt, and other forms of indebtedness, repayment measures can induce lower income levels because of lower spending. This process sets off further rounds of debt reduction as borrowers devote increasing percentages of their diminished income to meeting principal and interest payments. Such periods may see liquidity crises in the domestic and international corporate and banking sectors as well as in governments and government agencies.

The spending school places great emphasis on the decline in business and consumer spending just prior to and during the 1930s. This drop in spending was partly caused and partly accompanied by a number of factors. The first and perhaps the most widely discussed influence on consumer and business spending was the massive decline in equity prices. Between the third quarter of 1929 and the second quarter of 1932, the Standard & Poor's Composite Index fell by 77 percent, and the total market value of all corporate equities declined by $74 billion. The Dow Jones Average of Industrial Stock Prices declined by 89 percent, from 381.17 in 1929 to 41.22 in 1932.

Second, a severe decline took place in the income of the agricultural labor force (which represented 25 percent of the total labor force in the late 1920s, compared with 4 percent in the late 1970s). The producer price index declined by 31 percent in the Great Depression, and the consumer price index fell by 25 percent.

Third, partly as a result of a so-called shift to profits during much of the 1920s decade, businesses had greatly expanded capacity, particularly in automobiles and other durable goods. In the early 1930s, overcapacity led many businesses to reduce prices in order to expand or maintain sales, keep plants operating, and reduce inventory levels. The amount of new investment in plant and equipment and the rate of return on investment declined significantly. This situation was aggravated by several governmental initiatives in the early 1930s to maintain wage levels even as prices were falling. Many businesses were forced to reduce drastically the size of their labor forces.

The failure of some businesses tended to reduce further overall output and employment and to maintain downward pressure on prices. Such uncertainty reinforced the cautious consumer-spending environment, which led consumers to delay or cancel their spending outlays, especially on high-priced purchases.

Reduced spending by consumers, businesses, and governments can cause even lower output levels, which can have particularly devastating financial and operational effects following a period of large expansion in such areas as industrial capacity, residential building, and commercial construction. Falling industrial production and declining price levels may raise *real* hourly wage levels but put downward pressure on *nominal* wages and employment levels. If several industrial countries all experience deflationary conditions simultaneously, it becomes extremely difficult for one major nation to extend assistance to try to arrest the downward spiral, whether through loans, outright grants, or increased purchases of the deflationary countries' exports. Large numbers of new entrants into the labor force through immigration, population growth, or societal changes (as when more than one member of a household seeks work) may accelerate the decline in hours worked and/or wage rates and total income.

Provided that government spending accounts for a sufficiently large percentage of GNP, a major source of deflation can stem from deliberately restrictive policies instituted by the government. Such policies can put downward pressure on prices through (1) restraints on demand or (2) strong incentives to greater supplies of goods and services.

Demand restraints include substantial tax increases, large cuts in government spending, and the removal of governmental programs which serve to stimulate consumption. Such measures may originate from a shift in national priorities toward combating or reversing excessive price increases even at the expense of a possible rise in the unemployment rate. One such example occurred in Germany in 1948, when government spending was sharply curtailed at the same time that wage-price controls were lifted, leading to a rapid decline in the inflation rate. In some cases, tax-oriented incomes policies (TIP), with restraint exercised through tax penalties or bonuses, may be applied in an attempt to reduce prices without resorting to mandatory controls or to large declines in employment levels.

Examples of governmental policies which can reduce prices by *stimulating supplies* of goods and services include (1) deregulation and the encouragement of price competition in regulated industries with a previously fixed pricing structure, (2) training and injection into the labor force of various groups of professional, technical, or skilled workers in short supply, (3) suspension of acreage allotments and other governmental agricultural price support programs, and (4) removal of immigration controls and import restrictions on categories of laborers and products that enter the marketplace at wage and price levels much lower than those in force domestically.

Certain circumstances which are normally thought of as tending to maintain or drive up price levels may carry sharply deflationary consequences when carried to their extremes. If several major trading nations erect overly restrictive tariffs, quotas, and other barriers to the free flow of international trade, total employment in these and other countries may fall off sharply in response to lowered aggregate production levels. These conditions are discussed below in further detail.

Several additional factors are frequently hypothesized to have played an important part in converting what would otherwise have been a deep recession of the 1929–1930 era into the Great Depression. Some of these factors have more plausibility than others. The falloff in home construction is alleged to have contributed to the protraction of the economic decline, but in reality the home-building boom had reached a peak several years before the 1929 stock market crash. Perhaps more relevant was the burdensome level and short maturity of most home mortgage debt in the United States. For example, the average maturity of residential mortgages was only 7.5 years in 1929. When individuals were unable to repay or service this debt because of unemployment or when the banks tried to call in certain mortgages to shore up their own liquidity, a large number of foreclosures resulted.

In recent years, increased attention has been devoted to the international aspects of the deflationary years of the early 1930s. The end of the 1920s and the beginning of the 1930s witnessed a significant increase in protectionistic sentiment and the establishment of trade barriers as many nations sought to solve their economic problems at the expense of other countries. In the United States, the Smoot-Hawley Tariff Act of 1930 increased import duties on more than 20,000 types of goods. Within such a contentious climate, the failure of the Austrian commercial bank Creditanstalt-Bankverein in May 1931 was a greatly publicized instance in a wave of defaults on international borrowings in 1931 and the immediately succeeding years. These conditions greatly restricted international credit, trade, and capital flows. By 1933 total world trade had declined by almost 66 percent from the levels of 1929.

Historical events have demonstrated the unfailing periodicity of both deflation and inflation, even though at a given point in time each set of economic conditions may seem as if it will persist indefinitely. With greatly varying degrees of speed and momentum, the events of both inflations and deflations create countervailing forces which gradually build up and eventually themselves gain ascendancy, only to be replaced again in time by opposing trends.

Once past a certain point, deflations may be quite difficult to bring to a halt. They often require new directions of public opinion about the future economic outlook and about the role of the principal sectors of society in moving the economy toward greater price stability. Major deflations, while similar to earlier periods of price declines, often originate and unfold in patterns which are different from those of preceding cycles. Thus the investor should take heed of the lessons of earlier events but not rely overly on them as an exact guide to future economic developments.

Effects of Deflation

Many of the effects of deflation, and particularly of a serious and protracted deflationary period such as the Great Depression, are closely linked with their causes and have been mentioned in the immediately preceding section of this chapter. The actual effects of deflation depend upon the absolute amount and rate of change of price decline as well as upon expectations about future deflationary trends and their impact on economic activity.

Deflation, particularly if it is severe and extends over a long period of time, may see a reduction in government activity due to a shortfall in income accruing to the public sector. In deflationary periods, with declining levels of production and spending, practically every sector of society receives lower income. Lenders, savers, and recipients of fixed monetary payments enjoy greater purchasing power provided that the payers of their income do not reduce their contractual payments because of bankruptcy or other forms of debt renegotiation. Those sectors of the economy which suffer the greatest unemployment and are hardest hit by the economic contractions of a deflationary cycle usually call on the government for various forms of aid, but governmental help may be hindered by a lack of tax receipts or by public disagreement over the ways and means of halting deflation.

Extended deflation reduces demand in the personal and corporate sector. Because of falling incomes, debt repayment obligations, uncertainty about future economic developments, and expectations that prices will be lower in the future, producers may supply greater than normal quantities of goods and services to the marketplace. In the face of reduced consumer demand, prices fall further. As mentioned earlier, borrowers seek to repay their debt or to liquidate it through reorganization proceedings. Often, assets are sold off by consumers and corporations to generate cash. Persistent selling pressure serves to exacerbate price declines, particularly on types of goods which may have been accumulated for speculative reasons during inflationary periods. Liquidity, safety, and cash balances are sought as a hedge against falling measures of economic activity.

Moderate deflationary conditions enhance the real value of fixed-income securities, partly because bond prices rise during periods of falling interest rates and partly because fixed dollar payments increase in real terms during a deflation. The investor should keep in mind that when interest rates fall, bond prices rise, but the extent of the rise may be limited by (1) the bond's call feature, (2) any sinking-fund provisions which allow the issuer to repurchase bonds, and (3) the eventual maturity of the bond. In circumstances of falling prices, an issuer which is able to refinance its debt at lower interest rates gains an advantage over a competitor which is locked into noncallable, long-term, high-coupon debt. Table 5-5 below shows the gains in purchasing power which result from declines in the general price level.

In extreme deflationary conditions, the issuer's ability to repay becomes paramount in selecting fixed-income investments. When deflation is under way, if a borrower is able to service its debt without any default or perceived risk thereof, its bonds should rise in price and in purchasing power. At the same time, risk premiums expand between various bond quality ratings. As shown in Figure 5-1, which inversely plots industrial bond yields for the period 1929–1976 according to quality rating, during the 1930–1932 period Moody's Aaa-rated bonds rose in yield (declined in price) from an average of 4.69 percent in 1930 to an average of 5.09 percent in 1932, at which time they began to recover in price. However, Moody's Baa-rated bonds rose in yield (declined in price) much more precipitously than the Aaa-rated bonds, moving from an average of 6.09 percent to an average of 8.76 percent in the 1930–1932 period.

For a certain period in the early 1930s, the prices of very high-quality corporate bonds rose by as much as 30 to 40 percent or more (their yields were declining), while the prices of corporate issues rated A or less simul-

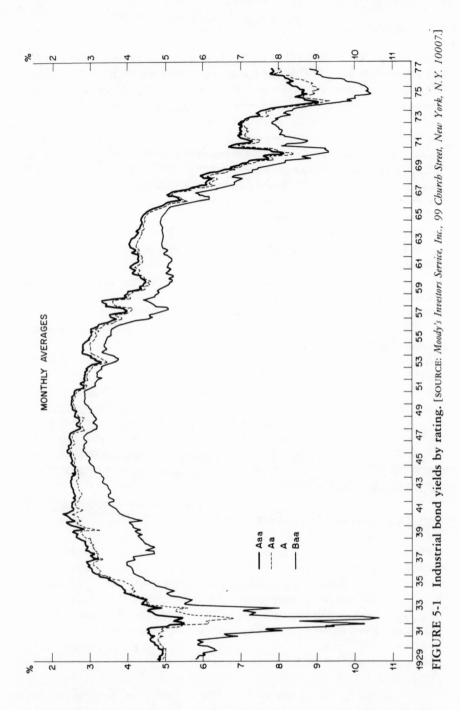

FIGURE 5-1 Industrial bond yields by rating. [SOURCE: *Moody's Investors Service, Inc., 99 Church Street, New York, N.Y. 10007.*]

taneously *declined* by 50 to 60 percent or more (their yields were rising). Similar divergences in the price performance of high-quality issues compared with lower-quality bonds have been witnessed in other periods of severe credit stringency and/or deflation.

According to *Corporate Bond Quality and Investor Experience,* [1] a total of $71 billion of nonconvertible corporate bonds were issued in the 1900–1943 period. Of this amount, 12 percent were paid in full upon maturity, 37 percent were called, 26 percent were still outstanding as of 1943 without having had defaults of any kind, and 18 percent defaulted. Such experience underscores the need for investors to investigate closely the quality of their fixed-income investments and relate them to their own quality preferences and risk profile.

At the beginning of the 1980s, even though many nations were more deeply concerned about the risks of high inflation than about the possibilities of severe deflation, several potentially deflationary factors could not be ruled out. Balanced against the deflationary risks of the early 1980s were many improved structural elements of the economic system in the early 1980s that did not exist in the early 1930s. First, central banks and certain other governmental institutions appeared more willing to provide funds as lenders of last resort and worked cooperatively with one another internationally in currency matters and other policies. Second, many industrialized countries had a larger percentage of the labor force employed in service industries (as opposed to production or transportation), with a substantially higher incidence of more than one working member in each household. Third, many nations had instituted or broadened unemployment compensation, social security, and other income transfer programs (such as agricultural price supports) that were expected to provide some measure of stabilization in deflationary cycles. Fourth, various governmental deposit insurance agencies (such as the Federal Deposit Insurance Corporation and the Securities Investor Protection Corporation) offered some degree of deposit insurance and securities protection to savers and investors. The Securities and Exchange Commission provided an additional form of safeguard against many of the practices that had been prevalent in the late 1920s and early 1930s. Fifth, much greater and more timely amounts of data were available on the health of the economy than had been available several decades ago. Nevertheless, quite a few major deflationary phases have originated in unexpected patterns, precisely because most people have expected events to unfold in the same way as in previous cycles.

Some potentially destabilizing forces at the beginning of the 1980s are summarized below. First, a not insignificant number of developing countries

---

[1] W. Braddock Hickman, *Corporate Bond Quality and Investor Experience,* National Bureau of Economic Research, Inc., New York, 1958.

carry large debt burdens, often at floating rates of interest. Restrictive international financial conditions could sharply increase the costs of debt service and the risks of unavailability of funds. Second, the sharp increases in world oil prices in late 1979 and in early 1980 carried the threat of ultimately deflationary consequences for developing and developed countries alike. In fact, increasing national recriminations and geopolitical disagreements over oil prices and availability have exhibited many similarities to the post-World War I era of international discord over war debts and reparations payments. Any sharp reduction in world trade and/or world commodities prices could be expected to fall especially heavily on the developing countries. At the same time, any major reductions in oil production would have deleterious ramifications for economic growth in the developing countries. Third, if major defaults occur in any sectors of the economy (such as corporations or consumers) which have large amounts of debt outstanding, confidence in the banking system would be severely strained. Fourth, if hyperinflation should strike any of the major international currencies, international trade and capital flows could be severely curtailed. Such circumstances would severely damage many national economies that depend in varying degrees on world trade. Fifth, a major error in governmental policy could lead to any of the previously mentioned possibilities or to other unexpected deflationary consequences.

The Effects of Inflation and Deflation on Capital Values

The effects of continued inflation or deflation on the purchasing power of money can be observed by computing the gain or loss in purchasing power which results from selected compound annual increases or decreases in a particular price index. The international investor may also look at such purchasing-power gains or losses as revaluations or devaluations of the currency of the investment relative to the investor's domestic currency.

Although the assumption of a constant rate of price change over a period of years is rarely if ever valid, it does help to direct attention to the real rate of return on an investment rather than merely focusing on nominal yields. In addition, the possibility of extreme values of deflation or inflation (or foreign currency appreciation or depreciation) over a period of years may seem remote, but the 1970s have witnessed such occurrences in a number of countries. The investor should keep in mind the charm and yet the difficulty of compound-interest calculations. It is one thing to live through an additional 10 years of continually declining or rising prices and quite another to enter 40 years rather than 30 years into a computer program.

Table 5-4 shows the decline in purchasing power which results from 1, 2, 4, 6, 8, 10, 12, and 20 percent compound rates of increase in a selected price index for 1, 2, 4, 5, 10, 12, 15, 20, 30, or 40 years. The relationship between price index changes and purchasing-power changes has been discussed earlier in this chapter. In Tables 5-4, 5-5, and 5-6, the appropriate rates of change in purchasing power are used in the calculations even though the column headings show the compound rates of change in the price index, since investors commonly think in terms of the latter. Investors should also keep in mind that the columns and rows in the tables progress in value by varying, not constant, percentages of the previous column's or row's value. While results have been rounded off to 2 places in the tables, figures in the calculations have been carried out to 10 places.

If a 4 percent annual rate of inflation persists for 10 years, the original purchasing power of $10,000 will have been reduced by 32.5 percent, to $6755.64. Such a calculation shows the ravages which even an apparently modest rate of inflation can exert if allowed to continue over long stretches of time. A 6 percent rate of inflation lasting 15 years wipes out 58.3 percent of the original purchasing power of $10,000, leaving $4172.65 in real terms.

Through interpolation, Tables 5-4 and 5-5 can also be used to approximate values which are not found in the tables. Because the functions which produce these calculations are exponential and not arithmetic, exact values will tend to stray in varying degrees from the interpolated values, with greater margins of error for greater numbers of years and for greater rates of change in the price indices. For example, in Table 5-4, if the investor wishes to find the effect of a 2 percent increase in the price index on the purchasing power of $10,000 over 3 years, the arithmetic average of the values for 2 and 4 years gives $9425.07, which differs by 0.02 percent from the correct value of $9423.22. On the other hand, if the investor wishes to find the effect of a 20 percent increase in the price index on $10,000 over 25 years, the arithmetic average of the values for 20 and 30 years gives $151.49, which differs by 44.5 percent from the correct value, $104.83. In spite of the wide margin of error between the two approximate and actual values in the latter example, the absolute amount of the error, $46.66, represents 0.47 percent of the original $10,000.

Table 5-5 shows the increase in purchasing power which results from 1, 2, 4, 6, 8, 10, and 20 percent compound rates of decrease in a selected price index for 1, 2, 4, 5, 10, 12, 15, 20, 30, or 40 years. If the price index deflates by 4 percent compounded annually, at the end of 5 years the purchasing power of $10,000 will have grown by 22.6 percent, to $12,264.33. Tables 5-4 and 5-5 can also be used to calculate how much money an investor would need to equal $10,000 of current purchasing power at the end of a specified time period. This can be accomplished through dividing $10,000 by the appropriate number shown in Table 5-4 or Table 5-5 and multiplying the

TABLE 5-4
Effects of Inflation on Capital Value
(Purchasing power of $10,000)

Years			Compound annual percentage increase in price index					
	+ 1.00 percent	+ 2.00 percent	+ 4.00 percent	+ 6.00 percent	+ 8.00 percent	+ 10.00 percent	+ 12.00 percent	+ 20.00 percent
1	9900.99	9803.92	9615.38	9433.96	9259.26	9090.91	8928.57	8333.33
2	9802.96	9611.69	9245.56	8899.96	8573.39	8264.46	7971.94	6944.44
4	9609.80	9238.45	8548.04	7920.94	7350.30	6830.13	6355.18	4822.53
5	9514.66	9057.31	8219.27	7472.58	6805.83	6209.21	5674.27	4018.78
10	9052.87	8203.48	6755.64	5583.95	4631.93	3855.43	3219.73	1615.06
12	8874.49	7884.93	6245.97	4969.69	3971.14	3186.31	2566.75	1121.57
15	8613.49	7430.15	5552.65	4172.65	3152.41	2393.92	1826.96	649.05
20	8195.44	6729.71	4563.87	3118.05	2145.48	1486.44	1036.67	260.84
30	7419.23	5520.71	3083.19	1741.10	993.77	573.09	333.78	42.13
40	6716.53	4528.90	2082.89	972.22	460.31	220.95	107.48	6.80

TABLE 5-5
Effects of Deflation on Capital Value
(Purchasing power of $10,000)

				Compound annual percentage decline in price index				
Years	− 1.00 percent	− 2.00 percent	− 4.00 percent	− 6.00 percent	− 8.00 percent	− 10.00 percent	− 12.00 percent	− 20.00 percent
1	10,101.01	10,204.08	10,416.67	10,638.30	10,869.57	11,111.11	11,363.63	12,500.00
2	10,203.04	10,412.33	10,850.69	11,317.34	11,814.74	12,345.68	12,913.22	15,625.00
4	10,410.20	10,841.66	11,773.76	12,808.21	13,958.82	15,241.58	16,675.13	24,414.06
5	10,515.36	11,062.92	12,264.33	13,625.76	15,172.63	16,935.09	18,949.01	30,517.58
10	11,057.27	12,238.81	15,041.38	18,566.13	23,020.87	28,679.72	35,906.52	93,132.26
12	11,281.78	12,743.45	16,320.94	21,011.92	27,198.57	35,407.06	46,366.89	145,519.15
15	11,627.19	13,539.69	18,447.24	25,297.77	34,928.71	48,569.36	68,039.31	284,217.09
20	12,226.33	14,978.85	22,624.31	34,470.13	52,996.04	82,252.63	128,927.80	867,361.74
30	13,518.99	18,332.33	34,030.08	63,997.70	122,001.50	235,898.25	462,934.81	8,077,935.67
40	14,948.31	22,436.60	51,185.94	118,818.99	280,858.07	676,549.57	1,662,237.65	75,231,638.45

resultant fraction by $10,000. For example, if the price index is expected to *decline* at 6 percent per annum for the next 4 years, the investor needs $\frac{\$10,000.00}{\$12,808.21} \times \$10,000 = \$7807.49$ at the end of that time period to equal $10,000 of current purchasing power. Similarly, from Table 5-4, if the price index is expected to *increase* at 4 percent per year for the next 15 years, the investor needs $\frac{\$10,000.00}{\$5552.65} \times \$10,000 = \$18,009.42$ at the end of that time period to equal $10,000 of current purchasing power.

Table 5-6 shows the real purchasing-power rate of return, independent of maturity, which results from annual coupons of 2, 4, 6, 8, and 10 percent and annual price index increases or decreases of 2, 4, 6, 8, and 10 percent. Table 5-6 can be of value because changes in real purchasing power are slightly different from changes in price indices.

If an investor holds a security with a 4 percent annual coupon for a period of time during which the annual rate of price decrease is 6 percent, the real

TABLE 5-6
Real Purchasing Power Rate of Interest Return

Coupon / Annual price index change	2 percent	4 percent	6 percent	8 percent	10 percent
−2	+4.1	+6.1	+8.2	+10.2	+12.2
+2	0	+2.0	+3.9	+5.9	+7.8
−4	+6.3	+8.3	+10.4	+12.5	+14.6
+4	−1.9	0	+1.9	+3.8	+5.8
−6	+8.5	+10.6	+12.8	+14.9	+17.0
+6	−3.8	−1.9	0	+1.8	+3.8
−8	+10.9	+13.0	+15.2	+17.4	+19.6
+8	−5.6	−3.7	−1.9	0	+1.9
−10	+13.3	+15.6	+17.8	+20.0	+22.2
+10	−7.3	−5.5	−3.6	−1.8	0

purchasing-power rate of interest return (changes in the capital value of the security are ignored) for such an investment is 10.6 percent. Alternatively, if an investor holds a security with a 6 percent annual coupon for a time period during which the annual rate of price increase is 4 percent, the real purchasing-power rate of interest return is 1.9 percent.

In practice, Table 5-6 is more useful for short periods of time than for a long time span because interest rates are likely to change as a result of continued price inflation or deflation. Such interest rate shifts lead to changes in the capital value of the security and the interest rates at which coupon income can be reinvested. Both of these factors exert a large influence upon the total holding-period yield produced by a fixed-income investment.

Taxes have been ignored in these calculations. If interest income is taxable to the investor, taxes must be paid on the interest received at whatever the investor's marginal tax bracket is. Over long periods of inflation, the increase in nominal earnings must far exceed the depreciation of the currency's purchasing power, especially when combined with a progressive tax rate schedule which shifts investors into higher tax brackets with increasing nominal income. The investor can calculate a target nominal rate of interest, given a desired real aftertax rate of interest, the expected price change, and the incremental tax bracket, according to the following formula:

Target nominal rate of interest =

$$\frac{\text{desired real aftertax rate of interest in percentage points} \pm \text{price change in percentage points}}{1 - \text{incremental tax bracket}}$$

Thus with inflation at 3 percent, if the investor desires a 2 percent real aftertax rate of interest and the tax bracket is 40 percent, the target nominal rate works out to be:

$$\frac{2 \text{ percent} + 3 \text{ percent}}{1 - 0.40} = \frac{5 \text{ percent}}{0.6} = 8.33 \text{ percent}$$

If an 8.33 percent target rate of interest cannot be obtained within the investor's safety, maturity, and liquidity parameters, a real aftertax rate of interest lower than desired may have to be accepted. Such acquiescences are one of the lamentable plights of an inflationary period for the fixed-income investor. Nevertheless, such analysis is useful because it directs the investor's attention to the concept of real rather than nominal, and aftertax rather than pretax, interest returns.

6

Financial Intermediation in the Credit and Capital Markets

Overview

The credit and capital markets are as marvelous and complex as the double helices which underlie genetic activity. An understanding of their structure and patterns of change can help investors grasp and anticipate the favorable and unfavorable influences which affect specific groups of securities and suppliers of funds. In broad terms, households, nonfinancial corporations, and financial institutions own a great part of the total outstanding debt, which can be classified into a similarly small number of investment vehicles. On an even broader scale, *individuals* can be said to provide the funds employed by the *corporate* and *governmental* borrowing sectors of the economy. Yet investor preferences and the ingenuity of capital market participants have created many varieties of financial instruments, a great diversity of borrowers and lenders, and countless subtle interactions between and among the principal components of the investment system.

For each economic unit, flows of money into and out of the financial markets reflect decisions on consumption, borrowing, lending, and investment. The manner in which these flows take place has evolved considerably since 1900. During the first few decades of this century, individuals usually invested as much as 50 percent or more of their total annual additions to financial assets directly in the securities of the entities which actually employed the capital. In the past 30 years, the situation has changed. Individual investors now place a very large share of their annual investment flows into financial institutions which act as intermediaries in redeploying the funds thus received. The trend toward greater financial intermediation has been aided by the wide array of instruments which have been created by financial institutions and which offer (1) relatively low transaction costs and economies of scale, (2) professional supervision of the investor's funds, (3) small and easily divisible denominations, (4) liquidity, (5) diversification of assets, (6) accessibility, and (7) safety, often backed up by numerous forms of governmental insurance or guarantees.

Financial intermediaries normally attract funds through deposit facilities offered to the individual, through securities issues, or through other means such as pension contributions or the sale of insurance contracts. This money is then lent to or invested in the securities of corporations and governmental borrowers. From the 1950s through the early 1980s, financial intermediaries of all types accounted for more than 87 percent of all funds invested in capital markets. The share of private financial intermediation as a percentage of total private domestic funds advanced to credit markets in the United States for each year from 1950 through 1979 is shown in Table 6-1.

Major shortfalls from the 87 percent average intermediation rate occurred in 1953, 1955, 1959, 1966, 1969, 1974, and 1975. These years generally were periods of strong credit demands and/or policies of monetary restraint pursued by the Federal Reserve Board. The resultant high market interest rates temporarily exceeded the returns which financial institutions could legally offer individual investors and caused *disintermediation,* in which individual investors invest their funds directly in the securities of ultimate borrowers rather than channeling their funds through financial institutions.

Quasi intermediation takes place when a governmental body or occasionally a corporate entity borrows funds which are then *relent* to another part of the economy. Perhaps the most common example occurs when government agencies raise capital to provide money to the housing industry or the agricultural sector. *Layered intermediation* arises when a financial institution such as a commercial bank raises money which is not advanced to an ultimate user of the funds but instead to another financial intermediary.

Until the 1960s financial intermediaries usually specialized in the specific types of borrowing, lending, and investing in which they were primarily engaged. Beginning in the late 1960s and the early 1970s, a number of factors led to greater flexibility in both asset and liability composition and to a blurring of many of the distinctions between the various types of financial intermediaries. Among these factors were (1) increased management sophistication and the use of technological innovations, (2) gradual synchronization of dissimilar regulatory and legal constraints (although the overall level of regulatory involvement appeared to rise), (3) expanding inflows of funds at higher costs, (4) trends toward an equalization of the tax provisions affecting different groups of financial intermediaries, and (5) the necessity of earning higher investment yields.

Such changes produced less differentiation between alternative forms of

TABLE 6-1
Private Financial Intermediation, 1950–1979
(In billions of dollars)

Year	(1) Total private domestic funds advanced to credit markets	(2) Total private financial intermediation	(3) Percentage private financial intermediation (2) ÷ (1)
1950	20.496	17.122	83.5
1951	17.956	15.597	86.9
1952	27.212	23.542	86.5
1953	25.399	19.767	77.8
1954	26.179	25.233	96.4
1955	34.530	24.734	71.6
1956	25.163	21.855	86.9
1957	27.466	22.978	83.7
1958	36.053	33.099	91.8
1959	45.705	28.780	63.0
1960	33.608	32.882	97.8
1961	41.196	38.482	93.4
1962	48.966	47.964	98.0
1963	54.376	49.615	91.2
1964	60.653	57.469	94.8
1965	64.531	61.706	95.6
1966	61.002	46.701	76.6
1967	69.459	63.375	91.2
1968	89.332	75.539	84.6
1969	82.535	57.403	69.5
1970	75.509	77.035	102.0
1971	102.129	109.693	107.4
1972	155.013	149.638	96.4
1973	180.200	164.900	91.5
1974	156.100	126.300	80.9
1975	164.800	119.900	72.8
1976	221.800	187.200	84.4
1977	269.000	242.700	90.2
1978	330.000	296.900	90.0
1979	378.180	328.764	86.9

SOURCE: *Flow of Funds Accounts,* Board of Governors of the Federal Reserve System.

consumer credit and between demand deposits, time deposits, and direct-market investments at commercial banks and thrift institutions. To attract the individual investor's funds, a more intense competitive environment emerged between different categories of financial institutions and among similar firms within a given category. This increased rivalry often tended to reduce the average margin between the realized return on the funds invested by a financial intermediary and the rate which the intermediary had to pay in order to attract funds inflows from individual investors and other sources.

Partly in response to a more competitive environment and to pressures to earn higher returns, financial institutions have introduced new investment instruments and new internal and external operating strategies. For example, many depositary institutions have reduced their holdings of governmental securities as a percentage of total assets, no longer relying upon such investments as a form of liquid reserve which can be drawn upon when necessary. Instead, these institutions have turned from *asset* management to *liability* management, using their own borrowings in the short-term federal funds market, the short-term money markets, or even the longer-maturity portions of the capital markets as sources of funds to meet liquidity requirements.

Analyzing Investment Behavior of Capital Market Participants

Investors should be aware of such shifts in management practice, since prevailing supply-demand relationships can be significantly affected both in the institutions' normal investment outlets and in the markets where the institutions choose to raise funds themselves. Equally important factors to consider in analyzing the investment behavior of major capital market participants are (1) the diversity, safety, and degree of regularity in their sources of funds and (2) the way in which they are influenced by and react to conditions of monetary ease or tightness. Among the principal sources of investment funds for financial intermediaries are (1) governmental, foreign, and private-sector deposit inflows, including possible redeposits of interest earned on existing deposits; (2) dividend and interest payments as well as principal repayments from investments already made; (3) insurance and retirement plan contributions; (4) borrowing by a given intermediary in the credit and capital markets; and (5) earnings after outflows to individual depositors, after expense payments, and after taxes and dividends.

The growth of individual firms and of specific categories of financial institutions and the amounts of funds which they can supply to various types of investments depend upon a number of factors. Among other factors, these influences include (1) their success in capturing savings flows, (2) their inclination to borrow money or issue securities when suitable and prudent, (3) internal profit growth, and (4) their disposition to supply funds on appropriate credit and interest rate risk terms to satisfy the funds requirements of their major current and targeted borrowing constituencies.

In this chapter and the five succeeding chapters, the investment activities of the major investor groups in fixed-income securities are examined, with some peripheral treatment of these investors' activities in the mortgage and equity markets. Credit instruments such as mortgages and consumer credit, which are not included in the strict definition of fixed-income securities, are considered whenever such an analysis provides a better comprehension of the network of forces acting upon a specific investor group. For example, a more profound understanding of the investment activities of mutual savings banks in corporate bonds (these banks' second-largest investment outlet) is obtained by careful scrutiny of the dynamics of the mortgage market (their largest investment outlet).

Equities are not analyzed in as great detail as fixed-income securities since they represent residual claims of ownership and thus do not have many of the contractual elements of debt instruments. By knowing who are the principal holders of each type of security, the reasons for and the uses of their investments, and the pressures acting on these holders, investors can appreciate and often anticipate the ebb and flow of buying and selling interest in each subsector of the fixed-income securities markets.

As mentioned earlier, some financial intermediaries can be both borrowers and suppliers of funds in a given year. For example, in the late 1970s savings institutions issued mortgage-backed securities and/or subordinated capital notes in order to invest in further real estate lending activities. At about the same time, state and local governments, commercial banks, and corporations borrowed funds through securities issues which were temporarily reinvested in short-term money market instruments and other securities of the United States government or federal agencies. While the primary focus of analysis in Chapters 8 through 11 is on investors' *asset structures,* which represent their contribution to the supply side of the credit and capital markets, their *liability structures* will be examined to the extent that such an examination contributes to an improved understanding of these investors' portfolio distributions.

While investors tend to buy fixed-income instruments in general because of the level and predictability of these instruments' interest payments, their relative safety in periods of economic recession, and their contribution to balance within a diversified portfolio, the specific motives for investing in one sector of the fixed-income markets as opposed to another are considerably more intricate. For each of the major categories of funds suppliers, investors should investigate some or all of the following factors which influence the distribution of lending and investment: (1) the sensitivity, diversification, and predictability of money flows and reflows to and from the investor category in response to changed economic conditions in the United States and other countries; (2) limitations placed on suppliers' investment behavior by their form of ownership, their charter and bylaws, the personal preferences of key decision makers, and other organizational factors; (3) the formal regulatory and legal framework as well as the formal or informal supervisory system under which they operate; (4) tax laws at the federal, state, local, and occasionally international level; (5) competitive practices and traditional asset and liability distributions among other entities in the same investor category; (6) secular, cyclical, and seasonal shifts in the supply of incremental investment funds; (7) the degree of definition and ease of attainment of stated objectives and liquidity positions; (8) the rate of return generated from investments and, if applicable, the profitability of the investment entity; (9) normal accounting practices and asset valuation rules; (10) the ability to take investment losses and gains and any effects of realized or unrealized gains or losses on the investor's financial statements; (11) how often and by whom the investor's activities are sanctioned and evaluated; (12) if applicable, the cost of money raised to be reinvested; (13) whether the liabilities issued by the investor group are for a fixed or a variable sum of money and whether the return on these liabilities is fixed or variable; and (14) the investor's desired levels of current income, capital gains, safety, marketability, liquidity, and taxation.

For various reasons, a specific investor may adopt an investment course which differs widely from the normative patterns described in Chapters 8 through 11 for each broad investor grouping. Besides the factors mentioned above, such differences may relate to (1) the long-term orientation of that investor toward the credit and capital markets, as opposed to other forms and venues of investing such as physical assets, real estate, art, commodities, and other investment vehicles; (2) tactical shifts of the portfolio into or out of market sectors to avoid losses or to seek above-average gains; and (3) the actual choice of individual investments for the portfolio.

Over 20 to 30 years, an investor group may place funds in a relatively broad range of investment assets in response to changing circumstances. The primary emphasis of Chapters 6 through 11 is on the analysis of aggregate investment behavior and the way in which it can shift over time. This approach is followed in order to identify the considerable similarities among investment entities of the same type. Nevertheless, it is useful to remember that the specific investment actions of a large, well-established, and highly capitalized entity will often vary from those of a small, newly formed, and less substantially capitalized one.

Once the analyst has gained an understanding of how a particular investor group allocates its funds in the marketplace, it is possible to gauge the effects on various sectors of the capital market when one or more investor groups act in concert or in opposition to one another. For instance, when several investor groups simultaneously desire to earn tax-exempt income by investing in tax-exempt securities, this segment of the fixed-income market can appreciate in price even though other sectors may be declining or remaining stable in price.

This phenomenon occurred during one period in the late 1970s when all the following groups were substantial net purchasers of tax-exempt fixed-income securities: (1) the household sector, both directly and through tax-exempt bond funds; (2) the commercial banks, which were encountering relatively slack loan demand and fewer loan losses (the latter sometimes shelter a portion of banks' earnings from taxes); and (3) property-casualty insurance companies, which were experiencing a time of favorable underwriting profitability. Such purchasing activity enabled the tax-exempt securities sector generally to outperform the other sectors of the fixed-income securities market for a prolonged span of months.

Similar events can occur in other sectors of the market with the same effect if numerous investor groups simultaneously decide to buy a specific type of security or with the opposite effect if a number of investor groups decide at the same time to liquidate or to discontinue buying a certain type of security. When exceptional buying or selling phases are localized in one particular sector of the market, they can often cause a countervailing reaction in another sector or sectors, as investors may have proportionately lesser or greater amounts of funds to place in a specific group of securities. The extent of the reaction depends upon the magnitude of the funds flows involved as well as on the relative ease of shifting funds from one sector of the fixed-income securities market to another.

In very general terms, the American financial system described in the preceding pages might be simply diagramed as in Figure 6-1. In general, households and other providers of capital invest in the deposits, contracts, or securities of financial intermediaries (point A in the figure), which in turn channel these funds into the securities, mortgages, or other liabilities of corporate, governmental, and other borrowers (point B). As mentioned earlier, under certain conditions households may choose not to place their savings with a financial intermediary but instead to invest these funds directly in the securities, mortgages, or other liabilities of corporations, governmental bodies, and other issuers (point C). Figure 6-1 does not account for a number of details which reflect actual conditions in the debt markets, including (1) so-called negative financial flows, such as debt repayments or reductions in financial asset holdings by an investor group, and (2) cases in which

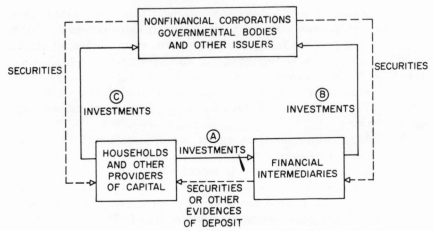

FIGURE 6-1   Simplified diagram of flows in the U.S. financial system.

governments, corporations, and other borrowers supply funds to financial intermediaries or to households and other providers of capital.

Effective and realistic analysis of the investment patterns in many different sectors of the fixed-income securities area is not an easy task. The difficulty is due to (1) conflicting and sometimes-redundant data sources covering both investor categories and the instruments in which they invest, (2) the need to differentiate between information as of a certain moment in time (so-called balances, or stock data) and information covering a certain period of time (so-called flow data), and (3) the sheer quantity of data and the difficulty of grasping the absolute magnitudes of the figures involved. An additional complication arises from the need to view credit and capital market developments over several years in order to gain a true perspective on changing modes of investment preferences.

Classification Conventions in Financial Markets

As in any technical field, questions of nomenclature can cause confusion in studying investment folkways. Thus far in this chapter, "credit markets" has been used practically interchangeably with the term "capital markets." Many investors interpret credit markets or "money markets" to include instruments of short-term maturity (up to 1 year or slightly longer) as well as bank loans, trade credit, and other forms of indebtedness of reasonably short duration. On the other hand, capital markets or "bond markets" are usually interpreted to encompass notes, bonds, and most other forms of intermediate- and longer-term indebtedness. In this book credit markets and capital markets are used *interchangeably* unless they are modified by an adjective which refers only to the short-term or long-term sectors of the market. On the other hand, money markets and bond markets are used to delineate *separate* maturity subdivisions of the fixed-income securities markets.

Another classification problem revolves about the definition of "savings." One of the principal descriptions of savings emanates from the National Income Accounts of the U.S. Department of Commerce, which define savings as personal aftertax disposable income minus personal outlays for goods and services by families and individuals. The Flow of Funds Accounts of the Federal Reserve System employ a similar method of defining savings, except that purchases of consumer durable goods are not treated as a *consumption* item but as a *capital* expenditure. Such a division produces a smaller aggregate amount of current consumption and a larger overall amount of savings than are shown by the Department of Commerce data. A third measure of savings portrays actual over-the-counter savings flows to depositary institutions, and these figures are collected and disseminated by such agencies as the Federal Deposit Insurance Corporation and the Federal Home Loan Bank Board.

Even a seemingly precise term for a group of investors can be subject to varying shades of meaning. For example, a question arises whether "private insured pension funds" should be classified and discussed with *pension funds* or with *insurance companies.* A mention of "pension funds" can refer to one or all of several distinct categories of investor, each within widely separate investor groups: (1) state and local government retirement funds, (2) federal government pension accounts, (3) private-sector noninsured pension funds, and (4) private-sector insured pension funds. Because the investment decisions for these four categories are made by different groups, they are treated separately in Chapters 8 and 10. Other, more subtle lines of demarcation between investors are also utilized. Certain investors such as endowments and pension funds can be characterized as having an *indefinitely long lifetime,* while investors such as individuals and limited-term trusts have a *specific time span* during which their funds are deployed. Similarly, investors can be grouped according to whether they supply predominantly short-term capital or long-term capital.

A very broad and commonly employed means of classifying financial intermediaries uses two main categories. First, there are *depositary* institutions, such as credit unions, commercial banks, mutual savings banks, and savings and loan associations. These institutions draw most of their funds from deposits and various other forms of certificates, and the saver relies upon them primarily for liquidity. Second, there are *contractual* institutions, such as life insurance companies, corporate pension funds, and state and local government retirement plans. These institutions obtain most of their funds under conditions agreed upon between the institution and the contributor. The contributor generally relies upon this form of saving as *protection* against longer-term contingencies. In practice, rigid lines of separation are not as accurate as in earlier years because of the diversification of many groups of investors' lending and investing activities.

Classification by Financial Assets

Table 6-2 classifies the major groups of investors according to the total amount of their financial assets, which include credit extensions, corporate equities, mortgages, demand deposits, time deposits, currency, and all types of fixed-income securities for selected years during the period from 1950 through 1979. This table and most of the tables in Chapters 6 through 11 employ arbitrarily selected dates (1950, 1955, 1960, 1965, 1975, and 1979) for comparison purposes. It is helpful to remember that in intervening years there may have been variations or reversals from the broad trends displayed by the data for the years chosen. Most important is the development of an understanding of broad trends over this time period rather than an attempt to explain every single variation in the data during each 5-year span.

As of the end of 1975, the eight largest holders of financial assets listed in Table 6-2 and ranked according to size were:

Investor category	Financial assets in billions of dollars (end of 1975)
Households, personal trusts, and nonprofit organizations	$2496.8
Commercial banks	873.6
Nonfinancial business	629.0
Savings and loan associations	338.4
Life insurance companies	279.9
Private pension funds	148.9
Mutual savings banks	121.1
State and local government employee retirement funds	106.0

These investor groups could properly be called the richest in terms of financial assets at the end of 1975. Partly because some of the 13 different groups of investors listed in Table 6-2 started from a relatively low base at the end of 1950, a ranking of the eight highest compound annual rates of growth from 1950 through 1975 for the investor groups produces a different distribution:

Investor category	Compound annual rate of growth, 1950–1975 (percent)
Credit unions	15.5
State and local government employee retirement funds	13.1
Private pension funds	12.9
Savings and loan associations	12.7
Open-end investment companies	10.7
Finance companies	9.9
Other insurance companies	7.9
Commercial banks	7.3

To provide perspective on more recent trends in total financial asset holdings, compound annual growth rates have also been computed for the period from 1965 through 1975. With the exception of commercial banks, nonfinancial business, and mutual savings banks, compound annual growth rates in financial asset holdings for the period from 1965 through 1975 were lower than for the entire period from 1950 through 1975. As shown in Table 6-2, the eight fastest-growing holders of financial assets during the 1965–1975 period were:

Investor category	Compound annual rate of growth, 1965–1975 (percent)
Credit unions	12.9
State and local government employee retirement funds	12.0
Savings and loan associations	10.1
Commercial banks	9.8
Finance companies	8.2
Nonfinancial business	8.0
Other insurance companies	7.8
Mutual savings banks	7.4

A comparison of this list and the preceding one shows that private pension funds and open-end investment companies were among the fastest-growing holders of financial assets during the 1950–1975 period but were not among the fastest-growing holders of financial assets during the 1965–1975 period. Conversely, nonfinancial business and mutual savings banks were among the fastest-growing holders of financial assets during the 1965–1975 period but were not among the fastest-growing holders of financial assets during the 1950–1975 period.

Certain admonitions should also be added concerning Table 6-2. As mentioned earlier, the financial assets of one group, such as the time deposits and savings accounts held by the household sector, may well provide the funds

TABLE 6-2
Financial asset holdings of investor groups for selected years, 1950–1979
(In billions of dollars)

Category	1950	1955	1960	1965	1970	1975	1979	Compound annual growth rates (percent)	
								1950–1975	1965–1975
Households, personal trusts, nonprofit organizations	445.7	707.6	972.1	1465.3	1922.8	2496.8	3827.1	7.1	5.5
Nonfinancial business	125.6	168.1	210.2	291.3	408.8	629.0	944.8	6.7	8.0
Commercial banks	150.3	188.5	230.0	343.6	518.2	873.6	1252.7	7.3	9.8
Savings and loan associations	16.9	37.7	71.5	129.6	176.2	338.4	579.1	12.7	10.1
Mutual savings banks	22.4	31.7	41.4	59.1	79.3	121.1	165.0	7.0	7.4
Credit unions	1.0	2.9	6.3	11.0	18.0	37.0	62.3	15.5	12.9

Life insurance companies	62.6	87.9	115.8	154.2	200.9	279.9	420.5	6.2	6.1
Private pension funds	7.1	18.3	38.1	73.6	110.6	148.9	236.8	12.9	7.3
State and local government retirement funds	4.9	10.8	19.7	34.1	60.3	106.0	178.9	13.1	12.0
Other insurance companies	11.7	19.4	26.2	36.5	50.6	77.4	156.7	7.9	7.8
Finance companies	9.3	18.3	27.6	44.7	64.6	98.4	168.9	9.9	8.2
Open-end investment companies	3.3	7.8	17.0	35.2	47.6	42.2	46.2	10.7	1.8
Security brokers and dealers	4.0	5.9	6.7	10.3	16.2	17.2	30.6	6.0	5.3

SOURCE: *Flow of Funds Accounts*, Board of Governors of the Federal Reserve System. Data for all periods through 1975 are taken from the *Flow of Funds Accounts, 1946–1975*, issued in December 1976; data for periods subsequent to 1975 are taken from the *Flow of Funds Accounts, 1969–1979*, issued in February 1980. Because of occasional revisions in the Flow of Funds Accounts data, certain statistics from the latter source and subsequent releases may vary somewhat from those contained in the *Flow of Funds Accounts, 1946–1975*.

which enable another sector such as savings and loan associations to invest in mortgages. In turn, a large portion of mortgage debt is a liability of the household sector and other groups. The intertwining of investors and borrowers with each other points up the need for a systematic way of analyzing the financial markets. Such a system is described in Chapter 7. It is also worth repeating that the *year-end figures* for the 7 specific years selected for Table 6-2 and numerous tables in the following chapters may not accurately portray the importance of *funds flows* during any one of these years or the significance of developments which occurred during periods of time which are not displayed.

Because of their small size, quite a few investor groups have not been included in Table 6-2. Certain other investor groups have not been included because their total financial asset holdings include gold, Special Drawing Rights, and reserves of foreign currency, which are not covered in depth in this book. The primary emphasis of Chapters 7 through 11 is on *credit market instruments,* which are in fact a subcategory of financial asset holdings. Investor groups not listed in Table 6-2 but discussed in connection with their provision of funds to the credit and capital markets include the United States government, the Federal Reserve System, the general funds of state and local governments, federally sponsored credit agencies and mortgage pools, and foreign official and private holders of debt instruments.

Classification by Credit Market Assets

Table 6-3 provides a compilation of total credit market assets for selected years from 1950 through 1979 for a broader range of investor groups than in Table 6-2. To arrive at total credit market asset holdings, Table 6-3 excludes all official reserves of foreign currency, currency held by the U.S. Treasury, and Special Drawing Rights certificates. In addition, it excludes certain financial assets such as currency, demand deposits, time deposits and negotiable certificates of deposit, savings deposits in the commercial banking system and at savings institutions, government and private insurance and pension reserves owned by households, security credit, trade debt, profit taxes payable, interbank claims and other floats, corporate equities and investment company shares, and miscellaneous other liabilities not allocated as assets and financial assets not included in borrowing. Because most of these categories are not actually a part of organized credit markets, they are not analyzed in detail in Chapters 7 through 11 even though many of these categories play an important role in financing certain transactions in the economy.

When analyzing the ownership of total *credit market instruments* portrayed in Table 6-3, a somewhat different picture emerges than when analyzing the ownership of total *financial assets* (a much broader and more encompassing category) as presented in Table 6-2. Credit market instruments include U.S. government securities and federal agency issues, state and local government obligations, corporate and foreign bonds, extensions of consumer credit, bank loans not elsewhere classified, open-market paper such as bankers' acceptances and commercial paper, federal funds, repurchase agreements, and several other evidences of debt ownership.

As of the end of 1975, the 10 largest holders of credit market instruments were:

Investor category	Credit market instruments in billions of dollars (end of 1975)
Commercial banks	$745.4
Households, personal trusts, and nonprofit organizations	346.8
Savings and loan associations	310.5
Life insurance companies	234.8
Mutual savings banks	111.2
Federal Reserve System	95.2
Finance companies	94.5
Federally sponsored credit agencies	91.5
United States government	88.2
State and local government employee retirement funds	78.5

The principal reasons for differences between the figures and the rankings in Tables 6-3 and 6-2 involve the degree of ownership by a particular group of investors of assets which are classified as financial assets but not as credit market instruments. Such sectors include equities, cash, time deposits, negotiable certificates of deposit, and the other assets mentioned previously. Perhaps the most striking differences are in the household and nonfinancial corporate business sectors because of their heavy ownership of these latter assets.

Another large difference stems from the fact that a much greater component of the total financial assets held by private pension funds (as opposed to state and local government employee retirement funds) was represented by equities at the end of 1975. Thus, the total financial assets of private pension funds as listed in Table 6-2 exceeds those of state and local government employee retirement funds, but since the latter own more *debt* instruments than private pension funds, they are ranked ahead of private pension funds in Table 6-3. The specific mix of holdings of credit market instruments of each of the major investor groups is analyzed in greater detail in Chapters 8 through 11.

The most rapid growth in ownership of credit market instruments during

TABLE 6-3
Credit Market Instrument Holdings of Investor Groups for Selected Years, 1950–1979
(In billions of dollars)

Category	1950	1955	1960	1965	1970	1975	1979	Compound annual growth rates (percent)	
								1950–1975	1965–1975
Households, personal trusts, nonprofit organizations	99.8	117.2	148.2	176.5	240.0	346.8	552.5	5.1	7.0
Nonfarm noncorporate business	3.1	4.2	5.4	7.4	9.2	12.6	18.8	5.8	5.5
Nonfinancial corporate business	23.6	31.2	30.8	33.7	47.1	72.9	90.8	4.6	8.0
State and local governments: general funds	9.0	14.6	18.9	23.7	32.5	70.1	97.6	8.6	11.5
Rest of the world (foreign sector)	3.4	6.5	12.5	15.9	25.7	77.5	164.6	13.3	17.2
United States government	16.0	21.1	26.8	37.9	57.8	88.2	152.4	7.1	8.8
Federally sponsored credit agencies	3.1	5.0	11.1	18.3	44.9	91.5	156.6	14.5	17.5
Mortgage pools	...*	0.1	0.2	0.9	4.8	34.1	118.0	N.M.†	43.8
Federal Reserve System	20.8	24.8	27.5	41.0	62.2	95.2	126.9	6.3	8.8

Commercial banks‡	125.5	158.4	197.9	301.2	445.5	745.4	1147.1	7.4	9.5
Savings and loan associations	15.3	34.3	66.2	119.8	164.9	310.5	542.7	12.8	10.0
Mutual savings banks	21.4	29.5	38.5	55.0	73.9	111.2	151.5	6.8	7.3
Credit unions	0.7	2.0	4.5	8.2	15.2	32.0	56.7	16.5	14.6
Life insurance companies	57.9	80.5	105.6	137.8	174.6	234.8	353.8	5.8	5.5
Private pension funds	5.3	11.2	19.7	29.1	36.9	51.0	84.1	9.5	5.8
State and local government retirement funds	4.7	10.5	18.9	31.3	49.6	78.5	131.6	11.9	9.6
Other insurance companies	7.2	11.5	15.5	20.6	31.6	53.7	115.9	8.4	10.1
Finance companies	8.2	17.0	25.9	42.7	61.9	94.5	164.3	10.3	8.3
Open-end investment companies	0.3	0.8	2.0	3.8	7.2	7.3	11.7	13.6	6.7
Security brokers and dealers	1.4	1.9	2.4	6.0	4.2	8.4		4.5	5.8
Total§	427.3	582.0	777.9	1107.2	1595.3	2626.7	4246.0	7.5	9.0

SOURCE: *Flow of Funds Accounts*, Board of Governors of the Federal Reserve System. Data for all periods through 1975 are taken from the *Flow of Funds Accounts, 1946–1975*, issued in December 1976; data for periods subsequent to 1975 are taken from the *Flow of Funds Accounts, 1969–1979*, issued in February 1980. Because of occasional revisions in the Flow of Funds Accounts data, certain statistics from the latter source and subsequent releases may vary somewhat from those contained in the *Flow of Funds Accounts, 1946–1975*.

*Less than $50 million.

†Not measurable from data in the table.

‡Includes chartered commercial banks, their domestic affiliates, Edge Act corporations, agencies of foreign banks, and banks in United States possessions.

§Includes categories listed above, plus Real Estate Investment Trusts and money market funds.

the period from 1950 through 1975 was exhibited by the following investor groups:

Investor category	Compound annual rate of growth, 1950–1975 (percent)
Credit unions	16.5
Federally sponsored credit agencies	14.5
Rest of the world (foreign sector)	13.3
Savings and loan associations	12.8
State and local government employee retirement funds	11.9
Finance companies	10.3
Private pension funds	9.5
State and local governments: general funds	8.6
Other insurance companies	8.4
Commercial banks	7.4

With the exception of nonfarm noncorporate business, savings and loan associations, credit unions, life insurance companies, private pension funds, state and local government employee retirement funds, finance companies, and open-end investment companies, all the investor groups shown in Table 6-3 had higher growth rates in ownership of credit market instruments during the period from 1965 through 1975 than in the period from 1950 through 1975. The fastest-growing ownership of credit market instruments during the period from 1965 through 1975 was demonstrated by the following investor groups:

Investor category	Compound annual rate of growth, 1965–1975 (percent)
Mortgage pools	43.8
Federally sponsored credit agencies	17.5
Rest of the world (foreign sector)	17.2
Credit unions	14.6
State and local governments: general funds	11.5
Other insurance companies	10.1
Savings and loan associations	10.0
State and local government employee retirement funds	9.6
Commercial banks	9.5
Federal Reserve System	8.8
United States government	8.8

A comparison of this list and the preceding one shows that finance companies and private pension funds were among the fastest-growing holders of credit market instruments during the 1950–1975 period but were not among the fastest-growing holders of credit market instruments during the 1965–1975 period. Conversely, the Federal Reserve System and the United States government were among the fastest-growing holders of credit market instruments during the 1965–1975 period but were not among the fastest-growing holders of credit market instruments during the 1950–1975 period.

Although one investor group may seem small in the absolute amount of its financial assets or credit market asset holdings, its *incremental* importance may loom large in a particular sector of the fixed-income securities markets, either at one point in time or over a span of several years. Various methods of ranking investor groups may reveal differing aspects of their actual and potential purchasing power in the financial markets. These ranking systems might classify investor groups by (1) total holdings of credit market instruments or of financial assets, (2) total annual flows of money into the credit and capital markets, either including or excluding the reflows of funds which derive from existing asset holdings, and (3) compound annual rates of growth with methods 1 or 2 over a selected time period. Finally, these aggregate statistics do not provide insight into the number of individual entities and their size range within each investor group. For example, the number of private pension funds is greater than the number of open-end investment companies, and the largest private pension fund is greater in size than the largest open-end investment company, but these distributions cannot be directly ascertained from the data presented in this chapter.

7

Macroanalysis of Credit Market Instruments

Overview

A detailed examination of the growth, ownership patterns, and classification systems of the major groups of credit market instruments can provide greater understanding of the evolution of capital markets and the relative investment importance of each of the investor groups treated in Chapters 8 through 11. Table 7-1 sets forth the amounts of securities, mortgages, bank loans, and other credit market instruments outstanding at the end of selected years during the period from 1950 through 1979. From the table it can be seen that total credit market instruments outstanding grew from $405.9 billion at the end of 1950 to $2460.1 billion at the end of 1975. For comparison purposes, total amounts outstanding are listed at the bottom of the table for the same years for corporate equities (including both common and preferred stocks), demand deposits and currency, and time deposits and savings accounts. The total of these three financial assets grew from $342 billion (84.5 percent of the total amount of credit market instruments outstanding) in 1950 to $2064.2 billion (83.9 percent of the total amount of credit market instruments outstanding) in 1975.

As of the end of 1975, the six groups of credit market instruments with the largest total amounts outstanding were:

Credit market instrument category	Amount outstanding in billions of dollars (end of 1975)
Mortgages	$803.3
U.S. government securities	445.2
Corporate and foreign bonds	317.2
Bank loans not classified elsewhere	277.0
State and local government securities	230.5
Consumer credit	197.3

TABLE 7-1
Credit Market Instruments Outstanding for Selected Years, 1950–1979
(In billions of dollars)

Category	1950	1955	1960	1965	1970	1975	1979	Compound annual growth rates (percent)	
								1950–1975	1965–1975
U.S. government securities	216.5	230.0	235.0	260.6	299.3	445.2	662.9	2.9	5.5
Federally sponsored agency issues	1.8	3.0	7.9	13.9	38.9	78.8	135.9	16.3	18.9
Mortgage pool securities	..*	0.1	0.2	0.9	4.8	34.1	118.0	..†	43.8
State and local government securities	24.4	45.9	70.8	100.3	144.4	230.5	312.7	9.4	8.7
Corporate and foreign bonds	39.2	60.9	90.0	123.0	201.6	317.2	455.7	8.7	9.9
Mortgages	73.0	130.1	208.9	335.3	473.1	803.3	1333.7	10.1	9.1
Consumer credit	21.5	38.8	56.1	89.9	127.0	197.3	382.3	9.3	8.2

Bank loans not classified elsewhere	28.2	42.8	62.9	106.2	161.5	277.0	406.8	9.6	10.1
Commercial paper	0.9	2.1	4.5	9.3	33.1	47.8	106.5	17.2	17.8
Bankers' acceptances	0.4	0.6	2.0	3.4	7.1	18.7	49.9	16.6	18.6
Federal funds and security repurchase agreements	0.0	...*	...*	0.6	1.6	10.2	99.8	...†	32.8
Total	405.9	554.3	738.3	1043.4	1492.4	2460.1	4064.2	7.5	9.0
Memorandum:									
Corporate equities	146.0	317.0	451.0	749.0	907.0	854.6	1198.3	7.3	1.3
Demand deposits and currency	124.1	144.7	155.5	187.5	241.8	325.0	425.6	3.9	5.7
Time deposits and savings accounts	71.9	113.3	177.1	319.7	466.6	884.6	1340.0	10.6	10.7
Total	342.0	575.0	783.6	1256.2	1615.4	2064.2	2963.9	7.5	5.1

SOURCE: *Flow of Funds Accounts*, Board of Governors of the Federal Reserve System. Data for all periods through 1975 are taken from the *Flow of Funds Accounts, 1946–1975*, issued in December 1976; data for periods subsequent to 1975 are taken from the *Flow of Funds Accounts, 1969–1979*, issued in February 1980. Because of occasional revisions in the Flow of Funds Accounts data, certain statistics from the latter source and subsequent releases may vary somewhat from those contained in the *Flow of Funds Accounts, 1946–1975*.

*Less than $50 million.

†Not measurable from data in the table.

Mortgages were by far the largest outstanding credit market instrument at the end of 1975, representing 1.8 times the amount of the next largest instrument, U.S. government securities. During the period from 1950 through 1975, the most rapid growth rates in total amounts outstanding were exhibited by the following credit market instruments:

Credit market instrument category	Compound annual rate of growth, 1950–1975 (percent)
Commercial paper	17.2
Bankers' acceptances	16.6
Federally sponsored agency issues	16.3
Mortgages	10.1
Bank loans not classified elsewhere	9.6
State and local government securities	9.4

Commercial paper, bankers' acceptances, and federally sponsored agency issues were the three credit market instruments which showed the fastest compound annual rates of growth in total outstandings during the *1950–1975 period.* While each of these credit market instruments and the other three categories of instruments also demonstrated rapid rates of compound annual growth in total outstandings during the *1965–1975 period,* a number of other categories exhibited even faster growth rates:

Credit market instrument category	Compound annual rate of growth, 1965–1975 (percent)
Mortgage pool securities	43.8
Federal funds and security repurchase agreements	32.8
Federally sponsored agency issues	18.9
Bankers' acceptances	18.6
Commercial paper	17.8
Bank loans not classified elsewhere	10.1

With compound annual growth rates in total amounts outstanding of 43.8 and 32.8 percent respectively, mortgage pool securities and federal funds and security repurchase agreements were the two fastest-growing categories of credit market instruments during the 1965–1975 period.

A number of other interesting conclusions can be drawn from Table 7-1. First, the compound annual rate of growth in total credit market instruments outstanding was 9 percent in the 1965–1975 period, representing a considerable increase from the 7.5 percent rate over the entire 1950–1975 period and indicating an acceleration in the use of debt financing in recent years.

Second, direct obligations of the United States government declined from 53.3 percent of the total credit market instruments listed in Table 7-1 at the end of 1950 to 18.1 percent at the end of 1975. However, this trend was partially offset by substantial growth in the total amount of federally sponsored agency issues outstanding over the same period. In addition, from 1950 through 1975 virtually every other financial vehicle listed in Table 7-1 expanded its proportion of total credit market instruments outstanding at the expense of the share represented by U.S. Treasury obligations.

Third, the sum of the market value of corporate equities, demand deposits and currency, and time deposits and savings accounts was 15.7 percent less than the sum of total credit market instruments outstanding in 1950 and 16.1 percent less than this total in 1975 but was greater by 3.7 percent in 1955, 6.1 percent in 1960, 20.4 percent in 1965, and 8.2 percent in 1970. Aside from variations in the volume of debt financing, a major reason for such fluctuations derived from cyclical changes in the market value of corporate equities. As mentioned earlier, the amount of outstanding preferred stock, which is usually categorized as a fixed-income security, is included in the figures for corporate equities. Because preferred stock and common stock are classified as *financial assets* but not as *credit market instruments,* they will not be treated separately in the discussion of credit market instruments. When available, amounts of corporate equities outstanding and held by various categories of investors will be shown.

Fourth and finally, the total amounts of credit market instruments outstanding by category of issuer in Table 7-1 are about 5 to 6 percent less than the total amounts of credit market instruments outstanding as shown by category of ownership in Table 6-3, since certain types of credit market instruments such as the "other loans" classification have been excluded from Table 7-1.

Flow of Funds Accounts

To aid the investor in organizing and monitoring the many categories of debt issuers and debt holders over a period of time, the Federal Reserve Board has developed a national statistical system called the Flow of Funds Accounts, which has been published regularly in various forms since it was initiated in 1947. The Flow of Funds Accounts are constructed so that the financial activities of the United States economy can be related to the nonfinancial economic functions that turn out income, savings, and goods and services.

Perhaps more important for the investor, the Flow of Funds Accounts have been planned so that the various amounts of debt and equities held by investors and marketed by issuers can be analyzed in relation to each other and in relation to the types of credit instruments involved. To the greatest possible degree, the Flow of Funds Accounts attempt to portray in broad categories practically every investor group and every major type of financial transaction in the economy. They include financial assets and liabilities but do not encompass ownership of physical assets. At some point in the future, when the issues of data collection and valuation of physical assets have been resolved, the Federal Reserve Board plans to include data on physical assets, which will allow balance sheets for various financial sectors of the economy to be constructed from Flow of Funds Accounts data.

A summary of Flow of Funds Accounts in matrix form for the year 1975 is shown in Table 7-2. To a large degree, analysis of the various sectors shown as columns across the top of the table will concentrate on rows 27 through 36 of the table, which depict transactions in nine summary categories of credit market instruments. The *U* and the *S* on the left- and right-hand sides of each column heading indicate the amount of funds invested (a use of funds) or raised (a source of funds) by that particular sector.

For example, during 1975 households invested $10.5 billion in U.S. Treasury securities, businesses invested $9 billion, and state and local governments invested $6.3 billion, yielding a total of $25.8 billion invested by all private domestic nonfinancial sectors in these securities. (These numbers are shown reading from left to right in line 28 of Table 7-2.)

The category rest of the world (foreign sector) invested $8.1 billion in U.S. Treasury securities, as shown at the intersection of column 5 and line 28. The next column to the right, column 6, shows that the United States government sector issued $85.8 billion in U.S. Treasury securities (shown as a source of funds rather than as a use of funds, since the United States government was on balance raising money through the sale of U.S. Treasury securities rather than investing in U.S. Treasury securities).

Continuing to the right across line 28, it can be seen that financial sectors in total invested $52 billion in U.S. Treasury securities, divided in the next four columns as (a) $1.5 billion by (federally) sponsored agencies and mortgage pools, (b) $7.4 billion by the monetary authority (the Federal Reserve Board), (c) $28.8 billion by commercial banking, and (d) $14.3 billion by private nonbank financial sources such as savings and loan associations, mutual savings banks, credit unions, life insurance companies, private pension funds, state and local government employee retirement funds, and other sources. In the summary column for all sectors, it can be seen that $85.8 billion in U.S. Treasury securities was issued by the United States government and that an equivalent amount was invested in these securities by all groups of investors. By reading down the same "All sectors" column (the third column from the right), it is possible to note the total amounts borrowed in each major transaction category (lines 28 through 36) during 1975.

A *negative* sign in the "All sectors" column indicates a *net repayment* of the particular credit market instrument by that specific sector or sectors. In 1975 all sectors (columns 1 through 11) in the aggregate paid back $14.4 billion in bank loans not classified elsewhere (the intersection of line 34 and column 12). When the intersection of a column and a row contains entries under both the *U* and the *S* headings, certain entities within a sector were *investing* in a specific type of security while simultaneously the same or other entities

TABLE 7-2
Summary of Flow of Funds Accounts for the Year 1975
(In billions of dollars)

Transaction category	(1) Households U	(1) Households S	(2) Business U	(2) Business S	(3) State and local governments U	(3) S	(4) Total U	(4) S	(5) Rest of the world U	(5) S	(6) United States government U	(6) S	(7) Total U	(7) S	(8) Sponsored agencies and mortgage pools U	(8) S	(9) Monetary authority U	(9) S	(10) Commercial banking U	(10) S	(11) Private nonbank finance U	(11) S	(12) All sectors U	(12) S	(13) Discrepancy U	(13) S	(14) National saving and investment
1 Gross saving		256.5		138.7		-4.1		391.1		-11.9		-75.0		6.8		.6		.2		.2		2.2		311.0		-6.6	323.0
2 Capital consumption		149.6		131.1				280.7						4.3						2.2		2.1		285.0		-4.4	285.0
3 Net saving (1-2)		106.9		7.6		-4.1		110.4		-11.9		-75.0		2.4		.6		.2		*		1.6		26.0			37.9
4 Gross investment (5+11)	280.9		124.2		-5.4		399.7		-16.2		-75.2		9.4		.3		.2		6.5		2.4		317.6				331.6
5 Private capital expenditures	179.2		127.6				306.9				-1.3		9.9						4.6		5.3		315.4				315.4
6 Consumer durables	131.7						131.7																131.7				131.7
7 Residential construction	42.4		7.8				50.2						1.0								1.0		51.2				51.2
8 Plant and equipment	5.1		133.2				138.3						8.9						4.6		4.3		147.1				147.1
9 Inventory change			-14.6				-14.6																-14.6				-14.6
10 Mineral rights			1.3				1.3				-1.3																
11 Net financial investment (12-13)	101.6		-3.4		-5.4		92.8		-16.2		-73.9		-.5		.3		.2		1.9		-2.9		2.2			-2.2	16.2
12 Financial uses	154.8		38.4		10.4		203.6		15.1		17.0		171.0		15.5		11.2		34.0		110.3		406.7				31.3
13 Financial sources		53.1		41.9		15.8		110.8		31.3		90.9		171.5		15.2		11.0		32.1		113.2		404.4		-2.2	15.1
14 Gold and official foreign exchange										.5	.3						.3						.5			.5	
15 Treasury currency											.3	.9	.3	1.0			1.0						.5	.9		*	
16 Demand deposits and currency	6.7		2.9		.3		10.0		.1		2.9		1.3	16.1				10.6	.1	5.4	1.2	1.2	14.3	16.1			
17 Private domestic	6.7		2.9		.3		10.0						1.3	13.2				6.2	.1	7.0	1.2	1.2	11.3	13.2			
18 Foreign									.1					.1				*		.2			.1	.1			
19 United States government														2.8				4.5		-1.7			2.9	2.8			
20 Time and savings accounts	84.9		1.9		-2.0		84.8		.7					89.9						30.1	4.3	59.8	89.9	89.9			
21 At commercial banks	25.7		1.9		-2.0		25.7		.7		.1			30.1						30.1	3.7		30.1	30.1			
22 At savings institutions	59.2						59.2				.1			59.8							.6	59.8	59.8	59.8			
23 Life insurance reserves	7.6						7.6							7.6								7.6	7.6	7.6			

TABLE 7-2
Summary of Flow of Funds Accounts for the Year 1975 (continued)
(In billions of dollars)

Transaction category	(1) Households U	(1) S	(2) Business U	(2) S	(3) State and local governments U	(3) S	(4) Total U	(4) S	(5) Rest of the world U	(5) S	(6) United States government U	(6) S	(7) Total U	(7) S	(8) Sponsored agencies and mortgage pools U	(8) S	(9) Monetary authority U	(9) S	(10) Commercial banking U	(10) S	(11) Private nonbank finance U	(11) S	(12) All sectors U	(12) S	(13) Discrepancy U	(13) S	(14) National saving and investment U	(14) S
24 Pension fund reserves	36.1						36.1					3.6		32.4								32.4	36.1	36.1				
25 Interbank claims													-3.3	-3.3			1.6	.8	-4.9	-4.1								
26 Corporate equities	-1.8			9.9			-1.8	9.9	4.7	.1			8.3	1.2							8.3	.2	11.2	11.2				
27 Credit market instruments	27.2	49.7	14.4	37.7	12.1	14.9	53.7	102.3	6.1	12.8	15.1	85.2	139.1	13.7	14.5	13.5	8.5		27.6		88.5		214.0	214.0				
28 U.S. Treasury securities	10.5		9.0		6.3		25.8		8.1			85.8	52.0		1.5		7.4		28.8		14.3		85.8	85.8				
29 Federal agency securities	-4.8		-.7		2.7		-2.8				4.5	-.6	10.4	12.7		12.7	1.0		1.4		8.1		12.1	12.1				
30 State and local government securities	8.7			2.6	1.5	14.7	9.9	17.3					7.3						1.7		5.6		17.3	17.3				
31 Corporate and foreign bonds	10.4		2.6	27.2			10.4	27.2	.6	6.2			25.3	2.9					1.8		23.5	2.7	36.3	36.3				
32 Mortgages	4.4	40.5		16.4	1.6		6.0	56.8			3.2		49.8	2.3	15.7				4.3		29.8	2.3	59.0	59.0				
33 Consumer credit		8.5					1.3	8.5					7.2						2.9		4.3		8.5	8.5				
34 Bank loans not elsewhere classified				-13.0		-1.5		-14.5	4.0	-.1			-14.4						-14.4				-14.4	-14.4				
35 Private short-term paper	-1.9		5.0	-2.2			3.1	-2.2		.1				2.8		-.2			1.1		-1.0							
36 Other loans	2.2			6.7		.2		9.1	2.8	7.3			1.4	-3.1		-2.4		.1			3.8	-4.0	8.7	8.7				
37 Security credit	.1	2.2					.1	2.2					4.4	2.2					1.9		2.5		4.5	4.5				
38 Trade credit	.6		4.8	-3.2			7.9	6.3	1.6	2.1	1.2	-3.3	.6	-.1								.6	11.5	10.1		-1.4		
39 Taxes payable		.7					-.1	-3.2				1.7											-3.4	-3.4				
40 Equity in noncorporate business	-9.9			-9.9			-9.9	-9.9																				
41 Miscellaneous	3.7	11.3	5.0	2.4	.9		15.1	3.1	1.8	15.6	.7	-.7	15.0	12.0	.9	1.6	-.2	-.4	9.4	-.7	4.9	11.4	32.6	30.0		-2.6		
42 Sector discrepancies (1–4)	-24.3	14.5					-8.5	4.3	4.3			.3	-2.6			.3		-4.3		1.4			-6.6	-8.7				

SOURCE: *Flow of Funds Accounts*, Board of Governors of the Federal Reserve System.

142

within that category were *issuing* that type of security. For instance, at the intersection of the "Corporate and foreign bonds" row with the "Private nonbank finance" column (the meeting point of line 31 and column 11) it can be noted that nonbank financial institutions as a group *invested* a total of $23.5 billion in corporate and foreign bonds during the same year in which they were *issuing* $2.7 billion worth of the same securities.

Whereas Table 7-2 shows a summary of flows of funds *during a given year* (1975), Table 7-3 contains total amounts of financial assets and liabilities outstanding *as of a certain date* (December 31, 1975). Table 7-3 permits examination of the ownership of credit market instruments as of a specific *point* in time, while Table 7-2 reveals details concerning short-term and long-term capital raised and supplied over a selected *period* of time. Similarities in construction facilitate analysis and comparison between the two tables. Many of the row and column headings are the same for both tables, except that the *A* and the *L* at the top of each column in Table 7-3 refer to whether the sector owns the instrument in question (in which case it is classified as an asset) or owes it (in which case it is categorized as a liability).

If we allow for combinations of certain more detailed sector amounts in Table 6-3 to fit into the summary headings of Table 7-3, the total amounts of credit market instruments held as assets by each of the investor sectors, listed across line 19 of Table 7-3, generally conform to the amounts presented under the column labeled "1975" in Table 6-3. In similar fashion, if we allow for combinations of certain more detailed credit market instrument categories in Table 7-1 to fit into the summary row titles for lines 20 through 28 in Table 7-3, the total amounts of credit market instruments outstanding as shown in the "All sectors" column (12) of Table 7-3 (lines 20 through 28) generally conform to the amounts presented under the column labeled "1975" in Table 7-1.

Line 20 of Table 7-3 shows that as of December 31, 1975, the households sector owned $114.3 billion worth of U.S. Treasury securities, including U.S. savings bonds; the business sector owned $14.3 billion in U.S. Treasury securities; the general funds of state and local governments owned $30.6 billion; the rest of the world (foreign sector) owned $66.5 billion; the United States government had issued $437.3 billion in U.S. Treasury securities (this amount is thus shown on the liability side of column 6); and all *financial* sectors taken together owned $211.6 billion in U.S. Treasury securities, broken down as *(a)* $2.9 billion held by federally sponsored agencies and mortgage pools, *(b)* $87.9 billion owned by the monetary authority (the Federal Reserve System), *(c)* $85.4 billion held by the commercial banking sector, and *(d)* $35.3 billion held by the various groups of financial institutions which comprise the private nonbank financial sector.

Under the conventions of flow-of-funds accounting, it should be noted that the holdings of U.S. government securities by the various federal gov-

TABLE 7-3
Summary of Financial Assets and Liabilities as of December 31, 1975 (Continued)
(Amounts outstanding in billions of dollars)

Transaction category	(1) Households		(2) Business		(3) State and local governments		(4) Total		(5) Rest of the world		(6) United States government		(7) Total		(8) Sponsored agencies and mortgage pools		(9) Monetary authority		(10) Commercial banking		(11) Private nonbank finance		(12) All sectors		(13) Floats and discrepancies
	A	L	A	L	A	L	A	L	A	L	A	L	A	L	A	L	A	L	A	L	A	L	A	L	A
1 Total financial assets	2496.9		629.0		139.2		3265.0		247.7		122.4		2407.1		127.1		124.7		873.6		1281.6		6042.1		37.3
2 Total liabilities		782.8		1109.3		240.3		2132.4		271.0		510.8		2291.7		124.9		124.7		826.5		1215.6		5205.9	
3 Gold									38.1				11.6				11.6						49.7		
4 Special Drawing Rights									8.9								2.3						11.2	11.2	
5 IMF position									2.2			2.2											2.2	2.2	
6 Official foreign exchange									.1								.1						.1	.1	
7 Treasury currency												8.7	10.6	8.7			10.6				.1		10.6	8.7	−1.9
8 Demand deposits and currency	165.6		67.4		14.3		247.3		14.0		11.2		17.8	325.0	.3			82.5	.9	242.5	16.7		290.3	325.0	34.7
9 Private domestic	165.6		67.4		14.3		247.3						17.8	300.1	.3			74.3	.9	225.8	16.7		265.2	300.1	35.0
10 United States government											11.2			10.9				7.8		3.1			11.2	10.9	
11 Foreign									14.0					14.0				.5		13.5			14.0	14.0	−.3

144

12 Time and savings accounts	776.2			846.7		20.9		.6		16.4 884.6			455.6		16.4 429.0 884.6 884.6
13 At commercial banks	350.7	22.4		421.1		20.9		.6		13.0 455.6			455.6		13.0 455.6 455.6
14 At savings institutions	425.6	22.4	48.1	425.6						3.4 429.0					3.4 429.0 429.0
15 Life insurance reserves	164.6			164.6				7.7		156.9					156.9 164.6 164.6
16 Pension fund reserves	368.6			368.6				41.9		326.7					326.7 368.6 368.6
17 Interbank claims									3.9	58.6 58.6		38.3	54.7 20.3		58.6 58.6
18 Corporate equities	630.5			630.5		26.7				197.4 42.2			.9	196.5	42.2 854.7 42.2
19 Credit market instruments	346.8 753.5	85.5 834.4	70.1 229.6	502.4 1817.5	77.5	94.2	88.2	446.3 1958.6	268.7 125.7 114.5	95.3	745.4	33.9	992.4	120.3 2626.7 2626.7
20 U.S. Treasury securities	114.3	14.3	30.6	159.2	66.5		7.0	437.3 211.6	2.9	87.9	85.4	35.3	437.3 437.3
21 Federal agency securities	9.1	3.2	22.3	34.6				7.9 79.2 112.9	.4 112.9	6.2	34.5	38.0	120.8 120.8
22 State and local government securities	74.2	4.5 6.7	4.4 223.8	83.1 230.5				147.4			102.8	44.6	230.5 230.5
23 Corporate and foreign bonds	65.9	254.3		65.9 254.3	2.6	25.6		248.7 37.3			8.6	4.5 240.2	32.8 317.2 317.2
24 Mortgages	72.7 508.2	286.8	12.8	85.6 795.0			13.5	1.1 704.2 7.2	87.5		136.5	480.3	7.2 803.3 803.3
25 Consumer credit	197.3	30.9		30.9 197.3				166.4			90.3	76.1	197.3 197.3
26 Bank loans not elsewhere classified	16.5	198.2		214.7		21.8		277.0	40.5	1.1	277.0		29.9 277.0 277.0
27 Private short-term paper	10.5	32.6 17.8		43.1 17.8	8.4	11.1		28.7 51.4	3.0		10.3	10.5 18.9	14.4	32.5 80.3 80.3
28 Other loans	31.5	70.6	5.8	107.9		35.7	67.7	95.3 19.4	31.8 1.6			63.5	17.8 163.0 163.0
29 Security credit	4.0 13.7	13.7		4.0 13.7	.4	.3		24.6 15.0			14.6	10.1	15.0 29.0 29.0
30 Trade credit	7.9 283.3 234.8	10.7	283.3 253.4	11.6	14.2	6.4	5.2 7.7				7.7	29.9 272.8 −36.2
31 Taxes payable	13.4	6.6	6.6 13.4	5.3		2.7				.6	2.1 12.0 4.1
32 Miscellaneous	40.5 7.7 170.5	26.7	211.1 34.5	49.5 160.0	6.1	1.2	103.6 211.3	1.2 10.5	3.2	3.8	57.1	73.6	42.0 123.5 370.3 406.9

SOURCE: *Flow of Funds Accounts*, Board of Governors of the Federal Reserve System.

ernment insurance and trust funds are *excluded* from the $437.3 billion listed as total U.S. government securities outstanding. Approximately $120 billion of additional U.S. government securities were held in federal government insurance and trust funds as of the end of 1975.

Although the flow-of-funds accounting system does produce some differences in data classification from certain of the conventions commonly employed on a day-to-day basis in specific investor categories, its breadth, uniformity, continuity over a period of years, and reliability argue greatly in favor of its use by fixed-income securities investors. Utilization of Flow of Funds Accounts in this book also permits the investor to update the data by obtaining tables showing annual total funds flows as well as year-end financial assets and liabilities.[1]

In reviewing the investment behavior of the principal investor groups in Chapters 8 through 11, the year-end totals are used somewhat more frequently than the annual total investment flows. The latter represent net changes in the year-end totals and are the actual route used by the financial markets to attract funds from national income totals and redirect them for spending purposes. The investor should keep in mind that a strict comparison of year-end totals for two successive years may not completely reflect flows which take place during that particular year. For example, savings and loan associations temporarily invest in commercial paper for several months during the year in anticipation of investing their funds in mortgages or other credit market instruments in the latter part of the calendar year. The year-end total holdings of commercial paper by savings and loan associations may remain unchanged, giving an erroneous picture of no activity in commercial paper on the part of the associations. In addition, for certain investors such as life insurance companies, net asset changes may reflect valuation adjustments in designated parts of their securities holdings as well as actual investment flows during the year.

With some differences from the flow-of-funds methodology in classifying investor groups and credit market instruments, year-end totals for the period from 1900 through 1958 are contained in *Studies in the National Balance Sheet of the United States.*[2] In general, the analysis of credit market instruments and investor sectors in this and the following chapters concentrates primarily on the period since 1945, the first year for which flow-of-funds figures are available. Certain investor groups, such as investment-counseling organizations and hedge funds, are not covered in detail because of a lack of separately classified data.

Table 7-4 shows the various groupings of financial claims for which sepa-

---

[1]Such statistics are available from the Division of Research and Statistics, Board of Governors of the Federal Reserve System, Division of Research and Statistics, Flow of Funds and Savings Section, Washington, D.C. 20551.

[2]Raymond W. Goldsmith and Robert E. Lipsey, *Studies in the National Balance Sheet of the United States,* 2 vols., Princeton University Press, Princeton, N.J., 1963.

TABLE 7-4
Financial Transaction Categories Used in the Flow of Funds Accounts
(Continued)

Financial transaction category	Also occasionally grouped together as

Gold and Special Drawing Rights
Official foreign exchange position
  IMF gold tranche position
  Convertible foreign exchange
Treasury currency
	Monetary reserves

Demand deposits and currency
  Private domestic
  United States government
  Foreign
Time deposits at commercial banks
Savings accounts at savings institutions
	Deposit claims on
	financial institutions

Life insurance reserves Pension fund reserves	Insurance and pension reserves
Interbank claims Corporate equities	

U.S. government securities
  Treasury issues
    Short-term
    Other marketable
    Savings bonds
  Nonguaranteed agency issues
  Loan participation certificates
State and local obligations
Corporate and foreign bonds
Mortgages
  Home (one- to four-family) mortgages
  Other mortgages
  Multifamily residential mortgages
  Commercial mortgages
  Farm mortgages
Consumer credit
  Installment
  Noninstallment
Bank loans not classified elsewhere
Other loans
  Open-market paper
  Finance company loans to business
  U.S. government loans
  Sponsored credit agency loans
  Loans on insurance policies
	Credit market instruments

TABLE 7-4
Financial Transaction Categories Used in the Flow of Funds Accounts
(Continued)

Financial transaction category	Also occasionally grouped together as
Security credit	
Owed by brokers and dealers	
Owed by others	
Taxes payable	
Trade credit	
Equity in noncorporate business	Other claims
Miscellaneous	
Deposit claims	
Equities	
Insurance claims	
Unallocated claims and bank floats	
Sector discrepancies	

rate listings are kept in the flow-of-funds accounting system, with boldface type denoting the categories that are discussed in this chapter. In the following sections of this chapter, historical growth and ownership patterns are reviewed for U.S. government and federal agency securities, state and local government obligations, corporate and foreign bonds, mortgages, consumer credit, bank loans not classified elsewhere, and other loans.

U.S. Government and Federal Agency Securities

Because of the frequent intermingling of the securities of the United States government and federally sponsored credit agencies in many investors' portfolios, these two categories are treated together here and shown separately when detailed breakdowns are available. The securities which comprise the United States government and federally sponsored credit agency categories include U.S. savings bonds; foreign currency issues of the U.S. Treasury, such as the securities issued in such overseas capital markets as Germany and Switzerland by the United States government in the late 1970s and early 1980s; so-called federal budget agencies, including the issues of the Export-Import Bank, the U.S. Postal Service, the Federal Housing Administration (FHA), the General Services Administration (GSA), the Washington Metropolitan Area Transit Authority, the Tennessee Valley Authority (TVA), and the Federal Financing Bank (FFB); Commodity Credit Corporation (CCC)–guaranteed bank loans and certificates of interest; loan participation certificates issued by the Government National Mortgage Association (GNMA; "Ginnie Mae") and the Export-Import Bank; pass-through securities backed by mortgage pools and guaranteed by GNMA; Farmers Home Administration–insured notes; and issues by the so-called nonbudget federally sponsored credit agencies: the Federal Home Loan Banks, the Federal National Mortgage Association (FNMA; "Fannie Mae"), the Federal Land Banks, the Federal Intermediate Credit Banks, the Banks for Cooperatives, the Student Loan Marketing Association (SLMA), the Farm Credit Banks, and the Federal Home Loan Mortgage Association (FHLMC).

The entities in the last-named group raise funds for their lending activities primarily through issues of their own debt securities. Together with GNMA, they comprise the strict definition of the category known as federally sponsored credit agencies, or federal agencies. Debt issues of the United States government or the federal agencies held respectively by the United States government or the federal agencies have been netted out and are excluded from the aggregates for each of these two categories, but issues of the U.S. Treasury sector held by the federal agency sector, or vice versa, are included in the statistics discussed below.

Table 7-5 shows the ownership of U.S. government and federal agency securities for selected years during the period from 1950 through 1979. Even though yields and other characteristics of agency issues often differ from those of Treasury securities, they are grouped together in Table 7-5 because of the degree of homogeneity perceived by many investors. The shifting composition of ownership of U.S. government and federal agency securities over the 1950–1975 period can readily be seen in the table. For Treasury issues, the broad picture is one of declining percentage ownership by large private-sector investor groups such as households and corporations and increasing percentage ownership by the Federal Reserve System and foreign holders, chiefly the central banks of other nations.

When analyzing Table 7-5 and similar tables, it should be kept in mind that the *absolute* amount of securities held by a particular investment group may increase even while the *percentage* of total securities under discussion held by that investor category declines. This is due to a slower growth rate in securities held by the specific investor group than the rate for the overall amount of these securities held by all investor categories taken together.

Trust funds controlled by the United States government have also vastly increased their percentage ownership of Treasury debt, but as noted earlier, such holdings are netted out and thus are not included under flow-of-funds accounting conventions. The largest holder of U.S. Treasury securities in 1950 was the household sector, with 31.5 percent of total Treasury issues outstanding. By the end of 1975 households still owned the largest portion

TABLE 7-5
Ownership of U.S. Government and Federal Agency Securities for Selected Years, 1950–1979
(In billions of dollars)

Investor category	1950		1955		1960		1965		1970		1975		1979	
	US	FA	US	FA	US	FA	US	FA	US	FA	US	FA	US	FA
United States government	0.0	0.0	0.0	...*	0.0	...*	0.0	...*	0.0	...*	0.0	7.0	0.0	32.1
Federally sponsored credit agencies	0.3	0.0	0.9	0.0	1.5	0.0	1.9	0.0	3.2	0.0	3.4	0.0	1.7	0.4
Federal Reserve System	20.8	0.0	24.8	0.0	27.4	0.0	40.8	0.0	62.1	0.0	87.9	6.2	117.5	8.7
Rest of the world (foreign sector)	3.1	NS	5.8	NS	10.6	NS	13.2	NS	19.7	NS	66.5	NS	124.2	NS
Households†	68.1	0.1	68.7	0.6	71.5	2.5	87.1	6.0	82.8	22.3	114.3	9.1	189.4	53.6
Nonfinancial corporate business	17.9	0.0	21.3	0.3	15.8	1.1	7.5	1.2	8.3	1.2	14.3	3.2	6.5	3.0
State and local governments: general funds	6.6	0.2	10.8	0.6	13.4	1.1	18.0	0.9	23.2	2.3	30.6	22.3	49.3	19.4
Commercial banks	62.6	1.9	62.3	2.9	61.6	2.3	60.2	5.8	62.5	13.9	85.4	34.5	97.2	51.0
Savings and loan associations	1.5	0.0	2.4	...*	4.6	0.6	7.4	0.8	6.8	4.1	5.4	17.2	4.7	32.1

Mutual savings banks	10.9	...*	8.5	0.1	6.2	0.5	5.5	0.8	3.2	2.2	4.7	6.1	4.3	15.5
Credit unions	...*	0.0	0.1	0.0	0.2	0.0	0.3	...*	0.6	0.8	1.5	3.5	1.3	3.4
Life insurance companies	13.5	0.0	8.6	...*	6.4	0.1	5.1	0.2	4.0	0.5	4.7	1.4	4.8	8.8
Private pension funds	2.3	0.0	3.0	...*	2.4	0.3	2.5	0.5	2.1	0.9	7.9	2.9	18.4	7.0
State and local government retirement funds	2.5	0.0	4.7	...*	5.7	0.2	7.2	0.5	5.1	1.5	2.2	4.6	15.0	17.1
Other insurance companies	5.3	0.0	6.0	0.0	5.4	0.1	5.5	0.6	3.4	1.6	4.7	2.3	11.9	6.8
Open-end investment companies	0.1	NS	0.2	NS	0.6	NS	0.8	NS	0.9	NS	1.0	NS	1.4	NS
Money market funds	0.0	0.0	0.0	0.0	0.0	0.0	0.0	0.0	0.0	0.0	0.9	NS	5.6	NS
Security brokers and dealers	0.5	NS	0.2	NS	1.0	NS	1.1	NS	3.4	NS	2.2	NS	5.0	NS
Total	216.0	2.2	228.3	4.5	234.3	8.8	264.1	17.3	291.3	51.3	437.6	120.3	658.2	258.9

SOURCE: *Flow of Funds Accounts*, Board of Governors of the Federal Reserve System. Data for all periods through 1975 are taken from the *Flow of Funds Accounts, 1946–1975*, issued in December 1976; data for periods subsequent to 1975 are taken from the *Flow of Funds Accounts, 1969–1979*, issued in February 1980. Because of occasional revisions in the Flow of Funds Accounts data, certain statistics from the latter source and subsequent releases may vary somewhat from those contained in the *Flow of Funds Accounts, 1946–1975*.

NOTE: US = U.S. government securities; FA = Federal agency securities; NS = Separate federal agency securities holdings, if any, not supplied.

*Less than $50 million.

†In this table and all succeeding tables, the "households" category includes personal trusts and nonprofit organizations unless otherwise noted.

of U.S. Treasury debt, accounting for 26.1 percent of the total. It is interesting to note that 54 percent of households' total holdings of Treasury issues were savings bonds in 1950 and that this proportion increased to 59 percent by 1975.

The second-largest holder of U.S. government debt in 1950 was the commercial banking sector, with 29 percent of the total outstanding. At the end of 1975, commercial banks held 19.5 percent of U.S. Treasury debt and were the third-largest investor in Treasury issues. In 1975 the second-largest holder of U.S. government debt was the Federal Reserve System, with 20.1 percent of the total, up from third place and 9.6 percent of the total in 1950. The foreign sector, primarily foreign central banks, was the fourth-largest investor in U.S. Treasury securities at the end of 1975, holding 15.2 percent of total Treasury debt, up sharply from 1.4 percent of the total in 1950. The general funds of state and local governments were the fifth-largest investor in U.S. government issues in 1975, with 7 percent of the total, up from 3.1 percent in 1950.

Major declines in the proportion of total Treasury debt outstanding held by investor groups at the end of 1975 as compared with the end of 1950 were exhibited by (1) life insurance companies, whose share of total Treasury debt declined from 6.3 to 1.1 percent of the total; (2) mutual savings banks, whose share of total Treasury debt declined from 5 to 1.1 percent; and (3) other insurance companies, whose share of total Treasury debt declined from 2.5 to 1.1 percent. Less than 1 percent of the total Treasury debt at the end of 1975 was held by each of the following investor categories: (1) federally sponsored credit agencies (0.8 percent), (2) securities brokers and dealers (0.5 percent), (3) state and local government employee retirement funds (0.5 percent), (4) credit unions (0.3 percent), (5) open-end investment companies (0.2 percent), and (6) money market mutual funds (0.2 percent).

For federal agency securities, Table 7-5 reveals enormous growth during the 1950–1975 period. By growing at a 17.4 percent compound annual rate in total outstanding debt compared with a 2.9 compound annual rate of growth for U.S. Treasury securities outstanding, total federal agency debt increased from slightly more than 1 percent of total Treasury debt in 1950 to 27.5 percent of total Treasury debt outstanding at the end of 1975. During the 1970–1975 period, the rise in federal agency debt outstanding was particularly dramatic, exhibiting a 32.9 percent compound annual rate of growth.

In broad terms, the huge expansion of the federal agency securities market from 1965 through 1975 can be said to have been financed by its three largest investor groups: (1) commercial banks, which accounted for 28.7 percent of total federal agency debt outstanding in 1975 (down from 33.5 percent of the total in 1965); (2) the general funds of state and local governments, which represented 18.2 percent of total federal agency debt outstanding at the end of 1975 (up from 5.2 percent in 1965); and (3) savings and loan associations, which held 14.3 percent of total agency debt in 1975 (up from 4.6 percent in 1965). Other major holders of federal agency debt at the end of 1975 included (1) households (7.6 percent of total federal agency debt outstanding), (2) the United States government (with 5.8 percent), (3) the Federal Reserve System (with 5.2 percent), (4) mutual savings banks (with 5.1 percent), and (5) state and local government employee retirement funds (with 3.8 percent).

Table 7-5 provides information about long-term trends in the ownership distribution of U.S. government and federal agency securities. To gain some perspective on the year-to-year changes in credit demands and the supply of funds to meet such demands, Tables 7-6 and 7-7 have been included. Slight differences in format arise from the fact that these data have been supplied and gathered from the U.S. Treasury and the Bankers Trust Company rather than the Federal Reserve System. Table 7-6 shows, for the years 1972 through 1979, the total amount of funds raised and supplied in U.S. Treasury securities.

The amount of new credit raised by the United States government during the period exhibits a wide degree of variability, ranging from a low of $7.9 billion in 1973 to a high of $85.8 billion in 1975. A similar degree of variability characterizes the shifting investment patterns of the suppliers of funds to the U.S. government securities markets. For example, the Federal Reserve System shifted from the position of being a net seller of $300 million worth of U.S. government securities in 1972 to one of being a net buyer in 1973 of $8.6 billion worth of U.S. Treasury issues, or more than the total of new purchases of U.S. government securities from all sources combined in 1973.

For varying reasons in the domestic and world economy, in the investors' own spheres of activity, and in the U.S. government securities market itself, the largest sources of funds supplied to Treasury issues and their share of the total have changed frequently. Foreign investors, chiefly foreign central banks, were the largest source of funds to the U.S. Treasury securities market in 1972, 1977, and 1978, providing 44.2, 54.7, and 54.7 percent respectively of the total. Commercial banks were the leading supplier of funds in 1975 and in 1976, providing 33.6 and 26.3 percent respectively of the total amount invested in U.S. government issues. Although not the largest single contributor of funds in any of the years shown, state and local government general funds were major contributors both in 1972 and in 1977, supplying more than 23 percent of the total amount raised by the U.S. Treasury in each of those years.

The total amount of funds raised by federal agencies during the 1972–

1979 period, which demonstrates a degree of variability similar to that of the aggregates for U.S. government securities, is shown in Table 7-7. As an example of variability, federal agencies raised $16.8 billion in 1973 and $16.9 billion in 1974 but then raised only $2.4 billion and $2.3 billion in the two succeeding years. The amounts raised by federal agencies as a percentage of the amounts raised by the U.S. Treasury vary widely:

Year	Total funds raised by federal agencies as a percentage of total funds raised by the U.S. Treasury
1972	25.8
1973	212.7
1974	140.8
1975	2.8
1976	3.3
1977	9.8
1978	19.1

Commercial banks were the largest suppliers of funds in 1972 and 1973, accounting for 83.7 and 44 percent respectively of total funds invested in federal agency securities. Individuals and others were the leading supplier of funds in 1974 and 1978, representing 46.2 and 34.3 percent respectively of the total invested in agency issues, but they liquidated $6.4 billion worth of federal agency issues over the 1975–1977 period, for a net sell-off of 55.6 percent of total funds raised during that time span by federal agencies. Business corporations were the largest supplier of funds in 1976, providing 65.2 percent of the total federal agency investment.

State and Local Government Securities

Table 7-8 shows the ownership of state and local government securities (also called municipal securities or tax-exempt securities) for selected years during the period from 1950 through 1979. As defined in the Flow of Funds Accounts, state and local government securities include the aggregate short-term and long-term debt of all state and local governmental entities. Trade debt and debt owed to the United States government are not included. Any state and local government issues held by state and local governments are incorporated in the data.

A major factor in the relative attractiveness of municipal securities to investor groups is the incremental income tax rate of the investor at the federal level and, to a lesser degree, at state and local levels. The marginal income tax rates affecting investors are usually determined by (1) their aggregate level of income and/or (2) legislative action which increases or

TABLE 7-6
Funds Raised and Supplied in U.S. Government Securities, 1972–1979
(*In billions of dollars*)

	1972	1973	1974	1975	1976	1977	1978 (estimated)	1979 (projected)
FUNDS RAISED								
U.S. government debt	19.0	7.9	12.0	85.8	69.1	57.6	54.8	56.0
FUNDS SUPPLIED								
Federal Reserve System	-.3	8.6	2.0	7.4	9.0	5.5	6.8	7.5
Insurance companies and pension funds								
Life insurance companies	--	-.4	-.1	1.4	.6	-.1	--	.1
Private noninsured pension funds	.7	-.4	-.7	3.4	1.6	2.1	.5	1.2
State and local government retirement funds	-.4	-1.1	-1.1	1.0	1.6	2.4	3.0	2.8
Fire and casualty insurance companies	.1	-.1	.4	2.5	3.1	3.1	.8	1.5
Total	.5	-2.0	-1.5	8.3	6.9	7.6	4.3	5.6

TABLE 7-6
Funds Raised and Supplied in U.S. Government Securities, 1972–1979 (Continued)
(In billions of dollars)

	1972	1973	1974	1975	1976	1977	1978 (estimated)	1979 (projected)
Thrift institutions								
Savings and loan associations	-.5	-2.4	--	1.8	2.7	1.4	-1.0	.5
Mutual savings banks	.2	-.6	-.4	2.2	1.0	.1	-.8	--
Credit unions	-.1	.3	.4	.8	.4	-.5	.1	.2
Total	-.4	-2.6	--	4.7	4.2	.9	-1.7	.7
Investment companies	.1	.4	.1	.8	.1	-.1	.6	.3
Commercial banks	2.4	-8.8	-2.6	28.8	18.2	-.9	-7.0	-5.5
Business corporations	-2.6	-5.3	2.1	9.0	8.1	-6.0	-2.6	--
Government								
Nonbudget agencies	-.3	-.8	--	-.3	1.7	-2.5	--	--
State and local government: general funds	4.4	.9	--	4.8	6.0	12.9	10.5	3.5
Total	4.1	.1	--	4.5	7.7	10.4	10.5	3.5
Foreign investors	8.4	.2	4.1	7.7	11.6	31.5	30.0	28.0
Individuals and others	6.8	17.3	7.9	14.6	3.4	8.7	13.9	15.9
Total	19.0	7.9	12.0	85.8	69.1	57.6	54.8	56.0

SOURCE: Bankers Trust Company and the U.S. Department of the Treasury.

TABLE 7-7
Funds Raised and Supplied in Federal Agency Securities, 1972–1979
(In billions of dollars)

	1972	1973	1974	1975	1976	1977	1978 (estimated)	1979 (projected)
FUNDS RAISED								
Budget agencies								
Export-Import Bank	1.2	...	.4	-.2	-.2	-.4	-.6	-.6
Government National Mortgage Association	-1.1	-.4	-.1	-.1	-.1	-.4	-.6	-.2
General Services Administration	.4	.2	.1	...	...	...	...	...
Tennessee Valley Authority	.5	.4	-.3	-.1	-.2	...	...	...
Other*	.2	...	.2	.1	...	...	...	...
Total	1.2	.1	.3	-.3	-.5	-.8	-1.2	-.8
Less U.S. government investment accounts	-.2	-.3	...	...	...	-.1	...	...
Total	1.4	.4	.3	-.3	-.5	-.6	-1.2	-.8
Nonbudget agencies								
Banks for cooperatives	.1	.7	.9	.1	.7	.1	...	-4.1
Federal Home Loan Banks	-.2	8.4	6.5	-3.0	-2.1	1.5	10.0	9.0
Federal Home Loan Mortgage Corporation	.8	.4	-.2	.5	...	...	...	.3
Federal Intermediate Credit Banks	.3	1.1	1.7	.7	1.2	.7	.2	-8.6
Federal Land Banks	1.0	1.9	2.6	2.4	2.1	2.0	1.2	-4.4
Federal National Mortgage Association	1.5	3.8	5.2	1.8	.6	1.3	9.3	6.8
Other†	...	.2	...	.3	.3	1.8	3.2	22.0
Total	3.5	16.4	16.6	2.7	2.8	7.4	23.9	21.0
Total funds raised	4.9	16.8	16.9	2.4	2.3	6.8	22.7	20.2

TABLE 7-7
Funds Raised and Supplied in Federal Agency Securities, 1972–1979 *(Continued)*
(In billions of dollars)

	1972	1973	1974	1975	1976	1977	1978 (estimated)	1979 (projected)
FUNDS SUPPLIED								
Federal Reserve System	0.7	0.5	3.1	0.9	1.0	1.5	−.6	...
Insurance companies and pension funds								
Life insurance companies	−.3	...	.2	.4	.9	1.7	2.3	1.2
Private noninsured pension funds	.1	.5	1.1	.3	.6	.6	.5	1.0
State and local retirement funds	−.2	.5	.4	−.3	.5	1.0	1.5	1.9
Fire and casualty insurance companies	−.1	...	.3	.2	.3	.3	.2	.3
Total	−.5	1.0	2.0	.6	2.3	3.6	4.5	4.4
Thrift institutions								
Savings and loan associations	1.5	1.8	−.2	.8	.6	1.3	2.2	1.5
Mutual savings banks	.5	−.5	−.1	.6	.5	.1	.1	.2
Credit unions	.5	.2	...	.5	.1	.2	...	...
Total	2.5	1.5	−.3	1.9	1.2	1.6	2.3	1.7
Commercial banks	4.1	7.4	3.3	1.2	.6	−1.2	4.7	2.0
Business corporations	.1	1.5	1.4	−.7	1.5	−.4	.8	.5
State and local general funds	.7	1.3	.1	.4	−.3	.6	2.0	1.5
Foreign investors	.1	...	−.5	−1.0	...	2.7	1.2	1.5
Individuals and others	−2.9	3.5	7.8	−.9	−4.0	−1.5	7.8	8.6
Total funds supplied	4.9	16.8	16.9	2.4	2.3	6.8	22.7	20.2

SOURCE: Bankers Trust Company and the U.S. Department of the Treasury.

*Includes Federal Housing Administration, U.S. Postal Service, and Washington Metropolitan Area Transit Authority.

†Includes Student Loan Marketing Association and Farm Credit Banks.

TABLE 7-8

Ownership of State and Local Government Securities for Selected Years, 1950–1979

(In billions of dollars)

Investor category	1950	1955	1960	1965	1970	1975	1979
Households	9.2	19.3	30.8	36.4	45.2	74.2	74.3
Nonfinancial corporate business	0.7	1.2	2.4	4.6	2.2	4.5	4.0
State and local governments:							
general funds	2.0	2.5	2.7	2.2	2.4	4.4	8.2
Commercial banks	8.2	12.9	17.7	38.8	70.2	102.8	135.9
Savings and loan associations	0.0	0.0	0.0	0.0	0.1	1.1	1.2
Mutual savings banks	. . .*	0.6	0.7	0.3	0.2	1.5	3.2
Life insurance companies	1.2	2.0	3.6	3.5	3.3	4.5	6.4
State and local government							
retirement funds	1.5	2.7	4.4	2.6	2.0	2.5	4.0
Other insurance companies	1.1	4.2	8.1	11.3	17.8	34.3	74.7
Security brokers and dealers	0.4	0.3	0.4	0.5	0.9	0.6	1.0
Total	24.4	45.9	70.8	100.3	144.4	230.5	312.7

SOURCE: *Flow of Funds Accounts,* Board of Governors of the Federal Reserve System. Data for all periods through 1975 are taken from the *Flow of Funds Accounts, 1946–1975,* issued in December 1976; data for periods subsequent to 1975 are taken from the *Flow of Funds Accounts, 1969–1979,* issued in February 1980. Because of occasional revisions in the Flow of Funds Accounts data, certain statistics from the latter source and subsequent releases may vary somewhat from those contained in the *Flow of Funds Accounts, 1946–1975.*

*Less than $50 million.

decreases tax rates in general or for specific sectors of the economy. At the end of 1975, the three dominant investor groups in the municipal securities markets were (1) commercial banks, with $102.8 billion, or 44.6 percent of the total outstanding (up from 33.6 percent in 1950); (2) households, with $74.2 billion, or 32.2 percent of the total outstanding (down from 37.7 percent in 1950); and (3) the category of other insurance companies, primarily representing property-casualty insurers, with $34.3 billion, or 14.9 percent of the total outstanding (up significantly from 4.9 percent in 1950).

During the 1950–1975 period, several investor groups reduced their percentage share of the total amount of state and local government securities outstanding. The general funds of state and local governments lowered their proportion of the total from 8.2 percent in 1950 to 1.9 percent in 1975. Over the same time span, state and local government retirement funds decreased their share of the total from 6.1 to 1 percent, and the share of the total held by life insurance companies declined from 4.9 to 2 percent. Nonfinancial corporate businesses' percentage of the total moved downward from 2.9

percent in 1950 to 2 percent in 1975. At the end of 1975, small amounts of municipal securities (less than 1 percent of the total outstanding for each investor group) were held by mutual savings banks, savings and loan associations, and security brokers and dealers.

For the years from 1972 through 1979, Table 7-9 sets forth the specific breakdowns of funds raised by maturity, with short-term debt classified as having an original maturity of less than 1 year and long-term debt classified as having an original maturity in excess of 1 year. Breakdowns of funds supplied, organized by investor category, are also included.

The total amount of funds supplied ranged from $14.7 billion in 1972 to $29.4 billion in 1977. The most important source of funds to municipal securities was not always the same investor group. Commercial banks provided the largest percentage of total funds raised in the state and local government securities markets in 1972 and 1973, with 49 and 37 percent of the total respectively. Individuals and others supplied the largest investment flow in 1974, with 41 percent of the total, and fire and casualty insurance companies provided the largest portion of investment funds in 1975, 1976, 1977, and 1978, contributing 15.2, 24.2, 34.7, and 50.2 percent of the total respectively.

Corporate and Foreign Bonds

Corporate and foreign bonds comprise the convertible and nonconvertible funded debt of American private corporations and the bonds held in the United States of foreign governments, private corporations, and international agencies. Table 7-10 shows the ownership of corporate and foreign bonds for selected years during the period from 1950 through 1979.

At the end of 1975, the four dominant investor groups in corporate and foreign bonds (for most of the years covered, the vast majority of foreign bonds represented Canadian issues) were (1) life insurance companies, with $105.5 billion, or 33.1 percent of the total outstanding (down considerably from the 63.3 percent level in 1950); (2) households (a fair share of this category's holdings were represented by personal trusts and nonprofit corporations), with $65.9 billion, or 20.8 percent of the total outstanding (up from 12.2 percent of the total in 1950); (3) state and local government retirement funds, with $60.9 billion, or 19.2 percent of the total outstanding (representing a significant proportional gain from the 1.5 percent level in 1950); and (4) private pension funds, with $37.8 billion, or 11.9 percent of the total (up from 7.1 percent in 1950).

As of the end of 1975, mutual savings banks held 5.5 percent of total corporate and foreign bonds outstanding, but savings and loan associations

TABLE 7-9

Funds Raised and Supplied in State and Local Government Obligations, 1972–1979

(In billions of dollars)

	1972	1973	1974	1975	1976	1977	1978 (estimated)	1979 (projected)
FUNDS RAISED								
Long-term debt								
New offerings								
Industrial bonds	0.5	2.4	2.5	3.0	3.0	4.3	3.9	3.5
Other	22.5	20.6	20.3	26.3	30.8	40.8	42.0	37.1
Total	22.9	23.0	22.8	29.3	33.8	45.1	45.9	40.6
Less retirements, refundings, and adjustments	8.3	8.6	9.1	13.5	13.9	16.8	17.0	17.2
Net	14.6	14.4	13.7	15.8	19.9	28.3	28.9	23.4
Short-term debt								
New offerings	25.2	24.7	29.0	29.0	21.9	21.3	21.6	23.0
Less retirements and adjustments	25.1	24.1	26.3	29.3	22.8	20.4	21.6	22.5
Net	0.1	0.6	2.7	−0.3	−0.9	0.9	…	0.5
United States government loans	…	0.3	0.7	0.2	2.0	0.2	−1.4	0.5
Total	14.7	15.3	17.1	15.8	21.0	29.4	27.5	24.4
FUNDS SUPPLIED								
Insurance companies and pension funds								
Life insurance companies	…	…	0.3	0.8	1.1	0.5	0.1	0.2
State and local government retirement funds	−0.1	−0.4	−0.7	1.9	1.4	0.3	0.5	0.5
Fire and casualty insurance companies	4.4	3.3	1.9	2.4	5.1	10.2	13.8	13.2
Total	4.3	2.9	1.5	5.2	7.4	11.0	14.4	13.9

TABLE 7-9

Funds Raised and Supplied in State and Local Government Obligations, 1972–1979 *(Continued)*

(In billions of dollars)

	1972	1973	1974	1975	1976	1977	1978 (estimated)	1979 (projected)
Thrift institutions								
Savings and loan associations	...	...	0.3	0.6	...	...	...	...
Mutual savings banks	0.5	0.1	...	0.6	0.9	0.4	0.4	0.2
Total	0.5	0.1	0.3	1.2	0.9	0.4	0.4	0.2
Investment companies	0.9	0.7	1.0	2.2	2.9	3.9	3.1	2.7
Commercial banks	7.2	5.7	5.5	1.7	3.0	9.2	7.9	4.5
Business corporations	1.0	−0.1	0.6	−0.2	−1.1	...	0.2	...
Government								
United States government	...	0.3	0.7	0.2	2.0	0.2	−1.4	0.5
State and local government general funds	−0.3	0.2	0.5	2.4	2.7	0.2	1.2	1.0
Total	−0.3	0.5	1.2	2.6	4.7	0.4	−0.2	1.5
Individuals and others	1.1	5.5	7.0	3.1	3.1	4.6	1.7	1.6
Total	14.7	15.3	17.1	15.8	21.0	29.4	27.5	24.4

SOURCE: Bankers Trust Company; *Flow of Funds Accounts,* Board of Governors of the Federal Reserve System; Securities Industry Association; *The Daily Bond Buyer; National Income Accounts,* U.S. Department of Commerce.

TABLE 7-10

Ownership of Corporate and Foreign Bonds for Selected Years, 1950–1979
(In billions of dollars)

Investor category	1950	1955	1960	1965	1970	1975	1979
Households	4.8	6.0	10.0	10.8	35.9	65.9	71.6
Rest of the world (foreign sector)	0.2	0.3	0.6	0.7	1.7	2.6	10.2
Commercial banks	2.6	1.9	1.3	1.1	2.4	8.6	7.7
Mutual savings banks	2.1	2.6	3.8	2.9	8.1	17.5	20.8
Life insurance companies	24.8	37.1	48.1	61.0	74.1	105.5	173.1
Private pension funds	2.8	7.9	15.7	22.7	29.7	37.8	55.2
State and local government retirement funds	0.6	2.7	7.1	17.2	35.1	60.9	86.2
Other insurance companies	0.7	1.2	1.7	3.0	8.6	12.2	22.2
Open-end investment companies	0.2	0.5	1.2	2.6	4.3	4.8	6.5
Security brokers and dealers	0.4	0.8	0.5	0.9	1.7	1.4	2.3
Total	39.2	60.9	90.0	123.0	201.6	317.2	455.7

SOURCE: *Flow of Funds Accounts*, Board of Governors of the Federal Reserve System. Data for all periods through 1975 are taken from the *Flow of Funds Accounts, 1946–1975*, issued in December 1976; data for periods subsequent to 1975 are taken from the *Flow of Funds Accounts, 1969–1979*, issued in February 1980. Because of occasional revisions in the Flow of Funds Accounts data, certain statistics from the latter source and subsequent releases may vary somewhat from those contained in the *Flow of Funds Accounts, 1946–1975*.

held no corporate and foreign bonds since they were not permitted to use this investment vehicle. Other insurance companies, principally property-casualty firms, owned 3.8 percent of the total of corporate and foreign bonds outstanding, and commercial banks owned 2.7 percent. Lesser amounts were held by open-end investment companies, the rest of the world, and security brokers and dealers.

Because of the use of the Securities and Exchange Commission rather than the Federal Reserve System as a data source, Table 7-11 has a slightly altered format and excludes foreign bond totals from the aggregate data for funds raised and supplied in corporate bonds during the 1972–1979 period. Life insurance companies and state and local government employee retirement funds provided the relatively steadiest flows of money into corporate bonds from 1972 through 1979, accounting for 42.8 and 21.1 percent respectively of all new corporate bonds issued during this 8-year interval. Individuals and others demonstrated the greatest variability in total net demand for corporate bonds, ranging from net purchases of $6.4 billion in 1974 and $5.6 billion in 1975 to net sales of $7.6 billion in 1978. Similar large swings in total net demand for corporate bonds were exhibited by mutual savings banks.

TABLE 7-11

Funds Raised and Supplied in Corporate Bonds, 1972–1979

(In billions of dollars)

	1972	1973	1974	1975	1976	1977	1978 (estimated)	1979 (projected)
FUNDS RAISED								
Gross new issues								
Manufacturing and extractive	5.5	4.5	10.2	17.3	13.6	11.7	10.1	14.1
Transportation	1.6	1.8	0.8	2.6	3.5	1.2	2.1	2.5
Electric, gas, and water	6.2	5.5	8.8	9.6	8.2	7.4	7.0	7.2
Communication	3.7	3.5	3.7	3.4	2.6	3.1	3.4	3.8
Financial and real estate	8.1	5.2	6.2	5.7	8.5	12.2	8.4	8.6
Commercial and other	1.9	1.0	1.6	1.9	2.6	2.8	3.0	3.2
Total	27.1	21.5	31.4	40.5	39.0	38.4	34.0	39.4
Less: Retirements								
Conversions	1.8	1.6	0.5	1.0	0.9	1.0	1.0	1.2
Other	6.2	7.2	5.8	7.6	8.2	6.2	6.5	6.5
Total	8.0	8.8	6.3	8.6	9.1	7.2	7.5	7.7
Net new issues	19.1	12.7	25.1	31.9	29.9	31.2	26.5	31.7
FUNDS RAISED BY								
Financial intermediaries								
Finance companies	3.7	1.9	1.9	1.1	4.7	3.7	6.0	4.7
Real Estate Investment Trusts	0.4	0.6	0.2	...	-0.2	-0.1	-0.1	

Commercial banks	2.4	0.9	2.3	1.3	1.9	2.3	1.1	1.5
Other	...	0.1	1.0	2.3	0.7	4.3	1.0	1.5
Total	6.5	3.5	5.4	4.7	7.1	10.2	8.0	7.7
Business corporations	12.6	9.2	19.7	27.2	22.8	21.0	18.5	24.0
FUNDS SUPPLIED								
Insurance companies and pension funds								
Life insurance companies	6.4	5.5	3.6	7.9	13.2	16.9	17.0	18.5
Private noninsured pension funds	1.5	2.0	2.7	4.6	2.3	6.2	7.0	8.0
State and local retirement funds	4.5	4.0	7.5	5.0	4.0	5.3	6.2	7.5
Fire and casualty insurance companies	-0.7	-0.2	2.0	2.1	3.8	3.4	2.5	3.2
Total	11.8	11.3	15.8	19.6	23.3	31.8	32.7	37.2
Mutual savings banks	2.1	-0.9	0.8	3.5	2.8	1.2	0.2	0.5
Investment companies	1.5	1.3	0.5	1.1	0.7	2.1	0.5	0.3
Commercial banks	1.7	0.4	1.1	1.8	-0.6	-0.1	-0.1	...
Foreign investors	-0.1	...	0.5	0.2	0.1	1.0	0.8	1.0
Individuals and others	2.1	0.6	6.4	5.6	3.6	-4.7	-7.6	-7.3
Total	19.1	12.7	25.1	31.9	29.9	31.2	26.5	31.7
Memorandum:								
Convertible bonds								
Gross new issues offered for cash	2.2	0.6	0.5	1.3	1.0	0.6	0.4	0.8
Conversions	1.8	1.6	0.5	1.0	0.9	1.0	1.0	1.2
Net increase in outstandings*	0.4	-1.0	...	0.3	0.1	-0.4	-0.6	-0.4

SOURCE: Bankers Trust Company; Securities and Exchange Commission.
*Excludes convertible bonds issued in exchange for stocks.

Mortgages

As defined in the Flow of Funds Accounts, the total amounts outstanding for mortgages include all debt secured by (1) one- to four-family nonfarm residential properties, whether insured by the FHA, guaranteed by the Veterans Administration, or without any governmental guarantee (the last-named are called conventional mortgages), which together represented 61.3 percent of total mortgages outstanding as of the end of 1975; (2) multifamily residential properties, which accounted for 2.5 percent of total mortgages outstanding; (3) commercial properties, amounting to 19.8 percent of total mortgages outstanding; and (4) farm properties, representing 6.4 percent of total mortgages outstanding.

Although mortgages are not technically fixed-income securities, any examination of the fixed-income securities markets should include an analysis of the mortgage markets as well. In recent years there has been a significant increase in the liquidity, marketability, variety of terms, and breadth of investor ownership of mortgages, with particular influence upon the funds flows of those investor groups that view mortgages as actual or potential substitutes for certain of their fixed-income securities investments.

During the late 1960s, the 1970s, and the early 1980s, greater investment interest developed in mortgages owing to (1) their frequently higher yields relative to high-quality corporate bonds, (2) the generally rising values of the real property securing mortgage debt, (3) the regular repayment of principal through amortization payments, and (4) the growth in the secondary market for home mortgages. As a result, the yield premium of mortgages over corporate bond issues narrowed considerably compared with the levels of the 1950s and the early 1960s (it was even negative at times, indicating that corporate bonds were yielding more than mortgages).

Governmental support of mortgage markets has often led to the issuance of substantial amounts of bonds and notes by several types of budget and nonbudget federal agencies. In addition, new mortgage features, such as variable-interest-rate mortgages, and new debt instruments, such as mortgage-backed bonds issued by the corporate sector to finance its activities in the mortgage markets, became somewhat more prevalent in the late 1970s.

In the late 1970s a number of states removed statutory mortgage interest rate ceilings or allowed a change in the calculation of residential mortgage interest payments from a fixed-rate basis to a variable-rate basis. Under the variable-rate-mortgage (VRM) system, the interest rate on home mortgages is generally permitted to rise or fall in accordance with prevailing yields on a selected index of medium- or long-term U.S. Treasury or corporate bonds. For some variable-rate mortgages, a maximum amount by which mortgage interest rates can rise or fall over the life of the mortgage is set. A variant of VRMs, renegotiated-rate mortgages, allows less frequent resetting of the interest rate on a mortgage, with a maximum specified increase or decrease in the rate from one renewal period to the next.

Such new terms and instruments tended to facilitate the flow of investor groups' funds into mortgages in periods of high interest rates. In addition, these terms allowed greater flexibility in structuring mortgage features such as down-payment amounts, maturities, and other aspects of the mortgage contract to take account of local property values, taxation rates, and the possibility for mortgage holders to package and sell mortgages if necessary to governmentally sponsored secondary-mortgage lending agencies.

Another development which aided the flow of investor funds into mortgages in the late 1970s and early 1980s was the rise of so-called conduit firms. With nicknames such as Maggie Mae (MGIC Mortgage Marketing Corp.), Pennie Mae (PMI Mortgage Corp.), and Connie Mac (Continental Mortgage Co.), these firms purchase pools of conventional mortgages from small- and medium-size savings and loan associations and other mortgage lenders. These mortgages are then assembled and used to pass through interest and principal payments on securities backed by the mortgages. Several groups of investors such as insurance companies have thus been able to invest in conventional mortgages without the administrative costs involved in originating and servicing loans.

Table 7-12 shows investor ownership of all types of mortgages grouped together for selected years during the period from 1950 through 1979. At the end of 1975 the seven largest investors in mortgages were (1) savings and loan associations, with $278.7 billion, or 34.7 percent of total mortgages outstanding (almost doubling their share from 18.8 percent of the total in 1950); (2) commercial banks, with $136.5 billion, or 17 percent of total mortgages outstanding (down slightly from 18.8 percent of the total in 1950); (3) life insurance companies, with $89.4 billion, or 11.1 percent of total mortgages outstanding (a sharp decline from 22.1 percent of the total in 1950); (4) mutual savings banks, with $77.2 billion, or 9.6 percent of total mortgages outstanding (a modest decline from 11.4 percent of the total in 1950); (5) households, with $72.7 billion, or 9.1 percent of total mortgages outstanding (down significantly from 24.1 percent of the total in 1950); (6) federally sponsored credit agencies, with $53.4 billion, or 6.6 percent of the total outstanding (up from 1.4 percent of the total in 1950); and (7) federally sponsored mortgage pools, consisting of GNMA, FHLMC, and Farmers Home Administration pools, with $34.1 billion, or 4.2 percent of total mortgages outstanding (up from an infinitesimal percentage of the total in 1950).

Five investor groups held between 1 and 2 percent of total mortgage debt outstanding at the end of 1975: (1) the United States government, with

TABLE 7-12
Ownership of Mortgages for Selected Years, 1950–1979*
(In billions of dollars)

Investor category	1950	1955	1960	1965	1970	1975	1979
Households	17.5	22.5	33.4	42.2	51.3	72.7	123.0
State and local governments: general funds	0.2	0.6	1.6	2.7	3.7	12.8	20.7
United States government	1.8	3.6	5.8	5.9	10.2	13.5	11.3
Federally sponsored credit agencies	1.0	1.6	5.5	6.8	17.7	53.4	86.4
Mortgage pools	. . .†	0.1	0.2	0.9	3.2	34.1	118.0
Commercial banks	13.7	21.0	28.8	49.7	70.5	136.5	246.8
Savings and loan associations	13.7	31.4	60.1	110.3	140.0	278.7	475.7
Mutual savings banks	8.3	17.5	26.9	44.6	56.1	77.2	98.7
Credit unions	. . .†	0.2	0.4	0.6	0.7	1.6	3.8
Life insurance companies	16.1	29.4	41.8	60.0	72.0	89.4	119.2
Private pension funds	0.1	0.3	1.3	3.4	4.2	2.4	3.5
State and local government retirement funds	. . .†	0.3	1.5	3.7	5.6	8.3	9.4
Other insurance companies	0.1	0.2	0.1	0.1	0.2	0.2	0.3
Finance companies	0.5	1.4	1.6	4.5	5.7	9.3	11.4
Real Estate Investment Trusts	0.0	0.0	0.0	0.0	2.0	13.2	5.6
Total	72.7	130.1	208.9	335.3	443.2	803.3	1333.7

SOURCE: *Flow of Funds Accounts,* Board of Governors of the Federal Reserve System. Data for all periods through 1975 are taken from the *Flow of Funds Accounts, 1946–1975,* issued in December 1976; data for periods subsequent to 1975 are taken from the *Flow of Funds Accounts, 1969–1979,* issued in February 1980. Because of occasional revisions in the Flow of Funds Accounts data, certain statistics from the latter source and subsequent releases may vary somewhat from those contained in the *Flow of Funds Accounts, 1946–1975.*

*Includes one- to four-family residential mortgages, multifamily residential mortgages, commercial mortgages, and farm mortgages.

†Less than $50 million.

$13.5 billion, or 1.7 percent of the total; (2) the general funds of state and local governments, with $12.8 billion, or 1.6 percent of the total; (3) Real Estate Investment Trusts, with $13.2 billion, or 1.6 percent of the total; (4) finance companies, with $9.3 billion, or 1.2 percent of the total; and (5) state and local government retirement funds, with $8.3 billion, or 1 percent of the total. Three investor groups held substantially less than 1 percent of the total at the end of 1975: (1) private pension funds, with $2.4 billion, or 0.3 percent of the total; (2) credit unions, with $1.6 billion, or 0.2 percent of the total; and (3) other insurance companies, with $0.2 billion, a minuscule percentage of the total.

Table 7-13 shows total annual flows into the mortgage market during the

TABLE 7-13
Funds Raised and Supplied in Mortgages, 1972–1979
(In billions of dollars)

	1972	1973	1974	1975	1976	1977	1978 (estimated)	1979 (projected)
FUNDS RAISED								
Residential mortgages								
Home	43.2	44.1	33.3	41.4	65.2	99.5	95.0	89.5
Multifamily	13.0	10.3	6.9	0.6	3.7	7.3	10.3	9.5
Total	56.2	54.4	40.2	42.0	68.9	106.8	105.3	99.0
Commercial mortgages	17.2	19.1	15.3	12.4	12.3	18.4	25.2	26.8
Farm mortgages	3.6	5.5	5.0	4.6	6.4	8.8	10.5	11.0
Total	77.0	78.9	60.5	59.0	87.6	134.0	141.0	136.8
FUNDS SUPPLIED								
Insurance companies and pension funds								
Life insurance companies	1.8	4.5	4.9	2.9	2.4	5.3	9.2	11.0
Private noninsured pension funds	−0.8	0.4	0.7	1.5	1.8	2.9	2.4	3.0
State and local government retirement funds	−0.3	0.1	−0.7	0.5	1.1	1.0	1.6	2.0
Total	0.7	5.0	4.9	4.9	5.3	9.2	13.2	16.0
Thrift institutions								
Savings and loan associations	33.3	26.4	18.8	32.0	47.2	60.8	57.0	54.0
Mutual savings banks	6.2	6.1	2.6	3.5	6.5	9.1	7.8	6.6
Credit unions	0.5	0.5	0.5	0.1	0.5	1.9	1.9	1.2
Total	39.9	33.0	21.8	35.6	54.2	71.8	66.7	61.8

TABLE 7-13
Funds Raised and Supplied in Mortgages, 1972–1979 *(Continued)*
(In billions of dollars)

	1972	1973	1974	1975	1976	1977	1978 (estimated)	1979 (projected)
Other financial intermediaries								
Mortgage brokers	2.0	2.2	−1.4	1.2	2.7	4.0	−1.0	2.0
Real Estate Investment Trusts	4.1	5.6	0.2	−4.9	−3.7	−2.4	−1.3	−0.6
Total	6.1	7.8	−1.2	−3.7	−1.0	1.6	−2.3	1.4
Commercial banks	16.8	20.0	13.1	4.5	15.6	29.4	35.2	30.0
Government								
United States government	−0.7	−0.6	3.9	6.2	−0.8	2.0	2.5	2.0
Nonbudget agencies	4.0	7.2	10.2	5.3	2.9	3.5	11.9	9.4
State and local government general funds	1.4	1.7	2.5	1.6	0.9	0.6	1.2	2.0
Total	4.7	8.3	16.6	13.2	3.1	6.1	15.6	13.4
Individuals and others	8.7	4.9	5.3	4.5	10.5	16.0	12.6	14.2
Total	77.0	78.9	60.5	59.0	87.6	134.0	141.0	136.8
Memoranda:								
Private housing starts (in thousands of units)	2357	2045	1338	1160	1538	1987	2018	1650
Mortgage pools	4.9	3.6	5.8	10.3	15.7	20.5	18.2	19.0

SOURCE: Bankers Trust Company.

years from 1972 through 1979. A slight alteration in format from that followed in Table 7-12 has allocated the ownership of mortgage pools evidenced by GNMA-guaranteed pass-through securities, FHLMC–guaranteed mortgage certificates, and certificates of beneficial interest issued by the Farmers Home Administration among the investor groups shown as supplying funds in Table 7-13. One of the two memoranda at the bottom of the table shows total amounts flowing into the mortgage market via investor purchases of these pool-type securities and the subsequent relending of the money into the mortgage market by the pools.

As can be seen in Table 7-13, flows of funds into mortgages fluctuate widely. For example total funds raised and supplied dropped from the $77 billion to $79 billion annual level in 1972 and 1973 to roughly $60 billion per year in 1974 and 1975, only to rebound strongly to $88 billion in 1976 and to a $134 billion to $141 billion annual level in 1977 and 1978. Such variability in large part derives from the withdrawal and diversion of funds from savings and loan associations, mutual savings banks, and the savings departments of commercial banks when disintermediation occurs. Total mortgage funds that were supplied by these three investor groups dropped from $53.0 billion in 1973 to $34.9 billion in 1974, or by 34.2 percent.

During periods of disintermediation, the United States government (primarily on-budget agencies) and nonbudget agencies provide buying support to the mortgage market. In 1974 the United States government and nonbudget agencies supplied $14.1 billion to the mortgage market, representing an increase of 114 percent from the $6.6 billion provided in 1973. From being a consistent net buyer of mortgages prior to 1974, Real Estate Investment Trusts (REITs) became net sellers of mortgages in the 1975–1979 period. The lessened activity of REITs was more than offset by increased mortgage-purchasing activity by individuals and others in the years from 1975 through 1979, when their net acquisition of mortgages reached an annual average of $12 billion, up from $6 billion annually from 1972 through 1974.

Consumer Credit

Although technically not fixed-income securities, consumer short-term and intermediate-term installment and noninstallment credit is important in the asset structure of business entities, commercial banks, savings and loan associations, mutual savings banks, credit unions, and finance companies. For this reason and because changes in consumer credit demands can influence the amounts of funds which these investors may have available for fixed-

TABLE 7-14
Ownership of Consumer Credit for Selected Years, 1950–1979
(In billions of dollars)

Investor category	1950	1955	1960	1965	1970	1975	1979
Businesses*	7.9	11.5	14.3	20.3	24.4	30.9	49.3
Commercial banks	7.4	13.2	20.6	35.7	53.9	90.3	184.2
Savings and loan associations	0.2	0.5	1.0	1.4	2.1	2.8	14.3
Mutual savings banks	0.1	0.1	0.2	0.5	1.1	1.8	3.6
Credit unions	0.6	1.7	3.9	7.3	13.0	25.4	48.2
Finance companies	5.3	11.8	16.1	24.7	32.5	46.1	82.6
Total	21.5	38.8	56.1	89.9	127.0	197.3	382.3

SOURCE: *Flow of Funds Accounts,* Board of Governors of the Federal Reserve System. Data for all periods through 1975 are taken from the *Flow of Funds Accounts, 1946–1975,* issued in December 1976; data for periods subsequent to 1975 are taken from the *Flow of Funds Accounts, 1969–1979,* issued in February 1980. Because of occasional revisions in the Flow of Funds Accounts data, certain statistics from the latter source and subsequent releases may vary somewhat from those contained in the *Flow of Funds Accounts, 1946–1975.*

*Includes nonfarm noncorporate business and nonfinancial corporate business.

income securities investments, the ownership of consumer credit as of the end of selected years from 1950 through 1979 is reviewed in Table 7-14. Installment and noninstallment credit have been combined in the table. Installment credit represents the largest component of consumer credit, rising from 68.5 percent of the total at the end of 1950 to 82.2 percent at the end of 1975. By and large, credit unions and finance companies are not active in the provision of noninstallment consumer credit, restricting their lending primarily to installment consumer credit.

As of the end of 1975, the four largest holders of consumer credit outstanding were (1) commercial banks, with $90.3 billion, or 45.8 percent of the total (up strongly from 34.4 percent at the end of 1950); (2) finance companies, with $46.1 billion, or 23.4 percent of the total (approximately the same as the 24.7 percent level at the end of 1950); (3) nonfarm noncorporate business and nonfinancial corporate business, with $30.9 billion, or 15.7 percent of the total (down significantly from 36.7 percent at the end of 1950); and (4) credit unions, with $25.4 billion, or 12.9 percent of the total (up sharply from 2.8 percent at the end of 1950). Savings and loan associations and mutual savings banks each held a relatively small share of total consumer credit outstanding at the end of 1975, with 1.4 and 0.9 percent respectively of the aggregate.

Table 7-15 summarizes the total consumer credit demanded and supplied during the years from 1972 through 1979, showing also the main uses for which installment credit was borrowed and the yearly liquidations (repay-

TABLE 7-15
Funds Raised and Supplied in Consumer Credit, 1972–1979
(In billions of dollars)

	1972	1973	1974	1975	1976	1977	1978 (estimated)	1979 (projected)
FUNDS RAISED								
Installment credit								
Extensions (by type)								
Automobile	42.7	48.4	45.4	51.4	63.6	75.6	89.5	86.8
Revolving bank credit	12.9	17.2	21.3	24.5	30.6	38.3	51.0	53.0
Mobile home	6.0	7.1	5.8	4.3	4.8	5.4	6.1	5.5
Home improvement	4.1	4.8	5.2	5.6	6.8	N.A.	N.A.	N.A.
All other	72.3	80.4	79.5	78.4	88.5	125.5	142.9	145.5
Total	138.0	157.9	157.2	164.2	194.3	254.1	299.4	302.3
Less liquidations	122.1	138.2	147.9	156.7	172.8	218.8	255.0	270.0
Net	15.9	19.7	9.3	7.5	21.5	35.3	44.4	32.3
Noninstallment credit*	3.0	2.4	0.9	1.9	3.0	3.4	4.5	3.5
Total consumer credit	18.9	22.1	10.2	9.4	24.5	38.7	48.9	35.8
FUNDS SUPPLIED								
Thrift institutions								
Savings and loan associations	0.9	1.1	0.7	0.9	1.0	1.3	1.0	0.7
Mutual savings banks	0.1	0.2	0.2	0.2	0.2	0.4	0.6	0.3
Credit unions	2.2	2.7	2.3	3.8	5.9	6.4	8.2	6.8
Total	3.2	4.0	3.2	4.9	7.1	8.1	9.8	7.8
Finance companies (installment)	2.7	3.5	0.7	-0.1	2.6	5.9	9.6	6.0

TABLE 7-15
Funds Raised and Supplied in Consumer Credit, 1972–1979 *(continued)*
(In billions of dollars)

	1972	1973	1974	1975	1976	1977	1978 (estimated)	1979 (projected)
Commercial banks								
Installment	9.3	11.0	4.0	2.8	10.8	18.6	23.0	16.8
Noninstallment	1.6	0.6	−0.4	0.1	0.6	1.3	1.5	1.2
Total	10.8	11.6	3.6	2.9	11.4	19.9	24.5	18.0
Business corporations								
Installment	1.0	1.5	1.5	0.2	1.1	2.6	2.1	1.6
Noninstallment	0.6	0.5	0.5	0.6	1.1	0.6	1.2	0.9
Total	1.7	2.0	2.0	0.8	2.2	3.2	3.3	2.5
Noncorporate business								
Installment	−0.2	0.1	. . .	−0.1	. . .	0.2	0.2	0.2
Noninstallment	0.7	0.8	0.8	0.9	1.2	1.3	1.5	1.3
Total	0.5	0.9	0.7	0.8	1.2	1.6	1.7	1.5
Total	18.9	22.1	10.2	9.4	24.5	38.7	48.9	35.8

SOURCE: Bankers Trust Company; Board of Governors of the Federal Reserve System. NOTE: N.A. = not available.
*Comprises single-payment loans to individuals, charge accounts, including nonbank credit cards, and service credit.

ments) of installment debt. The total amount of incremental consumer credit borrowed each year correlates to some degree with economic activity. For example, total new consumer credit declined from an average of $20.5 billion annually during the expansionary years of 1972 and 1973 to an average of $9.8 billion during the recessionary years of 1974 and 1975, rebounding again to an average of $37.4 billion annually during the recovery years of 1976, 1977, and 1978. Savings and loan associations, mutual savings banks, and, in particular, credit unions have generally exhibited less variability in total consumer credit supplied during economic slowdowns, whereas commercial banks, finance companies, and business entities all tend to contract their consumer lending during periods of slower or negative economic growth.

Other factors which influence the total amount of consumer credit borrowed and supplied each year include (1) the spread between what a lending institution pays to raise money and the amount that it can earn by making consumer loans; (2) the relationship between market rates of interest on consumer credit and any applicable statutory interest rate ceilings on consumer borrowing; and (3) consumer psychology, which in turn is determined by the existing burden of consumer debt service as a percentage of income, the outlook for the economy and employment, and numerous other factors.

Bank Loans Not Classified Elsewhere

Another important credit market instrument consists of bank loans not already classified together with mortgages, consumer credit, security credit, or open-market paper. These so-called bank loans not classified elsewhere include most commercial loans to businesses as well as certain types of loans to farms, individuals, foreign banks, and other financial institutions. Total bank loans not classified elsewhere amounted to $277 billion at the end of 1975, up from $28.2 billion at the end of 1950, representing a compound annual rate of growth of 9.6 percent.

Because a division of total ownership of bank loans not classified elsewhere is not available in the Flow of Funds Accounts, this credit market instrument has not been analyzed in further depth in Chapters 8 through 11. For similar reasons, the Flow of Funds Accounts category other loans, which includes loans made by the United States government and federally sponsored credit agencies, loans by finance companies to businesses, and loans by life insurance companies, has not been treated in this chapter. Total credit included in the category of other loans amounted to $163 billion at the end of 1975, up from $21.2 billion at the end of 1950, representing an 8.5 percent compound annual rate of growth.

Open-Market Paper

Open-market paper includes primarily bankers' acceptances and commercial paper placed directly with investors by the issuer or placed with investors through securities dealers. Table 7-16 shows the principal owners of open-market paper for selected years from 1950 through 1979. As of the end of 1975, the five largest holders of bankers' acceptances and commercial paper were (1) nonfinancial corporate businesses, with $27.9 billion, or 42.9 percent of the total outstanding (a dramatic increase from 23 percent at the end of 1950), most of which represented investments in commercial paper; (2) commercial banks, with $10.3 billion, or 15.5 percent of the total outstanding (down sharply from 53.8 percent at the end of 1950); (3) foreign investors, with $8.4 billion, or 12.7 percent of the total outstanding (a slight decline from the 15.4 percent level at the end of 1950), primarily accounted

TABLE 7-16
Ownership of Open-Market Paper for Selected Years, 1950–1979
(In billions of dollars)

Investor category	1950	1955	1960	1965	1970	1975	1979
Households	...*	0.1	...*	...*	0.8	6.8	40.6
Nonfinancial corporate business	0.3	1.1	2.6	6.7	20.0	27.9	33.2
Rest of the world (foreign sector)†	0.2	0.4	1.3	2.0	4.3	8.4	30.2
Federally sponsored credit agencies	0.0	0.0	0.0	0.0	0.0	1.2	0.3
Monetary authority (Federal Reserve System)‡	0.0	...*	0.1	0.2	...*	1.1	0.7
Commercial banks	0.7	0.9	1.9	2.7	8.2	10.3	15.2
Savings and loan associations	0.0	0.0	0.0	0.0	1.8	2.7	3.4
Mutual savings banks	0.1	0.1	0.2	0.3	0.7	1.1	2.4
Life insurance companies	0.0	0.0	0.3	0.3	2.2	4.8	7.3
Open-end investment companies	0.0	0.1	0.1	0.5	2.1	1.5	3.8
Money market funds	0.0	0.0	0.0	0.0	0.0	0.5	19.3
Total	1.3	2.7	6.5	12.7	40.1	66.4	156.4
Memorandum (breakdown of above total):							
Commercial paper	0.9	2.1	4.5	9.3	33.1	47.7	106.5
Bankers' acceptances	0.4	0.6	2.0	3.4	7.0	18.7	49.9

SOURCE: *Flow of Funds Accounts*, Board of Governors of the Federal Reserve System. Data for all periods through 1975 are taken from the *Flow of Funds Accounts, 1946–1975*, issued in December 1976; data for periods subsequent to 1975 are taken from the *Flow of Funds Accounts, 1969–1979*, issued in February 1980. Because of occasional revisions in the Flow of Funds Accounts data, certain statistics from the latter source and subsequent releases may vary somewhat from those contained in the *Flow of Funds Accounts, 1946–1975*.

†Primarily bankers' acceptances.

‡Exclusively bankers' acceptances.

for by investments in bankers' acceptances; (4) households, with $6.8 billion, or 10.2 percent of the total outstanding (up significantly from virtually no investments in open-market paper at the end of 1950); and (5) life insurance companies, with $4.8 billion, or 7.2 percent of the total outstanding (a substantial rise from no investments in open-market paper at the end of 1950).

With the exception of mutual savings banks, which reduced their holdings of open-market paper to 1.7 percent of the total outstanding at the end of 1975 from 7.7 percent at the end of 1950, all the remaining investors in commercial paper and bankers' acceptances held modest percentages of the total amount of open-market paper outstanding, up from no investments in these securities at the end of 1950. These investors and their percentage holdings at the end of 1975 include (1) savings and loan associations, with 4.1 percent of the total; (2) open-end investment companies, which held 2.3 percent of the total; (3) federally sponsored credit agencies, with 1.8 percent of the total; (4) the Federal Reserve System (whose holdings of open-market paper were concentrated exclusively in bankers' acceptances), with 1.7 percent of the total; and (5) money market funds, with 0.8 percent of the total.

Table 7-17 provides a summary of funds raised and supplied in open-market paper. Like most short-term credit data, the total amount of new funds raised through open-market paper is highly volatile. For example, the total of new open-market paper issued in 1974 amounted to $16.2 billion, a 100 percent increase from the $8.1 billion issued in 1973. In 1975, however, issuers on balance paid back a net total of $1.5 billion in open-market paper. The supply of funds to open-market–paper investments exhibits a similar degree of fluctuation. Business corporations purchased on balance $6.5 billion of open-market paper in 1973 (80.2 percent of the total issued) but were net sellers of $600 million worth of open-market paper in 1974. By 1977 businesses had again swung to a position as net acquirers of open-market paper, purchasing $4 billion worth of such securities (26.7 percent of the total issued). Similarly, large year-to-year reversals in net investment flows to open-market paper were demonstrated from 1974 to 1975 by foreign investors and individuals. Together, these two investor categories went from a net acquisition of $11 billion in open-market paper in 1974 to a net disinvestment of $6 billion in 1975, for a total net shift of $17 billion.

Profile of Largest Holders of Credit Market Instruments

Table 7-18, which is derived from Tables 7-5, 7-8, 7-10, 7-12, 7-14, and 7-16, assembles some of the important data on the five largest investor groups

TABLE 7-17
Funds Raised and Supplied in Open-Market Paper, 1972–1979
(In billions of dollars)

	1972	1973	1974	1975	1976	1977	1978 (estimated)	1979 (projected)
FUNDS RAISED								
Commercial paper	2.6	6.4	6.8	−1.5	4.4	11.8	18.5	16.5
Bankers' acceptances	−1.0	1.7	9.6	0.2	3.8	3.1	7.8	6.5
Finance bills	0.2	0.1	−0.2	−0.3	...	0.1	...	...
+Total, open-market paper	1.8	8.1	16.2	−1.5	8.1	15.0	26.3	23.0
FUNDS RAISED BY								
Financial intermediaries								
Finance companies	−0.2	2.4	1.0	1.5	1.5	5.9	1.9	2.0
Real Estate Investment Trusts	2.5	0.7	−3.3	0.1	−0.3	...	0.1	...
Commercial bank holding companies and other affiliates	0.8	2.4	2.0	...	−0.8	1.3	6.7	6.0
Other	−1.0	−0.4	2.6	−0.9	1.8	2.4	6.1	4.0
Total	2.1	5.1	2.3	0.8	2.1	9.6	14.8	12.0
Nonfinancial sectors								
Business corporations	0.8	1.8	5.6	−2.4	3.4	2.4	4.1	5.0
Foreigners	−1.0	0.9	7.1	−0.1	1.2	2.4	6.1	4.5
Noncorporate business	...	0.4	1.3	0.2	1.3	0.6	1.3	1.5
Total	−0.3	3.1	13.9	−2.3	6.0	5.5	11.5	11.0

FUNDS SUPPLIED

Insurance companies and pension funds								
Life insurance companies	0.1	0.1	1.0	0.6	0.3	−0.2	0.7	0.5
Private noninsured pension funds	0.2	1.5	1.8	−1.5	−1.0	0.3	0.8	1.0
Total	0.3	1.6	2.8	−0.9	−0.7	0.1	1.5	1.5
Thrift institutions								
Savings and loan associations	0.5	−0.5	−0.1	0.2	0.4	0.2	0.3	0.1
Mutual savings banks	−0.1	−0.1	0.1	0.1	0.5	0.1	0.3	0.2
Total	0.4	−0.6	· · ·	0.3	0.9	0.3	0.6	0.3
Investment companies	−0.2	0.2	0.8	−0.4	−0.8	0.8	2.8	1.3
Commercial banks	−0.2	−1.3	2.2	1.1	3.7	0.3	−1.4	· · ·
Business corporations	1.4	6.5	−0.6	4.3	2.2	4.0	4.5	2.0
Foreign investors	−0.1	0.3	6.6	−2.6	2.7	4.4	6.0	4.8
Individuals and others	0.1	1.4	4.4	−3.4	0.2	5.1	12.3	13.1
Total	1.8	8.1	16.2	−1.5	8.1	15.0	26.3	23.0

SOURCE: Bankers Trust Company; Federal Reserve Bank of New York.

TABLE 7-18
Percentage Holdings of Credit Market Instruments, Year-End, 1975

Credit market instrument	Largest investor group	Percent	Second-largest investor group	Percent	Third-largest investor group	Percent	Fourth-largest investor group	Percent	Fifth-largest investor group	Percent
U.S. government securities	HH	26.1	FRS	20.1	CB	19.5	FS	15.2	SL-GF	7.0
Federal agency securities	CB	28.7	SL-GF	18.2	SL	14.3	HH	7.6	USG	5.8
State and local government securities	CB	44.6	HH	32.2	OIC	14.9	LIC	2.0	NCB	2.0
Corporate and foreign bonds	LIC	33.1	HH	20.8	SL-RF	19.2	PPF	11.9	MSB	5.5
Mortgages	SL	34.7	CB	17.0	LIC	11.1	MSB	9.6	HH	9.1
Consumer credit	CB	45.8	FC	23.4	NNCB	15.7	CU	12.9	SL	1.4
Open-market paper	NCB	42.0	CB	15.5	FS	12.7	HH	10.2	LIC	7.2
Memorandum:										
Corporate equities*	HH	68.8	PPF	10.4	OEIC	3.9	LIC	3.3	FS	3.1

KEY: HH = households, personal trusts, and nonprofit organizations; FRS = Federal Reserve System; CB = commercial banks; FS = foreign sector; SL-GF = state and local governments: general funds; SL = savings and loan associations; USG = United States government; OIC = other insurance companies; LIC = life insurance companies; NCB = nonfinancial corporate business; SL-RF = state and local government employee retirement funds; PPF = private pension funds; MSB = mutual savings banks; FC = finance companies; NNCB = nonfarm noncorporate business and nonfinancial corporate business; CU = credit unions; OEIC = open-end investment companies.

*Includes both convertible and nonconvertible preferred stock as well as common stock.

and their respective percentage holdings for the seven credit market instruments reviewed in this chapter as of the end of 1975. In addition, percentage holdings are shown for corporate equities.

Observation of the percentages of total outstanding credit market instruments held by various investor groups leads to insight into the degree of concentration and power exercised by specific investor categories. It should be stressed that these percentages represent holdings of instruments as of a specific point in time rather than relative annual amounts invested in a particular credit market instrument. Depending upon market conditions, financing demands, and other factors, the annual flows into or out of a credit market instrument initiated by an investor group, large or small, can assume much greater importance than its percentage holding of that credit market instrument.

To give some idea of the dispersal of investor importance for each category of credit market instrument, it is helpful to compare the degree of concentration represented by the largest investor group, the three largest investor groups taken together, and the five largest investor groups taken together. The rankings for the largest investor groups are as follows:

Credit market instrument	Percentage ownership represented by the single largest investor group
Consumer credit	45.8; commercial banks
State and local government securities	44.6; commercial banks
Open-market paper	42.0; nonfinancial corporate business
Mortgages	34.7; savings and loan associations
Corporate and foreign bonds	33.1; life insurance companies
Federal agency securities	28.7; commercial banks
U.S. government securities	26.1; households

If we consider only the single largest investor group on a percentage ownership basis rather than the absolute amount of its holdings of each instrument, we see that consumer credit, state and local government securities, and open-market paper have the highest degree of concentration of ownership. More than 40 percent of each of these three credit market instruments is held by the single largest investor group.

If the holdings of the three largest investor groups are taken together, the rankings are as follows:

Credit market instrument	Percentage ownership represented by the three largest investor groups
State and local government securities	91.7
Consumer credit	84.9
Corporate and foreign bonds	73.1
Open-market paper	70.2
U.S. government securities	65.7
Mortgages	62.8
Federal agency securities	61.2

The combined holdings of the three largest investor groups account for 91.7 percent of state and local government securities, 84.9 percent of consumer credit, and 73.1 percent of corporate and foreign bonds.

If the holdings of the five largest investor groups are taken together, the rankings are as follows:

Credit market instrument	Percentage ownership represented by the five largest investor groups
Consumer credit	99.2
State and local government securities	95.7
Corporate and foreign bonds	90.5
U.S. government securities	87.9
Open-market paper	87.6
Mortgages	81.2
Federal agency securities	74.6

The combined holdings of the five largest investor groups account for 99.2 percent of consumer credit, 95.7 percent of state and local government securities, and 90.5 percent of corporate and foreign bonds. It is worth keeping in mind that there are more than 18 categories of investors. Therefore, the degree of ownership of a given credit market instrument by the top one, three, and five investor groups can reveal one measure of the degree of influence which these investors can possibly exercise on funds flows into and out of such instruments.

Another instructive approach examines the number of times which any one investor group figures among the top five holders of the seven major categories of credit market instruments. Households and commercial banks each rank six times among the top five holders of each category of credit market instruments, followed by life insurance companies, which are counted four times among the top five holders of each category. The degree of frequency of these and the other investor groups represented among the top five holders of each category of credit market instruments is shown below:

Frequency of ranking among top five holders of major categories of credit market instruments	Investor category
Six times	Households
	Commercial banks
Four times	Life insurance companies
Three times	Savings and loan associations
	Nonfarm noncorporate business and nonfinancial corporate business (once) and nonfinancial corporate business (twice)
Twice	Mutual savings banks
	Rest of the world (foreign sector)
	State and local governments: general funds
Once	Federal Reserve System
	United States government
	Other insurance companies
	State and local government employee retirement funds
	Private pension funds
	Credit unions
	Finance companies

The degree of frequency of ranking among the top five holders of the major categories of credit market instruments provides a measure not only of the overall financial influence of a particular investor group but also of the susceptibility of that investor group to alter investments and funds flows in a specific sector of the credit markets in response to market conditions and funds flows in other sectors of the credit markets.

Participants in the Bond and Money Markets

8

The Investment Behavior of Households, the Business Sector, Governmental Bodies, and International Entities

Overview

Having analyzed the major markets for and the ownership of credit market instruments in Chapter 7, we shall find it useful in this chapter and in Chapters 9 through 11 to examine the principal investors in fixed-income securities, with particular emphasis on their portfolio mix and the factors which influence their investment behavior. Table 8-1 contains a listing of the investor groups (called sectors in Flow of Funds Accounts terminology) which are maintained in the Flow of Funds Accounts, with boldface type denoting sectors which are treated in this and the next three chapters.

Table 8-1 is also valuable in that it shows the 10 most commonly used groupings employed to combine the various categories of investors when discussing flows of funds within the credit and capital markets. For example, "savings institutions" in flow-of-funds terminology includes not only savings and loan associations and mutual savings banks but also credit unions. When the boldface type denominates a larger grouping in Table 8-1 (such as "commercial banking" or "nonfinancial business"), all the components of the larger grouping are discussed together in the appropriate chapter.

Households, Personal Trusts, and Nonprofit Organizations

In addition to the investment activities of individuals as members of households, the investor grouping usually referred to in flow-of-funds conventions as "households" includes a number of other entities. Unless other-

TABLE 8-1
Investor Sectors Used in the Flow of Funds Accounts

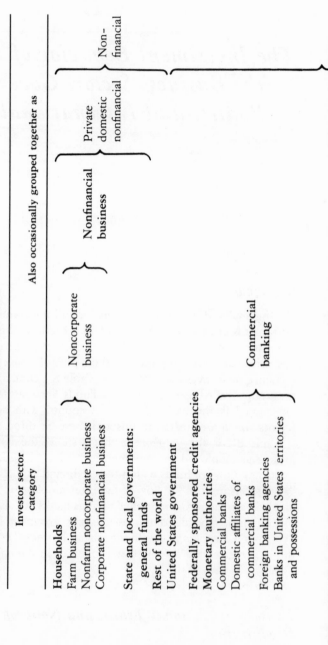

Savings and loan associations
Mutual savings banks
Credit unions
} Savings institutions

Life insurance companies
Other insurance companies
Private pension funds
State and local government employee retirement funds
} Insurance

Finance companies
Real Estate Investment Trusts
Open-end investment companies
Security brokers and dealers
} Finance not classified elsewhere

} Private nonbank finance

} Finance

wise noted, these entities are being referred to in the succeeding material whenever households are mentioned. Among other classes of investors, the household sector includes personal trusts, nonprofit organizations, foundations, investment advisory firms (investment counselors), labor unions, churches, charitable and philanthropic organizations, private schools and hospitals, and other nonprofit organizations serving individuals.

Separate data for each of these subgroups' investment holdings and funds flows are not produced on a continuing basis, but selected comments on their investment patterns are included when distinctive behavior can be noted. Table 8-2 presents the credit market investments of the overall household sector for selected years during the period from 1950 through 1979.

The broad picture which emerges from Table 8-2 is one of decreasing concentration in the range of credit market instruments held by the household investor category. As of the end of 1975, the household sector held the following credit market instruments, ranked in decreasing order of impor-

TABLE 8-2
Credit Market Instrument Holdings of the Household Sector for Selected Years, 1950–1979
(In billions of dollars)

Credit market instrument category	1950	1955	1960	1965	1970	1975	1979
U.S. savings bonds	49.4	50.2	45.6	49.7	52.1	67.4	79.9
Other U.S. Treasury securities	18.4	18.5	25.9	31.4	30.8	47.0	109.5
Federally sponsored agency issues	0.2	0.6	2.5	6.0	22.3	9.2	53.6
State and local government securities	9.2	19.3	30.8	36.4	45.2	74.2	74.3
Corporate and foreign bonds	4.8	6.0	10.0	10.8	35.9	65.9	71.6
Mortgages	17.4	22.5	33.4	42.2	52.9	72.7	123.0
Open-market paper	. . .*	0.1	. . .*	. . .*	0.8	6.8	40.6
Money market fund shares	0.0	0.0	0.0	0.0	0.0	3.6	45.2
Total	99.4	117.2	148.2	176.5	240.0	346.8	597.7
Memorandum:							
Investment company shares	3.3	7.8	17.0	35.2	47.6	42.2	46.2
Other corporate equities†	130.3	278.4	378.4	600.2	689.9	588.3	860.7

SOURCE: *Flow of Funds Accounts,* Board of Governors of the Federal Reserve System. Data for all periods through 1975 are taken from the *Flow of Funds Accounts, 1946–1975,* issued in December 1976; data for periods subsequent to 1975 are taken from the *Flow of Funds Accounts, 1969–1979,* issued in February 1980. Because of occasional revisions in the Flow of Funds Accounts data, certain statistics from the latter source and subsequent releases may vary somewhat from those contained in the *Flow of Funds Accounts, 1946–1975.*

*Less than $50 million.

†Includes both convertible and nonconvertible preferred stock and common stock.

tance: (1) state and local government securities, with $74.2 billion, or 21.4 percent of households' total investments (up from 9.3 percent in 1950); (2) mortgages, with $72.7 billion, or 21 percent of households' total investments (up somewhat from 17.5 percent in 1950); (3) U.S. savings bonds, representing $67.4 billion, or 19.4 percent of households' total investments (down significantly from 49.7 percent of the total in 1950); (4) corporate and foreign bonds, with $65.9 billion, or 19 percent of households' total investments (a strong increase from 4.8 percent of the total in 1950); (5) other U.S. Treasury securities, with $47 billion, or 13.4 percent of households' total investments (a modest decline from 18.5 percent in 1950); (6) federally sponsored credit agencies, with $9.2 billion, or 2.7 percent of households' total investments (up from 0.2 percent in 1950); (7) open-market paper, with $6.8 billion, or 2 percent of households' total investments (up from a negligible percentage in 1950); and (8) money market fund shares, with $3.6 billion, or 1 percent of households' total investments (up from 0 percent in 1950, since this investment category for all practical purposes came into existence only in 1974).

Figure 8-1 shows the growth rate in credit market instruments relative to other financial assets held by households in the period from 1946 until the mid-1970s. It can be seen that credit market instruments have grown more slowly and have been surpassed by life insurance and pension fund reserves, time and savings deposits at nonbank depositary institutions, and time and savings deposits at commercial banks. As mentioned in Chapter 7, households are by far the largest holder of *financial assets,* which include currency, savings and time deposits (including negotiable certificates of deposit), and corporate equities. However, households are a distant second behind commercial banks in total holdings of *credit market instruments.*

Table 8-3 shows the net annual flows of funds during the years from 1972 through 1979 from the entire household sector into various categories of credit market instruments, with U.S. savings bonds, other U.S. Treasury securities, and federally sponsored agency issues combined as one category. The household sector is a residual investor, in that it is generally called upon to satisfy borrowers' demands on a basis incremental to the flows into credit market instruments from institutional sources. Therefore, particularly attractive conditions must often be set on these instruments when borrowers are forced to induce households to divert their funds from normal savings and intermediation channels directly into the credit markets. Such attractions generally include higher interest rates than currently available on savings deposits at thrift institutions and occasionally longer call protection and other terms which are deemed favorable to the noninstitutional investor. This can be observed in the great variability of total funds flows and flows into each specific credit market instrument from the household sector.

For instance, in 1974 very high rates of interest and other special terms

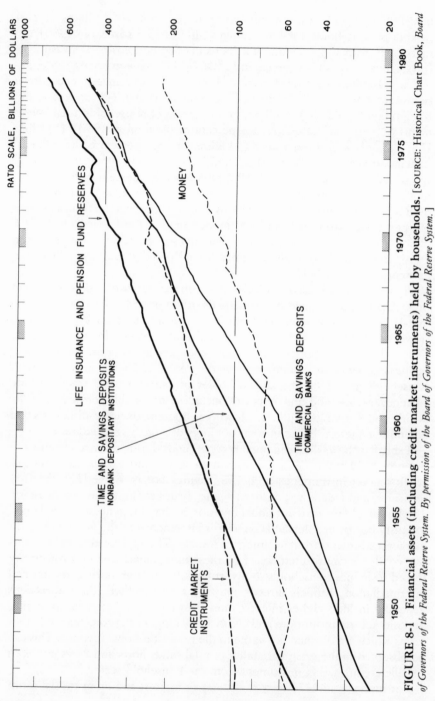

FIGURE 8-1 Financial assets (including credit market instruments) held by households. [SOURCE: Historical Chart Book, *Board of Governors of the Federal Reserve System. By permission of the Board of Governors of the Federal Reserve System.*]

TABLE 8-3
Annual Net Flows of Funds from the Household Sector into Credit Market Instruments, 1972–1979
(In billions of dollars)

Credit market instrument category	1972	1973	1974	1975	1976	1977	1978	1979
U.S. government and federal agency securities	−0.3	17.5	13.7	15.7	−1.0	6.2	27.0	40.6
State and local government securities	2.3	5.3	8.9	5.0	4.2	5.2	3.3	−0.8
Corporate and foreign bonds	4.4	1.3	4.7	8.2	4.0	0.2	−1.4	3.3
Mortgages	6.3	3.4	4.3	2.9	8.6	11.3	14.5	16.8
Open-market paper	−0.2	3.4	5.7	−6.0	−0.2	−1.5	14.6	4.4
Money market fund shares	NA	NA	2.4	1.3	−0.3	0.1	6.9	34.4
Total	12.5	30.9	39.6	27.0	15.3	21.7	64.9	98.8

SOURCE: *Flow of Funds Accounts,* Board of Governors of the Federal Reserve System. Data for 1978 and 1979 are taken from the *Flow of Funds Accounts* published in February 1980; data from 1972 to 1977 are taken from earlier years' *Flow of Funds Accounts* statistics.

NOTE: NA = Instrument not available for broad-scale investment until 1974.

were necessary to attract $39.6 billion of funds from the household sector into credit market instruments. This total was well over twice the $12.5 billion and $15.3 billion called forth from households in the less constricted overall capital-raising environment of 1972 and 1976 respectively. When we look at U.S. Treasury and federal agency securities, households swung from a net selling position of $300 million in 1972 to net purchases of $17.5 billion in 1973 and exhibited a similarly striking shift in the opposite direction when they veered from $15.7 billion in net purchases in 1975 to net sales of $1 billion in 1976.

It is especially difficult to characterize the investment portfolio policies of households because of their great numbers, their differences in tax brackets, and the diversity of their objectives. In general, individuals with high levels of net worth and substantial current income tend to concentrate their credit market investments in state and local government securities because of the tax-exempt status of these instruments. At lower levels of income and wealth, U.S. Treasury securities, particularly U.S. savings bonds, represent a preeminent portion of individuals' holdings. Corporate bonds are also important holdings for households in lower tax brackets and for other entities included in the households category that are tax-exempt.

In the aggregate, households tend toward more conservative and risk-averse management of their finances and investments than most other major investor groups. Psychological factors, unwillingness to take losses and/or pay income, capital gains, and estate taxes arising out of investment operations, and a general lack of uniformity in or knowledge about calculating true performance results hinder effective management of investment portfolios by the household sector.

Personal Trusts

One of the most important subcategories of the household sector, estimated by the Federal Reserve Board at between 5 and 10 percent of total household assets, consists of personal trusts. Most frequently administered by the trust departments of commercial banks or by separate trust companies, personal trusts are usually established for a continuous and stated period (in some cases, in perpetuity) to hold and manage financial and/or real property for the benefit of a specified individual or group of individuals. For example, personal trusts may arise from a will (these are called testamentary trusts) to provide for the guardian of the estate of a minor, or they may arise under court order, as a depositary for securities. At the end of 1977, total trust assets administered by banks amounted to $487 billion, spread among a very broad range of credit market instruments, financial assets, and other types of assets such as real estate.

The investment activities of trusts are bound by constraints established in the trust articles, by legal guidelines, and by court rulings. When the interests of the trust beneficiary and its remainderman diverge, capital and income are generally kept apart from one another. Among other attributes of the trust and/or its investment media which figure importantly in trust law are (1) the stated maturity of investments and the possibility of their being called or repaid prior to maturity, (2) the marketability and liquidity of investments, (3) expected market conditions during the life of the trust and at its projected termination date, (4) the investment mix and total value of the trust, (5) consequences of increased or decreased tax liability, and (6) the income level and income requirements of the beneficiary.

To provide economies of administration and greater portfolio diversification in areas such as mortgages or foreign bonds, many commercial banks and trust companies have set up pooled common trust funds for personal trusts and estates and commingled trust funds for employee benefit trusts. Such pooled vehicles usually combine a portion or all of the assets of numerous smaller trust units, with each unit sharing in the income and assets of the pooled trust according to its percentage contribution of the total common or commingled trust funds. Regulation F of the Federal Reserve Board governs the operation of common and commingled trust funds by commercial banks having a national charter.

At the end of the 1970s and in the early 1980s, a number of commercial bank trust departments and independent trust companies developed specialized fixed-income securities investment programs for marketing primarily to the supervisors of pension fund assets. Such programs, also known as immunization funds, were designed to reduce the volatility of returns from investing in bonds and thereby to reattract to bank trust departments pension moneys that had been captured by insurance companies. In the mid-1970s the latter group had attracted pension funds with guaranteed-income contracts (GICs) that offered insurance company–guaranteed rates of return to investors who placed funds with an insurance company for a specified minimum time.

Immunization funds offer pension fund supervisors a certain *probability* (but not a guarantee) that a specified rate of return will be earned on their investments. This somewhat greater uncertainty is compensated to some degree by the ability to withdraw money from a fund at any time. Trust institutions are able to compute the probability of the money's actually earning the expected return because of certain interest reinvestment practices and a carefully planned maturity spacing of the fixed-income securities portfolio underlying the immunization fund.

Nonprofit Organizations Serving Individuals

Difficulties also arise in describing normative investment activities for and restrictions affecting such widely differing entities as churches, labor unions, hospitals, private educational institutions, and other eleemosynary organizations. Nearly all these investors have some investment restrictions and/or guidelines written into their founding articles. Since their objectives frequently include the maximization of income and the maintenance of purchasing power to carry out the activities of the underlying organization, the investment activities of nonprofit organizations tend to concentrate on the taxable (often intermediate- and long-term) sector of the credit market spectrum. Equity investments may also comprise a significant portion of nonprofit organizations' holdings of total financial assets, although not as large a percentage as for individuals in the aggregate.

Foundations

As of January 1, 1980, approximately 29,000 private foundations with total assets of $32 billion were operating in the United States. Of this number, 1500 were *corporate* foundations, each of which generally remains under the control of the firm that established it rather than an independent group of trustees. *Community* foundations, numbering 230, usually direct their activities toward the specific area in which they are located. More than 24,000 *independent* foundations with a wide variety of sizes and objectives have been established.

In the aggregate, foundations annually award approximately 500,000 grants, amounting to $2.1 billion per year as of early 1980. The chief areas into which grants have been directed are education (28 percent of aggregate 1980 foundation grants), health care (21 percent), humanities (11 percent), international activities (6 percent), religion (2 percent), science and technology (17 percent), and other areas (15 percent). Because only 450 of the largest foundations publish annual reports of their activities, it is difficult to analyze their investment behavior in conclusive detail. Although many foundations have had a large proportion of their portfolios invested in equities, changing tax laws and market conditions led to greater investment in taxable fixed-income securities in the 1970s and early 1980s.

The Tax Reform Act of 1969 defined several requirements for private foundations to retain their tax-exempt status. A number of these regulations have directly influenced the investment activities of foundations. Restrictions include (1) limitations on the ownership of business enterprises by foundations, (2) special limitations on the tax deductibility of donations to foundations (except for community foundations), (3) regular reporting requirements for foundations at both the state and the federal levels, (4) excise taxes on the profits of foundations (the rate was 2 percent as of early 1980), (5) stipulation that a minimum of 5 percent of the market value of the assets of a foundation be paid out each year in grants, and (6) prohibition of direct and indirect lobbying activities by foundations to influence legislation.

In recent years, the investment supervisors of foundations and nonprofit organizations have faced a number of major policy questions concerning appropriate levels of liquidity, diversification, turnover, and quality for their investments. In addition, several nonprofit organizations have had to decide whether to manage their investments internally or to select an outside manager or managers. If the latter, proper means have had to be developed for selecting and supervising the results of the manager. Further questions have arisen about what portion of annual income from investments can be used toward the operating expenses and capital outlays of the institution. Finally, many nonprofit organizations have studied the feasibility and appropriateness of supplementing investment income through donations, governmental grants, or other activities indirectly related to the investment process. The latter activities include the lending of certain securities against full cash collateral, which is then invested to generate additional income for the life of the securities loan.

Nonfinancial Business

The nonfinancial business sector includes (1) corporate, noncorporate, and cooperative farm businesses, (2) nonfarm proprietorships and partnerships exclusive of any such financial entities, and (3) all nongovernmental corporations which are not included in the financial sectors of the Flow of Funds Accounts, and (4) all closed-end investment companies and holding companies. Because nonfinancial businesses in the aggregate are engaged in entrepreneurial activities, they tend to be much larger users than suppliers of capital. Their total holdings of credit market instruments are not large compared with the holdings of many other investor groups, and their credit market investments in mortgages and corporate and foreign bonds are relatively inconsequential. On the other hand, nonfinancial businesses hold more than 90 percent of total trade credit extended (trade credit is classified as a financial asset but not as a credit market instrument). Nonfinancial businesses' holdings of trade credit represented 3.3 times their total holdings of credit market instruments at the end of 1975, up from 1.5 times their total holdings of credit market instruments as of the end of 1950.

Table 8-4 presents a breakdown of credit market instrument holdings by nonfinancial businesses for selected years during the 1950–1979 period. With the exception of the "other" category, the four largest credit market instruments held by nonfinancial businesses at the end of 1975 were (1) commercial paper, representing 32.6 percent of total credit market instrument holdings (up sharply from 1.1 percent at the end of 1950); (2) U.S. government issues (of which 85 percent were Treasury bills and other issues with less than 1 year left to maturity), with 16.7 percent of total credit market instruments (down dramatically from 66.8 percent of the total at the end of 1950); (3) consumer credit extensions, representing 10.3 percent of total credit market instruments (almost no change from 10.8 percent at the end of 1950); and (4) bankers' acceptances, with 8.9 percent of total credit market instruments (up from 1.1 percent at the end of 1950). Other credit market instrument holdings at the end of 1975 were securities repurchase agreements (5.5 percent of total credit market instrument holdings by nonfinancial businesses), state and local government securities (5.3 percent of the total); and issues of federally sponsored agencies (3.7 percent of the total).

In general, nonfinancial businesses' investments in credit market instruments are heavily concentrated in conservative investments which can be sold or held to a relatively short maturity if the funds are needed in the business. As large buyers of commercial paper, nonfinancial businesses are in effect lending money on a short-term basis to other nonfinancial and financial business enterprises, who are the chief issuers of commercial paper. A small percentage of nonfinancial businesses' credit market instrument holdings are represented by closed-end investment companies, most of whose total assets are invested in corporate equities (a financial asset but not a credit market instrument).

Closed-end investment companies issue a limited number of shares and do not stand ready to repurchase, redeem, or issue new shares on a continuing basis. Under certain conditions, they are permitted to issue bonds (if the asset

TABLE 8-4
Credit Market Instrument Holdings of Nonfinancial Businesses for Selected Years, 1950–1979
(In billions of dollars)

Credit market instrument category	1950	1955	1960	1965	1970	1975	1979
U.S. Treasury issues*	17.9	21.3	15.8	7.5	8.3	14.3	6.5
Federally sponsored agency issues*	0.0	0.6	1.1	1.2	1.2	3.2	3.0
State and local government securities*	0.7	1.2	2.4	4.6	2.2	4.5	4.0
Commercial paper*	0.3	1.1	2.6	6.7	20.0	27.9	33.2
Securities repurchase agreements*	0.0	0.0	0.0	0.6	0.2	4.7	13.5
Consumer credit†	2.9	4.6	5.6	9.0	8.9	8.8	49.4
Bankers' acceptances‡	0.3	0.3	0.8	0.9	3.1	7.6	12.0
Other§	4.7	6.3	7.9	10.6	12.5	14.5	35.7
Total	26.8	35.4	36.2	41.1	56.4	85.5	157.3
Memorandum:							
Trade credit	40.4	59.0	83.0	121.2	190.9	283.3	420.1

SOURCE: *Flow of Funds Accounts,* Board of Governors of the Federal Reserve System. Data for all periods through 1975 are taken from the *Flow of Funds Accounts, 1946–1975,* issued in December 1976; data for periods subsequent to 1975 are taken from the *Flow of Funds Accounts, 1969–1979,* issued in February 1980. Because of occasional revisions in the Flow of Funds Accounts data, certain statistics from the latter source and subsequent releases may vary somewhat from those contained in the *Flow of Funds Accounts, 1946–1975.*

*Includes only nonfinancial corporate business; excludes farm business and nonfarm noncorporate business.

†Includes only nonfinancial corporate business and nonfarm noncorporate business; excludes farm business.

‡Includes nonfinancial corporate business, farm business, and nonfarm noncorporate business.

§Includes total nonfinancial corporate business holdings of selected credit market instruments not shown in this table (such as mortgages and corporate and foreign bonds), nonfarm noncorporate business and farm business holdings of credit market instruments denoted by the asterisked footnote, and farm business holdings of consumer credit.

coverage of the closed-end investment company exceeds 300 percent of the principal amount of such bonds) or preferred stock (if the asset coverage of the investment company exceeds 200 percent of the principal amount of such preferred stock).

As of the end of 1977, total assets of all closed-end investment companies amounted to $7.4 billion. An owner of closed-end investment company shares can dispose of them by selling the shares in the open market, with prices determined by the supply of and demand for the shares rather than by the underlying net asset value per share. Thus, the prices of closed-end investment company shares most frequently trade at a premium or a discount to the underlying net asset value per share. Because closed-end investment companies do not have the same needs as open-end investment funds to meet redemptions, they can sometimes adopt a broader range of investment goals.

Table 8-5 shows the net flows of funds during the years from 1972 through 1979 from the nonfinancial business sector into various categories of credit market instruments, with U.S. Treasury issues and federal agency securities grouped together as one category. The flows of investment funds from nonfinancial businesses into credit market instruments depend in large part upon the degree to which these businesses generate sufficient funds relative to (1) perceived needs arising from the operations of the business, (2) attractive direct and/or portfolio investment opportunities, (3) desired profitability measures, financial ratios, and liquidity levels, and (4) the cost of externally raised short-term and long-term capital.

Table 8-5 shows the variability in nonfinancial businesses' net flows of funds into credit market instruments. Total net investments by nonfinancial businesses in credit market instruments dropped from $6 billion in 1973 to $1.4 billion in 1974, only to rise sharply to $13.2 billion in 1975. Nonfinancial businesses' net purchases of U.S. Treasury and federal agency securities ranged from $9.6 billion in 1976 to net sales of $6.4 billion in 1978. Net flows into state and local government securities were relatively small, moving

TABLE 8-5
Annual Net Flows of Funds from Nonfinancial Businesses into Credit Market Instruments, 1972–1979
(In billions of dollars)

Credit market instrument category	1972	1973	1974	1975	1976	1977	1978	1979
U.S. Treasury and federal agency securities	− 2.4	− 3.8	3.5	5.4	9.6	− 4.9	− 6.4	5.4
State and local government securities	1.0	− 0.1	0.6	− 0.2	− 1.1	. . .*	0.2	0.3
Commercial paper	1.4	6.5	− 0.6	5.6	2.2	11.0	1.7	6.9
Security repurchase agreements	1.6	2.6	− 2.8	2.2	2.3	7.0	− 3.0	− 0.4
Consumer credit	0.9	0.8	0.7	0.2	1.1	2.7	3.1	5.7
Total	2.5	6.0	1.4	13.2	14.1	15.8	− 4.4	17.9

SOURCE: *Flow of Funds Accounts,* Board of Governors of the Federal Reserve System. Data for 1978 and 1979 are taken from the *Flow of Funds Accounts* published in February 1980; data from 1972 to 1977 are taken from earlier years' *Flow of Funds Accounts* statistics.
*Less than $50 million.

from $1 billion in 1972 to net sales of $1.1 billion in 1976. Nonfinancial businesses made large net acquisitions of commercial paper in 1973 ($6.5 billion), 1975 ($5.6 billion), and 1977 ($11 billion), but invested smaller amounts in 1972 ($1.4 billion) and 1976 ($2.2 billion), and were net sellers of $600 million in commercial-paper holdings in 1974.

Nonfinancial businesses provided $7 billion in security repurchase agreements in 1977, compared with net sales of $3.0 billion in 1977. In addition, nonfinancial businesses provided $5.7 billion worth of consumer credit extensions in 1979, up from $200 million in 1975.

State and Local Governments: General Funds

The general funds of state and local governments include all entities operated by political subdivisions of the United States except state and local government employee retirement funds, which are treated as a separate financial sector and discussed in Chapter 10. Any debt-issuing authorities, corporations, trust funds, or agencies operated by state and local governments are included here under the "general funds" category. Among the state and local government units in this category are funds set aside for debt service and debt retirement, funds for industrial accidents and sickness, and funds used by educational, transportation, and construction entities operating under the aegis of state and local governments.

In practice, the credit market investments of state and local governments are limited to governmental securities and, to a lesser degree, mortgages, and do not usually encompass corporate and foreign bonds, consumer credit, or open-market paper. Table 8-6 presents the credit market instrument holdings of the general funds of state and local governments for selected years during the period from 1950 through 1979.

As of the end of 1975, the four credit market instrument categories held by the general funds of state and local governments were, in order of importance, (1) U.S. Treasury securities, representing 43.7 percent of total credit market investments (down from 73.3 percent of the total at the end of 1950); (2) federal agency issues, with 31.8 percent of total credit market investments (up sharply from 2.2 percent at the end of 1950, with a major part of the increase occurring in in the 1970–1975 period); (3) mortgages (of which 54 percent were on multifamily residential dwellings, 32 percent on one- to four-family homes, 10 percent on commercial properties, and 4 percent on farm properties), with 18.3 percent of total credit market investments (up from 2.2 percent at the end of 1950); and (4) state and local government obligations, with 6.3 percent of total credit market investments (down from 22.2 percent at the end of 1950).

The investment policies of state and local government general funds are

TABLE 8-6

Credit Market Instrument Holdings of General Funds of State and Local Governments for Selected Years, 1950–1979

(In billions of dollars)

Credit market instrument category	1950	1955	1960	1965	1970	1975	1979
U.S. Treasury issues	6.6	10.9	13.4	18.0	23.3	30.6	49.3
Federally sponsored agency issues	0.2	0.6	1.1	0.9	2.3	22.3	19.4
State and local government securities	2.0	2.5	2.7	2.1	2.4	4.4	8.2
Mortgages	0.2	0.6	1.6	2.7	4.6	12.8	20.7
Total	9.0	14.6	18.8	23.7	32.5	70.1	97.6

SOURCE: *Flow of Funds Accounts,* Board of Governors of the Federal Reserve System. Data for all periods through 1975 are taken from the *Flow of Funds Accounts, 1946–1975,* issued in December 1976; data for periods subsequent to 1975 are taken from the *Flow of Funds Accounts, 1969–1979,* issued in February 1980. Because of occasional revisions in the Flow of Funds Accounts data, certain statistics from the latter source and subsequent releases may vary somewhat from those contained in the *Flow of Funds Accounts, 1946–1975.*

heavily oriented toward conservative holdings. Table 8-7 shows the net flows of funds into credit market instruments by the general funds of state and local governments during the years from 1972 through 1979.

To promote efficiency and to increase returns and liquidity in the management of local governments' short-term funds, a number of states have formed state-managed investment pools. Such pools are not secured by the states

TABLE 8-7

Annual Net Flows of Funds from General Funds of State and Local Governments into Credit Market Instruments, 1972–1979

(In billions of dollars)

Credit market instrument category	1972	1973	1974	1975	1976	1977	1978	1979
U.S. Treasury issues	4.1	1.4	− 1.9	2.8	7.4	17.2	9.8	6.9
Federally sponsored agency issues	2.6	4.4	2.8	− 1.8	3.8	5.3	2.8	3.1
State and local government securities	− 0.3	0.2	0.5	1.5	1.6	0.1	1.0	− 0.1
Mortgages	1.4	1.7	2.5	1.6	0.9	1.1	1.0	5.1
Total	7.8	7.8	4.0	4.1	13.3	23.7	14.6	15.0

SOURCE: *Flow of Funds Accounts,* Board of Governors of the Federal Reserve System. Data for 1978 and 1979 are taken from *Flow of Funds Accounts* published in February 1980; data from 1972 to 1977 are taken from earlier years' *Flow of Funds Accounts* statistics.

themselves, and their growth has been somewhat inhibited by many local governments' desires to maintain autonomy in their investment practices. Some influence on mortgage investments by the general funds of state and local governments is dictated by social considerations or occasionally by the goal of protecting or upgrading a particular community's property tax base. In part this explains the continuous net inflow of funds into the mortgage markets by state and local government general funds throughout the 1972–1979 period. An average of more than $1.9 billion of net purchases of mortgages was made by the general funds of state and local governments over this time span.

Until late 1978, a number of state and local governments were legally able to issue new tax-exempt securities having a large and early sinking-fund requirement that was met by placing escrow funds in new higher-yielding U.S. Treasury obligations. These so-called invested sinking-fund bonds (advance-refunding bonds) were a major factor behind the increase from $2.8 billion of net purchases of U.S. Treasury issues by the general funds of state and local governments to $17.2 billion in 1977. In addition, the large increase in aggregate budget surpluses (on the National Income Accounts basis) by state and local governments, from $5.9 billion in 1975 to $18.4 billion in 1976 and $29.2 billion in 1977, helped expand total purchases of credit market instruments by the general funds of state and local governments from $4.1 billion in 1975 to $13.3 billion in 1976 and $23.7 billion in 1977.

United States Government

The United States government includes all funds and governmental agencies which were included in the 1969 definition of the unified budget with the exception of the District of Columbia. Government-owned corporations are included in this category, as are federal employee retirement and life insurance funds and the Exchange Stabilization Fund. The Federal Reserve Board is not included in this category and is treated separately later in this chapter. By the conventions of the Flow of Funds Accounts system, U.S. government securities owned by federal retirement funds and other federal trust funds have been consolidated and are not included in either the investment activities of the United States government or in the Flow of Funds Accounts enumeration of total U.S. government securities outstanding. The various investment accounts administered by the United States government are restricted by law almost entirely to holdings in U.S. government obligations.

To give some perspective on the total amounts of U.S. Treasury securities held by federally administered funds, usually known as the Government Account Series, Table 8-8 presents such data for selected years during the

TABLE 8-8

Holdings of U.S. Government Securities by the Government Account Series for Selected Years, 1970–1979*

(In millions of dollars)

Fund category	1970	1975	1979
Airport and Airway Trust Fund	0	1,936	4,377
Exchange Stabilization Fund	0	1,451	4,266
Federal Deposit Insurance Corporation	74	1,367	7,835
Federal employees retirement funds	18,931	35,525	61,369
Federal Disability Insurance Trust Fund	4,435	7,843	5,286
Federal Home Loan Banks	199	0	0
Federal Hospital Insurance Trust Fund	2,583	9,711	13,144
Federal Old-Age and Survivors Insurance Trust Fund	25,939	35,815	23,251
Federal Supplementary Medical Insurance Trust Fund	13	1,378	4,974
Federal Savings and Loan Insurance Corporation	80	907	3,792
Government Life Insurance Fund	797	604	463
Highway Trust Fund	2,602	9,536	12,469
National Service Life Insurance Fund	5,915	6,716	7,825
Postal Service Fund	0	53	2,199
Railroad retirement accounts	3,751	3,466	2,794
Treasury deposit funds	0	836	1,731
Unemployment Trust Fund	10,520	4,557	12,048
Other†	484	2,470	8,567
Total	76,323	124,173	176,360

SOURCE: *Treasury Bulletin,* Table FD-4.

*Government fiscal years' totals are shown here.

†A full listing of the more than 40 funds and other entities contained in this category is contained in the footnotes to Table FD-4 of the *Treasury Bulletin.*

1970–1979 period. As of the end of the United States government fiscal year 1975, a total of $124.2 billion of U.S. Treasury securities was held by federal trust, retirement, and insurance funds. The four largest government holders of U.S. Treasury debt were (1) the Federal Old-Age and Survivors Insurance Trust Fund, with 28.8 percent of total federal holdings; (2) federal employees retirement funds, with 28.6 percent; (3) the Federal Hospital Insurance Trust Fund, with 8.8 percent; and (4) the Highway Trust Fund, with 7.7 percent.

The range of credit market instruments other than U.S. Treasury securities held by the United States government is relatively narrow, consisting primarily of (1) foreign aid loans, student loans, and small business loans, all of which are classified in the "other loans" category of credit market instruments, (2) mortgages, and (3) federally sponsored agency issues and mortgage pool securities. The United States government generally does not make investments in state and local government obligations, corporate and foreign bonds, consumer credit, or open-market paper. Table 8-9 shows the credit market instruments held by the United States government for selected years during the period from 1950 through 1979.

At the end of 1975, credit market instruments held by the United States government were divided as follows: (1) other loans (of which 53 percent were made to foreign entities and 47 percent to borrowers within the United States), representing 76.8 percent of total holdings (down from 88.7 percent as of the end of 1950); (2) mortgages (of which 51 percent were secured by one- to four-family homes, 44 percent by multifamily residential structures, 4 percent by farm properties, and 1 percent by commercial facilities), representing 15.3 percent of total holdings (up from 11.3 percent at the end of 1950); and (3) federal agency securities and mortgage pool securities, representing 7.9 percent of total holdings (up from no securities holdings in this category at the end of 1950 and insignificant levels until 1973).

For each of the years from 1972 through 1979, Table 8-10 shows the annual net flows by the United States government into credit market instruments.The total annual amounts invested in credit market instruments by the United States government during the 1972–1978 period were always positive, but they displayed a relatively wide variation, ranging from a low of

TABLE 8-9
Credit Market Instrument Holdings of the United States Government for Selected Years, 1950–1979
(In billions of dollars)

Credit market instrument category	1950	1955	1960	1965	1970	1975	1979
Federally sponsored agency issues and mortgage pool securities*	0.0	. . .†	. . .†	. . .†	. . .†	7.0	32.1
Mortgages	1.8	3.6	5.8	5.8	10.5	13.5	11.3
Other loans	14.1	17.5	20.9	32.1	47.2	67.7	109.1
Total	15.9	21.1	26.7	37.9	57.7	88.2	152.4

SOURCE: *Flow of Funds Accounts,* Board of Governors of the Federal Reserve System. Data for all periods through 1975 are taken from the *Flow of Funds Accounts, 1946–1975,* issued in December 1976; data for periods subsequent to 1975 are taken from the *Flow of Funds Accounts, 1969–1979,* issued in February 1980. Because of occasional revisions in the Flow of Funds Accounts data, certain statistics from the latter source and subsequent releases may vary somewhat from those contained in the *Flow of Funds Accounts, 1946–1975.*

*Beginning in 1974, United States government purchases of federal agency issues consisted mainly of Federal Financing Bank purchases of Farmers Home Administration mortgage pool securities.
†Less than $50 million.

TABLE 8-10
Annual Net Flows of Funds from the United States Government into Credit Market Instruments, 1972–1979
(In billions of dollars)

Credit market instrument category	1972	1973	1974	1975	1976	1977	1978	1979
Federally sponsored agency issues and mortgage pool securities*	. . .†	. . .†	2.5	4.5	3.7	4.6	7.7	8.2
Mortgages	− 0.7	− 0.6	1.4	3.2	− 3.0	− 0.1	− 0.4	1.4
Other loans	2.5	3.4	5.9	7.4	8.2	6.4	13.0	13.4
Total	1.8	2.8	9.8	15.1	8.9	10.9	20.4	23.0

SOURCE: *Flow of Funds Accounts,* Board of Governors of the Federal Reserve System. Data for 1978 and 1979 are taken from the *Flow of Funds Accounts* published in February 1980, and data from 1972 to 1977 are taken from earlier years' *Flow of Funds Accounts* statistics.

*Beginning in 1974, United States government purchases of federal agency issues consisted mainly of Federal Financing Bank purchases of Farmers Home Administration mortgage pool securities.

†Less than $50 million.

$1.8 billion in 1972 to a high of $23.0 billion in 1979. From 1974 onward, purchases of Farmers Home Administration mortgage pool securities by the Federal Financing Bank (part of the United States government) led to continuing net inflows of governmental funds into the federal agency issues and mortgage pool securities category, averaging $4.9 billion per year from 1974 through 1979. The government was not always a net acquirer of mortgages during the 1972–1979 time span, disposing of mortgages amounting to $700 million in 1972, $600 million in 1973, $3 billion in 1976, and $500 million in 1977–1978.

Rest of the World

The "rest of the world" category includes all foreign entities whose capital flows are measured in and defined by the balance-of-payments statement of the United States. Domestic or foreign purchases of securities issues of American entities in foreign markets, such as Eurobonds or foreign indigenous bonds, are not included in this category. Foreign investors include privately owned sources of funds, but beginning in the mid-1970s this category principally reflected the flows and holdings of official foreign institutions such as central banks and monetary authorities. These entities were reinvesting dollars accumulated primarily through oil payments imbalances or through currency intervention operations.

TABLE 8-11
Credit Market Instrument Holdings of the Rest of the World (International
Investors) for Selected Years, 1950–1979
(In billions of dollars)

Credit market instrument category	1950	1955	1960	1965	1970	1975	1979
U.S. Treasury and federally sponsored agency issues	3.0	5.8	10.6	13.2	19.7	66.5	124.2
Corporate and foreign bonds*	0.2	0.3	0.6	0.7	1.7	2.6	10.2
Open-market paper†	0.2	0.4	1.3	2.0	4.3	8.4	30.2
Total	3.4	6.5	12.5	15.9	25.7	77.5	164.6
Memorandum: United States corporate equities‡	2.9	6.6	9.3	14.6	18.7	26.8	49.9

SOURCE: *Flow of Funds Accounts,* Board of Governors of the Federal Reserve System. Data for all periods through 1975 are taken from the *Flow of Funds Accounts, 1946–1975,* issued in December 1976; data for periods subsequent to 1975 are taken from the *Flow of Funds Accounts, 1969–1979,* issued in February 1980. Because of occasional revisions in the Flow of Funds Accounts data, certain statistics from the latter source and subsequent releases may vary somewhat from those contained in the *Flow of Funds Accounts, 1946–1975.*
*Foreign bonds include only foreign bonds issued in the United States.
†A large part of this category is composed of bankers' acceptances.
‡Includes both convertible and nonconvertible preferred stock as well as common stock.

The holdings and flows of most international and regional organizations, such as the International Bank for Reconstruction and Development (World Bank), the European Investment Bank, the Asian Development Bank, the Inter-American Development Bank, and the Bank for International Settlements are also included. The Bank for International Settlements is a depositary for central bank reserves from 24 European countries, the United States, Canada, Japan, Australia, and South Africa. As of the end of 1979, its total assets amounted to $39 billion, a large part of which were invested for the account of its constituent members in government securities of the United States and other countries. Because of difficulties in gathering complete and timely data and because of errors and omissions, some *private* foreign investors' holdings of and flows in United States domestic credit market instruments are not covered by Flow of Funds Accounts data.

Table 8-11 presents the United States domestic credit market instrument holdings of the foreign sector (the rest of the world) for selected years during the period from 1950 through 1979. For taxation, safety, and other reasons, the foreign sector makes only minuscule reported investments in mortgages, state and local government obligations, and consumer credit, confining its credit market investments to U.S. Treasury and federally sponsored agency issues, corporate and foreign bonds issued in the United States, and open-market paper. Depending upon the maturity of the investment and the applicable tax treaties between the United States and the investor's country, a withholding tax may be levied on payments of interest and dividends to foreigners. For investors in some nations, the existence of the United States withholding tax and very conservative investment policies have directed them toward securities issued at a discount (such as Treasury bills, bankers' acceptances, and commercial paper) of sufficiently short maturity to qualify for an exemption from the tax. As of the end of 1975, a total of 53 percent of the international sector's holdings of U.S. Treasury and federally sponsored agency issues had a maturity of less than 1 year.

The percentage breakdown of international investors' holdings of credit market instruments at the end of 1975 was as follows: (1) 85.8 percent of their total holdings were in U.S. Treasury and federally sponsored agency issues (compared with 88.2 percent of the total as of the end of 1950); (2) 10.8 percent, in open-market paper (up from 5.9 percent at the end of 1950); and (3) 3.4 percent, in corporate and foreign bonds (down from 5.9 percent at the end of 1950).

Table 8-12 shows the net flows of funds during the years from 1972 through 1979 from the international sector into various categories of credit market instruments. Total foreign acquisition of credit market instruments expanded from $600 million in 1973 to $39.7 billion in 1977. In large part, this great increase was caused by reinvestment of payments surpluses by certain oil-producing nations and by the investment of dollars acquired by foreign official institutions in currency intervention operations. A substantial majority of such investments were directed into U.S. Treasury and federally

TABLE 8-12
Annual Net Flows of Funds from the Rest of the World (International Investors) into Credit Market Instruments, 1972–1979
(In billions of dollars)

Credit market instrument category	1972	1973	1974	1975	1976	1977	1978	1979
U.S. Treasury and federally sponsored agency issues	8.4	0.2	3.7	8.1	11.6	31.5	28.2	−13.6
Corporate and foreign bonds*	0.1	0.1	0.9	0.6	0.9	3.9	1.6	− 0.4
Open-market paper†	− 0.1	0.3	6.6	− 2.6	2.7	4.3	7.9	6.9
Total	8.4	0.6	11.2	6.1	15.2	39.7	37.7	− 7.2

SOURCE: *Flow of Funds Accounts,* Board of Governors of the Federal Reserve System. Data for 1978 and 1979 are taken from the *Flow of Funds Accounts* published in February 1980; data from 1972 to 1977 are taken from earlier years' *Flow of Funds Accounts* statistics.

*Foreign bonds include only foreign bonds issued in the United States.

†A large part of this category comprises bankers' acceptances.

sponsored agency issues, as foreign purchases of such instruments expanded from $200 million in 1973 to $31.5 billion in 1977.

Foreigners' purchases of open-market paper dropped from $6.6 billion in 1974 to net sales of $2.6 billion in 1975, swinging back again to an average net annual acquisition of $7.4 billion in 1978 and 1979. Foreigners' investments in corporate and foreign bonds ranged between $100 million in both 1972 and 1973 and $3.9 billion in 1977. Part of the increase was due to greater purchases of Yankee bonds by international investors including some foreign central banks. Yankee bonds are foreign bonds registered with the Securities and Exchange Commission and syndicated and sold within the United States and other countries; such issues are free of any United States withholding taxes.

Federally Sponsored Credit Agencies and Mortgage Pools

Federally sponsored agencies consist primarily of (1) the Federal Home Loan Bank System, which provides a central lending facility to supplement the resources of the savings and loan industry; (2) the Federal Land Bank System, which provides farm mortgage credit to eligible borrowers who purchase stock in associations owning shares in the System; (3) the Federal Intermediate Credit Banks, which provide short-term loans to qualifying agricultural entities; (4) the Banks for Cooperatives, which advance credit to eligible agricultural cooperative associations; and (5) the Federal National Mortgage Association (FNMA; "Fannie Mae"), which purchases and sells residential mortgages (primarily from and to private mortgage bankers) to stabilize mortgage flows and thus promote residential construction activity by enhancing the liquidity of mortgage holdings.

Although the Government National Mortgage Association (GNMA; "Ginnie Mae") is officially a part of the U.S. Department of Housing and Urban Development and thus its operations and funds flows are included with those of the United States government described earlier in this chapter, the mortgage-backed pass-through securities guaranteed by GNMA are classified as mortgage pools and are treated here for Flow of Funds Accounts purposes. The Federal Home Loan Mortgage Corporation (FHLMC; "Freddie Mac") is a federally sponsored credit agency whose activities encompass both mortgage pools and secondary market support for mortgages (primarily dealing with thrift institutions).

Taken together, FNMA, GNMA, and FHLMC are known as second-layer lenders in the mortgage markets, since they do not provide funds directly to the public but instead channel funds through mortgage bankers, commercial banks, savings and loan associations, and mutual savings banks. As an agency of the U.S. Department of Agriculture and thus part of the United States government, the Farmers Home Administration guarantees or directly extends mortgage credit for the purchase of farms or dwellings in rural areas. Its activities are classified with those of the United States government, but its mortgage pools are classified for Flow of Funds Accounts purposes with the "mortgage pools" category and are accordingly treated here. Two housing-related agencies which are not classified with the "federally sponsored credit agencies and mortgage pools" category but are totally included with the United States government are the Federal Housing Administration (FHA) and the Veterans Administration (VA). Neither agency provides mortgage credit, but both provide guarantees of mortgage payments for qualified individuals. In addition, the FHA administers interest rate subsidy programs and rent supplement programs.

Table 8-13 provides insight into the combined holdings of credit market instruments by federally sponsored credit agencies and mortgage pools. With a 16.6 percent compound annual rate of growth from 1950 through 1979, the holdings of credit market instruments by federally sponsored credit agencies and mortgage pools expanded from $3.2 billion at the end of 1950 to $274.6 billion at the end of 1979. Federally sponsored credit agencies and mortgage pools do not generally invest in other federal agency securities, corporate and foreign bonds, or state and local government obligations.

In order of importance, the credit market instruments held by federally

TABLE 8-13
Credit Market Instrument Holdings of Federally Sponsored Credit Agencies and Mortgage Pools for Selected Years, 1950–1979
(In billions of dollars)

Credit market instrument category	1950	1955	1960	1965	1970	1975	1979
U.S. Treasury issues	0.4	1.0	1.5	1.9	3.2	3.4	2.1
Open-market paper	0.0	0.0	0.0	0.0	0.0	1.2	0.3
Federal funds and securities repurchase agreements	0.0	. . .*	. . .*	0.0	1.0	1.8	4.1
Mortgages	1.0	1.7	5.7	7.7	27.8	87.5	209.8
Other loans	1.8	2.5	4.1	9.6	17.6	31.8	62.4
Total	3.2	5.2	11.3	19.2	49.6	125.7	274.6

SOURCE: *Flow of Funds Accounts,* Board of Governors of the Federal Reserve System. Data for all periods through 1975 are taken from the *Flow of Funds Accounts, 1946–1975,* issued in December 1976; data for periods subsequent to 1975 are taken from the *Flow of Funds Accounts, 1969–1979,* issued in February 1980. Because of occasional revisions in the Flow of Funds Accounts data, certain statistics from the latter source and subsequent releases may vary somewhat from those contained in the *Flow of Funds Accounts, 1946–1975.*
*Less than $50 million.

sponsored credit agencies and mortgage pools at the end of 1975 comprised (1) mortgages (of which 77 percent were made on one- to four-family homes, 22 percent on farm properties, and 1 percent on multifamily residential dwellings), representing 69.6 percent of total holdings (up sharply from 31.3 percent as of the end of 1950); (2) other loans (of which 56 percent represented advances to savings institutions, 31 percent to farmers, and 13 percent to agricultural cooperatives), with 25.3 percent of total holdings (down sharply from 56.2 percent at the end of 1950); (3) U.S. government securities, with 2.7 percent of total holdings (down substantially from 12.5 percent at the end of 1950); (4) federal funds and securities repurchase agreements, with 1.4 percent of total holdings (up from no holdings at the end of 1950); and (5) open-market paper, with 1 percent of total holdings (up from no holdings at the end of 1950).

Table 8-14 shows total net flows by federally sponsored credit agencies and mortgage pools into various categories of credit market instruments. Total annual flows into mortgages began at a relatively high level of $8.9 billion in 1972 and increased as federally sponsored credit agencies and mortgage pools stepped up their support to the mortgage market in the tightening credit conditions of late 1973 and 1974. After a small decline in 1975, flows into mortgages rose strongly in 1978 and 1979. In particular, total federal agency support to residential mortgage markets as a percentage of the total annual increase in residential mortgage debt outstanding has ranged from negative 7.6 percent and negative 4.2 percent (negative net support means that more mortgages were sold than were bought) in 1976

TABLE 8-14

Annual Net Flows of Funds from Federally Sponsored Credit Agencies and Mortgage Pools into Credit Market Instruments, 1972–1979
(In billions of dollars)

Credit market instrument category	1972	1973	1974	1975	1976	1977	1978	1979
U.S. Treasury issues	− 1.2	. . .*	0.4	1.5	1.5	− 3.5	0.6	0.4
Open-market paper	0.4	− 0.2	0.9	0.1	. . .*	0.2	−1.2	0.1
Federal funds and securities repurchase agreements	0.4	2.3	− 1.0	− 0.3	0.3	. . .*	1.4	0.5
Mortgages	8.9	10.7	16.0	15.7	18.6	23.8	39.2	44.0
Other loans	0.7	8.6	9.4	− 2.5	0.3	6.3	6.0	12.9
Total	9.2	21.4	25.7	14.5	20.7	26.7	44.6	57.5

SOURCE: *Flow of Funds Accounts,* Board of Governors of the Federal Reserve System. Data for 1978 and 1979 are taken from the *Flow of Funds Accounts* published in February 1980; data from 1972 to 1977 are taken from earlier years' *Flow of Funds Accounts* statistics.
*Less than $50 million.

and 1967 respectively, when mortgage-financing conditions were relatively easy, to 20.5 percent in 1966, 36.6 percent in 1969, 30 percent in 1970, 20.4 percent in 1973, and 36.9 percent in 1974. The latter five periods were all characterized by tight financing circumstances in residential mortgage markets. Similarly, loans extended to various specialized sectors of the economy rose from $700 million in 1972 to $8.6 billion and $9.4 billion in 1973 and 1974 respectively. Flows into or out of U.S. Treasury securities, open-market paper, and federal funds and securities repurchase agreements remained modest over the 1972–1979 time span. In general, the level of investment by federally sponsored credit agencies and mortgage pools in credit market instruments depends on (1) the secular and cyclical ability of certain identified high-priority sectors of the economy such as housing and agriculture to obtain sufficient credit through traditional private financial channels, (2) overall credit demands and interest rate levels, and (3) economic conditions and supply-demand relationships in sectors which currently receive assistance (or could receive assistance in the future) from federally sponsored credit agencies and mortgage pools.

Monetary Authority (Federal Reserve System)

The Federal Reserve System is by far the principal constituent of the "monetary authority" category, which also includes the gold, silver, and certain other monetary accounts of the U.S. Treasury. The Federal Reserve System investment portfolio in credit market instruments was originally intended to be a source of income, but it has evolved into a primary means of implementing monetary policy as set by the Federal Reserve Board. As such, credit market instrument investments are usually motivated in the first case by market operations conducted by the Federal Open Market Committee of the Federal Reserve Board and in the second case by the perceived necessity of directing support to a particular sector of the credit markets.

Practically without exception, the Federal Reserve System does not purchase state and local government obligations, corporate and foreign bonds, consumer credit, or commercial paper. When purchasing or selling those credit market instruments in which it conducts investment operations, the Federal Reserve System deals with foreign official entities, the U.S. Treasury, and a limited number of so-called recognized primary bank and nonbank dealers in U.S. Treasury and federal agency securities. Table 8-15 shows Federal Reserve System holdings of credit market instruments for selected years during the period from 1950 through 1979.

At the end of 1975, a total of 55 percent of Federal Reserve holdings of credit market instruments was in the form of U.S. Treasury bills and other Treasury issues with a maturity of under 1 year, compared with 56.9 percent at the end of 1950; 37.3 percent of Federal Reserve holdings were in Treasury issues with a maturity longer than 1 year (versus 43 percent at the end of 1950). Taken together, all Treasury issues represented 92.3 percent of the Federal Reserve System portfolio of credit market instruments at the end of 1975. Federal agency securities accounted for 6.5 percent of Federal Reserve holdings at the end of 1975. The Federal Reserve System had invested no funds in federal agency securities until 1966 and 1967, when very small amounts of federal agency securities were purchased. No additional purchases of federal agency securities were made until 1971, when the Federal Reserve System was authorized to accumulate agency issues in size. Bankers' acceptances represented 1.1 percent of the Federal Reserve System portfolio of credit market instruments at the end of 1975, up from no holdings at the end of 1950 and amounts under $200 million until 1971. Federal Reserve System holdings of bank loans not classified elsewhere were zero at the end of 1975, as they had been since the end of 1965, prior to which they were always an insignificant portion of the total credit market instrument portfolio. Since Federal Reserve System purchases of securities are paid for simply by crediting a member bank's account at the Federal Reserve, the total amount of Federal Reserve System holdings of U.S. Treasury and federal agency securities is one measure of the amount of money which has been created (monetized) by the Federal Reserve.

For the period from 1972 through 1979, the annual flows of investment funds into credit market instruments from the Federal Reserve System are

TABLE 8-15
Credit Market Instrument Holdings of the Federal Reserve System for
Selected Years, 1950–1979
(In billions of dollars)

Credit market instrument category	1950	1955	1960	1965	1970	1975	1979
U.S. Treasury issues	20.8	24.8	27.4	40.7	62.1	87.9	117.5
Federally sponsored agency securities	0.0	0.0	0.0	0.0	0.0	6.2	8.7
Bankers' acceptances	0.0	. . .*	. . .*	0.2	0.1	1.1	0.7
Bank loans not classified elsewhere	. . .*	. . .*	. . .*	. . .*	0.0	0.0	. . .*
Total	20.8	24.8	27.4	40.9	62.2	95.2	126.9

SOURCE: *Flow of Funds Accounts,* Board of Governors of the Federal Reserve System. Data for all periods through 1975 are taken from the *Flow of Funds Accounts, 1946–1975,* issued in December 1976; data for periods subsequent to 1975 are taken from the *Flow of Funds Accounts, 1969–1979,* issued in February 1980. Because of occasional revisions in the Flow of Funds Accounts data, certain statistics from the latter source and subsequent releases may vary somewhat from those contained in the *Flow of Funds Accounts, 1946–1975.*

*Less than $50 million.

TABLE 8-16
Annual Net Flows of Funds from the Federal Reserve System into Credit Market Instruments, 1972–1979
(In billions of dollars)

Credit market instrument category	1972	1973	1974	1975	1976	1977	1978	1979
U.S. Treasury issues	− 0.3	8.6	2.0	7.4	9.1	5.8	7.7	6.9
Federally sponsored agency issues	0.7	0.7	3.2	1.0	0.9	1.4	−0.4	0.7
Bankers' acceptances	− 0.2	. . .*	0.9	0.1	− 0.1	. . .*	−0.4	0.1
Total	0.2	9.3	6.1	8.5	9.9	7.2	7.0	7.7

SOURCE: *Flow of Funds Accounts,* Board of Governors of the Federal Reserve System. Data for 1978 and 1979 are taken from the *Flow of Funds Accounts* published in February 1980; data from 1972 to 1977 are taken from earlier years' *Flow of Funds Accounts* statistics.
*Less than $50 million.

shown in Table 8-16. With the exception of 1972, when the Federal Reserve System disposed of $300 million in U.S. Treasury securities, the monetary authority was a net purchaser of Treasury issues on balance throughout the 1973–1979 period. Purchases of federal agency securities by the Federal Reserve were also positive in each of the years from 1972 through 1977, with a high of $3.2 billion in 1974, when the Federal Reserve was providing support to this sector of the market. In 1974 the federal agency security market was experiencing large financing operations to aid the mortgage markets and other sectors of the economy such as agriculture. Federal Reserve System activity in bankers' acceptances remained relatively small in absolute terms during the 1972–1979 period, oscillating between net sales of $400 million in 1972 and net purchases of $900 million in 1974.

9

The Investment Behavior of Commercial Banks and Thrift Institutions

Overview

In recent years, commercial banks and thrift institutions have occupied a key position in the midst of the many changes that have transformed the financial system and the economy. This centrality has been rendered all the more important by the enormous holdings of both financial assets and credit market instruments of the thrift institutions (which in this book include the principal nonbank *depositary* institutions, such as savings and loan associations, mutual savings banks, and credit unions) and commercial banks.

The competition between and among commercial banks and thrift institutions has been intensified by the revision or elimination of many legislative provisions affecting interest rate ceilings, required reserve ratios behind various types of deposit and transaction accounts, investment guidelines, and geographical and functional barriers. At the same time that commercial banks and thrift institutions have been permitted to abandon many of the time-honored features of a fixed deposit rate structure, there has been a proliferation of savings instruments, securities, and funds transfer mechanisms offered by commercial banks and thrift institutions.

The following sections of this chapter devote attention to the many factors influencing the investment behavior of commercial banks, savings and loan associations, mutual savings banks, and credit unions. Some perspective on the pressures on and relative importance of these institutions in the bond and money markets can thereby be gained.

Commercial Banks

The commercial banking sector includes all domestic commercial banks, banking-related activities of bank holding companies, Edge Act subsidiaries

TABLE 9-1
Number and Total Assets of Commercial Banks in the United States as of June 30, 1978

Category	Number of banks	Total assets*
Insured banks		
Federal Reserve members		
State-chartered banks	1,005	217.4
Nationally chartered banks	4,616	671.2
Subtotal, Federal Reserve members	5,621	888.6
Nonmembers of Federal Reserve	8,760	284.2
Subtotal, insured banks	14,381	1,172.8
Noninsured Banks		
Banks of deposit	231	41.6
Nondeposit trust companies	86	0.7
Subtotal, noninsured banks	317	42.3
Total, all banks	14,698	1215.1

SOURCE: *Assets and Liabilities: 1978 Report of Income, Commercial and Mutual Savings Banks,* Federal Deposit Insurance Corporation.
*In billions of dollars.

of banks engaged in international banking, and banks located in United States territories and possessions. Loans and deposits between domestic commercial banks have been consolidated together and thus eliminated from the Flow of Funds Accounts. The total number and assets of various categories of commercial banks as of June 30, 1978, are shown in Table 9-1.

As can be seen in Table 9-1, there were 14,698 commercial banks in the United States as of June 30, 1978. Of this total, 5,621 banks were members of the Federal Reserve System (38.2 percent of all banks), and 8,914 banks were not members (61.8 percent). Federal Reserve System member banks had a total of $888.6 billion in assets (73.1 percent of all banks' assets, while banks that are not members of the System controlled $326.5 billion in assets (26.9 percent). The Federal Deposit Insurance Corporation (FDIC) covered 14,381 banks, or 97.8 percent of all commercial banks in the United States.

Under the McFadden Act, commercial banks have been prohibited from owning other commercial banks or from maintaining their own branches outside the state in which they conduct most of their business. In the late 1970s and early 1980s, a number of large commercial banks and some other savings institutions began to conduct a greater volume of activities outside their home states. These activities were undertaken through such facilities as out-of-state loan generation offices, the nationwide marketing of credit cards, expanded allowable services for Edge Act subsidiaries and consumer finance companies, and ownership of industrial banks (also known as Morris Plan banks) in other states. Industrial banks are prohibited from offering checking accounts but are allowed to offer such services as consumer loans and credit card facilities. Although not covered by federal deposit insurance, industrial banks are permitted to accept consumer savings deposits, which at these banks have generally not been subject to federally mandated interest rate ceilings whenever these have been in force.

The credit market instrument holdings of commercial banks for selected years during the period from 1950 through 1979 are shown in Table 9-2. The range of credit market instruments held by commercial banks is quite broad, with eight categories of investments represented throughout the 1950–1979 period. As of the end of 1975, the five largest categories of credit market instruments held by commercial banks were (1) bank loans not classified elsewhere, with 37.2 percent of total credit market instrument holdings (up strongly from 22.4 percent at the end of 1950); (2) mortgages, representing 18.3 percent of total credit market instrument holdings (a significant rise from 10.9 percent of the total at the end of 1950); (3) state and local government obligations, with 13.8 percent of total credit market instrument

TABLE 9-2
Credit Market Instrument Holdings of Commercial Banks for Selected Years, 1950–1979
(In billions of dollars)

Credit market instrument category	1950	1955	1960	1965	1970	1975	1979
U.S. government securities	62.6	62.3	61.3	60.2	62.5	85.4	97.2
Federally sponsored agency issues	1.9	2.9	2.3	5.8	13.9	34.5	51.0
State and local government securities	8.2	12.9	17.7	38.8	70.2	102.8	135.9
Corporate bonds	2.6	1.9	1.3	1.1	2.4	8.6	7.7
Mortgages	13.7	21.0	28.8	49.7	72.8	136.5	246.8
Consumer credit*	7.7	13.7	21.3	36.7	53.9	90.3	184.3
Bank loans not classified elsewhere	28.1	42.8	62.9	106.2	161.6	277.0	406.8
Open-market paper	0.7	0.9	2.0	2.7	8.2	10.3	15.2
Total	125.5	158.4	197.9	301.2	445.5	745.4	1144.9

SOURCE: *Flow of Funds Accounts,* Board of Governors of the Federal Reserve System. Data for all periods through 1975 are taken from the *Flow of Funds Accounts, 1946–1975,* issued in December 1976; data for periods subsequent to 1975 are taken from the *Flow of Funds Accounts, 1969–1979,* issued in February 1980. Because of occasional revisions in the Flow of Funds Accounts data, certain statistics from the latter source and subsequent releases may vary somewhat from those contained in the *Flow of Funds Accounts, 1946–1975.*

*Until 1966 includes consumer credit secured by hypothecated deposits.

holdings (more than double the 6.5 percent at the end of 1950); (4) consumer credit, representing 12.1 percent of total credit market instrument holdings (almost twice the 6.1 percent at the end of 1950); and (5) U.S. Treasury securities (of which 57 percent were issues of under 1-year maturity), with 11.5 percent of total credit market instrument holdings (down sharply from 49.9 percent at the end of 1950).

On a quarterly basis, the Federal Reserve Board conducts a survey of changes in lending practices at commercial banks. Known as the Senior Loan Officer Opinion Survey on Bank Lending Practice, this poll examines banks' willingness to extend consumer installment credit, mortgage loans, and business loans. In addition, information is gathered concerning *qualitative* factors that influence expected loan demand and loan pricing. A similar survey, the Survey of Terms of Bank Lending, gathers *quantitative* information on the maturity, interest rate structure, and volume of short-term and long-term loans extended by commercial banks. The results of both surveys are published regularly in the *Federal Reserve Bulletin.*

Other credit market instruments held by commercial banks at the end of 1975 were (1) federal agency issues, with 4.6 percent of credit market instrument holdings (triple the 1.5 percent share of the total as of the end of 1950); (2) open-market paper, representing 1.4 percent of credit market instrument holdings (up from 0.5 percent at the end of 1950); and (3) corporate and foreign bonds, with 1.2 percent of total holdings (down from 2.1 percent of the 1950 total).

Table 9-3 provides some perspective on commercial banks' investment flows into the various types of credit market instruments during the 1972–1979 period. Flows into U.S. Treasury securities ranged from negative $8.8 billion in 1973 (indicating net sales of Treasury issues on balance by commercial banks) to $28.8 billion in 1975, with demand for Treasury securities generally moving inversely to bank credit demands made by borrowers, as expressed in the categories bank loans not classified elsewhere and consumer credit. Taken together, these two categories represented $63.2 billion, or 73 percent of commercial banks' net acquisition of credit market instruments in 1973, but in response to net aggregate repayments of $14.4 billion in bank loans not classified elsewhere and a net increase of only $2.9 billion in consumer credit, these two categories accounted for a large part of the decline in the commercial banks' total net acquisition of credit market instruments from $64.6 billion in 1974 to $27.6 billion in 1975.

Commercial banks' net acquisitions of state and local government securities responds in large part to the banks' need for tax-exempt income. For example, in 1975, when loan losses and write-offs were quite substantial, banks acquired only $1.7 billion worth of state and local government securities, far below the $12.4 billion purchased on balance by the banks in 1977. Mortgages also account for a large and cyclical component of banks' net

TABLE 9-3
Annual Net Flows of Funds from Commercial Banks into Credit Market Instruments, 1972–1979
(In billions of dollars)

Credit market instrument category	1972	1973	1974	1975	1976	1977	1978	1979
U.S. government securities	2.4	− 8.8	− 2.6	28.8	18.2	− 2.1	− 6.5	2.0
Federally sponsored agency issues	4.1	7.6	3.6	1.4	1.5	− 1.5	7.0	7.1
State and local government securities	7.2	5.7	5.5	1.7	3.0	12.4	9.6	9.7
Corporate and foreign bonds	1.7	0.4	1.1	1.8	− 0.6	− 0.1	− 0.3	0.3
Mortgages	16.8	19.8	12.8	4.3	13.9	25.4	35.0	32.8
Consumer credit	10.8	11.6	3.6	2.9	11.4	17.0	26.9	17.0
Bank loans not classified elsewhere	27.8	51.6	38.4	−14.4	6.7	30.4	58.4	49.5
Open-market paper	− 0.2	− 1.3	2.2	1.1	3.7	− 1.7	− 1.3	2.2
Total	70.5	86.5	64.6	27.6	58.0	79.8	128.8	120.6

SOURCE: *Flow of Funds Accounts,* Board of Governors of the Federal Reserve System. Data for 1978 and 1979 are taken from the *Flow of Funds Accounts* published in February 1980; data from 1972 to 1977 are taken from earlier years' *Flow of Funds Accounts* statistics.

acquisition of credit market instruments, ranging from a low of $4.3 billion (16.1 percent of total net purchases of credit market instruments by banks) in 1975 to a high of $35.0 billion (27.2 percent of total net purchases) in 1978. Banks' net purchases of federal agency issues, open-market paper, and corporate and foreign bonds on average were smaller and more volatile than their net acquisition of other credit market instruments during the 1972–1979 period.

Investment Strategy

Because of commercial banks' large absolute size and their central position in the financial system when considered in the aggregate and because of the fact that they hold, acquire, and dispose of such a wide range of credit market instruments, it is worthwhile to explore their investment activities in some depth. Such an analysis will also provide insight into the competitive forces acting upon and generated by commercial banks in their quest with certain other financial intermediaries to obtain and supply funds. Each individual commercial bank, whether large or small, may be oriented in its money-raising and/or investing and lending activities toward a local community, a region, a major domestic money center, international financial markets, or some combination of these areas. This orientation, as well as a bank's capital adequacy, its asset and liability structure, its pledging requirements and liquidity needs, its tax outlook, and the nature of the loans which it primarily extends, whether in the commercial, industrial, consumer, or mortgage sectors, will influence the mix of federal, municipal, and corporate securities and other credit market instruments that it holds. These considerations are the topic of the remainder of this section.

At its most fundamental level, the investment strategy of a commercial bank usually sets (1) the proportion of bank assets to be placed in loans versus securities, (2) the amount of taxable versus tax-exempt securities holdings, and (3) an appropriate maturity spacing for the securities holdings and, to some degree, for the loan portfolio. A number of banks practice a form of balanced maturity spacing in which specified portions of a bank's investments are made in various securities which mature at different but regular intervals. This produces a steady movement of securities into the short-term–maturity sector.

Different banks may select a variety of methods to obtain and balance portfolio returns and risks. For example, one bank may elect to hold a high percentage of long-term loans in combination with a securities portfolio of short maturities, while another may utilize principally short-term loans while investing in longer-maturity securities. Desired proportions may change in response to a bank's current loan-deposit ratio, an inflow of funds created by loan repayments, the sale or maturity of securities holdings, or the expansion of bank liabilities such as customer deposits, bank capital, or other sources of borrowed funds.

Regulatory authorities, depositors, borrowers, and stockholders also impose constraints upon the investment activities of commercial banks. While borrowers desire an adequate supply of funds to meet their credit needs, depositors seek satisfactory levels of liquidity to respond to their withdrawals of funds. Bank shareholders desire a sufficient return on their investment. Regulatory authorities mandate the fulfillment of appropriate reserve levels and financial ratios to ensure bank soundness. Most banks combine the objectives of these varying constituencies by segregating the funds at their disposal into four categories listed in order of importance to the bank.

These categories are (1) non- or low-interest-earning *primary reserves,* consisting of vault cash and other earmarked assets, levels of which are legally established by the Federal Reserve System or by the state in which the bank operates if it is not a member of the System; (2) a short-term, high-quality, highly liquid portfolio of interest-earning *secondary reserves* (also called protective reserves), set aside by the bank to back up its primary-reserve position and to be converted immediately into cash to meet unforeseen contingencies; (3) funds used to meet the ongoing credit demands of the bank's existing and prospective customer base; and (4) investments made in the credit markets to provide income, some issues of which are readily convertible into cash on short notice and another part of which is somewhat less liquid and is expected to be held until maturity.

Each bank, in response to (1) its internal objectives, (2) its mix of funds sources from bank capital, from relatively stable, low-turnover savings accounts and time deposits, and from less stable, high-turnover demand deposits, (3) its ability to attract and redeploy new funds, and (4) the external environment, sets its own policies regarding the size, liquidity, maturity, and quality makeup of the secondary-reserve position, the loan portfolio, and the investment portfolio. For instance, a bank with a stable deposit base and high levels of shareholders' equity can adopt a loan and investment policy with longer maturities and less liquid assets than a bank with small capital resources of its own and an unstable deposit base. However, because the interest cost of obtaining savings deposits is generally higher than the interest cost of obtaining demand deposits, the funds gained from the former must generally be put into higher-yielding loans or investments than funds which come to the bank via low-interest demand deposits. In part, such considerations have often led the commercial banking industry to invest a substantial portion of the funds that it gains from the issuance of certificates of deposit into tax-exempt securities, which offer relatively high aftertax returns to banks.

Influence of Deposits

From the end of the Second World War until the mid-1960s, commercial banks tended to adjust their liquidity levels through *asset management* techniques. If more or less funds were needed in response to rising or falling loan demand, for example, a bank could increase or decrease its investments in Treasury bills, short-term federal agency securities, or open-market paper. Beginning in the mid-1960s and continuing through the 1970s, many banks began to use their governmental securities holdings more as collateral for governmental bank deposits.

To respond to variations in loan demand, banks began to rely more upon *liability management* procedures, in which funds were raised through (1) the issuance of certificates of deposit in the domestic or Eurodollar markets, (2) borrowings from the Federal Reserve System, (3) solicitation of deposits from and/or drawings on existing credit lines with correspondent banks and other banks, (4) the issuance of commercial paper by a bank holding company, (5) the sale of loan participations to other banks, or (6) the issuance of capital notes, subordinated debentures, or other securities such as floating-rate notes and small-denomination certificates of deposit with interest rates linked to short-term Treasury bill yields.

Particularly when the rate of interest earned on Treasury bills exceeds the federal funds rate, commercial banks have preferred to adjust their reserve positions by borrowing at the Federal Reserve System discount window (although banks are normally careful not to use this privilege excessively) or by purchasing federal funds rather than by selling Treasury bills from their portfolios. In recent years, the widening variety of bank liability alternatives has often obscured the difference for an investor between making a bank deposit and making an investment in bank securities.

Not only the type of deposits but also the sources of a bank's deposits can influence its loan and investment policies. Governmental deposits tend to vary a great deal in amount according to relatively predictable patterns. The tax and loan accounts of the federal government, as well as the regular outflows of revenue-sharing funds to state and local bodies, usually demonstrate large periodic movements. As mentioned earlier, governmental and certain other deposits require the recipient bank to maintain specified amounts of Treasury securities and, in some cases, other instruments as collateral (with the percentages usually set by the government) for (1) Treasury tax and loan accounts, (2) other federal, state, and local governmental deposits requiring collateral, and (3) specified trust assets. Whenever possible, banks generally pledge low-liquidity, higher-yielding, longer-term municipal issues or governmentally backed loans as collateral against that portion of governmental deposits (and other deposits requiring collateral) which is projected to remain stable over time, using more marketable, lower-yielding instruments as a part of their secondary reserves.

Corporate deposits and deposits made in one bank by another bank are also quite variable, although perhaps less so than governmental deposits. Corporations tend to have similar practices and timing in the payment of taxes, payrolls, and other invoices, in the sale and purchase of securities and deposits prior to the closing date for their financial statements (so-called window dressing), and in seasonal and holiday-caused payments and deposits, especially among retailing, agriculture, and finance companies. Corporations may also have large absolute inflows and outflows as funds are received or spent for large capital equipment outlays, mineral lease payments, construction projects, and other substantial direct investments. Finally, in the face of intense national competition among larger banks, large corporations are usually much more sensitive than individual depositors to the actual level of interest rates paid to or received from a particular bank.

Individuals' deposits in commercial banks tend to be more stable than corporate or governmental deposits. Significant changes occurred in the deposit structure of individuals and other entities at commercial banks and in the competitive climate between commercial banks and other thrift institutions in the 1970s. During this period, the continued secular rise in interest rates, growing pressures from the consumer movement, and financial entities' needs and desires for greater operational efficiency led to permission for banks and thrift institutions to inaugurate several new facilities affecting the composition and structure of savings and checking accounts. These measures included (1) preauthorized nonnegotiable transfer facilities from savings accounts to third parties for any purpose, (2) the installation of automated teller machines in states where these were permitted, (3) authorization for commercial banks to accept corporate and governmental savings accounts, and (4) allowance of telephone-ordered transfers from savings accounts to checking accounts.

In November 1978, commercial banks were allowed to introduce automatic-transfer-from-savings (ATS) facilities. The ATS mechanism permits a deposit holder to transfer funds from interest-bearing savings accounts to checking accounts, under varying fee structures, minimum balances in the checking and/or savings accounts, and methods of initiating transfer. ATS differs from interest-bearing checking accounts, which began to be introduced in late 1978, and from negotiable-order-of-withdrawal (NOW) accounts, which allow a depositor to write checks directly against a savings account.

Because savings deposits carry lower reserve requirements than demand (checking) deposits, commercial banks can experience changing levels of required reserves in response to funds transfers between savings and checking accounts. These changes in the mix of required reserves mirror some of the profound changes which NOW accounts, ATS facilities, money market certificates (MMCs), money market funds, and the wide variety of savings and demand deposits have had on the forms in which consumers, businesses, and other entities choose to hold a large portion of their financial assets. In 1979 and again in February 1980, the Federal Reserve Board took account of these new developments by adopting redefinitions of several monetary aggregates. The revised definitions provide more consistent coverage of similar types of deposits at both commercial banks and thrift institutions.

Commercial banks compete relatively aggressively with mutual savings banks and savings and loan associations in a specific local market or markets for individuals' savings accounts. Because of the variety of higher-yielding, longer-term instruments offered by mutual savings banks and savings and loan associations, in recent years they have usually experienced less disintermediation in periods of high interest rates than smaller and medium-size commercial banks that have not as aggressively promoted such higher-cost instruments. This has tended to limit the ability of smaller and medium-size commercial banks to direct substantial incremental flows of funds into longer-term, less liquid, higher-yielding assets such as mortgages. In states in which branch banking is permitted for commercial banks, individual depositors may exhibit a higher degree of importance relative to corporate depositors, and demand deposits may exhibit a higher ratio to time deposits than in states which do not allow branch banking.

Other Influences

Other important factors influencing a commercial bank's investment policies include (1) the economic growth of the region in which the bank is located, (2) the nature of the financing demands (such as industrial, consumer, or mortgage) placed upon the bank, (3) the size of the bank's own capital funds and savings department relative to its total assets, (4) any necessary reserves which the bank deems prudent to set aside for contingencies, and (5) the maturity structure of the bank's existing loan portfolio. Generally speaking, the greater the proportion of loans with long maturities (so-called term loans), the greater the need for the bank to maintain a higher level of liquidity in the securities portion of its credit market instrument holdings. As a matter of practice, commercial banks usually concentrate the bulk of their credit market investments in the short- to intermediate-maturity spectrum, with a modest proportion of investments in the maturity range of 20 years or more.

Prior to the Tax Reform Act of 1969, tax-swapping considerations exercised a much greater influence on banks' investment activities than in succeeding years. In executing tax swaps under the pre-1969 legislation, commercial banks could sell a securities holding (usually a municipal issue) at a book loss which was charged (after netting out against any capital gains realized that year) against operating income, reducing the bank's tax liability by the amount of its effective corporate tax rate. Unlike individuals and corporations, banks were not limited in the amount of capital losses that they could charge against operating income in a given year.

To avoid losing this tax benefit through so-called wash sales, the bank would then either wait 30 days before repurchasing the same securities or invest the proceeds of its sale in bonds which were considered to be substantially different securities by the Internal Revenue Service (IRS). If the bank then earned a profit on the new bond investment because of the maturity of the issue or a decline in interest rates, its gain was taxed as a capital gain, which incurred roughly one-half of the corporate tax rate. In periods of rising loan demand, rising interest rates, and rising operating income, banks were less reluctant to sell securities investments at a loss (because of the higher interest rates) to meet borrowers' credit needs, since in effect banks were able to offset capital losses (net of any capital gains that year) against operating income, thus saving the full corporate tax rate while paying only one-half of the corporate tax rate on any succeeding capital gains. Because banks had first to net out any capital losses against capital gains before deducting the losses from operating income, they generally attempted to realize primarily capital losses or primarily capital gains, but not both, in a given calendar year.

For this reason, depending upon the interest rate outlook and other factors, a given bank which followed such tax-swapping tactics generally denominated each calendar year a gain year or a loss year according to which type of transaction result it planned to try to achieve. Although tax benefits have been considerably reduced since 1969, commercial banks have continued to engage in the swapping of securities to some degree. Among other reasons, commercial banks engage in security swapping to reduce fluctuations in overall net income, to adjust the timing of capital gains tax payments, and to accommodate investment strategy considerations.

Because banks generally buy securities when loan demand is low, during periods of low and/or falling interest rates, and sell securities when loan demand is heavy, during periods of high and/or rising interest rates, they tend to emphasize maturity selection as an important element in the investment of their funds. Besides investing in tax-exempt securities, commercial banks use several other means to reduce their tax liabilities. One important source of tax shelter derives from the transfer of funds to bad-debt reserves to provide for expected future losses on loans. The lease-financing activities of commercial banks allow tax reductions for depreciation and the investment tax credit. In addition, the foreign operations of commercial banks provide tax deductions or tax credits for most taxes remitted to foreign governments.

Choice of Securities Investments

In directing their investment policies, commercial banks seek to balance the needs of their borrowing clientele against the less cost-intensive nature of their securities investment portfolio. An additional consideration in the loans-securities selection process is the relatively greater liquidity of securities as compared with loans. In making securities investments, banks tend to emphasize high credit quality, safety and predictability of income flow and principal repayment, diversification, and limited price volatility in response to a rise in interest rates. This emphasis is caused by the fact that banks do not hold fixed-income securities to maturity (as do many other financial intermediaries such as pension funds) but frequently sell them to meet loan demands, or for tax-swapping reasons, or because another issue or sector of the market appears to offer more advantageous relative values. In addition to managing the investment portfolio in Treasury, federal agency, municipal, and short-term money market securities, the fixed-income securities department of a large commercial bank may also serve as an underwriter and market maker in selected municipal issues or as a primary dealer (reporting regularly to the Federal Reserve Bank of New York) or dealer in U.S. government securities.

From time to time, the fixed-income securities department of a commercial bank may also (1) coordinate the fund-raising activities of the bank in the commercial-paper, certificates-of-deposit, federal funds, and Eurocurrency markets, (2) establish active trading positions on the long or the short side of the market to take advantage of downward or upward moves in interest rates as forecast by the bank, and (3) engage in arbitrage transactions (involving securities, funds borrowing and lending, and perhaps interest rate futures) to take advantage of momentary yield differentials on equivalent or similar securities. In carrying out all these functions, the securities-trading department is chiefly concerned with maintaining the overall liquidity of the bank and with earning an adequate return on that part of the bank's funds which is not used in its lending activities.

While gains and losses on the securities trading done by the *banking* and *investment* departments of commercial banks are treated for tax purposes as capital gains and losses, the operations of a bank's *trading* department are taxed as ordinary income. To sum up, U.S. government and federal agency securities are used by banks for adhering to solvency requirements, for collateral against certain government deposits, for tax switching, for the generation of investment income (often tax-exempt at the state and local level) and/or trading profits, and (primarily in U.S. government securities, although to a lesser degree in the era of liability management) for adjusting the banks' reserve position.

In the state and local government securities sector, commercial banks compare the aftertax equivalent of yields received from municipal issues with returns available from fully taxable investments. Because of the favorable aftertax returns offered by tax-exempt issues, banks' involvement in the underwriting and trading of municipal securities, and the wide variety of issues and serial maturities in the municipal market, banks have expanded the percentage of state and local government issues in their credit market investments, with primary emphasis on buying and holding to maturity good-quality issues of 10 years' maturity or less in the top four rating categories. With the exception of a few very marketable issues, banks generally do not rely on their municipal holdings as a principal source of liquidity. A bank's investment activity in municipal securities is highly influenced by its marginal income tax bracket at the federal, state, and local levels. For example, banks located in a particular city or state with high income taxes may buy securities of that city or state especially to earn income which is exempt from federal, state, or local taxes.

As noted earlier, banks buy relatively minuscule amounts of corporate and foreign bonds because these are classified as *risk assets* (as are municipal securities) by bank examiners, although they do not provide the aftertax yield advantage and staggered maturities offered by municipal securities. Corporate bonds are usually of long maturity. Short-maturity corporate bonds or notes are generally not as liquid as U.S. Treasury or federally sponsored credit agency issues which are *equivalently* taxed at the federal level but are *preferentially* taxed at the state and local level.

Banks very seldom buy convertible corporate bonds and generally may do so only when they are trading within 1 percent of the bond's estimated straight bond investment value as determined by its rating, maturity, and coupon. With the exception of certain exempted securities and so-called Article 12 banks, which are in fact investment companies with the ability to invest for their own account in convertible bonds, common stocks, and other securities, commercial banks are practically prohibited from investing in common stocks for their own investment account. Banks can invest in Federal Reserve System stock, in the equity of specified bank subsidiaries, and in a very small number of other exempt equities.

In addition, banks already have corporate *loans* in their portfolio of credit market instruments. Corporate bond holdings would limit the amount which can be lent by any one bank to the corporate issuer of the bonds, since a national bank is not allowed to invest more than 10 percent of its total capital and surplus in the loans and securities of any one obligor, with the sole exception of the federal government. In mortgages, commercial banks are a leading source of funds, particularly in one- to four-family home mortgages, short-term construction loans, and commercial mortgages. Commercial banks have placed more funds in commercial mortgages than the total invested in this area by both savings and loan associations and mutual savings banks. Banks tend to be a relatively variable source of mortgage funds because of their greater responsiveness to overall loan demands and monetary conditions and the lower marketability of mortgages compared with banks' liquidity needs.

Banks are required to carry their "legally eligible" securities investments on their books at cost, with regular amortization of any premium paid over par or the accrual of discounts from par if desired. Ineligible securities are required to be carried on the books at the lower of cost or market value. In a rising interest rate environment, ineligible securities investments can impair the capital adequacy ratios of a particular bank (since their prices must be marked down as interest rates rise). For this reason, banks' securities investments are highly concentrated in the legally eligible category, consisting of the four highest fixed-income securities quality categories of the debt-rating agencies. In some cases, nonrated bonds may qualify as eligible investments if supported by satisfactory financial statistics.

Federal Supervision

While banks' investment practices are supervised by the Office of the Comptroller of the Currency, the overall capital adequacy, asset quality, management ability, liquidity level, and earnings quantity and quality of a commercial bank are supervised (on the basis of data supplied by the banks) by the Federal Reserve System, the FDIC, or the Office of the Comptroller of the

Currency under the Uniform Interagency Bank Rating System adopted in May 1978. The Securities and Exchange Commission (SEC) works with these three agencies to see that banks provide adequate financial disclosure to investors. In addition, the International Banking Act of 1978 regulates United States commercial banks engaged in international banking and foreign banks operating in the United States. The act covers such areas as licensing and chartering of banks, multistate banking, deposit insurance, and nonbanking activities.

Under federal law, the Federal Reserve System supervises approximately 1000 Federal Reserve member banks which are chartered by state banking authorities and about 2000 domestic bank holding companies with one or more commercial banking subsidiaries, the Comptroller of the Currency oversees the approximately 4700 national banks, and the FDIC supervises approximately 8600 insured, state-chartered commercial banks that are not members of the Federal Reserve System. Federal Reserve control over all banking and thrift institutions was considerably broadened by the Depository Institutions Deregulation and Monetary Control Act of 1980.

Savings and Loan Associations

Savings and loan associations include both shareholder-owned and mutual associations which encourage thrift and accept savings deposits in the form of so-called share capital inflows (deposits) for lending and investment in mortgages (primarily to foster homeownership) and in other credit market instruments. At the end of 1978, there were 4053 savings and loan associations (of which 2000 were federally chartered and 2053 were state-chartered) insured by the Federal Savings and Loan Insurance Corporation (FSLIC). In addition, there were 670 savings and loan associations which either were noninsured or were insured by one of the four state-sanctioned savings and loan insurance bodies. Beginning in 1975, the Federal Home Loan Bank Board (FHLBB) initiated and continued to regulate a program allowing a number of savings and loan associations to convert from their usual status of mutual ownership by depositors to that of publicly held stockholder-owned corporations in order to raise additional capital.

In Table 9-4 the credit market investments of savings and loan associations are presented for selected years during the period from 1950 through 1979. The overwhelming dominance of mortgages in the credit market holdings of savings and loan associations can be seen in the table. At the end of 1975, mortgages (of which 81 percent were made against one- to four-family residences, and of which 10 percent were government-insured and 90 percent were conventional mortgages) represented 90 percent of savings and loan associations' total credit market investments, up from 89 percent as of the end of 1950.

TABLE 9-4

Credit Market Instrument Holdings of Savings and Loan Associations for Selected Years, 1950–1979

(In billions of dollars)

Credit market instrument category	1950	1955	1960	1965	1970	1975	1979
U.S. government securities	1.5	2.4	4.6	7.4	6.8	5.4	4.7
Federally sponsored agency issues	0.0	0.1	0.6	0.8	4.1	17.2	32.1
State and local government securities	0.0	0.0	0.0	0.0	0.1	1.1	1.2
Open-market paper	0.0	0.0	0.0	0.0	1.8	2.7	3.4
Mortgages	13.7	31.4	60.1	110.3	149.8	278.7	475.7
Consumer credit	0.2	0.5	1.0	1.4	2.1	2.8	14.3
Federal funds and securities repurchase agreements	0.0	0.0	0.0	0.0	0.0	2.6	11.5
Total	15.4	34.4	66.3	119.9	164.7	310.5	542.9

SOURCE: *Flow of Funds Accounts*, Board of Governors of the Federal Reserve System. Data for all periods through 1975 are taken from the *Flow of Funds Accounts, 1946–1975*, issued in December 1976; data for periods subsequent to 1975 are taken from the *Flow of Funds Accounts, 1969–1979*, issued in February 1980. Because of occasional revisions in the Flow of Funds Accounts data, certain statistics from the latter source and subsequent releases may vary somewhat from those contained in the *Flow of Funds Accounts, 1946–1975.*

After mortgages, the credit market instruments held by savings and loan associations at the end of 1975 included (1) federal agency securities, primarily Government National Mortgage Association (GNMA)–guaranteed pass-through securities, Federal Home Loan Mortgage Corporation (FHLMC)–guaranteed participation certificates, and Farmers Home Administration –insured notes, with 5.5 percent of total credit market instrument holdings (up from 0 percent at the end of 1950); (2) U.S. government securities, with 1.7 percent of total holdings (down from 9.7 percent of total holdings as of the end of 1950); (3) extensions of credit to consumers, representing 0.9 percent of total holdings (down from 1.3 percent at the end of 1950); (4) open-market paper, with 0.9 percent of total holdings (up from no holdings at the end of 1950); (5) federal funds and securities repurchase agreements, representing 0.8 percent of total holdings (compared with no holdings at the end of 1950); and (6) state and local government securities, with 0.4 percent of total holdings.

Until 1964 savings and loan associations were prohibited from owning state and local government securities. Since then tax-exempt income has not been a large incentive for savings and loan associations to buy municipal securities as long as their effective income tax rate has been sufficiently below the overall corporate tax rate. Nevertheless, in some cases savings and loan associations have increased their investments in tax-exempt securities that support real estate rehabilitation and development. With very few exceptions, the associations are prohibited from owning corporate and foreign bonds, although in the late 1970s and the early 1980s congressional proposals were made to allow federally chartered savings and loan associations to invest up to 10 percent of their assets in corporate bonds, consumer loans, and commercial paper.

Figure 9-1 graphically shows the principal earning assets and liabilities of savings and loan associations from 1946 through the mid-1970s. Of particular note are (1) the relatively rapid growth in mortgages other than residential mortgages held by savings and loan associations and (2) the variability in and growth of Federal Home Loan Bank (FHLB) advances to savings and loan associations.

Table 9-5 shows the principal flows of funds into credit market instruments by savings and loan associations during the period from 1972 through 1979. It can be seen that the total flow of funds correlates highly with the level of savings and loan associations' mortgage lending. When new acquisitions of mortgages declined (in part because of disintermediation) from $32 billion in 1972 to $17.6 billion in 1974, total net investments in credit market instruments by savings and loan associations also fell off, from $35.7 billion in 1972 to $21.4 billion in 1974. Similarly, total flows into credit market instruments by savings and loan associations rebounded to $67 billion in 1977, paced by $58.1 billion worth of net mortgage acquisitions by the associations that year.

One indicator of future flows into mortgages by savings and loan associations is the level of their mortgage commitments to residential builders. When savings inflows to savings and loan associations remain at high levels and their mortgage investment activity turns down, the associations may use the additional funds to repay Federal Home Loan Bank System (FHLBS) advances, which in turn can lead to reduced debt offerings or even to increased debt repayments by the FHLBS. After mortgages, the greatest proportion of savings and loan associations' flows into credit market instruments from 1972 to 1979 went to U.S. government securities and federally sponsored credit agency issues. State and local government securities, open-market paper, consumer credit, and federal funds and securities repurchase agreements accounted for a relatively small proportion of total credit flows, with certain of these categories exhibiting net sales.

Disintermediation and Interest Rate Restrictions

The degree of savings intermediation or disintermediation is one of the most important influences on the investment behavior of savings and loan associations. In turn, disintermediation occurs in large part as a result of the interest rate restrictions to which associations may be subject. To prevent excessive

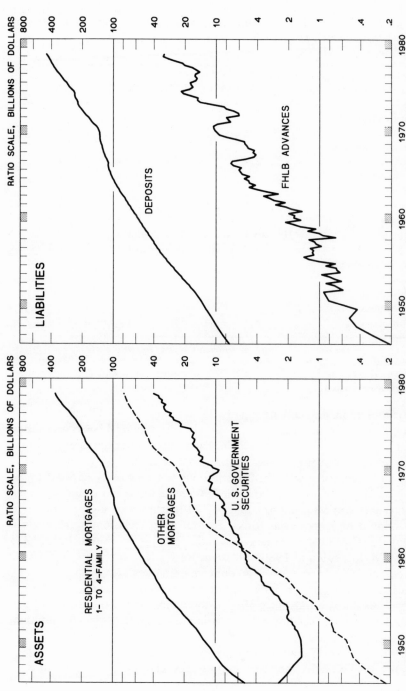

FIGURE 9-1 Principal earning assets and liabilities of savings and loan associations (amounts in billions of dollars). [SOURCE: Historical Chart Book, *Board of Governors of the Federal Reserve System. By permission of the Board of Governors of the Federal Reserve System.*]

TABLE 9-5

Annual Net Flows of Funds from Savings and Loan Associations into Credit Market Instruments, 1972–1979

(In billions of dollars)

Credit market instrument category	1972	1973	1974	1975	1976	1977	1978	1979
U.S. government securities	− 0.5	− 2.4	− 0.1	2.2	4.2	3.2	0.7	− 3.9
Federally sponsored agency issues	2.4	2.3	1.2	4.1	0.7	2.7	4.6	4.7
State and local government securities	. . .*	. . .*	0.3	0.6	0.1	− 0.1	0.1	− 0.1
Open-market paper	0.5	− 0.5	− 0.1	. . .*	− 0.1	0.9	0.4	0.7
Mortgages	32.0	26.5	17.6	29.5	45.0	58.1	51.7	42.8
Consumer credit	0.9	1.1	0.7	0.9	1.0	1.1	1.2	2.0
Federal funds and securities repurchase agreements	0.4	1.3	1.8	− 1.4	2.1	1.1	1.7	2.5
Total	35.7	28.3	21.4	35.9	53.0	67.0	60.4	48.7

SOURCE: *Flow of Funds Accounts,* Board of Governors of the Federal Reserve System. Data for 1978 and 1979 are taken from the *Flow of Funds Accounts* published in February 1980; data from 1972 to 1977 are taken from earlier years' *Flow of Funds Accounts* statistics.
*Less than $50 million.

rate competition, the Banking Act of 1933 (through Federal Reserve Regulation Q) stipulated interest rate ceilings which commercial banks and certain other institutions could offer on savings accounts. Under the Interest Adjustment Act of 1966, ceilings were broadened to cover savings and loan associations and several types of thrift institutions not previously affected by the 1933 legislation. Also included in the 1966 regulations was an allowance that savings and loan associations could pay a slight interest rate premium over that offered by commercial banks. Several major revisions were made in Regulation Q ceiling rates on savings and small time deposits in 1970, 1973, and 1978. In 1979 and 1980, initiatives were taken to phase out gradually all federal controls on savings account interest rates.

A list of the interest rate ceilings on FHLB member savings associations for various time periods since 1966 is shown in Table 9-6. As can be seen, savings and loan associations offer a variety of minimum-balance, minimum-term certificate accounts to savers. Such accounts pay a higher rate of interest than that paid on passbook accounts. In the late 1970s and early 1980s, congressional directives and market pressures reflected a trend toward even-

TABLE 9-6
Interest Rate Ceilings on Savings at Federal Home Loan Bank Member Savings Associations

Type of account	Effective month and rate ceiling (percent)						
	September 1966	January 1970	May 1973	July 1973	November 1973	December 1974[a]	June 1978[b]
Passbook	4.75	5.00	5.00	5.25	5.25	5.25	5.25
90-day notice	...[f]	5.25	5.25	5.75	5.75	5.75	5.75
Transaction (NOW)	...[f]	...[f]	...[f]	...[f]	...[f]	5.00[d]	5.00[d]
Certificate							
90 to 179 days							
No minimum	...[f]	5.25	5.25	5.25	5.75	5.75	5.75
$1000 minimum	...[f]	5.25	5.25	5.75	5.75	5.75	5.75
182 days							
$10,000 minimum	...[f]	...[f]	...[f]	...[f]	...[f]	...[f]	...[e]
180 to 364 days							
No minimum	...[f]	...[f]	...[f]	5.25	5.75	5.75	5.75
$1000 minimum	5.25	5.25	5.25	5.75	5.75	5.75	5.75
1 but less than 2 years							
No minimum	...[f]	...[f]	...[f]	5.25	5.75	5.75	5.75
$1000 minimum	5.25	5.75	5.75	6.50	6.50	6.50	6.50
2 but less than 2½ years							
No minimum	...[f]	...[f]	...[f]	5.25	5.75	5.75	5.75
$1000 minimum	5.25	5.75	5.75	5.75	6.50	6.50	6.50
$5000 minimum	5.25	6.00	6.00	6.50	6.50	6.50	6.50
2½ but less than 4 years							
No minimum	...[f]	...[f]	...[f]	5.25	5.75	5.75	5.75
$1000 minimum	5.25	5.75	5.75	5.75	6.75	6.75	6.75
$5000 minimum	5.25	6.00	6.00	6.75	6.75	6.75	6.75
4 but less than 6 years							
No minimum	...[f]	...[f]	...[f]	6.75	...[f]	5.75	5.75
$1000 minimum	5.25	5.75	5.75	None	7.50	7.50	7.50
$5000 minimum	5.25	6.00	6.00	None	7.50	7.50	7.50
6 but less than 8 years							
No minimum	...[f]	...[f]	...[f]	6.75	...[f]	5.75	5.75
$1000 minimum	5.25	5.75	5.75	None	7.50	7.75	7.75
$5000 minimum	5.25	6.00	6.00	None	7.50	7.75	7.75
8 or more years							
No minimum	...[f]	...[f]	...[f]	6.75	...[f]	5.75	5.75

TABLE 9-6

Interest Rate Ceilings on Savings at Federal Home Loan Bank Member Savings Associations *(Continued)*

Type of account	Effective month and rate ceiling (percent)						
	September 1966	January 1970	May 1973	July 1973	November 1973	December 1974[d]	June 1978[b]
8 or more years *(continued)*							
$1000 minimum	5.25	5.75	5.75	None	7.50	7.75	8.00
$5000 minimum	5.25	6.00	6.00	None	7.50	7.75	8.00
$100,000 minimum							
30- to 59-day maturity	. . .[c]	. . .[c]	. . .[c]	None	None	None	None
60- to 89-day maturity	. . .[c]	6.50	None	None	None	None	None
90- to 179-day maturity	. . .[c]	6.75	None	None	None	None	None
180- to 364-day maturity	5.25	7.00	None	None	None	None	None
1-year maturity or more	5.25	7.50	None	None	None	None	None

SOURCE: *Savings and Loan Fact Book 1979,* copyright 1979, United States League of Savings Associations; Federal Home Loan Bank Board.

NOTE: Certain technical details and rate ceilings applicable for a limited period of time or in special geographic regions have not been included. In July 1979, officially mandated minimum denominations were abolished for all savings certificates except money market certificates. On March 31, 1980, the Depository Institutions Deregulation and Monetary Control Act was signed into law. Among other provisions, the legislation (1) initiated a 6-year phasing out of interest rate ceilings on passbook accounts by commercial and mutual savings banks and savings and loan associations; (2) increased from $40,000 to $100,000 the amount of federal insurance on bank savings; (3) established a uniform system of banking reserves for all depository institutions (over a phase-in period of 8 years); (4) authorized the payment of interest on checking accounts (at the time permitted only in New England, New York, and New Jersey); and (5) eliminated or revised upward various state usury ceilings (subject to the states' ability to reenact such ceilings in certain cases).

[a] As of November 24, 1974, member associations were permitted to pay the maximum certificate rate on all governmental-unit certificate accounts with a 30-day minimum term and a balance under $100,000 and on all governmental-unit notice accounts.

[b] As of July 6, 1977, member associations were permitted to pay the maximum certificate rate on all individual retirement accounts and Keogh accounts with a 3-year minimum term.

[c] As of the date shown, this category was not authorized by the Federal Home Loan Bank Board.

[d] As of January 1, 1974, such accounts were permitted for certain member associations in certain states in New England.

[e] The maximum rate as of Thursday of each week is based on the average rate (discount basis) on 6-month U.S. Treasury bills as determined at the immediately preceding auction.

tual elimination of interest rate controls on some or all savings certificates and deposits, subject to emergency action by regulators to protect the financial soundness of institutions and the operation of monetary policy. In addition, such forces worked toward phasing out the deposit and certificate interest differential between thrift institutions and commercial banks.

As long as the ceiling rates remain competitive with or above interest rates on short-term money market instruments, there is little incentive for savers to shift existing deposits or new savings flows from savings and loan associations into short-term money market instruments. When market interest rates begin to exceed by a sufficiently wide margin the rates which can be paid by savings and loan associations on the various types of accounts which they offer, disintermediation occurs. Disintermediation results in a diversion of part or all of existing funds and/or new savings flows into higher-yielding short-term money market instruments. Although savings and loan associations can legally require advance written notice of withdrawals, in practice this convention has seldom been enforced.

The volatility of savings and loan associations' investment patterns which is caused by disintermediation was considerably reduced by the introduction of the certificate accounts listed in Table 9-6. At the end of 1978, such accounts represented more than 68 percent of total savings and loan associations' deposits. In the opinion of savers, many types of savings and loan deposits took on the character of an investment which had no nominal price risk (although certain penalties were assessed in the form of forfeited interest on premature withdrawals from minimum-term accounts) rather than that of a strict savings deposit.

To reduce further the variations in funds flows within the savings and loan industry, other sources of funds besides deposits are available to savings and loan associations. These include, first, advances (borrowings) from the FHLBS. Such advances amounted to 6.1 percent of total savings and loan associations' assets as of the end of 1978. Second, savings and loan associations can utilize mortgage sales and repurchase agreements (in mortgages or in other securities) with other financial institutions. Third, savings and loan associations can solicit time deposits by state and local governments and by other nonconsumer depositors. Fourth, savings and loan associations can sell mortgages to the Federal National Mortgage Association (FNMA), GNMA, and FHLMC. Fifth, savings and loan associations can issue mortgage-backed notes and bonds, mortgage pass-through securities, negotiable certificates of deposit, Eurocurrency securities, and commercial paper. Sixth, since June 1978 savings and loan associations have been able to issue 8-year minimum-term savings certificates offering a maximum 8 percent interest rate. Seventh, since June 1978 savings and loan associations have been able to issue 6-month floating-rate savings certificates.

The last-named certificates are also called money market certificates (MMCs). They pay a premium of up to 0.25 percent over the discount rate on 6-month Treasury bills (commercial banks are allowed to pay this Treasury bill rate but not the premium) as long as the Treasury bill rate is 8.75 percent or less. Above 8.75 percent, the 0.25 percent differential between savings and loan associations and commercial banks was eliminated as of March 15, 1979. The interest rate on newly issued MMCs is allowed to change weekly, but once a particular MMC has been purchased, the rate being paid on it is fixed until it matures. A total of $123.7 billion in MMCs was outstanding at commercial banks, savings and loan associations, and mutual savings banks as of April 1979.

Money market certificates and certificates with 8 percent maximum interest and 8-year minimum maturity (also known as 8 by 8s) were effective in reducing savings outflows in the environment of rising interest rates of 1978, 1979, and early 1980. However, they often represented merely a higher cost of funds to the savings institution offering them because of transfers of funds by savers out of existing lower-interest certificates or other savings accounts at the earliest nonpenalty date. The specific propensity of savers to transfer funds between accounts depends in part upon how much of their funds are in easily switchable accounts (for example, passbook accounts as opposed to time deposits) as well as their combined federal, state, and local incremental tax bracket (a high tax rate may reduce the relative attractiveness of increased taxable interest income).

In states where mortgage interest rates are limited to a maximum fixed or floating ceiling by law and where interest rates on existing mortgages held in the portfolio are much lower than current market rates of interest on many forms of deposits, savings institutions may be reluctant to promote actively floating-rate savings certificates when related Treasury security rates approach or exceed mortgage rates. In 1979 and 1980 the greater percentage of deposits in high-cost certificates and special accounts, coupled with lower returns from existing mortgages and new mortgages, created severe financial pressures on many savings and loan associations and mutual savings banks.

As of early 1980, almost half of the 50 states had various forms of usury laws which set maximum rates on loans to individuals. Under federal law, *nationally* chartered banks are allowed to make home mortgage loans at rates linked to the Federal Reserve System discount rate, but *state-* chartered banks usually are subject to any existing applicable usury ceilings in their state of operation. (For further details see Table Note (5), page 234.)

Floating-rate savings certificates of 6 months' maturity tend to shorten the average maturity of a savings and loan association's deposit structure, with outflows of funds from this savings vehicle in times of falling interest rates. In July 1979, the Federal Reserve Board and the FHLBB authorized a 4-year savings certificate paying interest 1 percentage point less than the average yield on 4-year U.S. Treasury securities. For commercial banks, the allowed rate is 1.25 percent less than the yield on 4-year Treasury securities. The rate is permitted to change every month for newly issued certificates, but once a specific certificate has been purchased, the rate being paid on it is fixed until the maturity of the certificate.

In late 1979, a 2½-year savings certificate was also authorized, with interest rates pegged to the return on equivalent-maturity U.S. Treasury securities. Savings institutions would be able to pay 50 basis points (0.5 percent) less than the Treasury return, and commercial banks would be able to pay 75 basis points (0.75 percent) less than the Treasury return. The rate on newly issued certificates is allowed to change monthly, but once a specific certificate has been purchased, the rate being paid on it is fixed until the maturity of the certificate.

Because of the relatively high percentage of savings and loan associations' credit market instruments represented by mortgages (which generally are less liquid than most of their fixed-income securities holdings), the need to assure ability to meet withdrawals by depositors, and the requirement to comply with certain regulatory standards, the associations must maintain adequate levels of liquidity in their investment policies. On average, amortization payments by mortgage debtors provide annual inflows of between 8 and 12 percent of average assets.

There is some seasonality to funds flows at savings and loan associations. Withdrawals generally increase at the end of quarterly interest payment periods as a result of the withdrawal of interest payments and/or a portion of the principal balance once the date which allows payment of interest at the stated rate has passed. Funds outflows demonstrate a slight seasonality as the mortgage demand for new homes and for home improvements or additions correlates to some degree with annual construction cycles. Consumer spending behavior and inflationary expectations also have an impact on savings inflows and withdrawals as well as on desired levels of investment liquidity by savings and loan associations. Some associations coordinate their funds flows and protect themselves against adverse interest rate fluctuations through the use of commitments to purchase mortgages, U.S. government securities, or securities issued by GNMA. Because of some speculation and improper use of such commitments, greater regulatory and industry-initiated scrutiny was focused upon this area in 1978, 1979, and 1980.

Effect of Tax Regulations

Tax regulations also have an influence on the operations and investments of savings and loan associations. To qualify for tax treatment as a savings and loan association, a savings institution must (1) derive at least 75 percent of its gross income from mortgage loans; (2) hold at least 60 percent of its assets in residential mortgages, cash, certificates of deposit (savings and loan associations were first allowed to buy certificates of deposit and include them in their liquidity tests in 1969, and in 1973 they were permitted to make unsecured short-term loans, through the federal funds market and otherwise, to commercial banks), and other specified types and maximum maturities of U.S. government and federal agency securities and other instruments; and (3) be insured by the FSLIC or be supervised by a state or federal thrift agency. In early 1979 the U.S. Treasury proposed that federally chartered thrift institutions be permitted to invest up to 10 percent of their assets in housing-related consumer loans.

Taken together, the Revenue Act of 1962, the Tax Reform Act of 1969, and the Tax Reform Act of 1976 raised the previously low tax liability of savings and loan associations. The corporate tax rates applied against savings and loan associations can be effectively reduced by an association's principal category of tax deductions, which can be taken for reasonable additions to its loss reserves, calculated under one of the following formulas: (1) as a certain percentage of net income (40 percent as of 1979), (2) as a certain percentage of outstanding mortgage loans (with such percentages declining every 6 years until 1987), or (3) by the actual amount of bad-debt losses averaged over a period of several years.

Particularly in the past, the positive yield spread on mortgages compared with most other credit market instruments, the assets and business operations qualifications tests for savings and loan associations, and the associations' relatively low effective income tax rates have sharply curtailed any attempt by the associations to seek tax-exempt income by investing in municipal securities or to seek partially reduced income taxes by investing in credit market instruments for capital gains. Under IRS regulations, total reserves of a savings and loan association are not allowed to exceed 12 percent of year-end savings balances or 6 percent of total qualifying mortgages held by the association, but the FSLIC mandates certain minimum reserve levels (generally 5 percent), incremental additions to reserves, and minimum net-worth requirements. The greater the degree of risk (as defined by the FSLIC) in a savings and loan association's portfolio of credit market instruments including mortgages, the higher the amount of net worth which must be set aside against such instruments. In general, savings and loan associations restrict their mortgage investments to areas near their own operating locales.

As of the end of 1975, 80.6 percent of savings and loan association mortgage lending activity, or $224.7 billion, was invested in one- to four-family residential mortgages (this was 45.6 percent of the total amount of one- to four-family residential mortgages held by all investors). A total of 9.1 percent of savings and loan association mortgage lending activity, or $25.4 billion, was directed toward multifamily residential mortgages (which accounted for 25.3 percent of total multifamily residential mortgages held by all investors). Commercial mortgages represented 10.3 percent of savings and loan association mortgage lending activity, or $28.6 billion, at the end of 1975; this total accounted for 18 percent of commercial mortgages held by all investors. A large portion of savings and loan association commercial mortgage lending is for short-term construction loans. Savings and loan associations provide only minuscule amounts of funds for farm mortgages.

Broadening of Asset and Liability Powers

Beginning in a selected number of states in the mid-1970s, savings and loan associations broadened their asset and liability powers. *Asset* alternatives were broadened with the expanded use of variable-rate mortgages. The interest on variable-rate mortgages is usually linked to a commonly accepted and regularly computed cost-of-funds index. The mortgage rate is generally permitted to *fall* as rapidly and as far as the index declines, but it is normally allowed to *rise* a maximum number of basis points in a specified period and by a maximum number of basis points throughout the duration of the mortgage. Variable-rate mortgages allow savings and loan associations in effect to pass on increases in their own costs of funds, thereby reducing possible operating and financial pressures which might constrain their investment behavior in credit market instruments.

Beginning in 1979, the FHLBB authorized federally chartered savings and loan associations to issue variable-rate mortgages. In some cases, limitations were placed on the amount of such mortgages as a percentage of total mortgages written or purchased by a savings and loan association in any one year and the number of times that the mortgage rate could be adjusted per year. Some variable-rate mortgages allow the mortgage borrower the option of absorbing an interest rate increase by extending the length of the loan, up to a maximum of one-third of the original maturity.

In the late 1970s the FHLBB also allowed graduated-payment mortgages, on which monthly payments increase over a period of time. For example, mortgage payments could increase by 7.5 percent annually for as many as 5 years, 6.5 percent annually for as many as 6 years, or 3 percent annually for as many as 10 years. Reverse-annuity mortgages, under which a homeowner with an already high equity position in a house can borrow against the value of the house, were also allowed. This is effected through monthly payments from the savings and loan association to the homeowner, the increasing amount of the loan being secured by the property itself.

British building societies, which are similar to savings and loan associations, have offered only variable-rate mortgages since 1932, and Canadian mortgage-issuing firms (mainly trust and insurance companies) primarily use roll-over mortgages, on which the terms of the mortgage are recalculated at 5-year intervals. Variable-rate mortgages have two main disadvantages from the point of view of the savings and loan association: (1) in periods of declining interest rates, mortgage interest income is lower than it would be under a fixed-rate mortgage, and (2) variable-rate mortgages can be difficult to resell in the secondary-mortgage market.

The *liability* powers of savings and loan associations were broadened beginning in the mid-1970s with the introduction of several new instruments described earlier in this section as well as NOW accounts (similar to checking accounts) and checking accounts themselves. The introduction of such products intensified competition for both the acquisition of savings inflows and the lending of money in the form of mortgages or otherwise between savings institutions and commercial banks in certain states, especially those in which branch banking is permitted for commercial banks. Commercial banks have responded through the introduction of remote-access banking terminals, automatic-payment services, and privileges for either telephonic or automatic funds transfer services between savings and checking accounts.

Federal Restrictions

Federally chartered savings and loan associations are required to be members in the FHLBS, organized by congressional action in 1932. The FHLBS also supervises and examines federally chartered member savings and loan associations, as well as state-chartered savings and loan associations, which are also subject to supervision and examination by state authorities. Besides overseeing the investment, lending, and deposit-gathering activities of savings and loan associations, the FHLB often augments and/or balances out the geographical, cyclical, and seasonal funds needs of savings and loan associations by issuing discount notes and consolidated obligations in the capital markets and advancing these funds (called advances) to member associations that qualify for such capital.

Among the restrictions which the FHLB places upon savings and loan associations are (1) maximum percentages which can be invested in conventional (as opposed to government-insured or -guaranteed) mortgages, (2) geographical restrictions on both government-backed and conventional mortgage lending, (3) maximum percentages which can be invested in multifamily or commercial mortgages as opposed to one- to four-family residential mortgages, (4) maximum loan-value ratios for different types of mortgages, and (5) maximum percentages on the ratio of total borrowings to total assets. (For mutual savings banks, discussed in the next section, there is a legal list of eligible corporate issues whose senior securities must attain certain ratios of quality and earnings coverage.)

Mutual Savings Banks

A total of 473 mutual savings banks were in operation in 17 states (principally in Massachusetts, New York, Connecticut, Maine, New Hampshire, and New Jersey) at the end of 1978. Of these 76 were members of the FHLBS, 331 were insured by the FDIC, and 166 were insured by state funds (124 mutual savings banks were jointly insured by the FDIC and state funds). In contrast to savings and loan associations, commercial banks, and credit unions, mutual savings banks are exclusively state-chartered.

In many ways, the asset structures, flows into credit market instruments, and determinants of investment behavior of mutual savings banks are quite similar to those of savings and loan associations. In this section, particular attention is directed to the important differences between these two investor groups. It is highly recommended that an investor with an interest in either savings and loan associations or mutual savings banks read the sections both on mutual savings banks and on savings and loan associations. Figure 9-2 shows the principal earning assets and deposits of mutual savings banks from 1946 until the late 1970s. Of particular interest are the pickup in the growth rate in holdings of corporate and government securities beginning in 1967 and 1970 respectively, after flat or declining growth rates during the late 1950s and early 1960s.

Table 9-7 presents the holdings of credit market instruments by mutual savings banks for selected years during the 1950–1979 period. As of the end of 1975, the four largest categories of credit market instrument holdings by mutual savings banks were (1) mortgages (of which 65 percent were on one- to four-family residential dwellings, 18 percent on multifamily buildings, 17 percent on commercial properties, and less than 0.1 percent on farm properties), representing 69.5 percent of total credit market instrument holdings (well below the ratio of mortgages to total credit market investments for savings and loan associations but up substantially from 38.4 percent of total holdings as of the end of 1950); (2) corporate and foreign bonds (unlike savings and loan associations, mutual savings banks are permitted to own corporate and foreign bonds), with 15.8 percent of total credit market instrument holdings (up from 9.7 percent at the end of 1950); (3) federal agency securities, with 5.6 percent of total credit market instrument holdings (up from negligible holdings as of the end of 1950); and (4) U.S. government securities, representing 4.2 percent of total credit market instrument holdings (down sharply from 50.4 percent of the total at the end of 1950). In addition, at the end of 1975 mutual savings banks had between 1 and 2 percent of their total credit market instrument holdings in each of the following investment categories: (1) consumer credit, with 1.6 percent of the total (up from 0.5 percent at the end of 1950), (2) state and local government securities, representing 1.3 percent of the total (up from 0.5 percent at the end of 1950); (3) commercial paper, with 1.1 percent of the total (up from 0.5 percent as of the end of 1950); and (4) securities repurchase agreements, representing 1 percent of the total (up from no holdings at the end of 1950).

Table 9-8 summarizes annual net flows into credit market instruments by mutual savings banks for each year during the 1972–1979 period. In absolute terms, annual net flows into credit market instruments by mutual savings banks were much smaller than annual net flows of savings and loan associations, with the banks' flows ranging between 12 and 29 percent of the associations' flows from 1972 through 1979. The total flows of mutual savings banks into credit market instruments demonstrated a wide variability

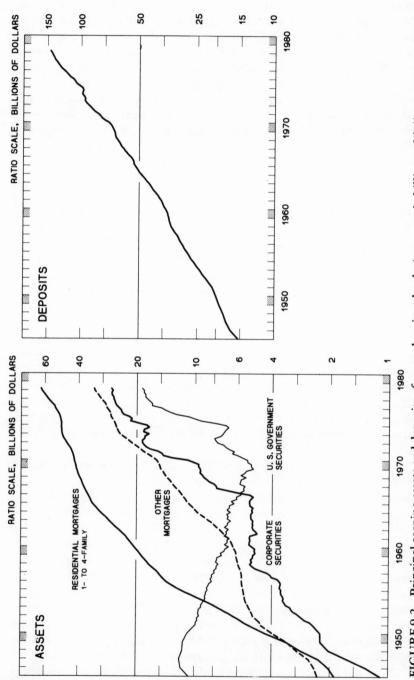

FIGURE 9-2 Principal earning assets and deposits of mutual savings banks (amounts in billions of dollars). [SOURCE: Historical Chart Book, *Board of Governors of the Federal Reserve System. By permission of the Board of Governors of the Federal Reserve System.*]

242

TABLE 9-7
Credit Market Instrument Holdings of Mutual Savings Banks for Selected
Years, 1950–1979
(In billions of dollars)

Credit market instrument category	1950	1955	1960	1965	1970	1975	1979
U.S. government securities	10.9	8.5	6.1	5.5	3.2	4.7	4.3
Federally sponsored agency issues	. . .*	0.1	0.1	0.8	2.2	6.2	15.5
State and local government securities	0.1	0.6	0.7	0.3	0.2	1.5	3.2
Corporate and foreign bonds	2.1	2.6	3.8	2.9	8.2	17.6	20.8
Mortgages	8.3	17.5	26.9	44.6	57.9	77.2	98.7
Consumer credit	0.1	0.1	0.2	0.5	1.1	1.8	3.6
Open-market paper	0.1	0.1	0.2	0.3	0.7	1.1	2.4
Securities repurchase agreements	0.0	0.0	0.0	0.0	0.4	1.1	3.0
Total	21.6	29.5	38.0	54.9	73.9	111.2	151.5
Memorandum: Corporate equities†	0.2	1.0	1.4	2.3	2.8	4.4	5.5

SOURCE: *Flow of Funds Accounts,* Board of Governors of the Federal Reserve System. Data for all periods through 1975 are taken from the *Flow of Funds Accounts, 1946–1975,* issued in December 1976; data for periods subsequent to 1975 are taken from the *Flow of Funds Accounts, 1969–1979,* issued in February 1980. Because of occasional revisions in the Flow of Funds Accounts data, certain statistics from the latter source and subsequent releases may vary somewhat from those contained in the *Flow of Funds Accounts, 1946–1975.*
*Less than $50 million.
†Includes both convertible and nonconvertible preferred stock as well as common stock.

and a high correlation with mortgage flows, similar to that of savings and loan associations. Accompanied in part by a decline in mortgage investments from $5.5 billion in 1972 to $2.2 billion in the tight-credit, disintermediative conditions of 1974, total net inflows into credit market instruments by mutual savings banks fell from $9.5 billion in 1972 to $2.9 billion in 1974. Net acquisitions of corporate bonds often picked up the slack in mortgage demand; they, too, were highly variable during the 1972–1979 period, swinging from net sales of corporate bonds amounting to $1.1 billion in 1973 to net purchases amounting to $3.5 billion in 1975. Flows into federal agency issues demonstrated patterns similar to corporate bond flows, moving from a low of $100 million in 1973 to a high of $2.9 billion in 1976. With the exception of net acquisitions of $2.2 billion and $1.1 billion in U.S. government securities in 1975 and 1976 respectively and a net acquisition of $1.5 billion in securities repurchase agreements in 1977, individual inflows into U.S. government securities, state and local government obligations, consumer credit, commercial paper, and securities repurchase agreements ranged between net sales of $600 million and net purchases of $2.1 billion from 1972 through 1979.

In slight contrast to the residential-home–financing objective of savings and loan associations, the functions and goals of mutual savings banks are (1) to protect and encourage the savings of depositors and (2) to redirect these funds into safe and productive investments that will earn a high rate of return consistent with the first objective. These goals, the form of ownership of mutual savings banks, and their geographical concentration in the Northeastern United States (where home building has been less active than in many areas of the country served by savings and loan associations) have led to a somewhat lesser concentration of credit market instrument holdings in mortgages for mutual savings banks than for savings and loan associations. Mutual savings banks are usually owned by their depositors and are managed by trustees for the depositors' benefit.

In general, as pointed out in the discussion of Table 9-7, mutual savings banks engage in proportionately more multifamily residential and commercial mortgage lending (including construction financing) than savings and loan associations. By examining mutual savings banks' mortgage holdings in

TABLE 9-8

Annual Net Flows of Funds from Mutual Savings Banks into Credit Market Instruments, 1972–1979

(In billions of dollars)

Credit market instrument category	1972	1973	1974	1975	1976	1977	1978	1979
U.S. government securities	0.2	− 0.5	− 0.4	2.2	1.1	0.3	− 0.9	− 0.7
Federally sponsored agency issues	1.1	0.1	0.2	1.7	2.9	2.2	1.7	2.1
State and local government securities	0.5	. . .*	. . .*	0.6	0.9	0.4	0.5	− 0.2
Corporate and foreign bonds	2.1	− 1.1	0.9	3.5	2.8	1.1	0.1	− 0.7
Mortgages	5.5	5.7	2.2	2.3	4.1	6.3	7.1	3.6
Consumer credit	0.1	0.2	0.2	0.2	0.2	0.4	0.7	− 0.2
Open-market paper	− 0.1	− 0.1	0.1	0.1	0.5	− 0.6	− 0.6	2.1
Securities repurchase agreements	0.1	0.7	− 0.3	− 0.1	0.4	1.5	0.9	. . .*
Total	9.5	5.0	2.9	10.5	12.9	11.6	9.4	5.9

SOURCE: *Flow of Funds Accounts,* Board of Governors of the Federal Reserve System. Data for 1978 and 1979 are taken from the *Flow of Funds Accounts* published in February 1980; data from 1972 to 1977 are taken from earlier years' *Flow of Funds Accounts* statistics.

*Less than $50 million.

another way, as a percentage of total mortgages outstanding, it can be seen that at the end of 1975 mutual savings banks held 10.2 percent of total one-to four-family residential mortgages outstanding, 13.7 percent of total multifamily residential mortgages outstanding, 8.4 percent of total commercial mortgages outstanding, and a minuscule amount (0.1 percent) of total farm mortgages outstanding.

The amount of funds directed into mortgages by mutual savings banks in any given year is a function of (1) mortgage credit demands in each of the three main subcategories of the mortgage lending markets, (2) total new deposit inflows to mutual savings banks, (3) the amounts of principal and credited interest left in mutual savings accounts, (4) current and future estimated yield spreads between mortgages (particularly federally insured or guaranteed mortgages, which often have an interest rate ceiling) and other credit market instruments, (5) repayments of principal by existing mortgage borrowers, and (6) mortgage interest rate ceilings imposed by various states.

Point 4 is particularly important for mutual savings banks, since federally insured or guaranteed mortgages represented a much larger percentage of their total mortgage investments as of the mid-1970s than they did for the mortgage investments of any of the other primary suppliers of mortgage funds such as commercial banks, savings and loan associations, or life insurance companies. In part, federally insured or guaranteed mortgages account for such a large proportion of total mortgage lending by mutual savings banks because of legislation passed in the 1950s by many of the states in which these banks are concentrated, allowing them to invest in mortgages outside their states only if the mortgages carried federal insurance or guarantees. In the 1970s some states also began to permit investing in conventional mortgages by mutual savings banks outside their own states of origin. As a result of such guidelines and sizable investments by mutual savings banks in certain mortgage-backed securities (particularly those guaranteed by GNMA), mutual savings banks tend to have a broader national geographic orientation of mortgages and mortgage-backed securities than savings and loan associations.

Generally, mutual savings bank purchases of corporate bonds (and to some degree, of U.S. government and federal agency issues) respond to the attractiveness of their interest rates (and, to a lesser degree, of their call provisions, sinking-fund features, and other terms) relative to returns available from mortgage investments. Other conditions being equal, when the yield spread narrows or turns negative between mortgages and taxable bonds, mutual savings banks usually increase the proportion of their funds directed toward bonds.

The liability structure of mutual savings banks, like that of savings and loan associations, underwent significant change beginning in the 1970s. By the beginning of 1977, various forms of high-interest-rate, longer-term time deposit accounts represented 39 percent of total deposits, up from 17 percent at the start of 1971. Also available were checking accounts and NOW accounts, automatic and/or telephonic funds transfer services, direct-deposit facilities for social security recipients' income, and tax-sheltered retirement accumulation programs for self-employed persons (such as Keogh plans and individual retirement accounts, or IRAs). While some of these new sources of funds have increased the competitiveness of mutual savings banks compared with savings and loan associations and commercial banks in securing short-term funds, amounts deposited in mutual savings banks and other approved thrift institutions by individuals in Keogh plans and IRAs tend to be quite long-term.

As mentioned earlier, all mutual savings banks are state-chartered and are governed by state legislation. In addition, mutual savings banks come under the supervision of state banking authorities. If a mutual savings bank is insured by the FDIC or if it is a member of the FHLBS, it is subject to the regulations and inspection of either or both of these bodies. The principal way in which states influence the investment behavior of mutual savings banks is through the establishment of approved lists of credit market instruments (so-called legal lists) as well as specified ceilings for certain credit market holdings as a percentage either of total deposits or of total assets for a given bank.

Credit Unions

Credit unions are cooperative associations organized to encourage savings among their members and to provide lending facilities for useful personal purposes. They can be established under either state or federal charter to accept share funds from and lend to 100 or more individuals having a common tie of residence, association, or employment. As of early 1978, it was estimated that 36 million United States citizens were members of one or more of the 22,448 credit unions in the country.

Credit union members purchase "shares," which are similar in most respects to savings accounts. Only members are entitled to borrow from a credit union. One of the chief attractions of credit unions derives from the fact that they are not subject to the interest rate payment ceilings imposed by Regulation Q of the Federal Reserve Board on accounts at commercial banks and savings institutions.

While credit unions accounted for more than 4.5 percent of total savings deposits in the United States as of the end of 1978, their market share vastly exceeded this percentage in a number of states. In Alaska credit unions had a 28 percent share of total savings deposits; in Washington, D.C., their share amounted to 16 percent; in Hawaii, to 15 percent; in Utah, to 14 percent;

and in Colorado, Michigan, New Mexico, Rhode Island, Tennessee, and Texas, to between 8 and 10 percent.

Table 9-9 presents the credit market instrument holdings of credit unions for selected years during the period from 1950 through 1979. As of the end of 1979, more than 85 percent of all credit unions consisted of groups whose common tie was the same employer. As can be seen from the table, total credit market investments of credit unions grew quite rapidly from a very low base of $600 million in 1950 to $57 billion in 1979. The range of credit market instruments held by credit unions is fairly narrow, with no holdings of state and local government obligations (except for property taxes, credit unions are fully exempt from federal, state, and local taxation, thus minimizing the benefit of tax-free income from municipal securities), corporate and foreign bonds, or open-market paper.

As of the end of 1975, the dominant credit market instruments held by credit unions were (1) consumer credit, representing 79.4 percent of total holdings (up from 66 percent as of the end of 1950); (2) federally sponsored agency issues, with 10.9 percent of total holdings (up from no holdings as of the end of 1950); (3) mortgages (primarily on one- to four-family residential dwellings), with 5 percent of total holdings (down from 17 percent as of the end of 1950); and (4) U.S. Treasury securities, representing 4.7 percent of total holdings (also down from 17 percent as of the end of 1950).

TABLE 9-9
Credit Market Instrument Holdings of Credit Unions for Selected Years, 1950–1979
(In billions of dollars)

Credit market instrument category	1950	1955	1960	1965	1970	1975	1979
U.S. government securities	0.1	0.1	0.2	0.3	0.6	1.5	1.3
Federally sponsored agency issues	0.0	0.0	0.0	. . .*	0.8	3.5	3.4
Mortgages†	0.1	0.2	0.4	0.6	0.8	1.6	3.8
Consumer credit	0.4	1.7	3.9	7.3	13.0	25.4	48.2
Total	0.6	2.0	4.5	8.2	15.2	32.0	56.7

SOURCE: *Flow of Funds Accounts,* Board of Governors of the Federal Reserve System. Data for all periods through 1975 are taken from the *Flow of Funds Accounts, 1946–1975,* issued in December 1976; data for periods subsequent to 1975 are taken from the *Flow of Funds Accounts, 1969–1979,* issued in February 1980. Because of occasional revisions in the Flow of Funds Accounts data, certain statistics from the latter source and subsequent releases may vary somewhat from those contained in the *Flow of Funds Accounts, 1946–1975.*

*Less than $50 million.

†Primarily one- to four-family home mortgages.

The investments and operations of federally chartered credit unions are regulated by the National Credit Union Administration. State-chartered credit unions are usually supervised by the state banking superintendent. Member deposits in all federally chartered credit unions and in a large number of state-chartered credit unions are protected by federal share insurance up to a specified limit. Because of extremely low effective taxation expenses (including exemption from federal taxation) and lower fixed and variable costs than those of many other depositary institutions and suppliers of consumer credit, credit unions have been able (1) to expand their deposit base by paying more attractive rates on deposits and (2) to expand their consumer lending efforts by offering credit at lower interest rates than competing lenders. Credit unions are also free of branching restrictions and are not required to maintain reserves at the Federal Reserve Bank.

Credit unions' share of total consumer loans rose from 12 percent at the end of 1969 to 17 percent at the beginning of 1978. Profits or surpluses on lending and investing operations may be distributed to credit union members in the form of rebates on loans or of higher interest rates paid on depositors' accounts.

Consumer credit extended by a credit union is subject to specified absolute limits, with larger amounts allowable for secured loans than for unsecured loans. Maximum lending rates are set for borrowers from federally chartered credit unions. When credit is tight, it is usually rationed through waiting lists rather than through the raising of interest rates charged to borrowers. Until the late 1970s, maturity limits were placed on the lending activity of credit unions, which tended to restrict their investments in mortgages. With the liberalization of some of the maturity limitations on credit union lending in early 1977, credit unions began to expand their lending in mortgages on one- to four-family homes and mobile homes as well as in home improvement loans.

The late 1970s also witnessed a greater diversification of credit union liabilities (and thus a need for increased flexibility in the investment strategy of credit unions) with credit union promotion of their own savings certificates, credit card facilities, and share drafts (which are in effect interest-bearing checking accounts). In 1978 Congress established a Central Liquidity Facility, which can draw funds from the U.S. Department of the Treasury and act as a lender of last resort to credit unions in difficulty. Such measures are necessary when some credit unions are not able to raise maximum interest rates on loans to members even though they may have to pay high rates for funds to supplement members' deposits. If excess funds are not invested in short-term Treasury bills or federal agency securities, credit unions tend to place them in loans to other credit unions, in deposits at savings and loan associations or mutual savings banks, or in deposits at a commercial bank insured by the FDIC. Certain so-called central credit unions act as a source

TABLE 9-10

Annual Net Flows of Funds from Credit Unions into Credit Market Instruments, 1972–1979

(In billions of dollars)

Credit market instrument category	1972	1973	1974	1975	1976	1977	1978	1979
U.S. government securities	. . .*	0.3	0.1	0.3	0.2	0.1	. . .*	− 0.1
Federally sponsored agency issues	0.6	0.2	0.3	0.8	0.5	0.9	. . .*	− 0.4
Mortgages†	0.2	0.4	0.1	0.5	0.2	0.3	0.4	0.5
Consumer credit	2.2	2.7	2.3	3.8	4.9	6.5	8.3	2.2
Total	3.0	3.6	2.8	5.4	5.8	7.8	8.8	2.2

SOURCE: *Flow of Funds Accounts,* Board of Governors of the Federal Reserve System. Data for 1978 and 1979 are taken from the *Flow of Funds Accounts* published in February 1980; data from 1972 to 1977 are taken from earlier years' *Flow of Funds Accounts* statistics.

*Less than $50 million.

†Primarily one- to four-family home mortgages.

of investment and borrowing for other credit unions and serve as a clearinghouse for funds lent by one credit union to another.

Table 9-10 shows the annual net flows of credit unions into credit market instruments for each year during the 1972–1979 period. With the exception of a slight downturn in overall annual credit market instrument flows and specifically flows into extensions of consumer credit in 1974, aggregates for both these measures exhibited steady growth from 1972 through 1977. Some variability in net investment flows was shown in mortgages, which ranged from $100 billion in 1974 to $500 million in 1975, as well as in federal agency issues, in which credit unions invested as little as $200 million in 1973 and as much as $800 million in 1975. Credit unions' net investment flows into U.S. government securities represented a relatively small part of total credit union flows, ranging between $100 million and $300 million from 1972 through 1978. Credit unions' net flows into credit market instruments fell 75 percent between 1978 and 1979, paced by a similarly large decline in their extensions of consumer credit.

10

The Investment Behavior of Insurance Companies and Pension Funds

Overview

Insurance companies and pension funds remain large and growing investors in the bond and money markets. Each of these two broad groups has many subgroups. For example, "insurance companies" include life insurance companies, property-casualty insurance companies, reinsurance companies, captive insurance companies, and several other types of insurance companies. Similarly, "pension funds" encompass private noninsured pension funds, employee benefit and profit sharing plans, and state and local government employee retirement funds.

In their primarily long-term investment orientation, insurance companies and pension funds differ somewhat from many other major classes of investors, but they compete for savings inflows with a wide variety of public and private institutions of both a short-term and a long-term nature. Many functional realignments, changes in tax laws, and regulatory shifts similar to those experienced by commercial banks and thrift institutions during the past decade have also affected the insurance industry and pension funds of all types. The following sections examine the influence of these changes and other factors on the investment behavior of the major groups of insurance companies and pension funds.

Life Insurance Companies

As of the end of 1978, 1824 legal-reserve life insurance companies were operating in the United States and had issued more than 96 percent of the total life insurance in force in the country. Mutual life insurance companies accounted for less than 10 percent of the total number of life insurance concerns and for more than 60 percent of their aggregate assets, whereas stockholder-owned companies represented more than 90 percent of the total number of companies and less than 40 percent of their aggregate assets. These totals and the analysis in this section exclude fraternal benefit societies and certain other organizations (such as savings banks) which also write life insurance. As discussed in connection with Table 8-10 in Chapter 8, the life insurance programs of the United States government are quite substantial. However, because of consolidation with the accounts of the federal government, they are not shown separately under Flow of Funds Accounts conventions.

Figure 10-1 shows the principal earning assets of life insurance companies from 1946 through the late 1970s. Of particular interest are (1) the relatively steady rate of increase in life insurance companies' holdings of corporate bonds (including private placements of corporate debt) and commercial mortgages, (2) a decline in their ownership of residential mortgage debt, and (3) an apparent leveling off in the growth rate in their holdings of multifamily residential mortgages.

Table 10-1 shows the holdings of credit market instruments by life insurance companies for selected years during the period from 1950 through 1979. These holdings are large and diverse. As of the end of 1975, the three largest categories of credit market instruments held by life insurance companies were (1) corporate and foreign bonds (including private placements of corporate debt, in which life insurance companies are by far the largest investors), with 44.9 percent of total credit market instrument holdings (up slightly from 42.8 percent as of the end of 1950); (2) mortgages (of which mortgages on one- to four-family homes accounted for 20 percent, mortgages on multifamily dwellings for 22 percent, mortgages on commercial properties for 50 percent, and mortgages on farm properties for 8 percent of total mortgages held by life insurance companies as a group), representing 38.1 percent of total credit market instrument holdings (up from 27.8 percent as of the end of 1950); and (3) loans (primarily loans made by life insurance companies against the cash surrender value of their policyholders' life insurance and certain limited-term loans to business concerns), representing 10.4 percent of total credit market instrument holdings (up substantially from 4.1 percent as of the end of 1950).

Among additional credit market instrument holdings of life insurance companies at the end of 1975 were (1) open-market paper, representing 2 percent of total credit market instrument holdings (up from no holdings as of the end of 1950); (2) U.S. Treasury securities, with 2 percent of total credit market instrument holdings (down sharply from 23.3 percent as of the end of 1950); (3) state and local government securities, representing 1.9 percent of total credit market instrument holdings (practically unchanged

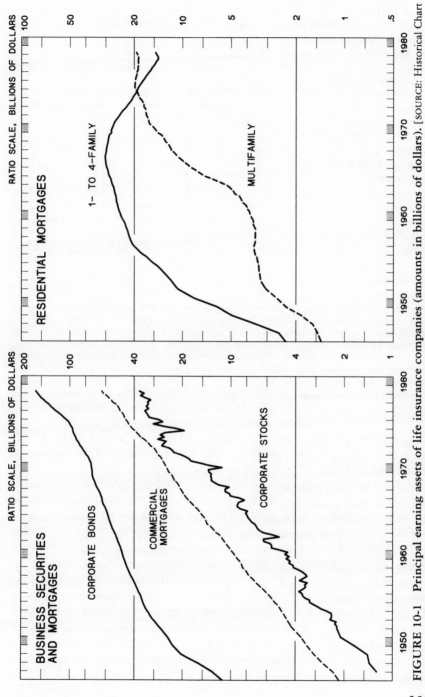

FIGURE 10-1 Principal earning assets of life insurance companies (amounts in billions of dollars). [SOURCE: Historical Chart Book, *Board of Governors of the Federal Reserve System. By permission of the Board of Governors of the Federal Reserve System.*]

TABLE 10-1

Credit Market Instrument Holdings of Life Insurance Companies for Selected Years, 1950–1979

(In billions of dollars)

Credit market instrument category	1950	1955	1960	1965	1970	1975	1979
U.S. Treasury securities	13.5	8.6	6.4	5.1	4.0	4.7	4.8
Federally sponsored agency issues	0.0	0.0	0.1	0.2	0.5	1.4	8.8
State and local government securities	1.2	2.0	3.6	3.5	3.3	4.5	6.4
Corporate and foreign bonds	24.8	37.1	48.1	61.0	74.1	105.5	173.1
Mortgages	16.1	29.4	41.8	60.0	74.4	89.4	119.2
Open-market paper	0.0	0.0	0.3	0.3	2.1	4.8	7.3
Other loans*	2.4	3.3	5.2	7.7	16.1	24.5	34.4
Total	58.0	80.4	105.5	137.8	174.5	234.8	353.8
Memorandum:							
Corporate equities†	2.1	3.6	5.0	9.1	15.4	28.1	40.1

SOURCE: *Flow of Funds Accounts,* Board of Governors of the Federal Reserve System. Data for all periods through 1975 are taken from the *Flow of Funds Accounts, 1946–1975,* issued in December 1976; data for periods subsequent to 1975 are taken from the *Flow of Funds Accounts, 1969–1979,* issued in February 1980. Because of occasional revisions in the Flow of Funds Accounts data, certain statistics from the latter source and subsequent releases may vary somewhat from those contained in the *Flow of Funds Accounts, 1946–1975.*

*Principally loans made against the cash surrender value of policyholders' life insurance.

†Includes both convertible and nonconvertible preferred stock as well as common stock.

from 2.1 percent at the end of 1950); and (4) federal agency issues, with 0.6 percent of total credit market instrument holdings (up from no holdings as of the end of 1950).

Table 10-2 shows the net annual flows of life insurance companies' funds into credit market instruments during the 1972–1979 period. Total flows by life insurance companies into credit market instruments increased throughout the 1972–1979 period, rising from $9.7 billion in 1972 to $35 billion in 1979. With the exception of 1974, when life insurance companies' investments in corporate and foreign bonds (including private placements) amounted to 31 percent of the companies' total purchases of credit market instruments, corporate and foreign bond investments accounted for between 45 and 72 percent of total annual investments in these instruments by life insurance companies. Relatively high purchases of mortgages, a cyclical high in loans extended to policyholders, and comparatively large investments in then high-yielding open-market paper helped account for the lower levels of corporate and foreign bond purchases in 1974.

The annual volume of mortgage investments by life insurance companies was relatively volatile during the 1972–1979 period, varying by more than 70 percent upward and downward from the $5.3 billion average for each year during this period. Loans made to policyholders usually accounted for less than 15 percent of annual net purchases of credit market instruments except for 1973 and 1974, when such loans amounted to $2.2 billion and $2.7 billion respectively and accounted for 18 and 21 percent respectively of total life insurance company net flows into credit market instruments. Life insurance companies' purchases of open-market paper, state and local government obligations, U.S. Treasury securities, and federal agency issues also varied relatively widely, with significant net sales of federal agency issues amounting to $900 million in 1976 and $1.4 billion in 1977.

The investment policies of life insurance companies are greatly influenced by (1) the long-term nature of their business, under which constant annual premiums received from the sale of multiyear policies are invested to meet actuarially determinable liabilities and other payments in the future because of death, disability, policy surrender, or dividend payments (representing a return of that part of insurance premiums which proved higher than necessary to meet obligations) made by certain life insurance companies to their owners and/or policyholders; and (2) substantial and regular inflows of cash in addition to premium payments, including prepayments and amortization

TABLE 10-2

Annual Net Flows of Funds from Life Insurance Companies into Credit Market Instruments, 1972–1979

(In billions of dollars)

Credit market instrument category	1972	1973	1974	1975	1976	1977	1978	1979
U.S. Treasury securities	. . .*	−0.4	−0.1	1.4	0.6	0.8	−0.5	. . .*
Federally sponsored agency issues	0.1	0.1	0.2	0.4	−0.9	−1.4	2.5	2.3
State and local government securities	. . .*	. . .*	0.3	0.8	1.1	0.5	0.4	. . .*
Corporate and foreign bonds	7.0	5.9	4.0	9.1	16.9	15.8	17.3	14.6
Mortgages	1.5	4.4	4.9	2.9	2.4	4.1	9.2	13.0
Open-market paper	0.2	. . .*	1.1	0.7	0.4	2.7	1.5	0.9
Other loans†	0.9	2.2	2.7	1.6	1.4	1.7	2.6	4.3
Total	9.7	12.3	13.1	16.9	23.7	27.0	32.9	34.9

SOURCE: *Flow of Funds Accounts,* Board of Governors of the Federal Reserve System. Data for 1978 and 1979 are taken from the *Flow of Funds Accounts* published in February 1980; data from 1972 to 1977 are taken from earlier years' *Flow of Funds Accounts* statistics.

*Less than $50 million.

†Principally loans made against the cash surrender value of policyholders' life insurance.

of mortgages and bonds, interest, and dividend receipts from portfolio investments.

Another moderate but growing influence on life insurance investment practices has been the introduction of new forms of insurance policies. Such insurance includes (1) adjustable life policies which permit policyholders to change the term and amount of coverage and to switch from term insurance to whole-life insurance and back again, (2) policies whose face amounts change annually, with periodically scheduled adjustments in premium payments, and (3) whole-life policies whose premiums are adjusted to reflect changing investment returns and mortality rates.

Of the $2.9 trillion of life insurance in force at the end of 1978, 50 percent was ordinary life insurance (including both *term* policies, which generally remain in force for a specified time period and do not build up cash surrender values, and other types of life policies, often called *whole-life, endowment,* or *permanent* insurance, most of which build up cash surrender values that represent premiums paid in excess of the costs of insurance protection and which can be drawn upon by a policyholder to meet special needs. Life insurance can also be divided into *nonparticipating* insurance, which does not pay dividends to policyholders, and *participating* insurance, which pays dividends based on a company's investment and underwriting performance.

Group life insurance (usually purchased in term form by unions, professional associations, and employers under master contracts for qualifying members or employees) accounted for 43 percent of total life insurance in force at the end of 1978; another 6 percent was *credit* life insurance (which is structured to repay the outstanding balance of debts of 10 years' maturity or less if the borrower should die), and 1 percent was *industrial,* or *debit,* life insurance (which is usually issued with small face amounts and is paid for on a monthly or even a weekly basis).

Life insurance companies also sell individual health insurance, group accident and health insurance, and annuities, which contract to provide annuitants with current or future regular income payments. According to the type of annuity purchased, these income payments may be for a fixed amount or for a variable amount (greater flexibility is allowed for the investment of reserves behind variable annuities).

In recent years, insurance companies have become active in three additional product lines. First, insurers act in some cases as guarantors of commercial paper issued by other firms. Second, insurers have issued surety bonds and other insurance policies to guarantee certain types of corporate and municipal debt securities. Third, as mentioned in Chapter 9, many insurance companies began in the 1970s to issue various forms of guaranteed-return plans, also known as guaranteed-income contracts (GICs). Such contracts generally offer a fixed interest rate on funds that must be kept with the insurance company for a specified number of years. These plans have received some degree of acceptance by pension fund sponsors.

TABLE 10-3
Income of United States Life Insurance Companies for Selected Years,
1950–1978
(In millions of dollars)

	Premium receipts						
Year	Life insurance premiums	Annuity considera- tions	Health insurance premiums*	Total premium receipts	Investment income†	Other income‡	Total income
1950	6,249	939	$1,001	8,189	2,075	1,073	11,337
1955	8,903	1,288	2,355	12,546	2,801	1,197	16,544
1960	11,998	1,341	4,026	17,365	4,304	1,338	23,007
1965	16,083	2,260	6,261	24,604	6,778	1,785	33,167
1966	17,160	2,416	7,244	26,820	7,353	1,961	36,134
1967	18,094	2,671	7,887	28,652	7,929	2,054	38,635
1968	19,364	2,993	8,730	31,087	8,613	2,163	41,863
1969	20,491	3,762	9,743	33,996	9,354	2,278	45,628
1970	21,679	3,721	11,367	36,767	10,144	2,143	49,054
1971	22,935	4,910	12,897	40,742	11,031	2,429	54,202
1972	24,678	5,503	14,318	44,499	12,127	2,222	58,848
1973	26,373	6,771	15,524	48,668	13,670	2,415	64,753
1974	27,750	7,737	17,123	52,610	15,144	2,256	70,010
1975	29,336	10,165	19,074	58,575	16,488	2,959	78,022
1976	31,358	13,962	21,059	66,379	18,758	3,421	88,558
1977	33,765	14,974	23,580	72,319	21,713	3,953	97,985
1978	36,592	16,339	25,829	78,760	25,294	4,152	108,206

SOURCES: *Spectator Year Book;* American Council of Life Insurance, *1980 Life Insurance Fact Book.*
*Includes some premiums for workmen's compensation and automobile and other liability insurance.
†After 1951 investment income is net of investment expenses.
‡Includes considerations for supplementary contracts with and without life contingencies. After 1975 other income includes commissions and expense allowance on reinsurance ceded.

Table 10-3 shows the relative importance of the various types of premium receipts, investment income, and other income for life insurance companies for selected years from 1950 through 1978. Total premium receipts (of which life insurance premiums represented 46.5 percent) accounted for 73 percent, investment income for 21 percent, and other income for 4 percent of the $108.2 billion in total income received by life insurance companies during 1978. As of the end of 1978, the policy reserves established by insurance companies to meet their future commitments to beneficiaries and-/or policyholders amounted to $318.5 billion, of which 56 percent, or $177.7 billion, covered life insurance policies, 3 percent, or $9.6 billion, covered health insurance policies, and 41 percent, or $131.2 billion, covered annuities, group policies, and other supplementary contracts.

The specific amount of policy reserves required to be maintained behind each type of insurance obligation, annuity, or other future contract liability is determined by state insurance regulations and actuarial assumptions concerning future interest rates, premium inflows, mortality experience, and other factors affecting the necessity and the ability of life insurance companies to meet policy obligations which fall due in the future. For example, lesser amounts of policy reserves are required to be held against term insurance in force than against nonterm insurance in force, since the insurance protection expires after a stated period for term insurance unless it is renewed for an additional period through additional premium payments by the policyholder. With the rapid growth of group life insurance in force (primarily term insurance), from 20 percent of total insurance in force at the end of 1950 to 30 percent, 39 percent, and 43 percent of total insurance in force at the end of 1960, 1970, and 1978 respectively, the policy reserves of life insurance companies have grown more slowly than the increase in total insurance in force.

In addition to policy reserves amounting to $318.5 billion as of the end of 1978, life insurance companies had (1) $11.3 billion in previously accumulated policy dividends left with the companies by policyholders to earn interest, (2) $6.4 billion earmarked for dividend payments or credits to policyholders during 1979, (3) $27.5 billion for liabilities such as policyholders' prepaid insurance premiums, required reserves for variations in security values, and expenses incurred but not yet paid, (4) $24.3 billion in special and unclassified surplus funds (established to meet contingencies and as additional backing for policy liabilities), and (5) $2 billion in capital funds of companies owned by stockholders. The year-end 1978 contingency reserves, capital, and surpluses of life insurance companies as a group amounted to just over 6.7 percent of their total assets. Taken together, the policy reserves, contingency reserves, capital, and surplus funds of the life insurance industry at the end of 1978 totaled $389.9 billion, of which $318.5 billion was invested in credit market instruments, $11.8 billion in real estate, $35.5 billion in common and preferred stocks, and $24.1 billion in miscellaneous assets.

Investment Policy

Reserve requirements, asset valuation rules, and regulatory constraints cause life insurance companies to emphasize solvency as the primary investment objective, followed by high and predictable rates of return on investment with minimum risk of loss. Income is of much greater relative importance than capital gains. Because policyholders of mutual life insurance companies can immediately share in higher realized portfolio yields, *mutual* companies tend to be less interested than *stockholder-owned* life insurance companies in capital gains.

Owing to relatively low income tax rates, both types of life insurance companies do not find that the 85 percent intercorporate dividend exclusion offers significant advantages from *dividend receipts* (which also can vary according to corporate and economic conditions) as opposed to *interest income* (which tends to be less variable than dividend income). In general, any sale of investments at a loss necessitates a reduction in a life insurance company's surplus unless it is offset by capital gains. These parameters, coupled with the fact that a substantial part of life insurance companies' obligations are of a fixed-dollar nature, have led to an investment concentration on intermediate-to long-term debt instruments such as mortgages and corporate and foreign bonds, but at the same time they have permitted a relatively wide range of investments, including real estate, common and preferred stocks, and seven different categories of credit market instruments.

Balanced against the needs of life insurance companies for steady and high income returns is a need for adequate levels of liquidity. In general, the liquidity needs of an insurance company depend upon (1) its size and experience in the industry; (2) the diversification of its investments by industry, by geographic area, and by type of instrument; (3) the mix of annuities and whole-life insurance in force as compared with group life and other types of short-term life insurance policies; (4) the quality of and the absolute rate of return from the investment portfolio; (5) expected policy claims, loans, and surrenders and the absolute amounts of cash outflow associated with each; (6) the cash demands of operating the business; and (7) management's judgment concerning the possibility of below-normal cash inflows, above-normal cash outflows, or especially attractive unforeseen investment opportunities.

As reviewed in the earlier discussion of Table 10-1, the levels of life insurance company holdings of U.S. Treasury and federal agency securities were considerably lower in the late 1960s and the 1970s than in the 1940s and early 1950s. In part, this was due to the higher yields on corporate securities than on equivalent-maturity U.S. Treasury and federal agency issues as well as to a relatively greater availability of current-coupon, long-maturity, deferred-redemption issues in the corporate sector.

In the corporate sector, a large part of life insurance companies' investments in bonds is accounted for by private placements, which provide a higher interest return than otherwise-equivalent corporate issues. The amount of yield advantage depends upon financial market conditions and other factors and represents compensation for lower liquidity in private placements than in corporate bonds and the flexibility in terms which private placements permit the borrowing entity to negotiate with the lender.

Since a certain amount of the private placements held by life insurance companies may be renegotiated as to interest rate, maturity, or other terms by the borrower in connection with additional financing, the acquisitions and disposals figures for corporate bonds in a given year may not accurately depict actual cash flows as much as transfers and other bookkeeping adjustments. Another part of the private-placement process is the so-called *forward commitment* (perhaps used even more frequently in mortgage lending by life insurance companies), which allows both the borrower and the lender to schedule their cash flows in advance (generally by 6 to 18 months) of the actual transfer of funds (this is sometimes called a *delayed takedown,* which also occurs from time to time in bond issues) at an agreed-upon interest rate usually relating more to current than to future yield levels.

As of the end of 1978, life insurance companies held $156 billion in corporate bonds, of which $105.5 billion consisted of industrial issues (in which most life insurance companies' private-placement activities are concentrated), $37.4 billion consisted of utility bonds (by law private placements are not permitted for certain utilities), and $4.3 billion consisted of railroad bonds. Investments in preferred stock amounted to $10.5 billion at the end of 1978.

Foreign governmental and foreign corporate bond investments are purchased by life insurance companies partly because of their attractive yield and largely to meet other countries' requirements that a specified amount of securities of issuers of a certain country be held in connection with operations conducted by the life insurance companies within that country. As of the end of 1978, United States domestic life insurance companies owned $8.8 billion in securities of foreign governments and international and regional organizations, of which $7 billion represented Canadian governmental issuers at all levels (federal, provincial, and municipal). Besides Canadian issues, the largest life insurance company holdings of foreign governmental issues were those of Australia, Israel, Japan, Mexico, and Panama. In addition to these Canadian and other foreign governmental issues, at the end of 1978 United States domestic life insurance companies owned $8.9 billion in securities of foreign corporate borrowers, primarily domiciled in Canada.

Owing to their relative security, generally long maturities, and high yields, mortgages are the second most important investment outlet for life insurance companies after corporate and foreign bonds. In contrast to an emphasis on one- to four-family residential mortgages in the early 1950s, life insurance companies became important factors in and directed greater amounts of funds into mortgages on multifamily housing properties, commercial facilities, and farm properties from the mid-1950s through the early 1980s. This trend was due in part to higher yields on farm, commercial, and multifamily residential mortgages than on one- to four-family residential mortgages and in part to increased lending competition in one- to four-family home mortgages from savings and loan associations and mutual savings banks.

As of the end of 1978, life insurance companies' holdings of mortgages on commercial properties, amounting to $62.4 billion, accounted for 29 percent of all such mortgages outstanding, and their holdings of mortgages on one- to four-family residential dwellings, amounting to $18.3 billion, accounted for 4 percent of all such mortgage debt. A total of 9 percent of all mortgages held by life insurance companies carried some form of governmental insurance or guarantees, the remaining 91 percent being represented by conventional mortgages. In the 1960s and 1970s, life insurance companies' mortgages on commercial properties exhibited particularly rapid growth in such areas as shopping centers, retail stores, medical facilities, and office buildings.

Life insurance company policy loans to policyholders against the accumulated cash value of their policies tend to increase in periods of high and rising interest rates because of the usually lower interest rates guaranteed in the terms of a life insurance policy. The actual interest rate on policy loans depends on when and in what state the policy was purchased as well as on the company writing the policy. Net increases in policy loans tend to divert funds which life insurance companies would otherwise have available for investment in corporate and foreign bonds, mortgages, or other credit market instruments. To meet unexpected short-term increases in policy loan demand, in the past some life insurance companies have been forced to reduce their investment commitments, to sell securities from their portfolios, or, in a number of cases, to draw upon borrowing facilities at commercial banks.

Beginning in the mid-1970s, a number of life insurance companies began to make short- and intermediate-term loans through their head offices and through regional lending offices to medium-size businesses. In addition, in the late 1970s life insurance companies selectively entered the market for construction loans (usually of up to 36 months' maturity) to real estate developers. Such an emphasis on corporate loans, with shorter (or nonexistent) forward commitment periods than those of many mortgage and private-placement investments, has tended to allow somewhat greater latitude in diverting funds to policy loans in periods of rising interest rates. As mentioned earlier, some insurance companies have also made loan standby commitments to guarantee certain companies' commercial paper, with a deductible provision mandating that, in the event of financial difficulty, the commercial-paper issuer will pay a stated part of the commercial-paper borrowing before the insurance company provides the additional funds promised under the guarantee program.

The level of investment by life insurance companies in corporate equities, including both common and preferred stocks, and in real estate can also influence funds flows by life insurance companies into credit market instruments. Because of legal restrictions and a high need for fixed-income flows, life insurance companies' investments in corporate equities have remained modest. Between 1970 and 1975 they represented between 9 and 12 percent of their total credit market instrument holdings (but were not included in such holdings). Because common stocks must be carried on life insurance companies' books at market value while preferred stocks, bonds, and mortgages can be carried at amortized cost or other relatively stable valuation methods, the price fluctuations of common stocks also affect the propensity of life insurance companies to invest in common equities. With greater management of private pension plans in accounts separate from life insurance companies' other assets and with increased offerings of variable annuities, life insurance companies gradually increased their investments in corporate equities during the 1970s.

Life insurance companies directly owned $11.8 billion in real estate at the end of 1978, up from $1.4 billion, $3.8 billion, and $6.3 billion at the end of 1950, 1960, and 1970 respectively. Approximately 21 percent of their real estate holdings represented offices for their own use, about 68 percent was accounted for by investment holdings of multifamily residential complexes and commercial properties, and roughly 11 percent represented properties acquired in settlement of mortgage debt and other types of properties.

Because all benefits payable to policyholders are tax-deductible by life insurance companies, tax exemption is not an important factor in investment selection. Since the investment income of life insurance companies becomes taxable only on that portion of income carried over into surplus accounts, the effective tax rate ranges from 0 percent to the full corporate income tax rate, depending upon the source; in the aggregate, the average tax rate on life insurance companies' total investment income ranges between 10 and 12 percent.

Federal income taxes rose significantly after the passage of the Life Insurance Company Income Tax Act of 1959, and the federal income tax treatment of life insurance companies began to be modified in the late 1970s as a result of the trend toward more equal taxation of various types of financial institutions. Of the $5.1 billion in taxes, licenses, and fees paid by life insurance companies in 1978, 59 percent represented federal income taxes, 21 percent state taxes on premium income, 8 percent federal social security taxes, 7 percent real estate taxes, and 5 percent other licenses, taxes, and fees.

Pension Plans Managed by Life Insurance Companies

As of the end of 1978, life insurance companies managed pension plans with total reserves of $119.1 billion (an increase of over 200 percent from the end of 1968), of which 77 percent represented group annuities, 3 percent terminal funded group plans, 5 percent individual policy pension trusts, 2 percent Keogh plans, 5 percent tax-sheltered annuities, 2 percent individual retirement accounts (IRAs), and 6 percent other forms of pension plans. Of the $119.1 billion of reserves behind private pension plans managed by life insurance companies, 84 percent represented reserves behind some form of insured or guaranteed annuity or other retirement plan, and 16 percent assets held in so-called special accounts.

As mentioned earlier, separate accounts permitting greater investment flexibility for the management of certain risk-sharing pension reserves (under the stewardship of life insurance companies) are allowed by most states, since (1) these funds carry no payment guarantee similar to that implied in the general accounts backing life insurance policies or guaranteed investment plans and (2) the beneficiary shares in the market risk of the investments. As of the end of 1978, a total of $19.3 billion was invested in separate accounts by life insurance companies; of this a very substantial proportion was in common stocks. In addition to the various types of group annuities reviewed earlier, individual annuities (including those set up as part of a Keogh plan or an IRA) can be purchased to provide a guaranteed income of a predetermined amount over a specified time period or for the remaining lifetime of the annuitant. *Variable annuities* may provide for variable income payments to the annuitant, with the amount of payment depending upon a chosen index or the performance of the separate investment account backing the annuity.

Regulation

Life insurance company operations and investments are regulated by insurance commissioners at the state level. The directors of state insurance commissions are often political appointees and usually stress conservative investment practices in the supervision of life insurance companies. State regulators also insist upon very conservative accounting rules for the insurance industry. These rules are somewhat different from the generally accepted accounting principles (GAAP) required by the Financial Accounting Standards Board (FASB) to be published by stockholder-owned insurance companies. In addition to compliance with the laws of the state in which they are chartered, life insurance companies must conform in many respects to the laws of the states in which they *write* insurance.

Because a number of the largest life insurance companies are headquartered in New York State and most of the large life insurance companies want to sell insurance there, the laws of New York State covering the insurance industry have been used as models by many other states. The National Association of Insurance Commissioners has also assisted in unifying many state regulations in such areas as agent licensing, issuance of debt securities, minimum and maximum premium rates on certain lines of insurance, and the evaluation and disposition of assets. These latter guidelines require each life insurance company to maintain so-called admitted assets at least equal to policy reserves. Furthermore, state regulations usually set forth (1) percentage limits on conventional mortgage holdings relative to total assets; (2) maximum loan-value ratios on mortgages (usually below those allowed for savings and loan associations and mutual savings banks); (3) reserve levels against holdings of lower-quality bonds as well as preferred stocks; (4) rules for valuing certain securities which have not met scheduled interest, dividend, or sinking-fund payments; (5) limitations on common stock and direct real estate ownership; and (6) an allowable percentage of assets (usually around 3 to 4 percent, in a provision often referred to as a basket clause) which can be invested in investments that otherwise are limited or ineligible.

Property-Casualty and Other Insurance Companies

As of late 1980, more than 1000 property-casualty insurance concerns were operating in the United States. Property-casualty insurance encompasses *consumer*-oriented insurance such as automobile, physical, bodily-injury, and property damage insurance and householders' fire, hail, windstorm, theft, and liability insurance, as well as *corporate*-related insurance products such as industrial fire insurance, marine and aviation insurance, general liability insurance (often purchased by such parties as doctors, accountants, company directors, aircraft-manufacturing firms, and others), engineering insurance, catastrophe insurance, workers' compensation, and fidelity and surety insurance.

Beginning in the 1970s, several property-casualty insurers began to offer various forms of *replacement-value* insurance coverage to homeowners and apartment dwellers. With a wide range of exclusions, ceilings, and deductibles, replacement-value insurance also varies considerably in its premiums with the type and location of dwelling units. Other conditions imposed on replacement-value insurance often include (1) exclusion of certain types of goods (such as antiques or art) which cannot easily be replaced by new articles, (2) maximum percentages of an article's value that will be paid at the time of loss, and (3) an option of replacing a lost or damaged article with a new item or accepting in cash the actual *depreciated* value of the item at the time of loss.

Approximately 25 percent of the property-casualty insurance companies are stockholder-owned; they account for 66 percent of all property-casualty insurance in force. The remaining 75 percent of the property-casualty insurance firms are mutual companies; they account for 34 percent of the property-casualty insurance in force. Both groups compete with some life insurance companies that write sickness and accident insurance, with nonprofit hospital-medical associations, and with state workmen's compensation funds.

Property-casualty insurance is also written by so-called *reciprocals,* which are cooperative nonprofit arrangements whereby participants contract to share the losses of fellow subscribers and the expenses of establishing a central office for the reciprocal. Another form of entity which writes property-casualty insurance is the so-called *domestic Lloyd's,* which is an association of unincorporated individual underwriters who share individually to varying extents in risks accepted by the association.

The property-casualty insurance companies (also known as property-liability, fire and casualty, or fire and accident insurance companies), together with a number of other insurance companies, comprise the "other insurance companies" category in the Flow of Funds Accounts. Because property-casualty insurance companies represent a very large proportion of aggregate investment data for this category, it is often referred to as "property-casualty and other insurance companies." Nevertheless, it is worth remembering that the activities of certain other types of insurance companies are included in this category; they will be discussed at the end of this section.

Table 10-4 shows the credit market instrument holdings of property-casualty and other insurance companies for selected years during the 1950–1979 period. As of the end of 1975, property-casualty insurance companies owned the following percentages of their total credit market instrument

TABLE 10-4
Credit Market Instrument Holdings of Property-Casualty and Other Insurance Companies for Selected Years, 1950–1979
(In billions of dollars)

Credit market instrument category	1950	1955	1960	1965	1970	1975	1979
U.S. Treasury securities	5.3	6.0	5.4	5.5	3.4	4.7	11.9
Federally sponsored agency issues	0.0	0.0	0.1	0.6	1.6	2.3	6.8
State and local government securities	1.1	4.2	8.2	11.3	17.8	34.3	74.7
Corporate and foreign bonds	0.7	1.2	1.7	3.0	8.6	12.2	22.2
Mortgages*	0.1	0.2	0.1	0.1	0.2	0.2	0.3
Total	7.2	11.6	15.5	20.5	31.6	53.7	115.9
Memorandum:							
Corporate equities†	2.6	5.4	7.5	12.0	13.2	14.3	25.6

SOURCE: *Flow of Funds Accounts,* Board of Governors of the Federal Reserve System. Data for all periods through 1975 are taken from the *Flow of Funds Accounts, 1946–1975,* issued in December 1976; data for periods subsequent to 1975 are taken from the *Flow of Funds Accounts, 1969–1979,* issued in February 1980. Because of occasional revisions in the Flow of Funds Accounts data, certain statistics from the latter source and subsequent releases may vary somewhat from those contained in the *Flow of Funds Accounts, 1946–1975.*

*Primarily mortgages against commercial properties.

†Includes both convertible and nonconvertible preferred stock as well as common stock.

holdings: (1) state and local government obligations (of which revenue bonds accounted for more than 60 percent of total municipal holdings by property-casualty insurance companies, up from under 30 percent at the end of 1950), with 63.9 percent of the total (up sharply from 15.3 percent of total credit market instrument holdings at the end of 1950); (2) corporate bonds, representing 22.7 percent of the total (more than twice the 9.7 percent share of total credit market instrument holdings at the end of 1950); (3) U.S. Treasury securities (of which 33 percent were Treasury bills and other issues with less than 1 year remaining to maturity), with 8.8 percent of the total (down sharply from 73.6 percent at the end of 1950); (4) federal agency issues, representing 4.3 percent of the total (up from no holdings at the end of 1950); and (5) mortgages on commercial property, with 0.4 percent of the total (down from 1.4 percent at the end of 1950).

Table 10-5 presents the flows into credit market instruments by property-casualty and other insurance companies for the years 1972 through 1979. With the exception of 1973, when total credit market investments by property-casualty and other insurance companies declined from the previous year, such investments by property-casualty and other insurance companies grew each year during the 1972–1979 period, from $3.7 billion in 1972 to $16.4 billion in 1979.

Property-casualty and other insurance companies' investments in state and local government securities moved steadily downward from $4.3 billion in 1972 to a low point of $2.2 billion in 1974, recovering each year to $16

TABLE 10-5
Annual Net Flows from Property-Casualty and Other Insurance Companies into Credit Market Instruments, 1972–1979
(In billions of dollars)

Credit market instrument category	1972	1973	1974	1975	1976	1977	1978	1979
U.S. Treasury securities	−0.3	−0.1	. . .*	1.9	2.0	2.4	0.9	1.2
Federally sponsored agency issues	0.4	. . .*	0.4	0.6	−0.4	−0.5	0.4	1.6
State and local government securities	4.3	3.6	2.2	2.6	4.2	9.4	13.1	12.3
Corporate and foreign bonds	−0.7	−0.1	2.0	2.2	2.0	0.3	1.6	0.9
Mortgages†	. . .*	. . .*	. . .*	0.1	. . .*	0.1	. . .*	−0.1
Total	3.7	3.4	4.6	7.4	7.8	11.7	15.3	16.4

SOURCE: *Flow of Funds Accounts,* Board of Governors of the Federal Reserve System. Data for 1978 and 1979 are taken from the *Flow of Funds Accounts* published in February 1980; data from 1972 to 1977 are taken from earlier years' *Flow of Funds Accounts* statistics.
*Less than $50 million.
†Primarily loans against commercial properties.

billion in 1979. As discussed later in this section, the propensity of property-casualty and other insurance companies to invest in municipal securities correlates with their need to earn tax-exempt income. When losses in other investment or operating areas can be used to shelter normally taxable income, property-casualty insurance companies tend to restrict acquisition of state and local issues in favor of corporate bonds. This was the case when property-casualty insurance companies shifted from net sales of $0.7 billion and $0.1 billion of corporate bonds in 1972 and 1973 respectively to net purchases of $2 billion and $2.2 billion in 1974 and 1975 respectively. As mentioned earlier, property-casualty and other insurance companies reduced their purchases of state and local government securities in 1974 and 1975 because of a lessened need for tax-exempt income. In part because of earnings pressures experienced during this period, the Tax Reform Act of 1976 permitted multiline property-casualty insurance companies to consolidate their life insurance operations with their property-casualty operations for tax purposes rather than filing separate returns. To some degree, this provision tended to reduce the wide swings between taxable and tax-exempt debt securities by multiline property-casualty insurance companies.

Nature of Property-Casualty Insurance

Property-casualty insurance is quite different from life insurance. While a life insurance contract usually involves the payment of a fixed premium extending for a known period of time (term insurance) or for the remaining lifetime of a policyholder (which is unknown in each individual case but which is calculable on the average for large numbers of policyholders through mortality tables and actuarial methods), the insurance contracts of property-casualty insurance companies usually last from 1 to 3 years, with revisions allowable in insurance rates when a contract is renewed. The new insurance rates are based upon the experience of the expiring contract period.

Payments to a beneficiary by a life insurance company are a known quantity and can be actuarially estimated to a fair degree of accuracy, whereas the size and timing of claims payments for a property-casualty insurance company are much more uncertain because of (1) variations in court awards in liability suits, (2) fluctuations in the costs of damage repair due to inflation or deflation, (3) the unpredictability of damage claims which might arise owing to severe weather, floods, or fire, and (4) possible delays between the time of an accident and the resultant payment by the property-casualty insurance company. Because of these uncertainties, a property-casualty insurance company generally must hold larger amounts available than a life insurance company does to be paid out quickly at an unknown time. Such liquidity needs tend to cause property-casualty insurance companies to hold proportionately more liquid assets (such as short-term U.S. Treasury and federal agency securities) than life insurance companies and are a major reason why they have invested only a nominal amount of funds in mortgages. Property-casualty insurance companies thus pay close attention to the ratio of (1) cash, accounts receivable, and bonds to total liabilities and (2) total liabilities to capital funds.

Underwriting

Property-casualty insurance companies usually divide their activities into *underwriting* operations and *investment* operations. The underwriting operations reflect the profitability of insurance activities after all claims and expenses have been subtracted from applicable premium income. The profitability of property-casualty insurance companies' underwriting operations is generally expressed in terms of the so-called *combined ratio* (also called the underwriting ratio), expressed as:

$$\text{Combined ratio} = \frac{\text{total claims and expenses}}{\text{total premium income}} \times 100$$

If the combined ratio is less than 100, underwriting operations are profitable, since total claims and expenses are less than premium income. If the combined ratio is greater than 100, underwriting operations are unprofitable, since total claims and expenses are greater than premium income. Among other factors, the profitability of underwriting operations depends upon (1) insurance premium rates, which are not fixed and are thus subject to competitive pressures but which tend to rise slowly because of the need to obtain approval for maximum rate levels on various kinds of insurance (rates on some types of commercial insurance are set by negotiation, not by regulation) from the appropriate state insurance commission (certain states require no prior approval for rate increases) and because of the fact that even when approval to raise rates has been granted, the property-casualty insurance company must often wait until existing insurance contracts expire before implementing the new rate schedules; (2) the presence or absence of severe weather and/or natural disasters; (3) price inflation or deflation in the costs of claims settlements; (4) the degree of participation in mandated risk-sharing pools which provide coverage to certain otherwise-uninsurable risks; and (5) the reserve structure of the property-casualty insurance company.

Investments

The profitability of underwriting operations tends to move in fairly consistent cycles of losses, succeeded by profits for a time and then succeeded by losses. This cyclicality is often accentuated by (1) intense price competition in years immediately following periods of high underwriting profits, (2) delays by state regulators in granting rate increases after high-profit years, (3) significant changes in claims settlement costs due to changes in the price level and in jury awards, and (4) regulatory rate relief and price increases caused by heavy underwriting losses, which lead to the restoration of profitability and the recommencement of a new profit cycle. During underwriting loss periods, investment income earned from the operations of the investment portfolio both represents the primary source of earnings and is a major factor in the long-term stability of a property-casualty insurance company. Whereas income from investment operations was originally intended to supplement the cyclicality of income from underwriting operations, by the 1970s on an ongoing aftertax basis investment income had become more important than underwriting income in the composition of total property-casualty insurance company income. In part this change was due to the growth of the investment portfolios of property-casualty insurance companies, the cyclicality of underwriting operations, and the fact that investment income is often partially or totally tax-exempt while income from underwriting operations is subject to the corporate tax rate except when previous years' losses from underwriting or investing operations can be used to offset such income.

In general, property-casualty insurance companies must invest 50 percent of all earned premiums plus all so-called *unearned premiums* (which represent policyholders' prepaid insurance premiums) in high-quality bonds and certain other specified credit market instruments, to be set aside as reserves for claims payments. Besides such premium reserves, investment income can be generated from *loss reserves* (also known as *claim reserves*), which are set aside to cover potential liabilities that have already occurred but whose full costs will not be completely investigated or settled for some time, perhaps for years. The amount of loss reserves tends to rise as more liability insurance (as opposed to property insurance) is written, since the delay between receiving premiums and paying off claims is longer on liability insurance. Much greater flexibility is allowed in the investment of capital reserves and surplus, which can be placed in a broader range of credit market instruments, some mortgages, and corporate equities (although common and preferred stocks must be valued at year-end market values while other investments can be valued at cost). Effective December 31, 1978, the National Association of Insurance Commissioners (NAIC) issued a ruling which allowed all non-life insurance companies to value preferred stock in good standing (as defined by the NAIC) at cost for statement purposes if the security was subject to a 100 percent mandatory sinking fund which fulfilled certain conditions as to the amount and timing of preferred stock sinking-fund purchases.

Among other factors, the level of aftertax investment income of a property-casualty insurance company is a function of (1) the company's effective tax rate, (2) capital gains or losses on its portfolio holdings, (3) the company's selection of investments, (4) the amount of new funds available for investment through growth in premium income and reserves as well as the insurance company's own capital and surplus, and (5) the absolute level of return generated from the portfolio in the form of interest and dividend receipts. Since both mutual and stockholder-owned property-casualty insurance companies are taxed (although somewhat differently) at the corporate tax rate and since their premium income, investment income, and contributions to reserves are fully taxable (while claims payments are deductible from taxable income), municipal securities are quite attractive to these companies during periods of increasing insurance rates and concomitant high or improving underwriting profitability because of their usual aftertax yield advantages compared with more highly taxable interest payments on corporate, federal agency, and U.S. Treasury securities.

Because of the 85 percent exclusion on intercorporate dividend payments, common and preferred stock dividend income is also attractive to property-casualty insurance companies. When underwriting operations produce losses, municipal interest income declines somewhat in relative attractiveness, since greater amounts of fully taxable income can be sheltered through deductions of such losses from taxable income. Thus, property-casualty insurance companies tend to purchase more corporate, federal agency, and U.S. Treasury securities and less municipal securities in periods of unprofitable underwriting activity. As of the end of 1977, with the maximum corporate tax rate at 48 percent, the effective tax rate for a corporate dividend recipient was equivalent to:

100 percent dividend income — 85 percent corporate dividend exclusion
= 15 percent taxable income × 48 percent corporate income tax rate
= 7.2 percent effective tax on corporate dividend receipts

A property-casualty insurance company usually seeks to lower its investment risk if its insurance risk is deemed to be substantial. Conversely, if its insurance risk is judged to be relatively low, a property-casualty insurance company usually allows itself to take a somewhat greater investment risk. The *insurance risk* of a property-casualty insurance company is measured in one way by the following ratio:

$$\text{Insurance risk} = \frac{\text{annual premium income}}{\text{total capital and surplus}}$$

The *investment risk* of a property-casualty insurance company is measured in one way by the following ratio:

$$\text{Investment risk} = \frac{\text{total common stock holdings}}{\text{total capital and surplus}}$$

A property-casualty insurance company with a high ratio of premium income relative to total capital and surplus may be subject to high claims, and thus it may seek to maintain higher levels of liquidity, safety, and predictability in its investment portfolio. This may lead to a correspondingly greater emphasis on credit market instruments and to a lesser emphasis on holdings of common stock. Similarly, a high growth rate in premium income may imply not only greater flows available for investment but also a quantitative increase in the insurance risk ratio. This may lead to a slackening in under-writing quality standards in order to generate business, in turn raising the probability of claims payouts by the property-casualty insurance company.

In the 1960s and 1970s the premium income of property-casualty insurance companies that write insurance directly through their own agents (so-called direct-writing companies) grew more rapidly than that of companies that write insurance through independent agents (so-called old-line insurers). Slow growth rates in premium income imply reduced flows for investment but fewer chances of losses due to lower levels of insurance liability.

The quality of premium income also affects the insurance risk of a given property-casualty insurance company and, among other factors, depends upon (1) the amount of the premium and the risk that is passed on to reinsurance companies or other parties, (2) the type of insurance underwrit-ten (for example, most fire insurance is less likely to result in a claim than automobile insurance and thus is considered of higher quality), (3) diversifi-cation of risks by type and location of the insured parties, and (4) the age and experience level of the company in writing a particular type of insurance. The quality of investment income, among other factors, depends upon (1) the credit quality of portfolio holdings, (2) the maturity and subjectivity to early redemption of portfolio holdings, and (3) the volatility of portfolio holdings in response to changes in interest rates or stock market fluctuations.

Reinsurance and Captive Insurance Companies

Besides property-casualty insurance companies, there are real estate title guaranty insurance companies, mortgage insurance companies, excess- and surplus-lines insurance companies (which issue special insurance written out-side the regulated market), reinsurance companies, and so-called captive insurance companies. The latter two groups often have sizable investment operations. Reinsurance companies insure direct insurance companies against excessive losses by sharing all or a part of large risks that direct insurers do not wish to underwrite on their own.

Reinsurance protects direct insurance companies from losses arising from a large individual catastrophe or from a series of claims arising from a single event such as a hurricane. Direct insurers are thus able to write a larger amount of business than otherwise could have been underwritten. "Reassur-ance" refers to the reinsurance of life insurance business. On average, rein-surance companies tend to experience longer periods of time between the receipt of premium income and the eventual claims payment than property-casualty insurance companies (this condition is termed having a long tail).

The growth rate and profitability of the reinsurance industry are in-fluenced by (1) the timing and magnitude of major catastrophes and whether such losses have been adequately funded for, (2) the degree of price competi-tion in reinsurance rates, (3) the reserve position of direct insurers (which often affects their willingness to reinsure risks), and (4) rates of return available on reinsurers' investments. The reinsurance business is international in scope and often involves important currency investment decisions. Its task is usually complicated by the fact that many risks may be coinsured, retroceded, re-retroceded, or reciprocally exchanged. In addition, some reinsurers purchase contingent insurance to cover reinsurance that may not be paid off in full. The three largest factors in the world reinsurance market (total annual nonlife reinsurance premiums amounted to $30 billion in 1980) are Lloyd's of London, the Swiss Reinsurance Company, and the Munich Reinsurance Company. Lloyd's had more than 17,000 individual members as of early 1980, compared with 6200 members 10 years earlier.

In the late 1970s the New York Insurance Exchange was established to conduct operations on a model similar to that of Lloyd's of London, with syndicates of underwriters operating on a trading floor. Lloyd's concentrates on reinsurance, foreign insurance risks, and unusual insurance risks that cannot be placed elsewhere. Another innovation in the reinsurance market during the early 1980s has been the formation of the Risk Exchange (REX). The Risk Exchange is a communications system that permits subscribers to cede and accept facultative reinsurance via computer terminals. *Facultative* reinsurance involves the coverage of large individual risks, whereas *treaty* reinsurance generally involves a long-term relationship between the reinsurer and the direct insurer.

In the mid-1970s a sizable number of large internationally oriented companies and other institutions, such as groups of hospitals and doctors, began to follow a trend begun by a few firms in the 1920s and formed so-called captive insurance companies. As of early 1980, more than 1000 captive insurance companies had been established, domiciled primarily in low-taxation areas such as Bermuda, the Bahamas, and the Channel Islands. These companies were collecting more than $4 billion per year in insurance premiums as of early 1980.

Such captive insurance companies were formed to (1) save a part of insurance costs, (2) create internal incentives for businesses to control and reduce losses, (3) handle unusually large, risky, complex, or new insurance lines such as those covering oil-drilling platforms, pollution losses, product liability, kidnapping, nuclear reactors, and criminal liability, and (4) maintain a degree of internal but separate control over the accumulating insurance premiums on risks which entail lengthy investigation and settlement periods.

Captive insurance companies often place a part of their insurance with reinsurance companies or with other coinsurers. A number of captive insurance companies insure risks unrelated to their parent institutions and have become sizable insurers on the open market. A large part of the reserves behind the insurance policies written by captive insurers is invested in intermediate- and long-term bonds as well as in short-term money market instruments. Because offshore captive insurers often are not allowed to invest in certain domestic markets without endangering their tax advantages, they generally keep large sums invested in Eurosecurities denominated in the currency in which their parent or parents calculate their liabilities. To a great degree, the specific mix of such investments depends upon the international domicile and tax status of the captive insurance company as well as that of its parent or parents.

Private Pension Funds

Private pension funds include pension and retirement plans administered by the private (nongovernmental) sector. Private pension funds may be further subdivided into insured and noninsured pension funds. Insured pension funds consist of the pension reserves managed by life insurance companies, which were treated earlier in the discussion of those companies. All other private pension funds are classified as noninsured. Table 10-6 illustrates the total book value of the two major categories of private pension funds, as well as that of the two principal classifications of public pension funds, from 1970 through 1977.

As of the end of 1977, private noninsured pension funds accounted for 36.1 percent of total pension fund assets, private insured pension funds represented 19.4 percent of the total, state and local government employee retirement funds accounted for 26.0 percent of the total, and federal government employee retirement funds represented 18.5 percent of the total. As mentioned earlier, federal government employee retirement funds are consolidated with other federal financial activities in the Flow of Funds Accounts and thus are treated together with the accounts of the United States government in this book.

TABLE 10-6
Book Value of Various Categories of Pension Funds, 1970–1977
(In billions of dollars)

Type of pension fund	1970	1971	1972	1973	1974	1975	1976	1977
Private noninsured	97.0	106.4	117.5	126.5	133.7	145.2	160.4	181.5
Private insured	41.2	46.4	52.3	56.1	60.8	71.7	88.4	98.1
Public state or local	58.2	64.8	73.4	82.7	92.4	103.7	117.3	130.8
Public U.S. government	65.6	71.1	76.1	79.7	84.1	86.1	90.0	91.1
Total	262.0	288.7	319.3	345.0	371.0	406.7	456.1	501.5

SOURCE: *Statistical Bulletin,* vol. 37, no. 5, Securities and Exchange Commission.

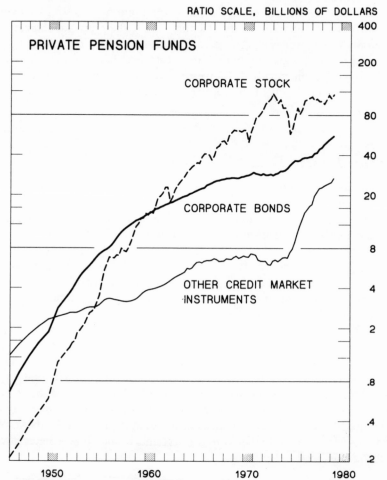

FIGURE 10-2 **Principal earning assets of private pension funds (amounts in billions of dollars).** [SOURCE: Historical Chart Book, *Board of Governors of the Federal Reserve System. By permission of the Board of Governors of the Federal Reserve System.*]

As of early 1978, 36 percent of the $501.5 billion in employee benefit and retirement funds shown in Table 10-6 was estimated to be internally managed, 25 percent was estimated to be managed by bank trust departments, 19 percent by insurance companies, 14 percent by private investment counselors (a particularly rapidly growing category in the late 1970s and early 1980s), and 6 percent by other sources such as unions (particularly in the trucking, apparel, and construction industries). A pension fund's "manager" is commonly defined as that entity with discretionary decision-making authority over the employee benefit and retirement funds, as distinct from an entity acting in a nondiscretionary or trustee capacity.

For the period from 1970 through 1977 private insured pension funds exhibited the greatest compound annual growth rate in the book value of total assets, with a 13.2 percent rate of increase. State and local government employee retirement funds showed a 12.3 percent annual compound rate of growth, private noninsured pension funds exhibited a 9.4 percent rate, and federal government employee retirement funds a 4.8 percent rate.

Figure 10-2 presents the principal earning asset categories of private pension funds during the period from 1946 until the early 1980s. Of particular note is the rapid growth in private pension funds' corporate stock investments during the period. From 1960 onward private pension funds' corporate equity investments exceeded their corporate bond investments, and from 1954 onward each of these two investment categories exceeded the total of other credit market instruments (excepting corporate bonds) taken together.

Table 10-7 shows the holdings of credit market instruments by private pension funds for selected years during the period from 1950 through 1979. Confirming the trend noted in Figure 10-2, the table shows that the equity investments of private pension funds demonstrated rapid growth in the

TABLE 10-7
Credit Market Instrument Holdings of Private Pension Funds for Selected Years, 1950–1979
(In billions of dollars)

Credit market instrument category	1950	1955	1960	1965	1970	1975	1979
U.S. treasury securities	2.3	3.0	2.4	2.5	2.1	7.9	18.4
Federally sponsored agency issues	0.0	. . .*	0.3	0.5	0.9	2.9	7.0
Corporate and foreign bonds	2.8	7.9	15.7	22.7	29.7	37.8	55.2
Mortgages	0.1	0.3	1.3	3.4	4.2	2.4	3.5
Total		5.2 11.2	19.7	29.1	36.9	51.0	84.1
Memorandum: Corporate equities†	1.1	6.1	16.5	40.8	67.1	88.6	136.4

SOURCE: *Flow of Funds Accounts*, Board of Governors of the Federal Reserve System. Data for all periods through 1975 are taken from the *Flow of Funds Accounts, 1946–1975*, issued in December 1976; data for periods subsequent to 1975 are taken from the *Flow of Funds Accounts, 1969–1979*, issued in February 1980. Because of occasional revisions in the Flow of Funds Accounts data, certain statistics from the latter source and subsequent releases may vary somewhat from those contained in the *Flow of Funds Accounts, 1946–1975*.

*Less than $50 million.

†Includes both convertible and nonconvertible preferred stock as well as common stock.

1950–1975 period, with total equity holdings by private pension funds exceeding the total of all their credit market instrument holdings in 1965, 1970, and 1975. As of the end of 1975, the credit market instrument holdings of private pension funds were divided as follows: (1) corporate bonds, representing 74.1 percent of the total (up substantially from 53.8 percent as of the end of 1950); (2) U.S. Treasury securities, with 15.5 percent of the total (down significantly from 44.2 percent as of the end of 1950); (3) federal agency issues, representing 5.7 percent of the total (up from no holdings at the end of 1950); and (4) mortgages (of which 49 percent were on commercial facilities, 28 percent on one- to four-family homes, 23 percent on multifamily residential dwellings, and virtually no mortgages on farm properties), with 4.7 percent of the total (up from 2 percent at the end of 1950). Also of interest is the fact that no holdings by private pension funds were registered in the Flow of Funds Accounts for state and local government obligations and for open-market paper. The tax-exempt income from municipal securities and the partially taxed dividends of preferred stocks (which allow special tax advantages to corporate investors) are not particularly attractive to tax-free pension funds.

Table 10-8 presents the flows of funds into credit market instruments by private pension funds during the period from 1972 through 1979. The range of total annual investments in credit market instruments by private pension funds is quite large, with a low of $800 million in net sales in 1972 and a high of $12.5 billion in net purchases in 1977. Flows into corporate bonds exhibited a fair amount of variability, swinging from net sales of $800 million in 1972 to net purchases of $4.7 billion in 1974, declining to net purchases

TABLE 10-8
Annual Net Flows from Private Pension Funds into Credit Market Instruments, 1972–1979
(In billions of dollars)

Credit market instrument category	1972	1973	1974	1975	1976	1977	1978	1979
U.S. Treasury securities	0.9	0.2	−0.2	4.5	3.7	5.3	1.6	0.9
Federally sponsored agency issues	0.1	0.6	1.3	0.7	0.3	1.5	0.5	2.2
Corporate and foreign bonds	−0.8	2.1	4.7	2.8	1.3	5.3	5.9	7.2
Mortgages	−0.9	−0.4	. . .*	. . .*	. . .*	0.4	0.6	0.5
Total	−0.8	2.5	5.8	8.0	5.3	12.5	8.6	10.8

SOURCE: *Flow of Funds Accounts,* Board of Governors of the Federal Reserve System. Data for 1978 and 1979 are taken from the *Flow of Funds Accounts* published in February 1980; data from 1972 to 1977 are taken from earlier years' *Flow of Funds Accounts* statistics.
*Less than $50 million.

of $1.3 billion in 1976, and then rising to $7.2 billion in net purchases in 1979. Flows into U.S. Treasury securities were large as a percentage of total flows for every year except 1973, 1974, and 1979.

Annual net purchases of federal agency issues were consistently smaller than net purchases of U.S. Treasury securities, except for 1973, 1974, and 1979. After a net liquidation of mortgage holdings amounting to $900 million in 1972 and $400 million in 1973, private pension funds' net acquisitions of mortgages were insignificant in 1974, 1975, and 1976, with a total of $600 million invested in mortgages in 1978. As of the beginning of the 1980s, private pension funds were not major factors in the single-family home mortgage, commercial mortgage, farm mortgage, or multifamily residential mortgage sectors of the mortgage market.

In addition to corporate *pension plans* for hourly and salaried employees, private retirement funds may also encompass employees' *profit sharing funds* or other forms of thrift plans. Private pension plans have a very long if not an indefinite lifetime and pay no income or capital gains taxes on their investment activities as long as they are considered by the Internal Revenue Service (IRS) to be outside the employer's control. This requirement can be met by placing the pension assets with an outside trustee such as a commercial bank or an independent trust company, by placing the assets with an insurance company or other investment management organization, or by obtaining IRS approval for a self-administered pension plan. Such a plan must be administered separately by certain authorized employees of the company in question.

Investment Strategy

Owing in part to their tax-free status, private pension funds have a relatively large amount of freedom in their investment choice, subject to certain legal statutes discussed later in this section which regulate their investment behavior. The prospect of large and possibly rising pension contributions in the future by employers and employees permits additional flexibility and somewhat less concern about liquidity needs than would otherwise be necessary. In aggregate terms for the years from 1972 through 1979, employer contributions represented 71 percent of total private pension fund receipts, employee contributions 6 percent, and investment income 23 percent. In turn, total pension benefit payments over this period accounted for 47 percent of total private pension fund flows, leaving 53 percent for investment in credit market instruments and other financial assets such as corporate equities and bank deposits.

The amount of employer contributions to pension funds is not fixed and depends upon (1) the overall investment performance, in terms of both income and capital gains, of the investment portfolio (the better the performance, the lower the annual contribution that must be made by the employer, and the poorer the performance, the greater the annual contribution that must be made by the employer); (2) the relationship of present and expected future pension benefit payments to employees' income levels; (3) the financial condition of the employer; (4) such pension plan features as vesting and portability; (5) actuarial assumptions about employee mortality, turnover, and hiring and retirement ages; (6) the outlook for inflation or deflation; and (7) the possibility of employee and/or union demands for more liberalized pension benefits and, if granted, the question of whether such liberalized benefits would have to be granted retroactively to already-retired employees. Also influencing these factors and thus affecting private pension funds' investment strategy is the current and future business outlook for the employer and the industry in which it operates, with particular emphasis on the age and numbers of employees likely to enter and leave the company and the industry in future years.

Deferred profit sharing funds usually have different investment objectives from those of pension funds. In general, taxes are not paid by profit sharing plans but are the responsibility of each beneficiary as income is received from the plan, usually after retirement. Legally, the employer's annual contributions to the plan may not exceed a specified percentage of its total wages and salaries and are normally set at some percentage of total yearly profits or of profits above a specified minimum level.

In a deferred profit sharing fund, the value of the employer's contribution remains relatively fixed in the short run, and the value of the employee's ownership in the fund fluctuates according to the market value of the entire fund (in practice, this value may vary rather widely). An increased investment return from the portfolio of a profit sharing plan usually does not lower the employer's contribution since such contributions depend upon the employer's level of profits. On the other hand, if the investment return of a profit sharing plan proves to be lower than expected, the company generally does not make additional contributions and the effects of the lower return are felt more directly by the beneficiaries of the plan.

This arrangement is unlike that of a pension fund, in which the value of the employee's benefit remains relatively fixed in the short run while the employer's level of contributions to the fund varies according to the investment performance of the fund and other factors reviewed earlier. Because the investment objectives and remaining career patterns of a company's employees may vary owing to age, current earnings, other income sources, family obligations, and other factors, many firms have established several different profit sharing fund portfolios with different asset mixes, risk levels, and investment goals. Employees are then given the option of choosing the fund or funds that best fit their needs. At specified intervals, fund participants may be allowed to switch the allocation of their own share of the assets between funds.

In addition to their large holdings of credit market instruments, private pension funds have large investments in corporate equities, as was shown in Figure 10-2 and Table 10-7. The amount of private pension funds' assets held in equities and the proportion of new money flowing into stocks is, among other factors, a function of (1) perceived risk-reward relationships in the equity markets as compared with other credit market instruments, (2) past performance and market valuations of equities versus other investments, (3) outside influences such as pension fund legislation or competition between various types of fund managers to gain additional private pension funds as clients, and (4) the profile of the employees covered by the pension fund with resultant requirements concerning liquidity, maturity, and the timing of income flows. While corporate equities represented more than 42 percent of total pension fund assets as of 1960, by 1975 their share had grown to 59 percent of the total.

Prior to the passage of the Employee Retirement Income Security Act (also known as the ERISA legislation) in September 1974, very few external restrictions other than the employer's own investment guidelines were imposed upon the management of private pension funds. ERISA contained provisions relating to enrollment eligibility, benefit vesting, reporting and disclosure of information, funding schedules, plan termination insurance (administered by the Pension Benefit Guaranty Corporation and financed through employer premium payments), and asset management.

In particular, ERISA established legal liability for losses caused by a fiduciary. In addition, the ERISA legislation made fiduciaries responsible for seeing that no cofiduciaries (if any) violate their obligations. Under ERISA, a "fiduciary" is defined as anyone who exercises any discretionary authority or control over the management of a private pension plan and/or the disposition of its assets or who provides investment advice for a fee or other compensation. Following the so-called prudent man guidelines, ERISA has also mandated that fiduciaries act with the skill, care, prudence, and diligence under the circumstances then prevailing that a prudent individual acting in a like capacity and familiar with such matters would use in the conduct of an enterprise of a similar character and aims.

The original prudent man rule was formulated in a Massachusetts court judgment in the early nineteenth century. The rule allows fiduciaries or trustees to purchase whatever they can prove is in conformity with the practices of individuals of prudence, intelligence, and discretion buying for the permanent disposition of their own funds, with due regard both to the probable safety and to the probable income of the investment. The ERISA legislation added an additional and more formalized degree of conservatism to the investment management of pension funds, and in the years immediately following its enactment the legislation led to increased emphasis on a diversified group of maturities and types of fixed-income securities and other credit market instruments, somewhat at the expense of the share of new and existing funds invested in corporate equities.

By the end of the 1970s and the beginning of the 1980s, pension fund managers had reduced somewhat the strong emphasis on fixed-income securities which initially occurred in the wake of the ERISA legislation. In addition, by 1979 the U.S. Department of Labor had issued regulations which under certain conditions allowed greater flexibility in choosing such alternative investments as precious metals, venture capital investments, and index funds for employee benefit and retirement funds, individual retirement accounts, and Keogh plans. Such action was predicated on the theory that the relative riskiness of a specific investment or investment strategy does not per se render it imprudent or prudent. Rather, the overall level of risk of an employee benefit and retirement portfolio should be taken into account. Another effect of the ERISA legislation was to spur the growth of pension consulting firms in the 1970s. Such firms usually provide counsel to corporate clients in such areas as performance measurement, the selection of professional investment managers, and other advisory services.

As mentioned earlier, the liquidity needs of a private pension fund are influenced by the degree to which the pension plan's current and future cash payout needs for benefit payments are covered by its total cash income flows from employer and employee pension contributions as well as from investment income. Because investment income and contributions usually exceed total benefit payments in the early years of a pension plan, liquidity considerations tend to become more important as the plan matures. In addition, precautionary considerations may dictate that some liquidity reserves be maintained to allow for unforeseen contingencies or to take advantage of attractive investment opportunities. Many private pension funds seek to balance their short-term assets against their short-term liabilities and to match their longer-term liabilities with their longer-term asset holdings.

State and Local Government Employee Retirement Funds

The retirement funds for the employees of state and local governments are classified separately from private pension plans in Flow of Funds Accounts conventions. Table 10-9 shows the total assets of the 25 largest state and local government employee retirement funds in the United States as of the end of 1979, compared with the 25 largest corporate-sponsored pension funds. As can be seen in the table, the largest fund was the California Public Employees Retirement System (consisting of the California Public Employees Fund and the California Teachers Fund), with total assets of $18 billion as of the end of 1979. This fund was followed by three funds for employees in New York. The total assets of the 25 largest state and local government employee retirement funds amounted to $114.2 billion.

TABLE 10-9

Total Assets of the 25 Largest State and Local Government Employee Retirement Funds and the 25 Largest Corporate-Sponsored Pension Funds, Year-End 1979
(In millions of dollars)

	Top 25 public employee funds			Top 25 corporate funds or sponsors	
Rank	Fund or sponsor	Assets*	Rank	Fund or sponsor	Assets
1	California Public Employees	17,958	1	General Motors Corp.	12,973
2	New York State Employees	14,356	2	General Electric Co.	6,023
3	New York City Employees/Teachers	10,461	3	Ford Motor Co.	4,900
4	New York State Teachers	6,463	4	Western Electric Co.	4,828
5	New Jersey Division of Investment	5,171	5	United States Steel and Carnegie Natural Gas Co.	4,700
6	Ohio State Teachers	4,611	6	IBM Corp.	4,476
7	Texas State Teachers	4,611	7	E. I. du Pont de Nemours & Co.	4,205
8	Pennsylvania School Employees	4,395	8	Exxon Corporation	3,624
9	Ohio Public Employees	4,300	9	Sears, Roebuck & Co.	2,676
10	Wisconsin Investment Board	4,229	10	Pacific Telephone & Telegraph Co.	2,541
11	Michigan State Employees	4,146	11	Rockwell International Corp.	2,494
12	Minnesota Investment Board	4,034	12	Eastman Kodak Co.	2,442
13	North Carolina Employees	3,940	13	Bell System Savings Plan†	2,350
14	Florida Retirement System	3,090	14	New York Telephone Co.	2,300
15	Washington Public Employees	2,750	15	Boeing Co.	2,169

TABLE 10-9
Total Assets of the 25 Largest State and Local Government Employee Retirement Funds and the 25 Largest Corporate-Sponsored Pension Funds, Year-End 1979 (*Continued*)
(*In millions of dollars*)

	Top 25 public employee funds			Top 25 corporate funds or sponsors	
Rank	Fund or sponsor	Assets*	Rank	Fund or sponsor	Assets
16	Los Angeles County Employees	2,539	16	Shell Oil Company	2,162
17	Pennsylvania State Employees	2,340	17	Mobil Oil Corp.	2,100
18	Illinois Teachers	2,179	18	General Telephone & Electronics Corporation	2,052
19	Maryland Public Employees	2,100	19	Chrysler Corporation	2,014
20	Georgia State Retirement	2,037	20	United Technologies	1,950
21	Alabama Public Employees	1,828	21	Bethlehem Steel Corp.	1,926
22	Colorado Public Employees	1,815	22	Standard Oil Co. (Indiana)	1,907
23	Arizona Public Employees	1,788	23	Southwestern Bell Telephone Co.	1,894
24	South Carolina Employees	1,632	24	McDonnell Douglas Corp.	1,829
25	Hawaii Public Employees	1,525	25	Westinghouse Electric Corp.	1,800
	Total	114,207		Total	82,335

SOURCE: *Pensions and Investments*, Jan. 21, 1980.

*Includes corporate equities and other financial assets as well as credit market instruments.

†The 25 separate funds of the Bell System amount to $27,090 million but are managed independently.

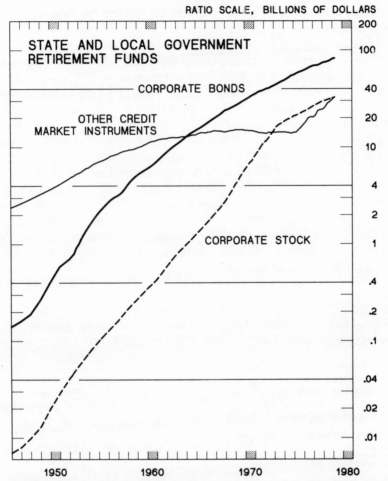

RATIO SCALE, BILLIONS OF DOLLARS

STATE AND LOCAL GOVERNMENT
RETIREMENT FUNDS

——— CORPORATE BONDS ———

OTHER CREDIT
MARKET INSTRUMENTS

CORPORATE STOCK

FIGURE 10-3   Principal earning assets of state and local government
employee retirement funds (amounts in billions of dollars). [SOURCE:
Historical Chart Book, *Board of Governors of the Federal Reserve System. By permission of
the Board of Governors of the Federal Reserve System.*]

Many of the features of state and local government employee retirement
funds are similar to those of private pension plans, and this section should
be considered in conjunction with the preceding section on private pension
plans. Figure 10-3 shows the principal earning assets of state and local government employee retirement funds from 1946 through the early 1980s. Of
particular note is the importance of corporate bondholdings and the growth
rate of corporate stockholdings relative to other credit market instruments.
By the mid-1970s corporate bondholdings were more than 3 times the total

combined holdings of all other credit market instruments by state and local government employee retirement funds.

Table 10-10 presents the holdings of credit market instruments by state and local government employee retirement funds for selected years during the period from 1950 through 1979. As of the end of 1975, the percentages of total credit market instruments held by state and local government employee retirement funds were (1) corporate bonds, 77.7 percent (up significantly from 12.8 percent of total credit market instrument holdings at the end of 1950); (2) mortgages (of which 39 percent were mortgages on one- to four-family homes, 29 percent were mortgages on multifamily residential dwellings, 28 percent were mortgages on commercial facilities, and 4 percent were mortgages on farm properties), 10.6 percent (up from 2.1 percent as of the end of 1950); (3) federal agency issues, 5.9 percent (up from no holdings at the end of 1950); (4) state and local government securities (which reached a peak in absolute amount of holdings by state and local government employee retirement funds in 1961), 3.2 percent (down sharply from 31.9 percent as of the end of 1950); and (5) U.S. Treasury securities, 2.8 percent (also down sharply from 53.2 percent as of the end of 1950).

TABLE 10-10
Credit Market Instrument Holdings of State and Local Government Employee Retirement Funds for Selected Years, 1950–1979
(In billions of dollars)

Credit market instrument category	1950	1955	1960	1965	1970	1975	1979
U.S. Treasury securities	2.5	4.6	5.7	7.1	5.1	2.2	15.0
Federally sponsored agency issues	0.0	0.1	0.2	0.5	1.5	4.6	17.1
State and local government securities	1.5	2.7	4.4	2.6	2.0	2.5	4.0
Corporate and foreign bonds	0.6	2.7	7.1	17.2	35.1	60.9	86.2
Mortgages	0.1	0.3	1.5	3.7	5.9	8.3	9.4
Total	4.7	10.4	18.9	31.1	49.6	78.4	131.6
Memorandum: Corporate equities*	. . .†	0.2	0.6	2.5	10.1	25.8	43.6

SOURCE: *Flow of Funds Accounts,* Board of Governors of the Federal Reserve System. Data for all periods through 1975 are taken from the *Flow of Funds Accounts, 1946–1975,* issued in December 1976; data for periods subsequent to 1975 are taken from the *Flow of Funds Accounts, 1969–1979,* issued in February 1980. Because of occasional revisions in the Flow of Funds Accounts data, certain statistics from the latter source and subsequent releases may vary somewhat from those contained in the *Flow of Funds Accounts, 1946–1975.*

*Includes both convertible and nonconvertible preferred stock as well as common stock.
†Less than $50 million.

Unlike private pension funds, state and local government employee retirement funds have investments in tax-exempt securities even though these funds are also exempt from taxes on their investment income. In part, such ownership of state and local government securities is due to political considerations, which together with state and local laws often dictate very conservative and/or locally oriented investment strategies, with a consequent close circumscription of possible investment alternatives for state and local government employee retirement funds.

An additional conservative influence and differentiating feature of state and local government employee retirement funds compared with private pension funds is the frequent requirement by state and local governments that employees make substantial contributions to a retirement plan. For example, for the period from 1972 through 1979 state and local government contributions averaged 47 percent of total state and local government employee retirement fund receipts, employee contributions amounted to 23 percent (versus 6 percent for private pension plans), and investment income represented 30 percent. In turn, retirement benefit payments over the same period accounted for 39 percent of total receipts, leaving 61 percent for investment in credit market instruments and other financial assets.

A summary of the flows into credit market instruments by state and local government employee retirement funds during the years from 1972 through 1979 is presented in Table 10-11. With the exception of 1977, when total flows declined compared with 1976 because of reduced net purchases of corporate bonds and net sales of state and local government securities, total

TABLE 10-11
Annual Net Flows from State and Local Government Employee Retirement Funds into Credit Market Instruments, 1972–1979
(In billions of dollars)

Credit market instrument category	1972	1973	1974	1975	1976	1977	1978	1979
U.S. Treasury securities	−0.3	−1.1	−0.9	1.0	2.2	3.2	3.8	3.6
Federally sponsored agency issues	0.6	0.9	1.0	1.0	0.8	1.7	2.5	2.7
State and local government securities	−0.1	−0.3	−0.7	1.0	0.9	−0.4	0.4	. . .*
Corporate and foreign bonds	4.2	5.6	6.8	6.1	6.8	4.9	8.6	8.2
Mortgages	0.2	0.7	0.6	0.2	0.3	0.5	0.7	0.7
Total	4.6	5.8	6.8	9.3	11.0	9.9	16.1	15.2

SOURCE: *Flow of Funds Accounts,* Board of Governors of the Federal Reserve System. Data for 1978 and 1979 are taken from the *Flow of Funds Accounts* published in February 1980; data from 1972 to 1977 are taken from earlier years' *Flow of Funds Accounts* statistics.
*Less than $50 million.

flows exhibited a steady uptrend, rising from $4.6 billion in 1972 to $16 billion in 1978, followed by another small decline to $15 billion in 1979. Net flows into corporate bonds remained strongly positive from 1972 through 1979, with slowdowns in the net acquisition of corporate bonds occurring in 1975, 1977, and 1979. Net purchases of federal agency securities and mortgages also remained positive each year from 1972 through 1979 and averaged 22 and 8 percent respectively of total net acquisitions of corporate bonds. State and local government employee retirement funds were net sellers of state and local government securities in 1972, 1973, 1974, and 1977 but acquired on balance a total of $2.3 billion in 1975, 1976, and 1978. After being net sellers of a total of $2.3 billion in U.S. Treasury securities from 1972 through 1974, state and local government employee retirement funds shifted sharply to the purchase side from 1975 through 1979, acquiring a combined net total of $13.8 billion of U.S. Treasury issues.

11

The Investment Behavior of Finance Companies, Real Estate Investment Trusts, Open-End Investment Companies, Money Market Funds, and Security Brokers and Dealers

Overview

The investment entities reviewed in this chapter are a diverse group, with widely differing asset structures, investment practices, and regulatory environments. Although smaller and in several instances newer than the investor groups discussed in Chapters 8, 9, and 10, they are often very important factors in selected areas of the bond and money markets. With few exceptions, a fairly narrow range of credit market instruments is held by finance companies, real estate investment companies, open-end investment companies, money market funds, and security brokers and dealers.

In a number of cases, the investor groups presented in this chapter compete actively with much larger investor groups. For example, in the consumer loan field, consumer finance companies engage in competition with commercial banks and credit unions. Similarly, money market funds compete with thrift institutions of all types and with commercial banks for the investor's short-term funds. In recent years, such competitive forces have been increasingly evident in virtually every sector of the financial system.

Finance Companies

Mortgage, consumer loan, commercial finance, and sales finance companies are included in the finance company category as defined in the Flow of Funds Accounts. According to a Federal Reserve survey conducted in 1975, approximately 55 percent of finance companies' lending was conducted with consumers and 45 percent with businesses. Of the total finance company credit supplied to businesses, 28.2 percent was used to finance retail business purchases, 27.9 percent was dealer inventory finance, 20.5 percent was in the

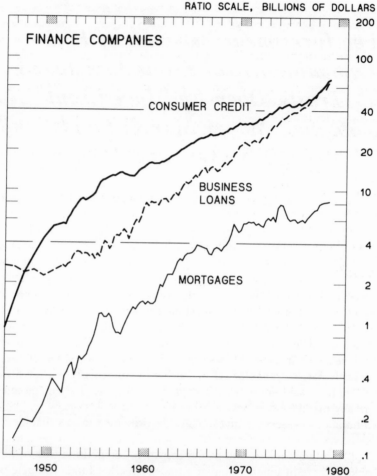

RATIO SCALE, BILLIONS OF DOLLARS

FINANCE COMPANIES

CONSUMER CREDIT

BUSINESS LOANS

MORTGAGES

1950   1960   1970   1980

FIGURE 11-1 Principal earning assets of finance companies (amounts in billions of dollars). [SOURCE: Historical Chart Book, *Board of Governors of the Federal Reserve System. By permission of the Board of Governors of the Federal Reserve System.*]

form of leasing, 8.6 percent was for loans against commercial accounts receivable, 4.1 percent was for loans to factored clients, and 10.7 percent was for all other business borrowers.

Another means of classifying finance companies is according to ownership. *Captive* finance companies are usually owned by a parent firm; their principal activity is to finance the products and/or services of the parent, often a company in the automotive or retailing industry. Many large bank holding companies have finance company subsidiaries. The relationship between the parent and its captive finance company is often spelled out in an *operating agreement* which may specify that the parent will maintain (1) certain minimum levels of pretax earnings relative to fixed charges, (2) minimum levels of equity investment in the captive, and (3) minimum standards of financial safety for the captive (this is known as a "keep well" clause), including a possible obligation to repurchase defaulted receivables from the captive.

Wholly owned finance companies are most often active in financing the products and/or services of firms other than their parent. *Independent* finance companies are usually engaged in financing activities on a completely autonomous basis. A number of finance companies have credit insurance subsidiaries which issue insurance covering any collateral held by the finance company and/or balances owed to the finance company in the event of death or disability of the borrower.

The principal earning assets of finance companies from 1946 through the early 1980s are shown in Figure 11-1. Of note is the importance of consumer credit, followed by business loans, as the major type of credit market instrument holdings of finance companies. Other credit market instruments are considerably less important than consumer credit and business loans in the portfolios of finance companies. To fund this lending activity, a number of finance companies are major *issuers* of commercial paper, often backed in full or in part by commercial bank lines of credit. Finance company commercial paper accounts for approximately 60 percent of the total amount of commercial paper outstanding.

Table 11-1 shows the holdings of credit market instruments by finance companies for selected years during the period from 1950 through 1979. As of the end of 1975, finance companies held three categories of credit market instruments, divided according to the following percentages: (1) consumer

TABLE 11-1
Credit Market Instrument Holdings of Finance Companies for Selected Years, 1950–1979
(In billions of dollars)

Credit market instrument category	1950	1955	1960	1965	1970	1975	1979
Mortgages	0.5	1.4	1.6	4.5	7.4	9.3	11.4
Consumer loans	5.3	11.8	16.1	24.7	32.5	46.1	82.6
Other loans*	2.5	3.8	8.2	13.5	22.0	39.0	70.3
Total	8.3	17.0	25.9	42.7	61.9	94.4	164.3

SOURCE: *Flow of Funds Accounts*, Board of Governors of the Federal Reserve System. Data for all periods through 1975 are taken from the *Flow of Funds Accounts, 1946–1975*, issued in December 1976; data for periods subsequent to 1975 are taken from the *Flow of Funds Accounts, 1969–1979*, issued in February 1980. Because of occasional revisions in the Flow of Funds Accounts data, certain statistics from the latter source and subsequent releases may vary somewhat from those contained in the *Flow of Funds Accounts, 1946–1975*.

*Principally loans made to businesses.

loans, with 48.8 percent of total credit market instrument holdings (down from 63.8 percent as of the end of 1950); (2) loans advanced to the business sector, representing 41.3 percent of the total (up from 30.2 percent as of the end of 1950); and (3) mortgages (of which 62 percent were mortgages on one- to four-family homes, 17 percent were mortgages on multifamily dwellings, 21 percent were mortgages on commercial facilities, and 0 percent were mortgages on farm properties), with 9.9 percent of the total (up from 6 percent as of the end of 1950).

At the end of 1975, finance companies held virtually no U.S. Treasury securities, federal agency issues, state and local government securities, corporate and foreign bonds, or open-market paper. In fact, finance companies were large net *issuers* of corporate bonds and open-market paper as of the end of 1975, with $30.7 billion of the former and $28 billion of the latter outstanding. Issues of bonds and open-market paper, together with loans to finance companies from banks, are the principal sources of finance companies' lendable and investable funds (besides the companies' retained earnings and allowances for loan-loss reserves).

Table 11-2 presents a summary of net flows into credit market instruments by finance companies for each of the years from 1972 through 1979. Total flows into credit market instruments were quite volatile in this period, dropping from $11.6 billion in 1973 to $1.3 billion in 1975 and then rising sharply to $23 billion in 1979. Business loans accounted for the least volatile and the major share (49 percent of total flows from 1972 through 1979) of finance companies' investments in credit market instruments. Consumer loans accounted in large part for the volatility of the companies' total net flows into credit market instruments, declining from $4.7 billion in 1973 to $0.5 billion in 1975 and then increasing to $15.5 billion in 1979.

When interest rates are rising and credit demands are high relative to the

TABLE 11-2
Annual Net Flows from Finance Companies into Credit Market
Instruments, 1972–1979
(In billions of dollars)

Credit market instrument category	1972	1973	1974	1975	1976	1977	1978	1979
Mortgages	1.7	1.9	−1.9	−1.3	−0.4	1.5	−0.2	0.6
Consumer loans	3.5	4.7	2.0	0.5	3.7	6.3	10.2	15.5
Other loans*	4.2	5.0	4.8	2.1	5.4	10.2	8.3	7.0
Total	9.4	11.6	4.9	1.3	8.7	18.0	18.3	23.0

SOURCE: *Flow of Funds Accounts,* Board of Governors of the Federal Reserve System. Data for 1978 and 1979 are taken from the *Flow of Funds Accounts* published in February 1980; data from 1972 to 1977 are taken from earlier years' *Flow of Funds Accounts* statistics.

*Principally loans made to businesses.

supply of funds, many lending institutions may begin to ration or even discontinue credit flows to a portion of their customers. These borrowers often turn to finance companies for credit. When interest rates are declining and the supply of funds exceeds credit demands, many lending institutions frequently seek to reattract customers away from finance companies, often through lower interest rates on loans.

During the 1972–1979 period, 22 percent of finance companies' *consumer* loans were extended to automobile dealers to carry inventories and 28 percent to individuals to purchase automobiles, 25 percent were made in connection with other retail sales, and 25 percent were extended for all other purposes.

Finance companies' *commercial* loans are generally asset-based, which means that they are secured by specifically identified assets of the borrower. These assets may be inventories, plants and equipment, or accounts receivable. The last-named category may be financed by *factoring,* whereby the factor actually purchases the receivables from the borrower and assumes the effort and risk of collection, or by *accounts-receivable financing,* whereby the finance company lends funds against specifically earmarked receivables. Commercial accounts-receivable financing and factoring are often used by companies in the apparel, textile, food-processing, electronics, and metals industries. As mentioned earlier, longer-term fixed assets are also financed by finance companies through leasing.

Mortgage investments by finance companies ranged from net purchases of $1.9 billion in 1973 to net sales of $1.9 billion in 1974. The major portion of mortgages sold by finance companies in the period from 1974 through 1976 consisted of mortgages on single-family and multifamily residences.

Most finance companies operate with a very leveraged capital structure, often with several classes of senior and subordinated (junior) debt. Because they usually finance larger loans, commercial finance companies are generally more highly leveraged than consumer finance companies. Finance companies frequently employ large amounts of short- and intermediate-term debt, in part because of the self-liquidating, high-turnover, short-term nature of a high proportion of finance companies' loan business. Nevertheless, at times of severe pressure in financial markets certain finance companies may experience difficulty in obtaining funds at desired maturities and interest rate levels. This situation is exacerbated for finance companies that have not properly matched the maturities and the fixed-rate versus floating-rate portions of their receivables with their debt liabilities.

In their consumer lending operations, finance companies are governed by state laws and by the Consumer Protection Act of 1969. In addition, a number of states have adopted the Uniform Consumer Credit Code (UCCC), which utilizes a common set of statutes and regulates interest calculation methods, debt collection practices, contract terms, and other aspects of consumer lending.

Real Estate Investment Trusts

Real Estate Investment Trusts (REITs) are a form of tax-sheltered investment fund authorized by Congress in 1960 (as a modification of similar trusts which operated around the turn of the century). REITs issue shares of beneficial interest to investors for the purpose of investing in a diversified portfolio of (1) mortgages, (2) real estate equity positions, or (3) some combination of mortgages and real estate equity positions. Of the more than 200 REITs in existence at the end of 1975, more than 120 had at least 50 percent of their assets in mortgage investments, and more than 60 had at least 75 percent of their assets in the equity ownership of real property.

Provided that certain conditions concerning share ownership, asset distribution, and income sourcing are met, the Internal Revenue Service (IRS) does not tax distributions to shareholders if at least 90 percent of trust taxable income is distributed, with any undistributed earnings being taxed at the corporate income tax rate. Although closed-end investment companies are comparatively limited in the amount of outside funds that they can borrow in relation to their shareholders' investment, REITs have tended to issue bonds and commercial paper and to borrow from commercial banks funds amounting to well over 100 percent of their equity base in order to augment their lendable funds and their earnings potential.

While several REITs were formed in the early 1960s, a large number were established in 1969 and 1970 in response to rising interest rates on and a demand for real estate construction and development loans and other forms of short-, intermediate-, and long-term mortgages. Many of these REITs were sponsored by insurance companies, commercial banks, mortgage banking and brokerage firms, and other financially related entities.

With wide interest rate fluctuations, greater competition from REITs and other groups of institutional investors for new mortgages, a cyclical oversupply in certain sectors of the real estate market, and the financial insolvency of a few builder-developers, several REITs were forced in 1974 to cut their dividends and shift their borrowings from the commercial-paper market to lines of credit at commercial banks. Such developments sharply reduced the real estate lending activities of many REITs and caused several of them to liquidate assets, to swap properties with lenders in return for cancellations of mortgages, and to renegotiate loan agreements in order to meet their commitments.

A few REITs filed for bankruptcy proceedings, and some REIT loans by commercial banks had to be written off. By early 1979 the real estate market had improved considerably, but the financial problems of a number of REITs had not yet been completely resolved. From a peak of $22 billion in assets (including $13.2 billion in mortgages and $8.8 billion in real estate equity holdings) in 1975, the REIT industry contracted to $13 billion in assets as of March 1979. For many of the financially troubled REITs this contraction led to differences and, in some cases, litigation between (1) commercial banks, as senior creditors to many REITs, and (2) public and private holders of the subordinated public and private debt of REITs. By early 1980, rising real estate values had attracted investor interest again to REIT securities. Particularly in the case of trusts which invest in equity ownership of real estate, certain investors purchased REIT securities in anticipation of possible takeovers, liquidations, or mergers of selected trusts because of undervaluation of REIT issues relative to the market value of their real estate properties.

Since the Flow of Funds Accounts did not list REITs separately until 1968, Table 11-3 shows holdings of credit market instruments by REITs for selected years from 1970 through 1979. REITs have practically no holdings of credit market instruments other than mortgages. As of the end of 1975, (1) 53 percent of REITs' mortgage holdings were on commercial facilities (virtually unchanged from 51.3 percent at the end of 1970), (2) 36.4 percent were on multifamily residential dwellings (up from 33.3 percent as of the end of 1970), and (3) 36.4 percent were on one- to four-family homes (down from 15.4 percent at the end of 1970).

As of the end of 1973, REITs' mortgage loans were classified according to the following types: (1) *land loans* (loans on unimproved real property held by borrwers for inventory or investment; because of the difficulty in forecasting the sale or development of such property, land loans have a higher element of risk than construction and development loans), with 7.2 percent of total mortgage loans; (2) *development loans* (loans advanced to finance the purchase of land and the development of unimproved property into finished sites for the construction of commercial or residential build-

TABLE 11-3

Credit Market Instrument Holdings of Real Estate Investment Trusts for Selected Years, 1970–1979

(In billions of dollars)

Credit market instrument category	1970	1975	1979
One- to four-family home mortgages	0.6	1.4	0.7
Commercial mortgages	2.0	7.0	3.0
Multifamily dwelling mortgages	1.3	4.8	1.9
Total	3.9	13.2	6.6

SOURCE: *Flow of Funds Accounts,* Board of Governors of the Federal Reserve System. Data for all periods through 1975 are taken from the *Flow of Funds Accounts, 1946–1975,* issued in December 1976; data for periods subsequent to 1975 are taken from the *Flow of Funds Accounts, 1969–1979,* issued in February 1980. Because of occasional revisions in the Flow of Funds Accounts data, certain statistics from the latter source and subsequent releases may vary somewhat from those contained in the *Flow of Funds Accounts, 1946–1975.*

ings; such loans are usually made in stages as work on a project progresses), with 15.2 percent of total mortgage loans; (3) *construction loans* (loans made usually on a first-mortgage basis to finance the construction of income-producing commercial or residential properties or, in some cases, one- to four-family home tract developments; such loans usually have a term of 12 to 36 months and are generally repaid by a long-term mortgage commitment), with 47.2 percent of total mortgage loans; (4) *mortgages on completed properties,* with 19.6 percent of total mortgage loans; (5) *junior mortgages* (loans whose lien priority is junior to that of a first-mortgage loan; such mortgages are often used for financing renovations or additions to existing properties and generally have a maturity of less than 10 years), with 0.2 percent of total mortgage loans; and (6) *land leasebacks* (such transactions usually involve a REIT's purchase of a property from a builder or a tenant and the simultaneous lease of the property back to the tenant), with 3.4 percent of total mortgage loans.

The specific distribution of loans by a given REIT is subject to change and depends, among other factors, on (1) the real estate market and general economic conditions, (2) interest returns, risk-reward relationships, and lending competition in each of these sectors of the mortgage market, and (3) the liquidity position, future cash flows, and overall financial status of each individual REIT.

Table 11-4 presents a summary of REITs' flows into credit market instruments for the years from 1972 through 1979. From a position of net mortgage purchases of $4.1 billion and $5.6 billion (of which a substantial majority represented net purchases of commercial and multifamily residential mortgages) in 1973 and 1974 respectively, REITs swung to heavy net dispo-

TABLE 11-4
Annual Net Flows from Real Estate Investment Trusts into Credit Market Instruments, 1972–1979
(In billions of dollars)

Credit market instrument category	1972	1973	1974	1975	1976	1977	1978	1979
One- to four-family home mortgages	0.4	0.7	−0.2	−0.5	−0.2	−0.3	−0.1	...*
Commercial mortgages	2.0	2.4	0.2	−2.6	−1.7	−1.3	−0.6	−0.2
Multifamily dwelling mortgages	1.7	2.5	0.2	−1.8	−1.8	−1.6	−0.3	−0.1
Total	4.1	5.6	0.2	−4.9	−3.7	−3.2	−1.0	−0.3

SOURCE: *Flow of Funds Accounts,* Board of Governors of the Federal Reserve System. Data for 1978 and 1979 are taken from the *Flow of Funds Accounts* published in February 1980; data from 1972 to 1977 are taken from earlier years' *Flow of Funds Accounts* statistics.

*Less than $50 million.

sitions of mortgages, amounting to $11.8 billion in total, in 1975, 1976, and 1977. These negative flows were due primarily to the unfavorable factors which affected the REIT industry beginning in the middle 1970s.

The major sources of regulation of REITs are the Securities and Exchange Commission (SEC) and any states in which REITs offer their shares to the public. As mentioned earlier, REITs must also comply with IRS statutes to preserve their exemption from federal corporate income taxes.

Open-End Investment Companies

As defined in the regulations of the Investment Company Act of 1940 and the Investment Company Amendments Act of 1970, an investment company operates a diversified portfolio for investment purposes and not to exercise or gain control of corporations through its portfolio holdings. The first open-end investment companies (also called mutual funds) in the United States were founded in the mid-1920s. In contrast to a closed-end investment company (included with and discussed together with nonfinancial business corporations in Chapter 8), an open-end investment company is obligated to make a continuous daily offering of its shares and to redeem its shares at net asset value. Since 1940 open-end investment companies have not been allowed to have senior securities (such as bonds or preferred stock) in their own capitalization.

A variation of the open-end fund is the *unit investment trust,* which is a fund that usually invests in a fixed list of securities and does not actively manage its portfolio holdings once they have been selected. In addition, a few *face-amount–certificate companies* buy securities as backing for the issuance of face-amount installment certificates, which are unsecured obligations to pay either a fixed amount to the certificate holder at a future date (provided the holder has made all payments) or specified cash values if the certificate is surrendered prior to its maturity.

As of the end of 1977, more than 650 mutual funds (exclusive of money market funds) were in operation. They included 427 mutual funds that reported to the Investment Company Institute and had a total of $48.3 billion under management, or 94 percent of the mutual fund industry's assets. These funds could be grouped by investment objective into the following classifications: (1) 44 funds in the Aggressive Growth category (invested primarily in common stocks), with 5.1 percent of the mutual fund industry's assets under management; (2) 143 funds in the Growth category (invested primarily in common stocks), with 26.3 percent of the industry's assets under management; (3) 87 funds in the Growth and Income category (invested in common stocks and to some degree in credit market instruments), with 35.4 percent of the industry's assets under management; (4) 22 funds in the

Balanced category (invested in a combination of common stocks, bonds, and preferred stocks), with 9 percent of the industry's assets under management; (5) 52 funds in the Income category (normally invested in high-yielding common stocks, preferred stocks, and bonds), with 9.7 percent of the industry's assets under management; (6) 40 funds in the Bond category (invested primarily in corporate, federal agency, foreign, and U.S. Treasury bonds), with 8.8 percent of the industry's assets under management; (7) 32 funds in the Municipal Bond category (invested in the tax-exempt securities of state and local governments), with 5 percent of the industry's assets under management; and (8) 7 funds in the Option Income category (invested chiefly in dividend-paying common stocks which have options listed on one of the main national securities exchanges, in order to generate income through various options investment strategies), with 0.7 percent of the industry's assets under management.

Table 11-5 presents the credit market instrument holdings of open-end investment companies for selected years during the period from 1950 through 1979. By comparing year-end 1975 holdings with year-end 1950 totals, it can be seen that while open-end investment companies' holdings of credit market instruments were much lower than their holdings of corporate equities (including both common and preferred stocks), they demonstrated

TABLE 11-5
Credit Market Instrument Holdings of Open-End Investment Companies for Selected Years, 1950–1979
(In billions of dollars)

Credit market instrument category	1950	1955	1960	1965	1970	1975	1979
U.S. Treasury and federal agency securities*	0.1	0.2	0.6	0.8	0.9	1.1	1.4
Corporate and foreign bonds	0.2	0.5	1.2	2.6	4.3	4.8	6.5
Open-market paper	0.0	0.1	0.1	0.4	2.1	1.5	3.8
Total	0.3	0.8	1.9	3.8	7.3	7.4	11.7
Memorandum: Corporate equities†	2.9	6.9	14.8	30.9	39.7	33.6‡	33.7

SOURCE: *Flow of Funds Accounts,* Board of Governors of the Federal Reserve System. Data for all periods through 1975 are taken from the *Flow of Funds Accounts, 1946–1975,* issued in December 1976; data for periods subsequent to 1975 are taken from the *Flow of Funds Accounts, 1969–1979,* issued in February 1980. Because of occasional revisions in the Flow of Funds Accounts data, certain statistics from the latter source and subsequent releases may vary somewhat from those contained in the *Flow of Funds Accounts, 1946–1975.*

*Principally U.S. Treasury securities.

†Includes both convertible and nonconvertible preferred stock as well as common stock.

‡Of which $0.5 billion represents preferred stock and $33.1 billion represents common stock.

a more rapid growth over the 1950–1975 time span, rising from 10.3 percent of equity holdings at the end of 1950 to 22 percent as of the end of 1975. In part this trend can be explained by (1) a growth in the number of income- and bond-oriented mutual funds, which tend to invest more of their assets in credit market instruments than in corporate equities; (2) slower rates of price appreciation (in some cases, price depreciation) in equity holdings; (3) generally higher levels of interest rates in the credit markets in the 1970s than in the preceding two decades; and (4) a need to maintain greater liquidity reserves to meet possible net redemptions of fund shares by share-holders (in 1972, for the first time in the postwar history of the mutual fund industry, redemptions exceeded new sales of conventional open-end investment company shares, and such net redemptions continued in each succeeding year through 1976).

As of the end of 1975, open-end investment companies held the following percentages of their total credit market investments in each of the following categories: (1) corporate bonds, 64.9 percent of total credit market instrument holdings (virtually unchanged from 66.7 percent at the end of 1950); (2) open-market paper, 20.2 percent of the total (up from no holdings at the end of 1950); (3) U.S. Treasury securities, 14.9 percent of the total (down from 33.3 percent at the end of 1950); and (4) state and local government securities, of which there were no recorded holdings from 1950 until 1976, when open-end mutual bond funds (as opposed to municipal bond unit trusts) were permitted to be established.

Table 11-6 presents a summary of open-end investment companies' total annual flows into credit market instruments for the years from 1972 through 1979, with the exclusion of flows into state and local government securities,

TABLE 11-6

Annual Net Flows from Open-End Investment Companies into Credit Market Instruments, 1972–1979

(In billions of dollars)

Credit market instrument category	1972	1973	1974	1975	1976	1977	1978	1979
U.S. Treasury and federal agency securities	0.1	0.5	−0.1	. . .*	. . .*	0.2	−0.2	−0.2
Corporate and foreign bonds	0.2	−0.9	−0.4	1.0	2.2	0.6	−0.9	1.0
Open-market paper	−0.3	0.2	0.1	−0.2	−1.1	0.9	1.3	0.4
Total	0.0	−0.2	−0.4	0.8	1.1	1.7	0.2	1.2

SOURCE: *Flow of Funds Accounts,* Board of Governors of the Federal Reserve System. Data for 1978 and 1979 are taken from the *Flow of Funds Accounts* published in February 1980; data from 1972 to 1977 are taken from earlier years' *Flow of Funds Accounts* statistics.

*Less than $50 million.

which were not included in the Flow of Funds Accounts of open-end investment companies until the late 1970s. In absolute terms, open-end investment companies' total net flows into credit market instruments were relatively small or negative for each of the years from 1972 through 1979, ranging from net sales of $400 million in 1974 to net acquisitions of $1.7 billion in 1977. Net acquisitions of corporate bonds amounted to a total of $3.2 billion in 1975 and 1976, when many new corporate bond funds were formed or began investing. During 1975 and 1976, open-end investment companies sold on balance a total of $1.3 billion in open-market paper, in partial reflection of the movement of temporary cash reserves into the stock and bond markets to take advantage of anticipated upward price movements. Total net activity in U.S. Treasury securities was relatively light during the 1972–1979 period.

Money Market Funds

Money market funds were begun in the early 1970s as a vehicle for investing in short-term money market instruments. They grew by almost $2 billion in both 1974 and 1975 as investors were attracted by their very competitive yields, safety, diversification, and certain other technical conveniences involving funds transfers by fundholders. As of mid-1978, there were more than 50 money market funds in operation, with total assets of $5.7 billion. By March 1979, total assets of money market funds amounted to $16.1 billion. As of the end of October 1979, their assets totaled $35 billion, spread among 67 different money market funds and representing 1,400,000 money market fund accounts. By July 1980, their assets reached $79.2 billion.

Table 11-7 shows the credit market instrument holdings of money market funds from 1974 (the first year for which such figures were available in the Flow of Funds Accounts) through 1979. As of the end of 1975, total holdings

TABLE 11-7
Credit Market Instrument Holdings of Money Market Funds, 1974–1979
(In billions of dollars)

Credit market instrument category	1974	1975	1976	1977	1978	1979
U.S. Treasury and federal agency securities	0.1	0.9	1.0	0.9	1.5	5.6
Open-market paper	0.6	0.5	0.8	1.1	3.7	19.3
Total	0.7	1.4	1.8	2.0	5.2	24.9

SOURCE: *Flow of Funds Accounts,* Board of Governors of the Federal Reserve System. Data for 1978 and 1979 are taken from the *Flow of Funds Accounts* published in February 1980; data from 1974 to 1977 are taken from earlier years' *Flow of Funds Accounts* statistics.

of credit market instruments by money market funds amounted to $1.4 billion, or double the total at the end of 1974. Such figures are less than the total amount of financial assets of the money market fund industry at the end of both years because money market funds' holdings of cash, time deposits (including certificates of deposit of all types), and demand deposits are not classified as credit market instruments in the Flow of Funds Accounts.

U.S. government securities (primarily U.S. Treasury issues) comprised 22.5 percent of total credit market instrument holdings by money market funds at the end of 1979, up from 14.3 percent of total holdings at the end of 1974. The proportion of money market funds' total credit market instrument holdings represented by U.S. government securities is influenced, among other factors, by (1) yield levels on U.S. Treasury and federal agency issues compared with short-term investment alternatives, (2) perceived safety and liquidity needs, and (3) the degree of ease or difficulty which money market funds may be experiencing in retaining or attracting fundholders, particularly in light of the funds' and fundholders' short-term interest rate expectations and orientation. At the end of 1979, open-market paper (of which approximately 92 percent was commercial paper and 8 percent was bankers' acceptances) represented 77.5 percent of total credit market investments of money market funds, down from 85.7 percent of the total at the end of 1974. The amount of commercial paper versus bankers' acceptances held by money market funds is variable (bankers' acceptances comprised 10 percent of the holdings of open-market paper by money market funds at the end of 1977) and is influenced by (1) internal supply-demand relationships in the commercial-paper and bankers' acceptance markets, (2) liquidity needs of the funds in relation to the current degree of trading liquidity in bankers' acceptances compared with commercial paper, and (3) the relative amounts of commercial paper or bankers' acceptances available for various segments of the short-term–maturity spectrum.

As of October 1979, 43.2 percent of total money market fund assets was invested in commercial bank certificates of deposit, which are classified in the Flow of Funds Accounts as financial assets but not as credit market instruments. Commercial paper accounted for 29.4 percent of total assets, U.S. Treasury bills for 3.4 percent, other Treasury and federal agency securities for 8.9 percent, bankers' acceptances for 10.5 percent, and cash reserves and other instruments for 4.5 percent. Money market funds can differ from one another in (1) their methodologies of calculating yields and share prices, (2) their investment strategies as to both liquidity reserves and the quality and maturity of investments, and (3) ancillary services and funds transfer mechanisms.

Table 11-8 presents flows into credit market instruments by money market funds from 1974 through 1979. The very fluid nature of short-term money market investment patterns by money market funds is evident in the

TABLE 11-8
Annual Net Flows from Money Market Funds into Credit Market
Instruments, 1974–1979
(In billions of dollars)

Credit market instrument category	1974	1975	1976	1977	1978	1979
U.S. Treasury and federal agency securities	0.1	0.8	0.1	−0.2	0.6	4.2
Open-market paper	0.6	−0.1	0.3	0.1	2.6	15.6
Total	0.7	0.7	0.4	−0.1	3.2	19.8

SOURCE: *Flow of Funds Accounts,* Board of Governors of the Federal Reserve System. Data for 1978 and 1979 are taken from the *Flow of Funds Accounts* published in February 1980; data from 1972 to 1977 are taken from earlier years' *Flow of Funds Accounts* statistics.

table. Assisted in part by new fund purchases by fundholders in response to attractive short-term yields, total flows by money market funds into credit market instruments amounted to $700 million both in 1974 and in 1975, yet dropped to $400 million in 1976, and turned to a net sales position of $100 million in 1977. The relative amounts of money invested by money market funds in U.S. government securities compared with open-market paper is also quite variable. In 1975 net purchases of U.S. government securities amounted to $800 million and substantially exceeded net sales of $100 million in open-market paper, but in 1974, 1976, and 1977 money market funds' net purchases of open-market paper were from $200 million to $500 million larger than net acquisitions of U.S. government securities. Net purchases of credit market instruments rose dramatically in 1978, 1979, and 1980.

Security Brokers and Dealers

Security brokers and dealers include those investment banking, securities brokerage, and other securities dealer firms registered with the SEC. Several thousand firms are active in the securities business. A large number of security brokers and dealers operate on a local or regional basis and specialize in over-the-counter securities and/or the marketing of mutual fund shares. Most of the credit market instrument holdings of security brokers and dealers are accounted for by a few hundred well-capitalized companies which are active in investment banking, market making, and securities brokerage. An even greater concentration of holdings is indicated by the fact that the 10 largest firms represented 43 percent of the capital, 33 percent of the commission revenues, and 41 percent of the total revenues of the securities industry as of June 30, 1977.

During the late 1960s and the 1970s, the securities industry underwent numerous significant changes. High securities trading volume in the late 1960s created varying degrees of operational problems for almost all securities firms. Subsequent sharp declines in both securities prices and transaction volume led to financial difficulties for some firms, which were forced to merge or liquidate. The advent of negotiated commission rates in May 1975, an increased degree of regulation by the SEC and other bodies with respect to net capital requirements and other financial measures, and the growing influence of institutional investors in the securities marketplace (with institutions' increased demands for the positioning of large blocks of equity and debt issues by security brokers and dealers in order to facilitate trades) tended to reduce the number of active firms while rendering the industry more capital-intensive.

Table 11-9 shows the credit market instrument holdings of security brokers and dealers for selected years during the period from 1950 through 1979. While total credit market instrument holdings of security brokers and dealers rose from $1.4 billion at the end of 1950 to $6 billion by the end of 1970, the total declined to $4.2 billion by 1975. As of the end of 1979, security brokers and dealers had the following percentages of their total credit market instrument holdings in the following instruments: (1) U.S. government securities, with 60.2 percent of total holdings (up from 42.9 percent as of the end of 1950), (2) corporate bonds, with 27.7 percent of total holdings (against 28.9 percent as of the end of 1950), and (3) state and

TABLE 11-9
Credit Market Instrument Holdings of Security Brokers and Dealers for Selected Years, 1950–1979
(In billions of dollars)

Credit market instrument category	1950	1955	1960	1965	1970	1975	1979
U.S. Treasury and federal agency securities	0.6	0.3	1.0	1.1	3.4	2.2	5.0
State and local government securities	0.4	0.3	0.4	0.5	0.9	0.6	1.0
Corporate and foreign bonds	0.4	0.8	0.5	0.9	1.7	1.4	2.3
Total	1.4	1.4	1.9	2.5	6.0	4.2	8.3
Memorandum: Corporate equities*	0.5	0.9	0.5	1.2	2.0	1.7	2.7

SOURCE: *Flow of Funds Accounts,* Board of Governors of the Federal Reserve System. Data for all periods through 1975 are taken from the *Flow of Funds Accounts, 1946–1975,* issued in December 1976; data for periods subsequent to 1975 are taken from the *Flow of Funds Accounts, 1969–1979,* issued in February 1980. Because of occasional revisions in the Flow of Funds Accounts data, certain statistics from the latter source and subsequent releases may vary somewhat from those contained in the *Flow of Funds Accounts, 1946–1975.*

*Includes both convertible and nonconvertible preferred stock as well as common stock.

local government obligations, representing 12.0 percent of total holdings (down from 28.9 percent at the end of 1950).

As mentioned earlier, security brokers' and dealers' holdings of credit market instruments more often represent dealer positions and inventories than long-term portfolio investments. For this reason, the level and mix of their holdings of credit market instruments depend on, among other factors, (1) security brokers' and dealers' judgments about which sectors of the securities market appear to offer the greatest profit potential under prevailing market conditions; (2) a possible desire to generate or offset tax losses or to gain tax-exempt income; (3) the outlook for interest rates; (4) investors' (including Federal Reserve System) buying and/or selling preferences and the possible need for security brokers and dealers to take securities into a long or short position in order to facilitate trading activity; (5) the level of competition in and the profitability of security brokers' and dealers' trading operations, as well as their overall level of profitability and rates of return in other parts of their business; and (6) coordination of the syndication and underwriting activities of securities firms with their trading operations and with the future supplies of each major type of credit market instrument which might be coming to market in the near future.

Table 11-10 presents a summary of the investment flows into credit market instruments by security brokers and dealers during the period from 1972 through 1979. Because of the rapidly changing and sometimes conflicting influences on their securities trading and underwriting activities, security brokers' and dealers' total annual investments in credit market instruments were quite variable and not always consistent with one another between

TABLE 11-10
Annual Net Flows from Security Brokers and Dealers into Credit Market Instruments, 1972–1979
(In billions of dollars)

Credit market instrument category	1972	1973	1974	1975	1976	1977	1978	1979
U.S. Treasury and federal agency securities	0.2	. . .*	0.2	−0.1	2.4	−0.7	−0.8	1.9
State and local government securities	−0.1	0.2	−0.4	−0.1	0.3	0.2	−0.2	0.2
Corporate and foreign bonds	0.2	0.4	−0.7	1.1	0.8	−0.3	−0.9	−0.5
Total	0.3	0.6	−0.9	0.9	3.5	−0.8	−1.9	1.6

SOURCE: *Flow of Funds Accounts,* Board of Governors of the Federal Reserve System. Data for 1978 and 1979 are taken from the *Flow of Funds Accounts* published in February 1980; data from 1972 to 1977 are taken from earlier years' *Flow of Funds Accounts* statistics.

*Less than $50 million.

1972 and 1979, ranging from net sales of $900 million in 1974 and $800 million in 1977 to net purchases of $900 million in 1975 and $3.5 billion in 1976. Security brokers' and dealers' net acquisitions of U.S. government securities demonstrated wide year-to-year swings, moving from annual net purchases of $2.4 billion in 1976 to annual net dispositions of $800 million in 1978. Annual corporate bond investments moved from purchases of $400 million in 1973 to sales of $700 million in 1974, followed by net purchases amounting to $1.1 billion in 1975 and $800 million in 1976. Security brokers and dealers were net sellers of state and local government securities on balance in 1972, 1974, 1975, and 1978 and were modest net purchasers of municipal securities in 1973, 1976, 1977, and 1979. Overall, security brokers and dealers purchased a net total of $100 million in state and local government securities during the 1972–1979 period.

*Investing in the Bond
and Money Markets*

12

Yield and Price Relationships for Fixed-Income Securities

One of the fundamental features of almost all commonly encountered fixed-income securities is the inverse correlation between their prices and their yields. When the prices of fixed-income securities rise, their yields decline. Conversely, when the prices of fixed-income securities decline, their yields rise. Because of the exponential nature of the mathematical formulas which underlie fixed-income securities' yield calculations, fixed-income securities' price changes generally do not vary in a linear fashion for a given change in one of the variables affecting their value. One version of the formula for calculating the yield and price of a bond is

$$P_c = c \sum_{1}^{n} \frac{1}{(1+i)^n} + \frac{P_d}{(1 + i)^n}$$

where
P_c = current price of the bond
n = number of coupons in the holding period of the bond
c = coupon income received per holding period
P_d = price of the bond upon disposition (almost always the par value of the bond if held until maturity)
i = yield discounting factor per coupon period (usually one-half of the yield to maturity for bonds with semiannual coupons)

The variables which affect the value of a fixed-income security include (1) its coupon, (2) its maturity, (3) the beginning yield level from which the change in interest rates occurs, and (4) the magnitude of the change in interest rates. A simplified formula for these relationships is

$$\triangle P = f (M, C, Y_b, \triangle i)$$

which can be described as

The change in the price of a fixed-income security = is a function of maturity, coupon, beginning-yield levels, magnitude of change in interest rates

Numerous refinements can be inserted into this equation, among them (1) changing the frequency, timing, and form of interest payments, (2) allowing for variable coupons, and (3) permitting different reinvestment rates for received coupon income. In addition, yields, accrued interest, and prices are calculated differently for various parts of the fixed-income securities markets and depend on, among other things, (1) the method of accounting for days between two dates, (2) the maturity and type of the security, and (3) the sector of the security (such as U.S. Treasury issues, federal agency issues, state and local government obligations, corporate bonds, foreign bonds, and other fixed-income instruments). The examples in this chapter are applicable for corporate, municipal, or federal agency bonds with a fixed semiannual coupon. To distinguish these examples from the other types of fixed-income securities such as Treasury bills and other kinds of short-term money market instruments, the word "bond" will be used rather than the broader term "fixed-income securities" throughout the remainder of this chapter. A further assumption is that all coupon income is reinvested at the same yield level as the yield to maturity implied by the bond's price.

While many investors possess some instinctive sense of how the major variables mentioned earlier affect bond prices and yields in a general way, it can be of great value to analyze the magnitude of influence on price levels caused by each of these variables, whether acting alone or in concert with one another. Unfortunately, very little perspective is gained by the cumbersome and time-consuming process of flipping through pages of financial tables which contain yields and prices for various combinations of coupons and maturities. Furthermore, because of space considerations many yield books contain only a limited range of yield and price information. In many cases, these books are discovered to have been constructed for a different interest rate environment than that which the investor happens to be experiencing or anticipating. When used merely to compute individual yields and prices, the otherwise most helpful electronic calculators provide very little perspective on the continuities and discontinuities of yields and prices as maturity, coupon, and other variables are allowed to range over a large number of neighboring values.

A more profound understanding of the forces which influence bond prices over a wide range of conditions (and, by implication, over more narrowly defined circumstances as well) can be gained by constructing a series of charts which bring together information normally contained in the front, middle, and back of several yield books. These regrouped data are most valuable in pointing out certain yield and price relationships which may otherwise be difficult to identify.

For bonds with coupons (half of whose values are paid semiannually) of 2 percent, 4 percent, 6 percent, 8 percent, and 10 percent and with 11 different maturities ranging from 3 months to 100 years, initial prices, ending prices, and net price changes have been computed for the following beginning and ending yield levels:

Table number	Beginning yield level (percent)	Ending yield levels (percent)
12-1	2	3 and 2.5
12-2	4	5 and 4.5
12-3	6	7 and 6.5
12-4	8	9 and 8.5
12-5	10	11 and 10.5

As can be seen, in all five tables the ending yield levels are 100 basis points and 50 basis points respectively higher than the beginning yield levels. Thus the tables show how bonds of 11 different maturities, with five different coupons, change in price for a rise in interest rates of either 100 basis points or 50 basis points, starting from five different initial yield levels. In the discussion of Tables 12-2 through 12-5, brief emphasis is given to the following topics: (1) in Table 12-2, the effect of a bond's *coupon* on its price fluctuations; (2) in Table 12-3, the effect of a bond's *maturity* on its price fluctuations; (3) in Table 12-4, the effect of the *magnitude of an interest rate change* on a bond's price fluctuations; and (4) in Table 12-5, the effect of a bond's *beginning yield level* on its price fluctuations. A schematic diagram of how the tables relate to each other is set forth in Figure 12-1.

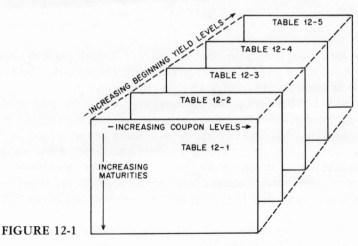

FIGURE 12-1

Tables 12-1 through 12-5 have been organized by beginning yield level rather than by coupon, since investors normally seek to compare several different coupon issues within a given interest rate environment. Before reviewing the tables in greater detail, it may be useful to describe some aspects of their construction.

First, all prices have been computed to three decimal places by using a Compucorp® 360/65 Bond Trader portable calculator.[1] A large number of randomly selected calculations have then been positively verified for accuracy with bond value tables published by the Financial Publishing Company.[2]

Second, there is a gradual escalation in maturity levels for each succeeding row in Tables 12-1 through 12-5. For example, a progression from the eighth row to the ninth row of any of the five tables causes an extension in maturity of 5 years (from 15 years' maturity to 20 years' maturity), which represents a 33 percent increase ($\frac{5}{15}$) in maturity. However, a shift from the ninth row to the tenth row of any of these tables causes an extension in maturity of 20 years (from 20 years' maturity to 40 years' maturity), which represents a 100 percent increase ($\frac{20}{20}$) in maturity.

Third, the 100-basis-point and 50-basis-point rises in interest rate levels represent varying proportions of the beginning yield levels and coupons. The extent of this variation is shown in the accompanying table:

100-basis-point rise		50-basis-point rise	
Beginning yield level or coupon (percent)	Percent change	Beginning yield level or coupon (percent)	Percent change
2	50.0	2	25.0
4	25.0	4	12.5
6	16.7	6	8.3
8	12.5	8	6.3
10	10.0	10	5.0

Thus, for a given maturity a 100-basis-point or 50-basis-point rise in interest rates represents a proportionately less dramatic change as the absolute value of the beginning yield level or coupon rises.

Fourth, 100-basis-point and 50-basis-point rises in interest rates, rather than specified percentage changes in interest rate levels, are used in Tables 12-1 through 12-5. This is done because many investors tend to think of interest rate changes in terms of basis points rather than in terms of a specified percentage change in interest rate levels. For example, with interest rates at 8 percent, bond market analysts may forecast a 25- to 50-basis-point fall in interest rates instead of predicting that interest rates will fall by 3.125 per-

---

[1]Manufactured by the Computer Design Corporation, Los Angeles, Calif. 90064.
[2]82 Brookline Ave., Boston, Mass. 02115.

cent $\left(\dfrac{0.25\ \text{percent}}{8.00\ \text{percent}} \right)$ to 6.25 percent $\left(\dfrac{0.50\ \text{percent}}{8.00\ \text{percent}} \right)$ in absolute percentage terms.

Nevertheless, because a 50-basis-point move upward or downward in interest rates from a beginning yield level of 4 percent implies as dramatic a shift as a 100-basis-point move upward or downward in interest rates from a beginning yield level of 8 percent, a number of bond market participants prefer to think of interest rate changes in terms of a *percentage* of beginning yield levels. For example, if interest rates rise by 60 basis points from a beginning yield level of 6 percent, they may be said to rise by 10 percent $\left(\dfrac{0.60\ \text{percent}}{6.00\ \text{percent}} \right)$. There is no entirely satisfactory solution to the issue of whether it is preferable to use basis-point changes or percentage changes in yield levels. Nevertheless, it may fairly be stated that basis-point changes in interest rates closely mirror actual bond price changes for low-coupon bonds and that percentage changes in interest rates accurately reflect actual bond price changes for sufficiently long-maturity bonds.

Fifth, rising yield levels rather than falling yield levels have been utilized in all calculations in the tables. In a later section of this chapter, ratios have been calculated for selected beginning yield levels, coupon rates, and maturities to show how the net price *loss* caused by a *rise* in interest rates compares with the net price *gain* caused by an equivalent basis-point *drop* in interest rates.

Sixth, Tables 12-1 through 12-5 concentrate on the *absolute* price change (in points) for bonds of varying coupons, maturities, and beginning yield levels. A similar series, Tables 12-6 through 12-10, provides information about the *percentage* price changes for these same bonds (although only 6 maturity categories are shown in Tables 12-6 through 12-10, compared with 11 maturity categories in Tables 12-1 through 12-5).

Point Changes in Bond Prices

In most of the following discussion concerning both point changes and percentage changes in bond prices, attention has been focused on the effects of a 100-basis-point, rather than a 50-basis-point, rise in interest levels. Later in this chapter, for selected beginning yield levels, coupon rates, and maturities, ratios are calculated for price changes resulting from a *100*-basis-point rise in interest rates as compared with a *50*-basis-point rise in interest rates.

Two Percent Beginning Yield Levels

Table 12-1 shows the price changes which occur when interest rate levels move from 2 percent to 3 percent and from 2 percent to 2.5 percent for

TABLE 12-1
Bond Price Changes from 2 Percent Beginning Yield Levels

Coupon	2 percent		4 percent		6 percent		8 percent		10 percent	
Beginning yield	2 percent		2 percent		2 percent		2 percent		2 percent	
Ending yields	2.5 percent	3.0 percent	2.5 percent	3.0 percent	2.5 percent	3.0 percent	2.5 percent	3.0 percent	2.5 percent	3.0 percent
3 months	100.000	100.000	100.492	100.492	100.987	100.987	101.482	101.482	101.977	101.977
	99.872	99.748	100.366	100.240	100.840	100.733	101.354	101.225	101.847	101.718
	−0.128	−0.252	−0.126	−0.252	−0.127	−0.234	−0.128	−0.257	−0.130	−0.259
6 months	100.000	100.000	100.990	100.990	101.980	101.980	102.970	102.970	103.960	103.960
	99.753	99.507	100.740	100.492	101.728	101.477	102.716	102.463	103.703	103.448
	−0.247	−0.493	−0.250	−0.498	−0.252	−0.503	−0.254	−0.507	−0.257	−0.512
1 year	100.000	100.000	101.970	101.970	103.940	103.940	105.911	105.911	107.881	107.881
	99.509	99.022	101.472	100.977	103.435	102.933	105.398	104.889	107.361	106.845
	−0.491	−0.978	−0.498	−0.993	−0.505	−1.007	−0.513	−1.022	−0.520	−1.036
2 years	100.000	100.000	103.901	103.901	107.803	107.803	111.705	111.705	115.607	115.607
	99.030	98.072	102.908	101.927	106.786	105.781	110.664	109.635	114.542	113.490
	−0.970	−1.928	−0.993	−1.974	−1.017	−2.022	−1.041	−2.070	−1.065	−2.117
3 years	100.000	100.000	105.795	105.795	111.590	111.590	117.386	117.386	123.181	123.181
	98.563	97.151	104.309	102.848	110.055	108.545	115.801	114.242	121.547	119.940
	−1.437	−2.849	−1.486	−2.947	−1.535	−3.045	−1.585	−3.144	−1.634	−3.241

5 years	100.000	100.000	109.471	109.471	118.942	118.942	128.413	128.413	137.885	137.885
	95.388	97.663	104.611	107.059	113.833	116.354	123.055	125.700	132.277	135.045
	−4.612	−2,337	−4.860	−2.462	−5.109	−2.588	−5.358	−2.713	−5.608	−2.840
10 years	100.000	100.000	118.045	118.045	136.091	136.091	154.136	154.136	172.182	172.182
	91.415	95.600	100.584	113.199	125.752	130.798	142.921	148.398	160.090	165.997
	−8.585	−4.400	−9.461	−4.846	−10.339	−5.293	−11.215	−5.738	−12.092	−6.185
15 years	100.000	100.000	125.807	125.807	151.615	151.615	177.423	177.423	203.230	203.230
	87.992	93.777	112.007	118.666	136.023	143.555	160.039	168.444	184.055	193.333
	−12.008	−6.223	−13.800	−7.141	−15.592	−8.060	−17.384	−8.979	−19.175	−9.897
20 years	100.000	100.000	132.834	132.834	165.669	165.669	198.504	198.504	231.338	231.338
	85.042	92.168	114.957	123.495	144.873	154.822	174.789	186.149	204.705	217.475
	−14.958	−7.832	−17.877	−9.339	−20.796	−10.847	−23.715	−12.355	−26.638	−13.863
40 years	100.000	100.000	154.888	154.888	209.776	209.776	264.664	264.664	319.552	319.552
	76.796	87.403	123.203	137.789	169.610	188.176	216.018	238.563	262.425	288.949
	−23.204	−12.597	−31.685	−17.099	−40.166	−21.600	−48.646	−26.101	−57.127	−30.603
100 years	100.000	100.000	186.331	186.331	272.662	272.662	358.994	358.994	445.325	445.325
	68.363	81.667	131.636	154.997	194.909	228.328	258.181	301.659	321.454	374.989
	−31.637	−18.333	−54.695	−31.334	−77.753	−44.334	−100.813	−57.335	−123.871	−70.336

bonds of (1) maturities ranging from 3 months to 100 years and (2) coupons of 2 percent, 4 percent, 6 percent, 8 percent, and 10 percent. To illustrate how Tables 12-1 through 12-5 can be used, it is worthwhile to consider a 6 percent, 10-year bond in a 2 percent yield environment. By looking at the intersection of the seventh row (10 years' maturity) and the third column (6 percent coupon) in Table 12-1, the investor can find a price of 136.091 (or $1360.91 per $1000 face-value bond). If interest rates rise from 2 percent to 3 percent, the 10-year-maturity, 6 percent bond will fall in price to 125.-752, producing a net loss of 10.339 points. If interest rates rise from 2 percent to 2.5 percent, the 10-year-maturity, 6 percent coupon bond will fall in price by a lesser amount to 130.798, causing a net loss of 5.293 points.

Because the beginning yield level of 2 percent is equal to or below all coupon levels shown in Table 12-1, all bonds in the table are priced initially either at par or at a premium to par. In addition, for a given maturity and coupon level, Table 12-1 contains the largest point declines in absolute terms of any bonds shown in Tables 12-1 through 12-5. The reason is that the 100-basis-point and 50-basis-point changes in interest rate levels represent a much larger proportion of the 2 percent beginning yield level than they would for a 4 percent, 6 percent, 8 percent, or 10 percent beginning yield level. The highest absolute price shown in any of Tables 12-1 through 12-5 is contained in Table 12-1: for a 10 percent coupon, 100-year-maturity bond at a 2 percent beginning yield level, the price is 445.325.

Four Percent Beginning Yield Levels

Table 12-2 shows the price changes which occur when interest rate levels move from 4 percent to 5 percent and from 4 percent to 4.5 percent for bonds of (1) maturities ranging from 3 months to 100 years and (2) coupons of 2 percent, 4 percent, 6 percent, 8 percent, and 10 percent. In a 4 percent beginning yield environment, the previously illustrated 10-year-maturity, 6 percent coupon bond is worth 116.351 (compared with a price of 136.091 in a 2 percent beginning yield climate). If interest rates rise by 100 basis points, to 5 percent, this bond adjusts in price to 107.794, resulting in a net loss of 8.557 points.

At beginning yield levels of 4 percent, all 2 percent bonds are valued below par, all 4 percent bonds are valued at par, and all bonds with coupons above 4 percent are valued at premiums over par. The influence of the interest coupon on bond prices can be briefly examined in Table 12-2. For example, for a 20-year bond in a 4 percent beginning yield environment, prices for issues with different coupons are shown below:

	Coupon				
	2 percent	4 percent	6 percent	8 percent	10 percent
Price	72.644	100.000	127.355	154.710	182.066

TABLE 12-2
Bond Price Changes from 4 Percent Beginning Yield Levels

Coupon	2 percent		4 percent		6 percent		8 percent		10 percent	
Beginning yield	4 percent		4 percent		4 percent		4 percent		4 percent	
Ending yield	5.0 percent	4.5 percent	5.0 percent	4.5 percent	5.0 percent	4.5 percent	5.0 percent	4.5 percent	5.0 percent	4.5 percent
3 months	99.500	99.500	100.000	100.000	100.480	100.480	100.970	100.970	101.460	101.460
	99.253	99.376	99.740	99.865	100.238	100.354	100.716	100.843	101.203	101.331
	−0.247	−0.124	−0.260	−0.135	−0.242	−0.126	−0.254	−0.127	−0.257	−0.129
6 months	99.019	99.019	100.000	100.000	100.980	100.980	101.960	101.960	102.941	102.941
	98.536	98.777	99.512	99.755	100.487	100.733	101.463	101.711	102.439	102.689
	−0.483	−0.242	−0.488	−0.245	−0.493	−0.247	−0.497	−0.249	−0.502	−0.252
1 year	98.058	98.058	100.000	100.000	101.941	101.941	103.883	103.883	105.824	105.824
	97.108	97.581	99.036	99.516	100.963	101.450	102.891	103.385	104.818	105.319
	−0.950	−0.477	−0.964	−0.484	−0.978	−0.491	−0.992	−0.498	−1.006	−0.505
2 years	96.192	96.192	100.000	100.000	103.807	103.807	107.615	107.615	111.423	111.423
	94.357	95.269	98.119	99.053	101.850	102.838	105.642	106.623	109.404	110.408
	−1.835	−0.923	−1.881	−0.947	−1.927	−0.969	−1.973	−0.992	−2.019	−1.015
3 years	94.398	94.398	100.000	100.000	105.601	105.601	111.202	111.202	116.804	116.804
	91.737	93.056	97.245	98.611	102.754	104.165	108.262	109.720	113.770	115.274
	−2.661	−1.342	−2.755	−1.389	−2.847	−1.436	−2.940	−1.482	−3.034	−1.530

TABLE 12-2
Bond Price Changes from 4 Percent Beginning Yield Levels (Continued)

Coupon	2 percent		4 percent		6 percent		8 percent		10 percent	
Beginning yield	4 percent		4 percent		4 percent		4 percent		4 percent	
Ending yield	5.0 percent	4.5 percent	5.0 percent	4.5 percent	5.0 percent	4.5 percent	5.0 percent	4.5 percent	5.0 percent	4.5 percent
5 years	91.017	91.017	100.000	100.000	108.982	108.982	117.965	117.965	126.947	126.947
	86.871	88.917	95.623	97.783	104.376	106.649	113.128	115.515	121.880	124.382
	−4.146	−2.100	−4.377	−2.217	−4.606	−2.333	−4.837	−2.450	−5.067	−2.565
10 years	83.648	83.648	100.000	100.000	116.351	116.351	132.702	132.702	149.054	149.054
	76.616	80.045	92.205	96.009	107.794	111.972	123.383	127.936	138.972	143.900
	−7.032	−3.603	−7.795	−3.991	−8.557	−4.379	−9.319	−4.766	−10.082	−5.154
15 years	77.603	77.603	100.000	100.000	122.396	122.396	144.792	144.792	167.189	167.189
	68.604	72.943	89.534	94.588	110.465	116.233	131.395	137.879	152.325	159.524
	−8.999	−4.660	−10.466	−5.412	−11.931	−6.163	−13.397	−6.913	−14.864	−7.665
20 years	72.644	72.644	100.000	100.000	127.355	127.355	154.710	154.710	182.066	182.066
	62.345	67.258	87.448	93.451	112.551	119.645	137.654	145.838	162.756	172.032
	−10.299	−5.386	−12.552	−6.549	−14.804	−7.710	−17.056	−8.872	−19.310	−10.034
40 years	60.255	60.255	100.000	100.000	139.744	139.744	179.489	179.489	219.233	219.233
	48.322	53.812	82.774	90.762	117.225	127.712	151.677	164.667	186.129	201.611
	−11.933	−6.443	−17.226	−9.238	−22.519	−12.032	−27.812	−14.827	−33.104	−17.622
100 years	50.952	50.952	100.000	100.000	149.047	149.047	198.094	198.094	247.142	247.142
	40.429	45.093	80.143	89.018	119.856	132.944	159.570	176.869	199.283	220.795
	−10.523	−5.859	−19.857	−10.982	−29.191	−16.103	−38.524	−21.225	−47.859	−26.347

For a 2 percent coupon, 20-year bond to produce a 4 percent yield to maturity (unless otherwise specified, all references to "yield" in this chapter refer to yield to maturity), it must sell at 72.644, which is a significant discount to par. On the other hand, if a 10 percent coupon, 20-year bond is to produce a 4 percent yield to maturity, its price works out to 182.066, which is a very large premium over par.

From this example and from the other bonds in Tables 12-1 through 12-5, it can be concluded that, all other factors being held constant, the higher the coupon relative to a bond's initial yield level, the higher that bond's price will be, and the lower the coupon relative to a bond's initial yield level, the lower that bond's price will be.

Six Percent Beginning Yield Levels

Table 12-3 shows the price changes which occur when interest rate levels move from 6 percent to 7 percent and from 6 percent to 6.5 percent for bonds of (1) maturities ranging from 3 months to 100 years and (2) coupons of 2 percent, 4 percent, 6 percent, 8 percent, and 10 percent. A 10-year-maturity, 6 percent coupon bond is valued at par at beginning interest rates of 6 percent. If interest rates rise by 100 basis points, this bond will drop by 7.107 points in price to 92.893.

At beginning yield levels of 6 percent, all 2 percent and 4 percent bonds are priced at a discount to par, all 6 percent bonds are valued at par, and bonds with coupons of 8 percent and 10 percent have prices above par. Table 12-3 can also show how Tables 12-1 through 12-5 can be used to examine the influence of maturity on bond prices. For instance, an 8 percent coupon bond at beginning yield levels of 6 percent will exhibit the following price behavior for the various maturities shown below:

	Maturity					
	3 months	1 year	3 years	5 years	15 years	40 years
Price	100.463	101.913	105.417	108.530	119.600	130.200

As maturities on the 8 percent coupon bond are lengthened, in a 4 percent beginning yield environment the absolute amount of the premium over par increases. Similarly, as maturities are increased on a bond whose coupon is *below* beginning yield levels, the absolute level of the *discount* to par increases. In the example shown above, an 8 percent, 1-year-maturity bond sells at a price of 101.913, whereas an 8 percent, 15-year-maturity bond is valued at a price of 119.600. On the other hand, from Table 12-3 it can be seen that a 4 percent, 1-year bond is valued at 98.086 in a beginning yield environment of 6 percent, while a 4 percent, 15-year bond under the same conditions sells for 80.399, which is a much greater discount than that

TABLE 12-3
Bond Price Changes from 6 Percent Beginning Yield Levels

Coupon	2 percent		4 percent		6 percent		8 percent		10 percent	
Beginning yield	6 percent		6 percent		6 percent		6 percent		6 percent	
Ending yield	7.0 percent	6.5 percent	7.0 percent	6.5 percent	7.0 percent	6.5 percent	7.0 percent	6.5 percent	7.0 percent	6.5 percent
3 months	99.007	99.007	99.492	99.492	100.000	100.000	100.463	100.463	100.948	100.948
	98.762	98.884	99.245	99.369	99.728	99.853	100.211	100.377	100.694	100.821
	−0.245	−0.123	−0.247	−0.123	−0.272	−0.147	−0.252	−0.126	−0.254	−0.127
6 months	98.058	98.058	99.029	99.029	100.000	100.000	100.970	100.970	101.841	101.841
	97.584	97.820	98.550	98.789	99.516	99.757	100.483	100.726	101.449	101.694
	−0.474	−0.238	−0.479	−0.240	−0.484	−0.243	−0.487	−0.244	−0.492	−0.247
1 year	96.173	96.173	98.086	98.086	100.000	100.000	101.913	101.913	103.826	103.826
	95.250	95.710	97.150	97.616	99.050	99.523	100.949	101.429	102.849	103.336
	−0.923	−0.463	−0.936	−0.470	−0.950	−0.477	−0.964	−0.484	−0.977	−0.490
2 years	92.565	92.565	96.282	96.282	100.000	100.000	103.717	103.717	107.434	107.434
	90.817	91.686	94.490	95.381	98.163	99.076	101.836	102.771	105.509	106.466
	−1.748	−0.879	−1.792	−0.901	−1.837	−0.924	−1.881	−0.946	−1.925	−0.968
3 years	89.165	89.165	94.582	94.582	100.000	100.000	105.417	105.417	110.834	110.834
	86.678	87.911	92.007	93.284	97.535	98.656	102.664	104.029	107.992	109.402
	−2.487	−1.254	−2.575	−1.298	−2.665	−1.344	−2.753	−1.388	−2.842	−1.432

5 years	82.939	82.939	91.469	91.469	100.000	100.000	108.530	108.530	117.060	117.060
	79.202	81.049	87.525	89.472	95.841	97.894	104.158	106.316	112.474	114.739
	−3.731	−1.890	−3.944	−1.997	−4.159	−2.106	−4.372	−2.214	−4.586	−2.321
10 years	70.245	70.245	85.122	85.122	100.000	100.000	114.877	114.877	129.754	129.754
	64.468	67.286	78.681	81.825	92.893	96.365	107.106	110.904	121.318	125.443
	−5.777	−2.959	−6.441	−3.297	−7.107	−3.635	−7.771	−3.973	−8.436	−4.311
15 years	60.799	60.799	80.399	80.399	100.000	100.000	119.600	119.600	139.200	139.200
	54.019	57.290	72.411	76.272	90.803	95.254	109.196	114.236	127.588	133.218
	−6.780	−3.509	−7.988	−4.127	−9.197	−4.746	−10.404	−5.364	−11.612	−5.982
20 years	53.770	53.770	76.885	76.885	100.000	100.000	123.114	123.114	146.229	146.229
	46.612	50.031	67.967	72.339	89.322	94.447	110.677	116.656	132.032	138.864
	−7.158	−3.739	−8.918	−4.646	−10.678	−5.553	−12.437	−6.458	−14.197	−7.365
40 years	39.598	39.598	69.799	69.799	100.000	100.000	130.200	130.200	160.401	160.401
	33.128	36.128	59.876	64.515	86.625	92.903	113.374	121.290	140.123	149.677
	−6.470	−3.470	−9.923	−5.284	−13.375	−7.097	−16.826	−8.910	−20.278	−10.724
100 years	33.513	33.513	66.756	66.756	100.000	100.000	133.243	133.243	166.486	166.486
	28.644	30.884	57.186	61.602	85.728	92.320	114.271	123.038	142.813	153.756
	−4.869	−2.629	−9.570	−5.154	−14.272	−7.680	−18.972	−10.205	−23.673	−12.730

exhibited by the shorter-maturity issue. It can be concluded from these examples and from most other cases (the exceptions will be treated in Chapter 13) that, all other factors being held constant, the longer the maturity of a bond, the greater its fall or rise in price as interest rates rise or decline.

Eight Percent Beginning Yield Levels

Table 12-4 shows the price changes which occur when interest rate levels move from 8 percent to 9 percent and from 8 percent to 8.5 percent for bonds of (1) maturities ranging from 3 months to 100 years and (2) coupons of 2 percent, 4 percent, 6 percent, 8 percent, and 10 percent. A 10-year-maturity, 6 percent coupon bond is valued at 86.409 at beginning yield levels of 8 percent. If interest rates rise by 100 basis points, this bond will fall in price to 80.488, for a loss of 5.921 points.

At beginning yield levels of 8 percent, all 2 percent, 4 percent, and 6 percent bonds are priced at a discount to par, all 8 percent issues are valued at par, and 10 percent bonds are priced at premiums over par. The influence of the magnitude of interest rate movements can be examined in Table 12-4. For example, for a 40-year-maturity, 6 percent bond in an 8 percent beginning yield environment, the greater price change for a 100-basis-point rise in interest rates as compared with a 50-basis-point rise is shown below:

	Magnitude of interest rate change	
	Rise from 8 to 9 percent	Rise from 8 to 8.5 percent
Price change	− 8.433	− 4.443

It can be seen from this example and from observation of all the other bonds in Tables 12-1 through 12-5 that, all other factors being held constant, the greater the magnitude of an interest rate change, the greater the resultant increase in bond prices.

Ten Percent Beginning Yield Levels

Table 12-5 shows the price changes which occur when interest rate levels move from 10 percent to 11 percent and from 10 percent to 10.5 percent for bonds of (1) maturities ranging from 3 months to 100 years and (2) coupons of 2 percent, 4 percent, 6 percent, 8 percent, and 10 percent. A 10-year-maturity, 6 percent coupon bond is valued at 75.075 at beginning yield levels of 10 percent. If interest rates rise by 100 basis points, this bond will fall in price to 70.124, for a loss of 4.951 points.

At beginning yield levels of 10 percent, the 2 percent, 4 percent, 6 percent, and 8 percent bonds all are priced at a discount to par, and the 10 percent bonds are priced at par. In addition, for a given maturity and coupon

TABLE 12-4
Bond price changes from 8 percent beginning yield levels

Coupon	2 percent		4 percent		6 percent		8 percent		10 percent	
Beginning yield	8 percent		8 percent		8 percent		8 percent		8 percent	
Ending yield	9.0 percent	8.5 percent	9.0 percent	8.5 percent	9.0 percent	8.5 percent	9.0 percent	8.5 percent	9.0 percent	8.5 percent
3 months	98.519	98.519	99.000	99.000	99.480	99.480	100.000	100.000	100.441	100.441
	98.277	98.398	98.755	98.877	99.233	99.356	99.711	99.835	100.189	100.315
	−0.392	−0.121	−0.245	−0.123	−0.247	−0.124	−0.289	−0.165	−0.252	−0.126
6 months	97.115	97.115	98.076	98.076	99.038	99.038	100.000	100.000	100.961	100.961
	96.650	96.882	97.607	97.841	98.564	98.800	99.521	99.760	100.478	100.719
	−0.465	−0.233	−0.469	−0.235	−0.474	−0.238	−0.479	−0.240	−0.483	−0.242
1 year	94.341	94.341	96.227	96.227	98.113	98.113	100.000	100.000	101.886	101.886
	93.445	93.892	95.315	95.771	97.190	97.650	99.063	99.530	100.936	101.409
	−0.896	−0.449	−0.909	−0.456	−0.923	−0.463	−0.937	−0.470	−0.950	−0.477
2 years	89.111	89.111	92.740	92.740	96.370	96.370	100.000	100.000	103.629	103.629
	87.443	88.272	91.031	91.820	94.618	95.489	98.206	99.097	101.793	103.706
	−1.668	−0.839	−1.709	−0.860	−1.752	−0.881	−1.794	−0.903	−1.836	−0.923
3 years	84.273	84.273	89.515	89.515	94.757	94.757	100.000	100.000	105.242	105.242
	81.947	83.100	87.105	88.300	92.263	93.500	97.421	98.700	102.578	103.899
	−2.326	−1.173	−2.410	−1.215	−2.494	−1.257	−2.599	−1.300	−2.664	−1.343

TABLE 12-4
Bond price changes from 8 percent beginning yield levels (Continued)

Coupon	2 percent		4 percent		6 percent		8 percent		10 percent	
Beginning yield	8 percent		8 percent		8 percent		8 percent		8 percent	
Ending yield	9.0 percent	8.5 percent	9.0 percent	8.5 percent	9.0 percent	8.5 percent	9.0 percent	8.5 percent	9.0 percent	8.5 percent
5 years	75.667	75.667	83.778	83.778	91.889	91.889	100.000	100.000	108.110	108.110
	72.305	73.964	80.218	81.975	88.130	89.986	96.043	97.997	103.956	106.008
	−3.362	−1.703	−3.560	−1.803	−3.759	−1.903	−3.957	−2.003	−4.154	−2.102
10 years	59.229	59.229	72.819	72.819	86.409	86.409	100.000	100.000	113.590	113.590
	54.472	56.793	67.480	70.087	80.488	83.382	93.496	96.676	106.503	109.970
	−4.757	−2.436	−5.339	−2.732	−5.921	−3.027	−6.504	−3.324	−7.087	−3.620
15 years	48.123	48.123	65.415	65.415	82.707	82.707	100.000	100.000	117.292	117.292
	42.988	45.468	59.227	62.247	75.566	79.026	91.855	95.805	108.144	112.584
	−5.135	−2.655	−6.138	−3.168	−7.141	−3.681	−8.145	−4.195	−9.148	−4.708
20 years	40.621	40.621	60.414	60.414	80.207	80.207	100.000	100.000	119.792	119.792
	35.594	37.998	53.996	57.076	72.397	76.153	90.799	95.230	109.200	114.307
	−5.027	−2.623	−6.418	−3.338	−7.810	−4.054	−9.201	−4.770	−10.592	−5.485
40 years	28.253	28.253	52.169	52.169	76.084	76.084	100.000	100.000	123.915	123.915
	24.521	26.267	46.086	48.954	67.651	71.641	89.217	94.328	110.782	117.015
	−3.732	−1.986	−6.083	−3.215	−8.433	−4.443	−10.783	−5.672	−13.133	−6.900
100 years	25.029	25.029	50.019	50.019	75.009	75.009	100.000	100.000	124.990	124.990
	22.233	23.547	44.452	47.071	66.671	70.595	88.890	94.119	111.109	117.642
	−2.796	−1.482	−5.567	−2.948	−8.338	−4.414	−11.110	−5.881	−13.881	−7.348

TABLE 12-5
Bond price changes from 10 percent beginning yield levels

Coupon	2 percent		4 percent		6 percent		8 percent		10 percent	
Beginning yield	10 percent		10 percent		10 percent		10 percent		10 percent	
Ending yield	11.0 percent	10.5 percent	11.0 percent	10.5 percent	11.0 percent	10.5 percent	11.0 percent	10.5 percent	11.0 percent	10.5 percent
3 months	98.036	98.036	98.512	98.512	98.987	98.987	99.463	99.463	100.000	100.000
	97.796	97.916	98.270	98.390	98.743	98.865	99.216	99.339	97.689	99.814
	−0.240	−0.120	−0.242	−0.122	−0.244	−0.122	−0.247	−0.124	−0.311	−0.186
6 months	96.190	96.190	97.142	97.142	98.095	98.095	98.047	98.047	100.000	100.000
	95.734	95.961	96.682	96.912	97.630	97.862	98.578	98.812	99.526	99.762
	−0.456	−0.229	−0.460	−0.230	−0.465	−0.233	−0.469	−0.235	−0.474	−0.238
1 year	92.562	97.552	94.421	94.421	96.281	96.281	98.140	98.140	100.000	100.000
	91.091	91.125	93.537	93.978	95.384	95.831	97.230	97.683	99.076	99.536
	−0.871	−0.437	−0.884	−0.443	−0.897	−0.450	−0.910	−0.457	−0.924	−0.464
2 years	85.816	85.816	89.362	89.362	92.908	92.908	96.454	96.454	100.000	100.000
	84.226	85.016	87.731	88.542	91.237	92.067	94.742	95.593	98.247	99.118
	−1.590	−0.800	−1.631	−0.820	−1.671	−0.841	−1.712	−0.861	−1.753	−0.882
3 years	79.697	79.697	84.772	84.772	89.848	89.848	94.924	94.924	100.000	100.000
	77.520	78.599	82.515	83.635	87.511	88.670	92.506	93.705	97.502	98.741
	−2.177	−1.098	−2.257	−1.137	−2.337	−1.178	−2.418	−1.219	−2.498	−1.259

TABLE 12-5
Bond price changes from 10 percent beginning yield levels (*Continued*)

Coupon	2 percent		4 percent		6 percent		8 percent		10 percent	
Beginning yield	10 percent		10 percent		10 percent		10 percent		10 percent	
Ending yield	11.0 percent	10.5 percent	11.0 percent	10.5 percent	11.0 percent	10.5 percent	11.0 percent	10.5 percent	11.0 percent	10.5 percent
5 years	69.113	69.113	76.834	76.834	84.556	84.556	92.278	92.278	100.000	100.000
	66.080	67.577	73.618	75.206	81.155	82.835	88.693	90.463	96.231	98.092
	−3.033	−1.536	−3.216	−1.628	−3.401	−1.721	−3.585	−1.815	−3.769	−1.908
10 years	50.151	50.151	62.613	62.613	75.075	75.075	87.537	87.537	100.000	100.000
	46.223	48.140	58.173	60.342	70.124	72.544	82.074	84.747	94.024	96.949
	−3.928	−2.011	−4.440	−2.271	−4.951	−2.531	−5.463	−2.790	−5.976	−3.051
15 years	38.510	38.510	53.882	53.882	69.255	69.255	84.627	84.627	100.000	100.000
	34.598	36.488	49.131	51.432	63.665	66.376	78.199	81.320	92.733	96.264
	−3.912	−2.022	−4.751	−2.450	−5.590	−2.879	−6.428	−3.307	−7.267	−3.736
20 years	31.363	31.363	48.522	48.522	65.681	65.681	82.840	82.840	100.000	100.000
	27.772	29.503	43.838	46.090	59.884	62.678	75.930	79.265	91.976	95.853
	−3.571	−1.860	−4.684	−2.432	−5.797	−3.003	−6.910	−3.575	−8.024	−4.147
40 years	21.614	21.614	41.210	41.210	60.807	60.807	80.403	80.403	100.000	100.000
	19.310	20.398	37.241	39.127	55.172	57.857	73.103	76.587	91.034	95.317
	−2.304	−1.216	−3.969	−2.083	−5.635	−2.950	−7.300	−3.816	−8.966	−4.683
100 years	20.004	20.004	40.003	40.003	60.002	60.002	80.001	80.001	100.000	100.000
	18.183	19.050	36.365	38.097	54.546	57.144	72.727	76.191	90.909	95.238
	−1.821	−0.954	−3.638	−1.906	−5.456	−2.858	−7.274	−3.810	−9.091	−4.762

level, Table 12-5 contains the smallest point declines of any of Tables 12-1 through 12-5. The reason is that the 100-basis-point and 50-basis-point changes in interest rate levels represent a much smaller proportion of the 10 percent beginning yield level than they would for a 2 percent, 4 percent, 6 percent, or 8 percent beginning yield level. The lowest price shown in any of the tables is contained in Table 12-5: for a 2 percent coupon, 100-year bond at an 11 percent ending yield level, the resultant price is 18.183.

By tracing the price performance of the 6 percent, 10-year-maturity bond through successively higher beginning yield levels, the following pattern can be observed for a 100-basis-point rise:

Beginning yield level (percent)	Price	Ending yield level (percent)	Price	Net price change (in points)
2	136.091	3	125.752	− 10.339
4	116.351	5	107.794	− 8.557
6	100.000	7	92.893	− 7.107
8	86.409	9	80.488	− 5.921
10	75.075	11	70.124	− 4.951

Thus, for a given coupon and maturity, the higher the beginning yield level, the lower the initial price of the bond. An additional very important conclusion can be drawn from observation of the price performance of the 6 percent coupon, 10-year bond: for a given maturity, coupon, and absolute value of change in interest rates, a bond's absolute price performance is influenced greatly by the beginning yield level.

For example, for a 100-basis-point rise in interest rates, a 6 percent, 10-year-maturity issue will lose 10.339 points (7.6 percent of its original capital value) in a 2 percent beginning yield environment, 7.107 points (7.1 percent of its original capital value) in a 6 percent beginning yield environment, and 4.951 points (6.6 percent of its original capital value) in a 10 percent beginning yield environment. In general, for a given basis-point rise in interest rates, maturity, and coupon, a bond's point and percentage price decline will decrease as beginning interest rate levels rise. This might have been expected, since as beginning yield levels rise, a fixed basis-point rise in interest rates accounts for progressively smaller percentages of the original interest level. In addition, as bond prices move lower, it takes less of a net point change to have an impact on the yield produced by the progressively lower starting prices.

Two additional conclusions can be drawn from looking at Tables 12-1 through 12-5 as a group. First, it can be seen that for very short maturities of 1 year or less, the price decline for a given change in interest rates is approximately the same regardless of the beginning coupon and yield level. Second, when the beginning yield level is less than or equal to the coupon rate, for a given basis-point rise in interest rates the absolute amount of point price decline experienced by a bond increases as the maturity is lengthened. For example, from Table 12-2, for a 100-basis-point rise in interest rates from a 4 percent beginning yield level, it can be seen that the 4 percent coupon, 3-month-maturity bond loses 0.260 points, and as maturity is lengthened, progressively greater price losses are incurred, reaching a loss of 19.857 points at 100 years' maturity.

However, when the beginning yield level is greater than the coupon rate, for a given basis-point rise in interest rates the absolute amount of point price decline at first increases, then decreases, as the maturity of the bond is lengthened. For example, from Table 12-4 it can be seen that in an 8 percent beginning yield environment, for a 100-basis-point rise in interest rates, a 4 percent coupon bond will decline by 0.245 points in price for an issue of 3 months' maturity. The decline increases to 6.418 points in price for an issue of 20 years' maturity and then decreases to 5.567 points in price for an issue of 100 years' maturity.

Factors Influencing the Magnitude of Bond Price Changes

In the discussion of Tables 12-1 through 12-5, the factors which influence the amount of change in a bond's price were held constant while only one factor, such as coupon, beginning yield level, maturity, or the magnitude of change in interest rates was allowed to vary. In a procedure deriving and deviating from this method, it is worthwhile to examine (1) those factors which have the most influence on the amount of change in a bond's price, (2) the causes underlying a particular factor's influence on a bond's price change, and (3) the way in which the effect on bond prices can be analyzed when more than one factor is allowed to vary.

To obtain further enlightenment on these questions and on the nature of bond price movements in general, it is useful to review the four main factors which influence the magnitude of a bond's price change:

1. Magnitude of change in interest rates
2. Beginning yield level
3. Coupon
4. Maturity

For the remainder of this chapter, it will be assumed that the first factor, the magnitude of change in interest rates, has been fixed (usually at 100 basis points). This leaves three factors which can vary in combination with one another. For purposes of analysis, only two possibilities have been assigned to each of the remaining three factors: (1) beginning yield level, high or low;

(2) coupon, high or low; and (3) maturity, long or short. By the laws of probability, there are thus 2^3, or 8 possible outcomes to review.

To provide some guidance as to what causes each of these three variables to influence the magnitude of a bond's price change in a certain way, it should be remembered that the yield to maturity on a bond is that internal discount rate which equates the present value of all future principal and interest payments with the market price of the bond. Thus a bond's yield to maturity is a *function* of (1) its purchase price and "disposition" price (usually par, if held to maturity), (2) the time remaining until maturity or disposition of the bond, (3) the coupon level, and (4) the interest level at which the coupons are reinvested (also known as the internal rate of return or the internal reinvestment rate).

These influences on a bond's yield to maturity may be grouped into two general categories which *comprise* yield to maturity: (1) *capital* considerations, which relate to the difference between a bond's purchase price and its disposition price; and (2) *income* considerations, which relate to the total coupon stream and the interest on the reinvestment of the coupons at the internal rate of return. As beginning yield level, coupon, and maturity are allowed to vary, it is possible to observe the part which each factor plays in the capital and income components of yield to maturity. This gives an insight into exactly how each variable exerts its influence on the price of a bond.

Each of the eight possible combinations of beginning yield level, coupon, and maturity has been analyzed for its impact on bond prices and considered as one of the alternatives numbered from 1 through 8 in Figure 12-2. In the figure, for each alternative the influence of a bond's characteristics and yield environment are divided into capital considerations and income considerations. It is possible for certain capital and/or income considerations to contradict or to reinforce one another in their effect on a given bond's price. For example, in the first alternative of Figure 12-2 (high beginning yield level, high coupon, long maturity), it can be seen that (1) the less the given basis-point change in interest rates relative to the beginning yield, the less dramatically the capital value must adjust upward or downward for a fall or rise in interest levels; (2) the later the capital is returned, the more its present value must be adjusted upward or downward for a fall or rise in interest levels (it should also be pointed out that past a certain maturity for a bond the relatively stable discounted value of its flow of coupons begins increasingly to outweigh the discounted value of the principal that is to be repaid at maturity); (3) the higher the coupon relative to initial yield levels, the lower the adjustment in price for a given change in interest rates; and (4) the longer the period during which interest is received, the greater the importance of coupon reinvestment. The effects of other combinations of beginning yield level, coupon, and maturity are also shown in Figure 12-2.

Percentage Changes in Bond Prices

To facilitate comparison of the magnitude of the price changes contained in Tables 12-1 through 12-5 and to analyze further the effect of beginning yield level, coupon, and maturity on bond prices, Tables 12-6 through 12-10 have been constructed in slightly abbreviated form (only 6 of the 11 maturities

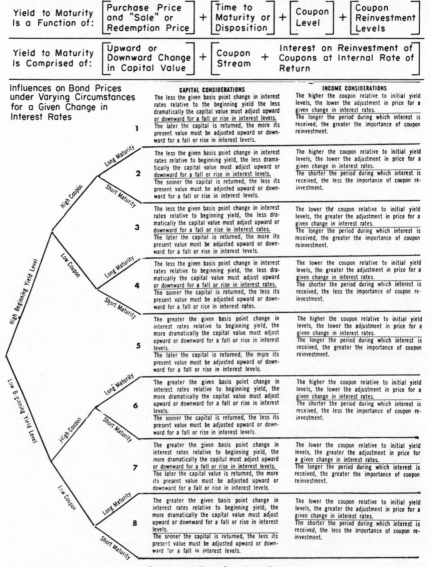

FIGURE 12-2   Factors influencing bond price changes

contained in Tables 12-1 through 12-5 have been included) to show the *percentage changes* according to coupon and maturity for a 100-basis-point rise in interest rates for the following beginning yield levels:

Table number	Beginning yield level (percent)
12-6	2
12-7	4
12-8	6
12-9	8
12-10	10

In Tables 12-6 through 12-10, the percentage price changes are rounded to the nearest tenth of 1 percent. The investor should keep in mind that the percentages in Tables 12-6 through 12-10 have been rounded, since seemingly equivalent values may in fact differ from one another.

To aid in the active comparison between Tables 12-6 through 12-10, they have been presented together. As an example of how to use the tables, an investor might wish to know what price risk would be incurred if interest rates rise by 100 basis points for a 40-year, 10 percent coupon bond (with 40-year bonds of the chosen quality level then trading at 8 percent yields) as compared with a 10-year, 4 percent coupon issue (with 10-year bonds of the chosen quality rating trading at 6 percent yields). If we assume an interest rate rise of 100 basis points on both issues, the percentage decline in principal for each issue can be located and compared as follows:

Initial yield level (percent)	Issue	Location	Percentage decline in principal
8	40-year, 10 percent coupon	Table 12-9, row 5, column 5	−10.6
6	10-year, 4 percent coupon	Table 12-8, row 3, column 2	−7.6

With the aid of the percentage tables, the investor can specifically gauge the additional capital risk (a decline of 10.6 percent versus a decline of 7.6 percent) which is incurred by buying the 40-year, 10 percent coupon bond at a beginning yield level of 8 percent as compared with the 10-year, 4 percent coupon bond at a beginning yield level of 6 percent. It should be remembered that this comparison does not consider the time during which the funds must be kept invested or any other aspects of the investor's time horizon parameters. Rather, the focus is on the capital loss that would be incurred under two alternative investment possibilities if interest rates in *both* the 10-year-and the 40-year-maturity sectors of the bond market suddenly rose by 100 basis points.

Tables 12-6 through 12-10 can also be used in conjunction with Figure

TABLE 12-6
**Percentage Price Changes, 2 Percent Beginning Yield Level, for
100-Basis-Point Rise in Interest Rates**

Maturity	Coupon (percent)				
	2	4	6	8	10
1 year	−1.0	−1.0	−1.0	−1.0	−1.0
5 years	−4.6	−4.4	−4.3	−4.2	−4.1
10 years	−8.6	−8.0	−7.6	−7.3	−7.0
20 years	−15.0	−13.5	−12.6	−11.9	−11.5
40 years	−23.2	−20.5	−19.1	−18.4	−17.9
100 years	−31.6	−29.4	−28.5	−28.1	−27.8

TABLE 12-7
**Percentage Price Changes, 4 Percent Beginning Yield Level, for
100-Basis-Point Rise in Interest Rates**

Maturity	Coupon (percent)				
	2	4	6	8	10
1 year	−1.0	−1.0	−1.0	−1.0	−1.0
5 years	−4.6	−4.4	−4.2	−4.1	−4.0
10 years	−8.4	−7.8	−7.4	−7.0	−6.8
20 years	−14.2	−12.6	−11.6	−11.0	−10.6
40 years	−19.8	−17.2	−16.1	−15.5	−15.1
100 years	−20.7	−19.9	−19.6	−19.4	−19.4

TABLE 12-8
**Percentage Price Changes, 6 Percent Beginning Yield Level, for
100-Basis-Point Rise in Interest Rates**

Maturity	Coupon (percent)				
	2	4	6	8	10
1 year	−1.0	−1.0	−1.0	−0.9	−0.9
5 years	−4.5	−4.3	−4.2	−4.0	−3.9
10 years	−8.2	−7.6	−7.1	−6.8	−6.5
20 years	−13.3	−11.6	−10.7	−10.1	−9.7
40 years	−16.3	−14.2	−13.4	−12.9	−12.6
100 years	−14.5	−14.4	−14.3	−14.2	−14.2

TABLE 12-9
Percentage Price Changes, 8 Percent Beginning Yield Level, for
100-Basis-Point Rise in Interest Rates

Maturity	Coupon (percent)				
	2	4	6	8	10
1 year	−0.9	−0.9	−0.9	−0.9	−0.9
5 years	−4.4	−4.3	−4.1	−4.0	−3.8
10 years	−8.0	−7.3	−6.9	−6.5	−6.2
20 years	−12.4	−10.6	−9.7	−9.2	−8.8
40 years	−13.2	−11.7	−11.1	−10.8	−10.6
100 years	−11.2	−11.1	−11.1	−11.1	−11.1

TABLE 12-10
Percentage Price Changes, 10 Percent Beginning Yield Level, for
100-Basis-Point Rise in Interest Rates

Maturity	Coupon (percent)				
	2	4	6	8	10
1 year	−0.9	−0.9	−0.9	−0.9	−0.9
5 years	−4.4	−4.2	−4.0	−3.9	−3.8
10 years	−7.8	−7.1	−6.6	−6.2	−6.0
20 years	−11.4	−9.7	−8.8	−8.3	−8.0
40 years	−10.7	−9.6	−9.3	−9.1	−9.0
100 years	−9.1	−9.1	−9.1	−9.1	−9.1

12-2 to evaluate the price performance of bonds with varying characteristics
if it is assumed that interest rates rise by 100 basis points across the entire
section of the maturity spectrum under comparison. An example is presented
in Figure 12-3.

By ranking each of the alternative bonds and yield conditions according
to the severity of price decline, the following array is obtained:

Beginning yield level (percent)	Coupon (percent)	Maturity (years)	Percentage price decline
2	2	40	−23.2
2	10	40	−17.9
10	2	40	−10.7
10	10	40	−9.0
2	2	5	−4.6
10	2	5	−4.4
2	10	5	−4.1
10	10	5	−3.8

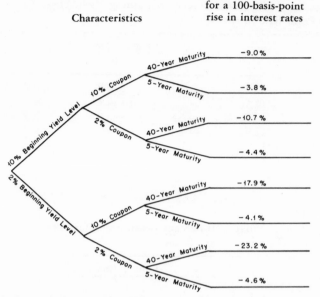

Percentage price decline
for a 100-basis-point
rise in interest rates

FIGURE 12-3   Percentage price changes for bonds of
varying coupons, maturities, and beginning yield levels

Arranging the bonds in this manner helps the investor draw conclusions
about which factors influence bond prices the most. For the particular sets of
conditions outlined in Figure 12-3, (1) maturity has the greatest influence on
bond price changes for all the bonds in the sample; (2) at *long* maturities the
beginning yield level is the second most important influence on bond prices,
followed by the coupon; and (3) at *short* maturities the coupon is the next
most important influence, followed by the beginning yield level. It is important to remember that these factors interact with one another, sometimes
reinforcing one another, sometimes vitiating each other's effect on bond
prices. By performing similar comparisons, the investor can more precisely
judge the risk associated with bonds of a wide range of coupons, maturities,
and beginning yield levels.

Tables 12-6 through 12-10 show the percentage decline in principal for
a 100-basis-point rise in interest rates with the beginning yield level held
constant while the coupon and maturity are allowed to vary. For conve-
nience, the investor may wish to reorganize the data contained in Tables 12-6
through 12-10 to produce either (1) a chart which holds the coupon constant

TABLE 12-11
Percentage Price Changes, 6 Percent Coupon, for 100-Basis-Point Rise in
Interest Rates

	Beginning yield level (percent)				
Maturity	2	4	6	8	10
1 year	−1.0	−1.0	−1.0	−0.9	−0.9
5 years	−4.3	−4.2	−4.2	−4.1	−4.0
10 years	−7.6	−7.4	−7.1	−6.9	−6.6
20 years	−12.6	−11.6	−10.7	−9.7	−8.8
40 years	−19.1	−16.1	−13.4	−11.1	−9.3
100 years	−28.5	−19.6	−14.3	−11.1	−9.1

TABLE 12-12
Percentage Price Changes, 10-Year Maturity, for 100-Basis-Point Rise in
Interest Rates

	Beginning yield level (percent)				
Coupon (percent)	2	4	6	8	10
2	−8.6	−8.4	−8.2	−8.0	−7.8
4	−8.0	−7.8	−7.6	−7.3	−7.1
6	−7.6	−7.4	−7.1	−6.9	−6.6
8	−7.3	−7.0	−6.8	−6.5	−6.2
10	−7.0	−6.8	−6.5	−6.2	−6.0

while allowing the beginning yield level to vary (an example is included as
Table 12-11, which holds the coupon constant at 6 percent) or (2) a chart
which holds the maturity constant while allowing the beginning yield level
and coupon to vary (an example is included as Table 12-12, which holds the
maturity constant at 10 years).

Table 12-12 allows a rapid comparison of the percentage price changes
for the 6 percent, 10-year bond discussed in conjunction with Tables 12-1
through 12-5. For instance, it can be seen that for a 100-basis-point rise in
interest rates a 6 percent, 10-year maturity bond will drop in price by the
following percentages:

Beginning yield level (percent)	Percentage price decline
2	−7.6
4	−7.4
6	−7.1
8	−6.9
10	−6.6

Thus, for a 100-basis-point rise in interest rates, a 6 percent, 10-year maturity bond will decline by 7.6 percent in a 2 percent beginning yield environment but only by 6.6 percent in a 10 percent beginning yield environment.

Tables 12-6 through 12-10 can be used to construct still another type of chart, which shows the *incremental* percentage price risk for a 100-basis-point rise in interest rates which is caused by extending maturity. Drawing a more limited number of samples from Tables 12-5 through 12-10, this table is included as Table 12-13. The investor can employ the table to judge how much additional price risk is being assumed by purchasing a longer-maturity issue. For example, under beginning interest rate conditions of 6 percent, if interest rates rise by 100 basis points, an investor who buys a 5-year issue will lose 3.2 percent more than an investor who purchases a 1-year issue. The percentage losses can be cumulated, allowing an investor to find that a 20-year-maturity, 6 percent coupon issue would incur 9.7 percent more capital risk (derived by adding losses of 3.2, 2.9, and 3.6 percent) than a 1-year maturity, 6 percent coupon issue for a 100-basis-point rise from beginning yield levels of 6 percent.

It can be seen that at low beginning yields (and, to a lesser degree, for low-coupon issues), extending maturity from 20 to 40 years and from 40 to 100 years involves significant additional capital risk if interest rates rise by 100 basis points. On the other hand, as beginning yield levels move upward (and, to some degree, as coupon levels move higher), extending maturity entails much less price risk. For example, if interest rates rise by 100 basis points from their beginning yield level, the incremental risk incurred by

TABLE 12-13
Incremental Percentage Decline in Principal Caused by Extending Maturity, for 100-Basis-Point Rise in Interest Rates

Maturity extension	Beginning yield (percent)								
	2	2	2	6	6	6	10	10	10
	Coupon (percent)								
	2	6	10	2	6	10	2	6	10
From 1 year out to 5 years	−3.6	−3.3	−3.1	−3.5	−3.2	−3.0	−3.5	−3.1	−2.8
From 5 years out to 10 years	−4.0	−3.3	−2.9	−3.7	−2.9	−2.6	−3.4	−2.6	−2.2
From 10 years out to 20 years	−6.4	−5.0	−4.5	−5.1	−3.6	−3.2	−3.6	−2.2	−2.0
From 20 years out to 40 years	−8.2	−6.5	−6.4	−3.0	−2.7	−2.9	+0.7	−0.5	−0.9
From 40 years out to 100 years	−8.4	−9.4	−9.9	+1.8	−0.9	−1.6	+1.6	+0.2	−0.1

having invested in a 100-year bond as compared with a 20-year bond would be as follows for the beginning yield levels and coupons listed below:

Beginning yield level (percent)	Coupon (percent)	Incremental price risk (percent)
2	2	$(-8.2 + -8.4) = -16.6$
6	6	$(-2.7 + -0.9) = -3.6$
10	10	$(-0.9 + -0.1) = -1.0$

Another rather surprising result can be gleaned from Table 12-13. Given a 100-basis-point rise in interest rates, when the coupon is low enough relative to beginning yield levels, less *incremental* price risk is incurred for certain sufficiently long maturity extensions. For example, should interest rates rise by 100 basis points, an investor who buys a 100-year, 2 percent bond at a beginning yield level of 10 percent assumes 1.6 percent *less* incremental capital risk than if a 40-year bond had been purchased. This is demonstrated by the following data, which have been retrieved from Tables 12-5 and 12-10 for a 2 percent coupon bond:

Maturity (years)	Price at 10 percent beginning yield	Price at 11 percent ending yield	Point change	Percentage change
40	21.614	19.310	− 2.304	− 10.7
100	20.004	18.183	− 1.821	− 9.1

The 2 percent coupon, 40-year bond has already been driven down so low in price in the high 10 percent beginning yield environment that extending maturity to 100 years entails less of a point change and less of a percentage change. As mentioned earlier in this chapter, at sufficiently long maturities this phenomenon derives from the much greater importance of coupon flow than that of principal repayment in the total discounted value of a bond. The investor should not confuse the discussion of what happens when maturity is extended with the fact that, given a *fixed* maturity and coupon, an increase in interest rates will always produce a lower absolute bond price.

In the preceding discussion, the primary emphasis on the price change effects generated by a *100*-basis-point *rise* in interest rates naturally raises questions concerning (1) whether bond prices will change by only half as much if interest rates rise by 50 basis points rather than by 100 basis points and (2) whether bond prices will *increase* by the same amount by which bond prices *decline* when interest rates *rise* by 100 basis points rather than *fall* by 100 basis points.

For a selection of beginning yields, coupons, and maturities, a calculation has been made of the ratio of the price change resulting from a *100*-basis-point rise in interest rates to the price change resulting from a *50*-basis-

TABLE 12-14

Ratio of Price Change Resulting from 100-Basis-Point Rise in Interest Rates to Price Change Resulting from 50-Basis-Point Rise in Interest Rates

	Beginning yield (percent)								
	2	2	2	6	6	6	10	10	10
	Coupon (percent)								
Maturity	2	6	10	2	6	10	2	6	10
1 year	1.99	1.99	1.99	1.99	1.99	1.99	1.99	1.99	1.99
15 years	1.93	1.93	1.96	1.93	1.94	1.96	1.93	1.94	1.96
100 years	1.73	1.75	1.76	1.85	1.86	1.86	1.91	1.91	1.91

point rise in interest rates. Since 100 basis points is exactly twice 50 basis points, it would be expected that the ratio of price changes would be $\frac{100 \text{ basis points}}{50 \text{ basis points}} = 2.00$. Such ratios are contained in Table 12-14. As can be seen, for a short maturity (1 year) the ratio (1.99) very closely approximates the 2.00 expected value regardless of beginning yield level and coupon.

At the 15-year maturity level, the ratio ranges between 1.93 and 1.96, with the higher ratio prevailing at the higher coupon and beginning yield levels. At 100 years' maturity, the ratio ranges from between 1.73 and 1.76 (at 2 percent beginning yield levels) to 1.91 (at 10 percent beginning yield levels). To generalize from these results, the lower the beginning yield level, the lower the coupon, and the longer the maturity of a bond, the less likely that a 100-basis-point change in interest rates will produce twice the price change of a 50-basis-point change in interest rates.

Table 12-15 is addressed to the question concerning the ratio of a bond's price decline (when interest rates rise) to its price increase (when interest rates fall by an equivalent number of basis points). For a selection of beginning yields, coupons, and maturities, a calculation has been made of the ratio of the absolute value of the price change resulting from a 100-basis-point *rise* in interest rates to the price change resulting from a 100-basis-point *decline* in interest rates. Since the absolute value of a 100-basis-point move upward in interest rates is equivalent to the absolute value of a 100-basis-point decline in interest rates, it might be expected that the ratio of the price changes resulting therefrom would be $\frac{100 \text{ basis points}}{100 \text{ basis points}} = 1.00$. As can be seen in Table 12-15, for a short maturity the ratio (0.99) very closely approximates the 1.00 expected value regardless of beginning yield and coupon. For a 15-year maturity bond, this ratio ranges between 0.87 and 0.89, with the higher ratio at higher coupons and beginning yield levels. For

TABLE 12-15
Absolute Value of Ratio of Price Change Resulting from 100-Basis-Point Rise in Interest Rates to Price Change Resulting from 100-Basis-Point Decline in Interest Rates

Maturity	Beginning yield (percent)								
	2	2	2	6	6	6	10	10	10
	Coupon (percent)								
	2	6	10	2	6	10	2	6	10
1 year	$\dfrac{-0.978}{+0.992}$	$\dfrac{-1.007}{+1.022}$	$\dfrac{-1.036}{+1.051}$	$\dfrac{-0.923}{+0.935}$	$\dfrac{-0.950}{+0.963}$	$\dfrac{-0.977}{+0.992}$	$\dfrac{-0.871}{+0.883}$	$\dfrac{-0.897}{+0.909}$	$\dfrac{-0.924}{+0.936}$
	0.99	0.99	0.99	0.99	0.99	0.99	0.99	0.99	0.99
15 years	$\dfrac{-12.003}{+13.897}$	$\dfrac{-15.592}{+17.870}$	$\dfrac{-19.175}{+21.843}$	$\dfrac{-6.780}{+7.805}$	$\dfrac{-9.197}{+10.465}$	$\dfrac{-11.612}{+13.125}$	$\dfrac{-3.912}{+4.478}$	$\dfrac{-5.590}{+6.311}$	$\dfrac{-7.267}{+8.144}$
	0.87	0.87	0.88	0.87	0.88	0.88	0.87	0.89	0.89
100 years	$\dfrac{-31.637}{+63.120}$	$\dfrac{-77.753}{+142.939}$	$\dfrac{-123.871}{-222.757}$	$\dfrac{-4.869}{+6.916}$	$\dfrac{-14.272}{+19.856}$	$\dfrac{-23.673}{+32.797}$	$\dfrac{-1.821}{+2.229}$	$\dfrac{-5.456}{+6.669}$	$\dfrac{-9.091}{+11.109}$
	0.50	0.54	0.56	0.70	0.72	0.72	0.82	0.82	0.82

337

a 100-year maturity bond, the ratio ranges from between 0.50 and 0.56 at the 2 percent beginning yield level to 0.82 at the 10 percent beginning yield level.

To generalize from these results, the lower the beginning yield level, the lower the coupon, and the longer the maturity of a bond, the less likely that the price change caused by a 100-basis-point *rise* in interest rates will be equal to the price change caused by a 100-basis-point *decline* in interest rates. In fact, at a 2 percent beginning yield level, a 2 percent coupon, 100-year maturity bond will *decline* by 31.367 points when interest rates *rise* by 100 basis points, which is just *half* the 63.120-point price *rise* which the same bond will experience if interest rates *drop* by 100 basis points.

Several caveats should be mentioned concerning the tables in this chapter. As extensive as they may seem, they are somewhat limited in scope. For coupons, maturities, beginning yield levels, and magnitudes of interest rate changes well outside those treated in this chapter, bond prices may not behave in exactly the same fashion as has been noted and commented upon. Nevertheless, by constructing similar tables and figures the investor can plumb the mysteries of bond price behavior in an organized way.

Interest rate changes have been assumed to occur virtually simultaneously, with either a 50-basis-point or a 100-basis-point adjustment taking place uniformly across the entire maturity spectrum of bonds. In practice, interest rate shifts may take several months or even years, during which time the maturities of the bonds under consideration become progressively shorter. Furthermore, these interest rate changes rarely occur uniformly over a broad spectrum of maturities. In spite of this, by concentrating attention on various maturity ranges and by allowing the fourth factor influencing bond prices (the magnitude of the expected interest rate shift) to vary (it has been fixed throughout most of this chapter) as forecasted by the investor along each preselected maturity segment, it is possible to compare bonds of widely varying coupons, maturities, and beginning yield levels.

The analysis in this chapter has not treated many of the practical considerations which strongly influence the actual net return to an investor, such as taxes and transaction costs. Moreover, because the main focus has been on the mathematical influences on bond prices, credit risk, liquidity, and other psychological factors have been ignored. These very factors, as well as call considerations, accrued interest, the effect of sinking funds on yield to average life, the importance of coupon reinvestment in the determination of total realized yield to maturity, and numerous other refinements may in the end cause a bond to trade far differently than it would according to its value on a theoretical basis.

13

Graphical Analysis of Bond Yields and Prices

Overview

By exhibiting many numerical values in a spatial context, graphs permit a greater understanding of the yield and price relationships for bonds. In addition, the figures used in this chapter have been constructed with several curves graphed on each figure to facilitate simultaneous comparisons of the yield and price relationships of bonds of varying characteristics. The graphs shown in Figures 13-1 through 13-5 present the prices of bonds with maturities of 30 years, 10 years, 5 years, and 1 year; coupons of 2 percent, 4 percent, 6 percent, 8 percent, and 10 percent; and yield-to-maturity levels ranging from 1 percent to 20 percent. The data from which Figures 13-1 through 13-5 have been constructed are shown in Tables 13-1 through 13-5 respectively. A schematic representation of the data displayed in Figures 13-1 through 13-5 and Tables 13-1 through 13-5 is shown below:

Figure number	Coupon level (percent)	Maturity (years)	Yield-to-maturity levels	Underlying data presented in table
13-1	2	30, 10, 5, 1	1 to 20 percent in 1 percent increments	13-1
13-2	4	30, 10, 5, 1	1 to 20 percent in 1 percent increments	13-2
13-3	6	30, 10, 5, 1	1 to 20 percent in 1 percent increments	13-3
13-4	8	30, 10, 5, 1	1 to 20 percent in 1 percent increments	13-4
13-5	10	30, 10, 5, 1	1 to 20 percent in 1 percent increments	13-5

It can be seen that in each of these figures and tables bond prices are calculated for a given constant coupon while maturity and yield to maturity are allowed to vary over a set range of values.

A broad and continuous spectrum of yield-to-maturity values is displayed in Tables 13-1 through 13-5, which support Figures 13-1 through 13-5, in contrast to the somewhat narrower (from 2 to 10 percent) and intermittent yield-to-maturity values shown in Tables 12-1 through 12-5 in Chapter 12. Another difference between these two sets of tables derives from the number of maturities under consideration. Tables 13-1 through 13-5 each show 4 maturities ranging from 1 year to 30 years, while Tables 12-1 through 12-5 each show 11 maturities ranging from 3 months to 100 years. If the investor wishes to analyze the yield and price behavior of bonds with maturities and/or coupons other than those shown in Tables 13-1 through 13-5, it is suggested that such values be computed and superimposed on the figure which displays a coupon value nearest to the one selected by the investor.

Figure 13-6 and its related Table 13-6 present a regrouping of data for 30-year-maturity bonds only at coupon levels of 2 percent, 4 percent, 6 percent, 8 percent, and 10 percent. Figure 13-7 and its related Table 13-7 display the price behavior, at a constant yield to maturity of 8 percent, of bonds ranging in maturity from 1 year to 100 years, with coupons of 2 percent, 4 percent, 6 percent, 8 percent, and 10 percent. Figure 13-8 and its related Table 13-8 show the prices of 30-year bonds, at yields to maturity of 2 percent, 4 percent, 6 percent, 8 percent, and 10 percent, with coupons ranging from 1 to 20 percent. A schematic representation of the data displayed in Figures 13-6 through 13-8 and Tables 13-6 through 13-8 is shown below:

Figure number	Coupon level (percent)	Maturity (years)	Yield-to-maturity levels (percent)	Underlying data presented in table
13-6	2, 4, 6, 8, 10	30	1 to 20 percent in 1 percent increments	13-6
13-7	2, 4, 6, 8, 10	1 to 100	8	13-6
13-8	1 to 20 percent in 1 percent increments	30	2, 4, 6, 8, 10	13-8

From this display it can be seen that bond prices are calculated under the following conditions: (1) in Figure 13-6, the maturity is kept constant while the coupon and yield to maturity are allowed to vary over a set range of values; (2) in Figure 13-7, the yield to maturity is kept constant while the coupon and maturity are allowed to vary over a set range of values; and (3) in Figure 13-8, the maturity is kept constant while the coupon and yield to maturity are allowed to vary over a set range of values.

The 35 individual graphical curves in Figures 13-1 through 13-8 provide much information about the yield and price behavior of bonds under many different combinations of coupon, maturity, and yield to maturity. At the same time, these graphs may give the investor an idea of the even greater number of variations in coupon, maturity, and yield to maturity which can be shown in figures to be constructed by the investor. Among these variations are (1) plotting in the same figure a number of graphical curves for which the coupon, maturity, and yield to maturity all are allowed to vary (for example, a figure might be constructed to include coupons of 2 percent, 6 percent, and 10 percent, maturities of 30 years, 10 years, 5 years, and 1 year, and yield-to-maturity levels of 1 percent to 20 percent in 1 percent increments); (2) further varying the price scale or using broken scales on the graphs to give greater emphasis to relatively small price changes; (3) plotting prices on a logarithmic scale, as opposed to the arithmetic scales used in this chapter, to emphasize rates of change, as opposed to absolute values; (4) using measures other than price as the dependent variable (for example, bond prices might be kept constant while various combinations of coupon, maturity, and yield to maturity are graphed); and (5) reversing the order of the values along either the x axis (the horizontal axis) or the y axis (the vertical axis) of the graph to produce bond values which rise rather than fall in price as the independent variables move out along the x axis.

Because Figures 13-1 through 13-5 employ different scales along the y axis, Table 13-9 has been constructed to compare the percentage price moves (rather than the absolute price moves) for bonds with coupons of 2 percent, 4 percent, 6 percent, 8 percent, and 10 percent and maturities of 30 years, 10 years, 5 years, and 1 year resulting from yield-to-maturity changes from (1) 1 percent to 2 percent, (2) 9 percent to 10 percent, and (3) 19 percent to 20 percent. Such yield changes have been chosen to illustrate bond price movements for interest rate shifts occurring at the low, medium, and high ends of the yield scale in many highly industrialized nations during this century, although it should also be pointed out that these extremes in interest rates have been met or exceeded in certain major industrialized countries since 1900. While much of the analysis in this chapter centers on the bond price declines resulting from *rising* yield levels, the figures and tables can also be employed (by using the methodology described in connection with Table 12-15 in Chapter 12) to analyze the bond price rises which result from *falling* yield levels. However, as discussed in Chapter 12, the percentage changes for falling interest rates will differ from those shown in connection with a scenario of rising interest rates.

In a similar manner to that utilized in constructing Table 13-9, Table 13-10 draws upon the data contained in Tables 13-1 through 13-5 to compare the percentage decline which results from a 50 percent rise in yield levels, from 2 percent to 3 percent, from 4 percent to 6 percent, from 6 percent to 9 percent, from 8 percent to 12 percent, and from 10 percent to 15 percent, for bonds with coupons of 2 percent, 4 percent, 6 percent, 8 percent, and 10 percent and maturities of 30 years, 10 years, 5 years, and 1 year. Table 13-11 approaches this subject in the same way except that the interest rate rise is not expressed as a constant *percentage* of the beginning yield levels but as a constant *increase of 100 basis points* over the original yields to maturity. Such rises are from 2 percent to 3 percent, from 4 percent to 5 percent, from 6 percent to 7 percent, from 8 percent to 9 percent, and from 10 percent to 11 percent.

Table 13-12 examines bond yield and price relationships from a somewhat different perspective, in that it analyzes the incremental basis-point move upward in interest rates which is necessary to cause a drop in a given bond's price from 100 to 95, from 100 to 90, from 100 to 85, and from 100 to 80. In graphical terms, Tables 13-10 and 13-11 can be thought of as showing the *vertical* move (decline in price) resulting from a specified *horizontal* move (rise in interest rates) in Figures 13-1 through 13-5, while Table 13-12 can be thought of as demonstrating the *horizontal* move (rise in interest rates) associated with a given *vertical* move (decline in price) in Figures 13-1 through 13-5.

A schematic representation of the data displayed in Tables 13-9 through 13-12 is shown below:

Table number	Derived from data in tables	Information shown in table
13-9	13-1 through 13-5	Percentage price decline resulting from yield increases from 1 to 2 percent, 9 to 10 percent, and 19 to 20 percent
13-10	13-1 through 13-5	Percentage price decline resulting from yield increases from 2 to 3 percent, 4 to 6 percent, 6 to 9 percent, 8 to 12 percent, and 10 to 15 percent
13-11	13-1 through 13-5	Percentage price decline resulting from yield increases from 2 to 3 percent, 4 to 5 percent, 6 to 7 percent, 8 to 9 percent, and 10 to 11 percent
13-12	13-1 through 13-5	Basis-point rise in yield to maturity resulting from bond price declines from 100 to 95, 100 to 90, 100 to 85, and 100 to 80

Graphs of Bond Yields and Prices

To facilitate comparison between bonds of varying coupons, maturities, and yields to maturity, Figures 13-1 through 13-5 and Tables 13-1 through 13-5 are presented together, followed by an analysis of all these figures and tables as a group. This analysis also draws upon the figures and tables presented later in this chapter.

Figure 13-1 graphically presents the prices of 2 percent coupon bonds with a maturity of 30 years, 10 years, 5 years, and 1 year for yields to maturity from 1 percent to 20 percent. The underlying data for Figure 13-1 are shown in Table 13-1.

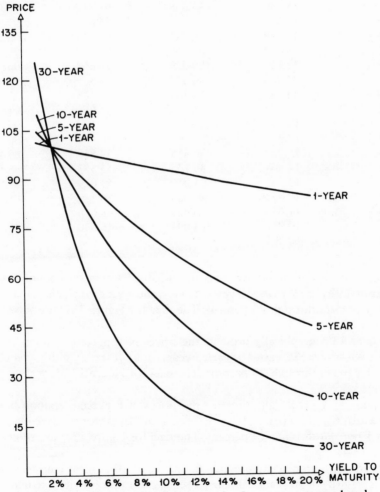

FIGURE 13-1 Prices of various-maturity 2 percent coupon bonds

TABLE 13-1
Prices of Various-Maturity 2 Percent Coupon Bonds

Coupon	2 percent	2 percent	2 percent	2 percent
Yield to maturity (percent)	30 years	Maturity 10 years	5 years	1 year
1	125.862	109.493	104.865	100.992
2	100.000	100.000	100.000	100.000
3	80.309	91.415	95.388	99.022
4	65.239	83.648	91.017	98.058
5	53.637	76.616	86.871	97.108
6	44.648	70.245	82.939	96.173
7	37.638	64.468	79.208	95.250
8	32.129	59.229	75.667	94.341
9	27.766	54.472	72.305	93.445
10	24.282	50.151	69.113	92.562
11	21.475	46.223	66.080	91.691
12	19.192	42.650	63.199	90.833
13	17.318	39.398	60.461	89.986
14	15.764	36.435	57.858	89.151
15	14.464	33.735	55.383	88.328
16	13.364	31.272	53.029	87.517
17	12.425	29.024	50.789	86.716
18	11.616	26.971	48.658	85.927
19	10.912	25.094	46.630	85.148
20	10.295	23.377	44.698	84.380

Figure 13-2 graphically presents the prices of 4 percent coupon bonds with a maturity of 30 years, 10 years, 5 years, and 1 year for yields to maturity from 1 percent through 20 percent. The data for Figure 13-2 are shown in Table 13-2.

Figure 13-3 graphically presents the prices of 6 percent coupon bonds with a maturity of 30 years, 10 years, 5 years, and 1 year for yields to maturity from 1 percent through 20 percent. The data for Figure 13-3 are shown in Table 13-3.

Figure 13-4 graphically presents the prices of 8 percent coupon bonds with a maturity of 30 years, 10 years, 5 years, and 1 year for yields to maturity from 1 percent through 20 percent. The data for Figure 13-4 are shown in Table 13-4.

Figure 13-5 graphically presents the prices of 10 percent coupon bonds with a maturity of 30 years, 10 years, 5 years, and 1 year for yields to maturity from 1 percent through 20 percent. The data for Figure 13-5 are shown in Table 13-5.

The graphs in Figures 13-1 through 13-5 and the data in Tables 13-1 through 13-5 can be rearranged to help the investor concentrate on selected maturity sectors and yield levels. An example of this methodology is provided in Figure 13-6, which graphically presents the prices of 30-year bonds only, with coupons of 2 percent, 4 percent, 6 percent, 8 percent, and 10 percent, for yields to maturity from 1 percent through 20 percent. The data for Figure 13-6 are shown in Table 13-6.

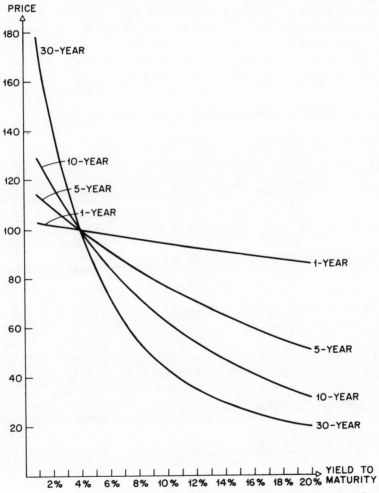

FIGURE 13-2   Prices of various-maturity 4 percent coupon bonds

Figure 13-7 maintains a constant yield to maturity of 8 percent and graph-ically presents the prices of bonds with coupons of 2 percent, 4 percent, 6 percent, 8 percent, and 10 percent for maturities ranging from 1 year to 100 years. Because the yield to maturity is held constant at 8 percent while the maturity is allowed to vary, the curves have a different shape from that of those displayed in Figures 13-1 through 13-6. At a constant yield to maturity of 8 percent, (1) those issues with coupons below 8 percent decline as maturity increases, with the 2 percent coupon bonds dropping the most steeply in price, followed by the 4 percent coupon bonds and the 6 percent coupon bonds respectively; (2) the 8 percent coupon bonds remain at par regardless of maturity; and (3) those issues with coupons above 8 percent rise as maturities are lengthened. It can also be seen that the greatest rate of price change for bonds with coupons above or below 8 percent occurs with issues of from 1 to 20 years' maturity. Issues of greater than 20 years' maturity

TABLE 13-2
Prices of Various-Maturity 4 Percent Coupon Bonds

Coupon	4 percent	4 percent	4 percent	4 percent
Yield to maturity (percent)	Maturity			
	30 years	10 years	5 years	1 year
1	177.588	128.481	114.595	102.977
2	144.955	118.045	109.471	101.970
3	119.690	108.584	104.611	100.977
4	100.000	100.000	100.000	100.000
5	84.545	92.205	95.623	99.036
6	72.324	85.122	91.469	98.086
7	62.582	78.681	87.525	97.150
8	54.753	72.819	83.778	96.227
9	48.404	67.480	80.218	95.318
10	43.212	62.613	76.834	94.421
11	38.925	58.173	73.618	93.537
12	35.354	54.120	70.559	92.666
13	32.351	50.416	67.650	91.807
14	29.804	47.029	64.882	90.959
15	27.623	43.930	62.247	90.124
16	25.740	41.091	59.739	89.300
17	24.101	38.488	57.351	88.487
18	22.664	36.100	55.076	87.686
19	21.393	33.907	52.909	86.895
20	20.262	31.891	50.843	86.115

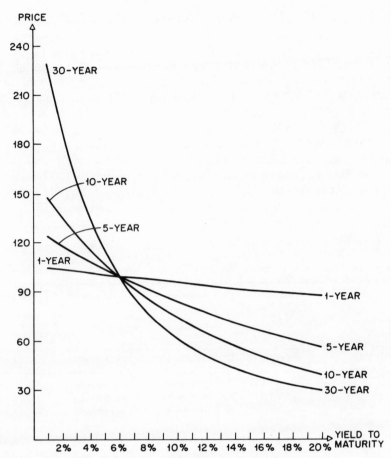

FIGURE 13-3   Prices of various-maturity 6 percent coupon bonds

generally exhibit ever-slower rates of price change as maturities are length-ened, particularly beyond 40 years. The data for Figure 13-7 are shown in Table 13-7.

As an example of still another shape, Figure 13-8 graphically presents the prices of bonds with a constant maturity of 30 years, with yields to maturity of 2 percent, 4 percent, 6 percent, 8 percent, and 10 percent, and with coupons of from 1 percent to 20 percent. As can be seen, with increasing coupon levels 30-year-maturity bond prices increase in a linear manner, with higher prices for lower levels of yield to maturity. The data for Figure 13-8 are shown in Table 13-8.

Analysis of Yield and Price Changes
Shown in Graphs

The data in Table 13-9 have been calculated from Tables 13-1 through 13-5 and present a unified analysis of Figures 13-1 through 13-5. Several conclusions can be drawn from the table concerning bond price and yield behavior with varying coupons, maturities, and yields to maturity. It can generally be stated that for any fixed coupon and maturity the percentage decline in bond prices resulting from a given rise in yield levels does not occur at a uniform rate all along the spectrum of yields to maturity. For example, for a 2 percent coupon, 30-year-maturity bond, when interest rates rise by 100 basis points, the resultant percentage price decline is 20.5 percent if the yield rise begins at 1 percent, 12.5 percent if the yield rise begins at 9 percent, and 5.7 percent if the yield rise begins at 19 percent.

TABLE 13-3
Prices of Various-Maturity 6 Percent Coupon Bonds

Coupon	6 percent	6 percent	6 percent	6 percent
Yield to maturity (percent)	Maturity			
	30 years	10 years	5 years	1 year
1	229.313	147.468	124.326	104.962
2	189.910	136.091	118.942	103.940
3	159.070	125.752	113.833	102.933
4	134.760	116.351	108.982	101.941
5	115.454	107.794	104.376	100.963
6	100.000	100.000	100.000	100.000
7	87.527	92.893	95.841	99.050
8	77.376	86.409	91.889	98.113
9	69.042	80.488	88.130	97.190
10	62.141	75.075	84.556	96.281
11	56.375	70.124	81.155	95.384
12	51.515	65.590	77.919	94.499
13	47.384	61.435	74.839	93.627
14	43.843	57.623	71.905	92.767
15	40.782	54.124	69.111	91.919
16	38.117	50.909	66.449	91.083
17	35.778	47.951	63.912	90.258
18	33.712	45.228	61.494	89.445
19	31.874	42.719	59.187	88.642
20	30.229	40.405	56.988	87.851

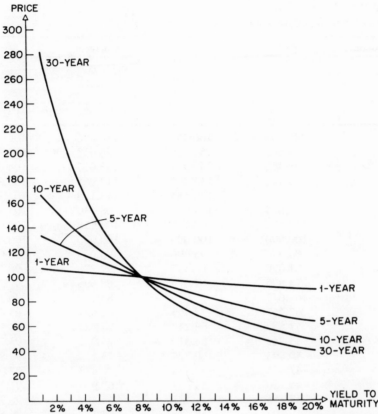

FIGURE 13-4   Prices of various-maturity 8 percent coupon bonds

A first case, involving a more specific application of the previous observation, holds that for any fixed coupon and maturity and for a given basis-point rise in interest rates bond prices fall less in percentage terms at higher beginning yield levels than at lower beginning yield levels. For example, for a 10 percent coupon, 5-year-maturity bond, when interest rates rise by 100 basis points, the resultant percentage price decline is 3.4 percent if the yield increase begins at a 19 percent yield to maturity, but the decline is a greater percentage amount (4.1 percent) if the yield rise begins at a 1 percent yield to maturity. This point was reviewed at some length in connection with Table 12-5 in Chapter 12.

In a second case, for a fixed coupon and beginning level of yield to

TABLE 13-4
Prices of Various-Maturity 8 Percent Coupon Bonds

Coupon	8 percent	8 percent	8 percent	8 percent
Yield to maturity (percent)	30 years	Maturity 10 years	5 years	1 year
1	281.039	166.455	134.056	106.947
2	234.865	154.136	128.413	105.911
3	198.450	142.921	123.055	104.889
4	169.521	132.702	117.965	103.883
5	146.362	123.383	113.128	102.891
6	127.675	114.877	108.530	101.913
7	112.472	107.106	104.158	100.949
8	100.000	100.000	100.000	100.000
9	88.680	93.496	96.043	99.063
10	81.070	87.537	92.278	98.140
11	73.825	82.074	88.693	97.230
12	67.677	77.060	85.279	96.333
13	62.417	72.453	82.027	95.448
14	57.882	68.217	78.929	94.575
15	53.942	64.319	75.975	93.715
16	50.493	60.727	73.159	92.866
17	47.455	57.414	70.473	92.029
18	44.760	54.357	67.911	91.204
19	42.355	51.531	65.466	90.390
20	40.197	48.918	63.132	89.586

maturity and for a given basis-point rise in interest rates, a longer-maturity bond will generally exhibit a larger percentage price decline than a short-maturity bond. For example, when interest rates rise from 9 percent to 10 percent, an 8 percent coupon, 10-year bond will decline by 6.4 percent while an 8 percent coupon, 30-year bond will decline by 9.6 percent. However, for certain combinations of low coupon, long maturity, and high beginning yield level, extending the maturity of a bond will not cause its price to decline more in percentage terms. This fact was also discussed briefly in Chapter 12.

For example, when interest rates rise from 19 percent to 20 percent, Table 13-9 shows that a 30-year bond declines *less* in percentage terms than a 10-year bond for coupon levels of 2 percent, 4 percent, and 6 percent.

In a third case, for any fixed maturity and beginning yield level and for a given basis-point rise in interest rates, bonds with high coupons will experience a lower percentage price decline than those with lower coupon levels. To illustrate, for an interest rate rise from 1 percent to 2 percent, an 8 percent coupon, 30-year bond will decline by 16.4 percent while a 4 percent coupon, 30-year bond will decline by 18.4 percent.

Even though Table 13-9 indicates that the percentage price decline is the same for certain short-maturity bonds with different coupons (for example, for a rise in yield levels from 9 percent to 10 percent, a 6 percent coupon, 1-year bond appears to decline by 0.94 percent, or by the same amount as a 4 percent coupon, 1-year bond or a 2 percent coupon, 1-year bond). In fact, the high-coupon issues decline less in price than the low-coupon issues of the same maturity, but the percentage changes appear equivalent because they have been rounded off to two decimal places.

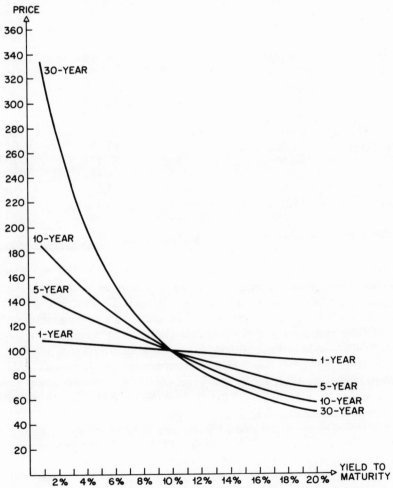

FIGURE 13-5   Prices of various-maturity 10 percent coupon bonds

TABLE 13-5
Prices of Various-Maturity 10 Percent Coupon Bonds

Coupon	10 percent	10 percent	10 percent	10 percent
Yield to maturity (percent)	Maturity			
	30 years	10 years	5 years	1 year
1	332.765	185.443	143.786	108.932
2	279.820	172.182	137.885	107.881
3	237.830	160.090	132.277	106.845
4	204.282	149.054	126.947	105.824
5	177.271	138.972	121.880	104.818
6	155.351	129.754	117.060	103.826
7	137.417	121.318	112.474	102.849
8	122.623	113.590	108.110	101.886
9	110.319	106.503	103.956	100.936
10	100.000	100.000	100.000	100.000
11	91.275	94.024	96.231	99.076
12	83.838	88.530	92.639	98.166
13	77.450	83.472	89.216	97.269
14	71.921	78.811	85.952	96.383
15	67.101	74.513	82.839	95.511
16	62.870	70.545	79.869	94.650
17	59.131	66.878	77.035	93.801
18	55.808	63.485	74.329	92.963
19	52.836	60.344	71.745	92.137
20	50.164	57.432	69.277	91.322

Table 13-10 presents a summary of the conditions for the one general conclusion and the three specific conclusions described in the text. Similar summaries can be constructed for other variations in the direction and/or the magnitude of change in (1) the coupon (possibly by assuming rising rather than falling coupons), (2) the maturity (possibly by assuming shortened rather than lengthened maturities), (3) basis-point movements (possibly by assuming falling rather than rising shifts in yields), (4) beginning yield-to-maturity levels (possibly by assuming consideration of declining rather than rising yields to maturity), and (5) percentage price changes (possibly by using rising rather than falling price changes).

Additional analysis of Table 13-9 can be accomplished by examining the *incremental* price changes which are due to (1) higher yield levels, (2) lengthening the maturity of a bond, and (3) lowering the coupon of a bond. Table 13-11 presents the incremental price changes resulting from each of these factors. Several conclusions can be drawn from the table.

First, for long-maturity (30-year) bonds and a given basis-point rise in interest rates, the amount of *incremental* price decline due to higher yield levels *decreases* with higher coupons and with higher absolute yield levels.

Second, for intermediate-maturity (10-year) bonds and a given basis-point rise in interest rates, the amount of *incremental* price decline due to higher yield levels *increases* with higher coupons but *decreases* with higher absolute yield levels.

Third, for a given basis-point rise in interest rates, the *incremental* price decline due to lengthening maturity *decreases* with higher coupons and with higher absolute yield levels.

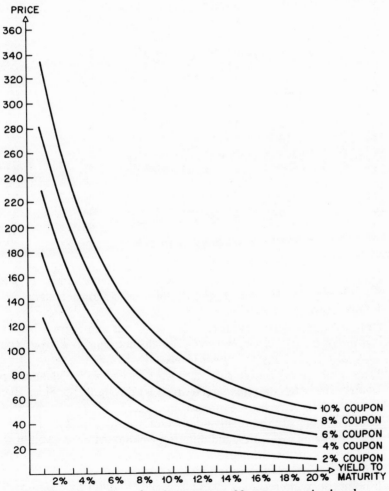

FIGURE 13-6   Prices of various-coupon 30-year–maturity bonds

TABLE 13-6
Prices of Various-Coupon 30-Year–Maturity bonds

Coupon	2 percent	4 percent	6 percent	8 percent	10 percent
Yield to maturity (percent)	Maturity 30 years	30 years	30 years	30 years	30 years
1	125.862	177.588	229.313	281.039	332.765
2	100.000	144.955	189.910	234.865	279.820
3	80.309	119.690	159.070	198.450	237.830
4	65.239	100.000	134.760	169.521	204.282
5	53.637	84.545	115.454	146.362	177.271
6	44.648	72.324	100.000	127.675	155.351
7	37.638	62.582	87.527	112.472	137.417
8	32.129	54.753	77.376	100.000	122.623
9	27.766	48.404	69.042	89.680	110.319
10	24.282	43.212	62.141	81.070	100.000
11	21.475	38.925	56.375	73.825	91.275
12	19.192	35.354	51.515	67.677	83.838
13	17.318	32.351	47.384	62.417	77.450
14	15.764	29.804	43.843	57.882	71.921
15	14.464	27.623	40.782	53.942	67.101
16	13.364	25.740	38.117	50.493	62.870
17	12.425	24.101	35.778	47.455	59.131
18	11.616	22.664	33.712	44.760	55.808
19	10.912	21.393	31.874	42.355	52.836
20	10.295	20.262	30.229	40.197	50.164

Fourth, for a given basis-point rise in interest rates and long-maturity (30-year) bonds, the *incremental* price decline due to a lower coupon *decreases* with higher absolute yield levels.

Fifth, for intermediate-maturity (10-year) bonds and a given basis-point rise in interest rates, the *incremental* price decline due to a lower coupon *decreases* with higher absolute yield levels.

Table 13-9 can be used in still other ways to analyze the yield and price behavior of the bonds described in Figures 13-1 through 13-5. Since all bond price movements have been expressed in percentage terms in this table, it is possible to compare the relative degree of price decline for (1) differing coupons, the same maturities, and differing yield-to-maturity levels at which a given basis-point rise in interest rates takes place; (2) the same coupons, differing maturities, and differing yield-to-maturity levels at which a given basis-point rise in interest rates takes place; and (3) differing coupons, differing maturities, and the same yield-to-maturity levels at which a given basis-point rise in interest rates takes place.

In Table 13-12, the ratios of the percentage price declines displayed in Table 13-9 have been computed for several bonds under varying conditions. Column 1 of the table shows the ratio of the price decline resulting from a yield rise from 19 to 20 percent to the price decline resulting from a yield rise from 1 to 2 percent, for a 30-year bond with the five different coupons shown along the left-hand margin. For a 2 percent coupon, 30-year issue, this ratio is 0.278 $\left(\dfrac{-\ 5.7\ \text{percent}}{-\ 20.5\ \text{percent}} \right)$; the ratio increases with increasing coupon levels, to 0.321 for a 10 percent coupon, 30-year issue. Thus for bonds of long maturity, the price decline caused by a yield rise from 19 to 20 percent relative to that caused by a yield increase from 1 to 2 percent tends to *increase* as coupon levels rise. A different result holds true for bonds of short maturity.

As shown in column 2 of Table 13-12, for a 1-year-maturity bond the ratio of the price decline resulting from a yield rise from 19 to 20 percent to the price decline resulting from a yield rise from 1 to 2 percent tends to *decrease*

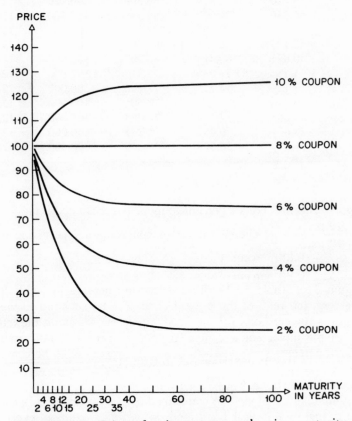

FIGURE 13-7   **Prices of various-coupon and various-maturity bonds at 8 percent yield to maturity**

TABLE 13-7
Prices of Various-Coupon and Various-Maturity Bonds at 8 Percent Yield to Maturity

Coupon	2 percent	4 percent	6 percent	8 percent	10 percent
Maturity (years)			Yield to maturity		
	8 percent	8 percent	8 percent	8 percent	8 percent
1	94.341	96.227	98.113	100.000	101.886
2	89.110	92.740	96.370	100.000	103.629
3	84.273	89.515	94.757	100.000	105.242
4	79.801	86.534	93.267	100.000	106.732
5	75.667	83.778	91.889	100.000	108.110
6	71.844	81.229	90.614	100.000	109.385
7	68.310	78.873	89.436	100.000	110.563
8	65.043	76.695	88.347	100.000	111.652
9	62.022	74.681	87.340	100.000	112.659
10	59.229	72.819	86.409	100.000	113.590
11	56.646	71.097	85.548	100.000	114.451
12	54.259	69.506	84.753	100.000	115.246
15	48.123	65.415	82.707	100.000	117.292
20	40.621	60.414	80.207	100.000	119.792
25	35.553	57.035	78.517	100.000	121.482
30	32.129	54.753	77.376	100.000	122.623
35	29.816	53.210	76.605	100.000	123.394
40	28.253	52.169	76.084	100.000	123.915
60	25.677	50.451	75.225	100.000	124.774
100	25.029	50.019	75.009	100.000	124.990

as coupon levels rise. For a 2 percent coupon, 1-year issue, this ratio is 0.918 $\left(\dfrac{-\ 0.90\ \text{percent}}{-\ 0.98\ \text{percent}} \right)$, whereas for a 10 percent coupon, 1-year issue the ratio is 0.917 $\left(\dfrac{-\ 0.88\ \text{percent}}{-\ 0.96\ \text{percent}} \right)$.

Column 3 of Table 13-12 displays, for an increase in yields from 1 to 2 percent, the ratio of the price decline of a 1-year bond to the price decline of a 30-year bond for the five coupons shown along the left-hand margin of the table. For a 2 percent coupon issue, this ratio is 0.0478 $\left(\dfrac{-\ 0.98\ \text{percent}}{-\ 20.50\ \text{percent}} \right)$; the ratio rises to 0.0604 $\left(\dfrac{-\ 0.96\ \text{percent}}{-\ 15.90\ \text{percent}} \right)$ for a 10 percent coupon bond. Thus for a given basis-point increase in yields from low beginning levels of yield to maturity, the price decline of a 1-year bond relative to that of a 30-year bond tends to *increase* as coupon levels rise.

A similar pattern emerges when the given basis-point increase in yields begins at high levels of yield to maturity. Column 4 of Table 13-12 sets forth, for an increase in yields from 19 to 20 percent, the ratio of the price decline of a 1-year bond to the price decline of a 30-year bond for the five coupons shown along the left-hand margin of the table. For a 2 percent coupon issue, this ratio is 0.158 $\left(\dfrac{-\ 0.90\ \text{percent}}{-\ 5.70\ \text{percent}} \right)$; the ratio rises to 0.1749 for a 10 percent coupon bond.

The latter ratio was computed to four significant figures from the original price data in Tables 13-4 and 13-5 and demonstrates the errors which

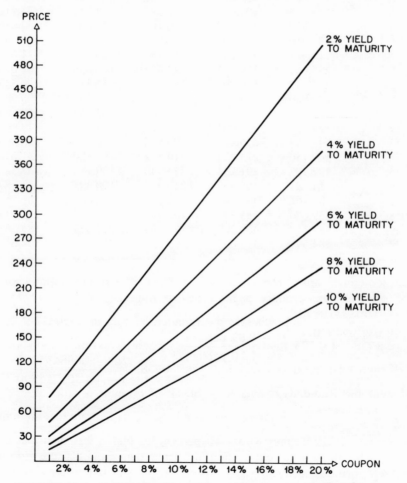

FIGURE 13-8   Prices of various-coupon 30-year–maturity bonds at various yields to maturity.

TABLE 13-8
Prices of Various-Coupon 30-Year–Maturity Bonds at Various Yields to
Maturity

Maturity	30 years	30 years	30 years	30 years	30 years
		Yield to maturity			
Coupon (percent)	2 percent	4 percent	6 percent	8 percent	10 percent
1	77.522	47.858	30.811	20.817	14.818
2	100.000	65.239	44.648	32.129	24.282
3	122.477	82.619	58.486	43.441	33.747
4	144.955	100.000	72.324	54.753	43.212
5	167.432	117.380	86.162	66.064	52.676
6	189.910	134.760	100.000	77.376	62.141
7	212.387	152.141	113.837	88.688	71.606
8	234.865	169.521	127.675	100.000	81.070
9	257.342	186.902	141.513	111.311	90.535
10	279.820	204.282	155.351	122.623	100.000
11	302.297	221.663	169.188	133.935	109.464
12	324.775	239.043	183.026	145.246	118.929
13	347.252	256.423	196.864	156.558	128.393
14	369.730	273.804	210.702	167.870	137.858
15	392.207	291.184	224.540	179.182	147.323
16	414.685	308.565	238.377	190.493	156.787
17	437.162	325.945	252.215	201.805	166.252
18	459.640	343.326	266.053	213.117	175.717
19	482.117	360.706	279.891	224.429	185.181
20	504.595	378.087	293.728	235.740	194.646

can sometimes arise from rounding. For an 8 percent coupon issue, the original data produce a ratio before rounding of 0.1745777566 $\left(\dfrac{-0.0089478920}{-0.0509503010} \right)$, whereas the rounded-off data in Table 13-9 produce a ratio of 0.175 $\left(\dfrac{-0.89 \text{ percent}}{-5.10 \text{ percent}} \right)$. For a 10 percent coupon bond, the original data produce a ratio of 0.1749109582 $\left(\dfrac{-0.0088455235}{-0.0505715800} \right)$, whereas the rounded-off data in Table 13-9 produce a ratio of 0.173 $\left(\dfrac{-0.88 \text{ percent}}{-5.10 \text{ percent}} \right)$. Although the rounded-off data indicate that the ratio of the two price declines with a 10 percent coupon is less than that experienced with an 8 percent coupon, the actual data show that the ratio of the two price declines with a 10 percent coupon is in fact *greater* than that experienced with an 8 percent coupon. Thus, for a given basis-point increase in yields from high beginning levels of yield to maturity, the price decline of a 1-year bond relative to that of a 30-year bond tends to *increase* as coupon levels rise.

A further use of Table 13-9 can derive from comparisons of the price change arising, for a given basis-point change in yields, from different combinations of coupon, maturity, and beginning yield level. For example, a 4 percent coupon, 10-year bond which rises from 9 to 10 percent in yield declines by approximately the same amount (7.2 percent) as a 10 percent coupon, 10-year bond which rises from 1 to 2 percent in yield. This is shown in Table 13-9, as is a similar example, in which a 2 percent coupon, 5-year bond which rises from a 19 percent yield to a 20 percent yield is seen to decline by roughly the same amount (4.1 percent) as a 6 percent coupon, 5-year bond which rises from 1 to 2 percent in yield. If the bonds in Table 13-9 are arranged in order of percentage price change, numerous other comparisons which provide insight into the price volatility of widely differing issues under varying interest rate conditions can be made.

TABLE 13-9
Percentage Bond Price Decline Resulting from 100-Basis-Point Interest Rate Rise from Various Yield Levels

Coupon (percent)	Maturity (years)	Percentage decline in price resulting from a yield change from		
		1 to 2 percent	9 to 10 percent	19 to 20 percent
2	30	−20.5	−12.5	−5.7
2	10	−8.7	−7.9	−6.8
2	5	−4.6	−4.4	−4.1
2	1	−0.98	−0.94	−0.90
4	30	−18.4	−10.7	−5.3
4	10	−8.1	−7.2	−5.9
4	5	−4.5	−4.2	−3.9
4	1	−0.98	−0.94	−0.90
6	30	−17.1	−10.0	−5.2
6	10	−7.7	−6.7	−5.4
6	5	−4.3	−4.1	−3.7
6	1	−0.97	−0.94	−0.89
8	30	−16.4	−9.6	−5.1
8	10	−7.4	−6.4	−5.1
8	5	−4.2	−3.9	−3.6
8	1	−0.97	−0.93	−0.89
10	30	−15.9	−9.4	−5.1
10	10	−7.2	−6.1	−4.8
10	5	−4.1	−3.8	−3.4
10	1	−0.96	−0.93	−0.88

TABLE 13-10
Summary of Bond Yield and Price Behavior for Fixed Basis-Point Yield
Increases

Category	General statement	Case 1	Case 2	Case 3
Coupon	Fixed	Fixed	Fixed	If rises
Maturity	Fixed	Fixed	If lengthens	Fixed
Amount of basis-point rise in yields	Fixed*	Fixed*	Fixed*	Fixed*
Yield-to-maturity level	If changes	If rises	Fixed	Fixed
Percentage fall in price	Will change	Will decline	Will generally rise†	Will decline‡

*Equivalent to a declining *percentage* of beginning yields as interest rate levels are allowed to rise.
†Except for certain combinations of low coupon, long maturity, and high beginning yield level.
‡Owing to rounding, at certain sufficiently short maturities the percentage fall in prices may appear in Table 13-9 to remain constant even though it is in fact declining.

Table 13-13 is similar to Table 13-9 and has also been computed from Tables 13-1 through 13-5. For coupons of 2 percent, 4 percent, 6 percent, 8 percent, and 10 percent and maturities of 1, 5, 10, and 30 years, Table 13-13 shows the percentage price decline resulting from a 100-basis-point rise in yield levels from 2 percent, 4 percent, 6 percent, 8 percent, and 10 percent respectively. In contrast to Table 13-9, which shows percentage price changes for widely separated parts of the yield spectrum, Table 13-13 has been constructed to portray percentage price changes over a continuous portion of the yield spectrum, from 2 to 11 percent.

The discussion thus far has concentrated on the percentage price changes in bonds resulting from a fixed *basis-point* change (a 100-basis-point rise) in yield levels. Using a somewhat different approach, Table 13-14 examines the bond price declines resulting from a given *percentage* change (a 50 percent increase) in yield levels, from 2 to 3 percent, from 4 to 6 percent, from 6 to 9 percent, from 8 to 12 percent, and from 10 to 15 percent. As can be seen in the table, a 50 percent increase in yield levels implies a rising absolute level of basis-point increases as the beginning yield level rises. Whereas a 50 percent rise in yields from a 2 percent beginning yield level translates into a *100*-basis-point increase in interest rates, a 50 percent rise in yields from a 10 percent beginning yield level translates into a *500*-basis-point increase in interest rates.

Analyzing bond price changes in terms of a fixed *percentage* change in yield levels rather than in terms of a fixed *basis-point* change in yield levels has one

TABLE 13-11
Incremental Bond Price Changes Due to Yield Level, Maturity, or Coupon

INCREMENTAL PRICE CHANGE DUE TO HIGHER YIELD LEVELS

Coupon (percent)	Maturity (years)	Additional percentage price change resulting from	
		Yield move from 1 to 2 compared with yield move from 9 to 10 (percent)	Yield move from 9 to 10 compared with yield move from 19 to 20 (percent)
2	30	-8.0	-6.8
2	10	-0.8	-1.1
2	5	-0.2	-0.3
2	1	-0.04	-0.04
4	30	-7.7	-5.4
4	10	-0.9	-1.3
4	5	-0.3	-3.3
4	1	-0.04	-0.04
6	30	-7.1	-4.8
6	10	-1.0	-1.3
6	5	-0.2	-0.4
6	1	-0.03	-0.05
8	30	-6.8	-4.5
8	10	-1.0	-1.3
8	5	-0.3	-0.3
8	1	-0.04	-0.04
10	30	-6.5	-4.3
10	10	-1.1	-1.3
10	5	-0.3	-0.4
10	1	-0.03	-0.05

INCREMENTAL PRICE CHANGE DUE TO LENGTHENING MATURITY

Coupon (percent)	Additional percentage price change resulting from lengthening maturity from	Yield move from		
		1 to 2 (percent)	9 to 10 (percent)	19 to 20 (percent)
2	10 to 30 years	-11.8	-4.6	+0.9
2	5 to 10 years	-4.1	-3.5	-2.7
2	1 to 5 years	-3.62	-3.46	-3.2
4	10 to 30 years	-10.3	-3.5	+0.6
4	5 to 10 years	-3.6	-3.0	-2.0
4	1 to 5 years	-3.52	-3.26	-3.0
6	10 to 30 years	-9.4	-3.3	+0.2
6	5 to 10 years	-3.4	-2.6	-1.7
6	1 to 5 years	-3.33	-3.16	-2.81
8	10 to 30 years	-9.0	-3.2	0.0*
8	5 to 10 years	-3.2	-2.5	-1.5
8	1 to 5 years	-3.23	-2.97	-2.71
10	10 to 30 years	-8.2	-3.2	-0.3
10	5 to 10 years	-3.1	-2.3	-1.4
10	1 to 5 years	-3.14	-2.87	-2.52

INCREMENTAL PRICE CHANGE DUE TO LOWER COUPON

Additional percentage price change resulting from decreasing coupon from	Maturity (years)	Yield move from		
		1 to 2 (percent)	9 to 10 (percent)	19 to 20 (percent)
4 to 2%	30	-2.1	-1.8	-0.4
4 to 2%	10	-0.6	-0.5	-0.9
4 to 2%	5	-0.1	-0.2	-0.2
4 to 2%	1	0.0*	0.0*	0.0*
6 to 4%	30	-1.3	-0.7	-0.1
6 to 4%	10	-0.4	-0.5	-0.5
6 to 4%	5	-0.2	-0.1	-0.2
6 to 4%	1	-0.01	0.0*	-0.01
8 to 6%	30	-0.7	-0.4	-0.1
8 to 6%	10	-0.3	-0.3	-0.3
8 to 6%	5	-0.1	-0.2	-0.1
8 to 6%	1	0.0*	-0.01	0.0*
10 to 8%	30	-0.5	-0.2	0.0*
10 to 8%	10	-0.2	-0.3	-0.3
10 to 8%	5	-0.1	-0.1	-0.2
10 to 8%	1	-0.01	0.0*	-0.01

*Difference may not exactly amount to zero since amounts being compared have been rounded off.

TABLE 13-12
Ratios of Bond Price Changes for Various Yield Levels, Maturities, and Coupons

Coupon (percent)	Ratio of percentage price declines for a rise in yields from 19 to 20 percent compared with a rise in yields from 1 to 2 percent		Ratio of percentage price declines for a 1-year-maturity bond compared with a 30-year-maturity bond	
	30-year maturity	1-year maturity	Yield rise from 1 to 2 percent	Yield rise from 19 to 20 percent
2	0.278	0.918	0.0478	0.158
4	0.288	0.918	0.0533	0.170
6	0.304	0.918	0.0567	0.171
8	0.311	0.918	0.0591	0.1746*
10	0.321	0.917	0.0604	0.1749†

*Computed by using original data in Table 13-4.
†Computed by using original data in Table 13-5.

TABLE 13-13
Percentage Bond Price Decline Resulting from 100-Basis-Point Interest Rate Rise from Various Yield Levels

Coupon (percent)	Maturity (years)	Percentage decline in price resulting from a 100-basis-point rise in yield levels from				
		2 to 3 percent	4 to 5 percent	6 to 7 percent	8 to 9 percent	10 to 11 percent
2	30	−19.7	−17.8	−15.7	−13.6	−11.6
2	10	−8.6	−8.4	−8.2	−8.0	−7.8
2	5	−4.6	−4.6	−4.5	−4.4	−4.4
2	1	−0.98	−0.97	−0.96	−0.95	−0.94
4	30	−17.4	−15.6	−13.5	−11.6	−9.9
4	10	−8.0	−7.8	−7.6	−7.3	−7.1
4	5	−4.4	−4.4	−4.3	−4.2	−4.2
4	1	−0.97	−0.96	−0.95	−0.94	−0.94
6	30	−16.2	−14.3	−12.5	−10.8	−9.3
6	10	−7.6	−7.4	−7.1	−6.9	−6.6
6	5	−4.3	−4.2	−4.2	−4.1	−4.0
6	1	−0.97	−0.96	−0.95	−0.94	−0.93
8	30	−15.5	−13.7	−11.9	−10.3	−8.9
8	10	−7.3	−7.0	−6.8	−6.5	−6.2
8	5	−4.2	−4.1	−4.0	−4.0	−3.9
8	1	−0.96	−0.95	−0.95	−0.94	−0.93
10	30	−15.0	−13.2	−11.5	−10.0	−8.7
10	10	−7.0	−6.8	−6.5	−6.2	−6.0
10	5	−4.1	−4.0	−3.9	−3.8	−3.8
10	1	−0.96	−0.95	−0.94	−0.93	−0.92

principal advantage. This advantage stems from the fact that this method takes into account the greater significance of a given basis-point change in yields at low interest rates than at high interest rates. Because of the much larger basis-point move (500 basis points) implied by a 50 percent rise in yields at a beginning yield level of 10 percent than at a beginning yield level of 2 percent (which results in a 100-basis-point move), bond prices fluctuate *more* as the beginning level of interest rates rises. For example, as shown in Table 13-14, an 8 percent coupon, 10-year bond declines in price by 7.3 percent for a 50 percent rise in yield levels beginning at 2 percent, but the same bond declines in price by 26.5 percent for a 50 percent rise in yield levels beginning at 10 percent.

By an approach similar to that used in the discussion of Table 13-9 (which reflects a fixed basis-point rise in yields), a summary can be constructed of the yield and price behavior of bonds under the conditions outlined in Table 13-14 (which uses fixed percentage rises in yields). A summary of these conditions is set forth in Table 13-15.

In case 1, for any fixed coupon and maturity and for a fixed percentage rise in yields, as the beginning yield level rises, the percentage fall in a bond's price will also increase. In case 2, for any fixed coupon, yield level, and percentage rise in yields, the percentage fall in a bond's price will rise as its maturity is increased. In case 3, for any fixed maturity, yield to maturity, and percentage rise in interest rates, the percentage fall in a bond's price will decrease as its coupon is increased.

Table 13-14 can also be used to compare the price volatility of bonds having various combinations of coupon, maturity, and changes in yield levels. For example, a 6 percent coupon, 5-year bond which moves from a 10 percent yield to maturity to a 15 percent yield to maturity declines by 18.3 percent in price. This is similar to the 18.6 percent decline for an 8 percent coupon, 10-year-maturity bond which moves from a 6 percent yield to maturity to a 9 percent yield to maturity. Many other similar price moves for widely differing circumstances can also be located in Table 13-14. The largest price decline shown in the table (40.4 percent) is for a 2 percent coupon, 30-year bond which moves from a 10 percent yield to maturity to a 15 percent yield to maturity. The smallest decline shown (0.96 percent) is for a 10 percent coupon, 1-year bond which moves from a 2 percent yield to maturity to a 3 percent yield to maturity.

A slightly different approach to the analysis of bond yield and price behavior is contained in Table 13-16. Rather than focusing on the *price* change resulting from a shift in *yield* levels, the table displays the *yield* changes which result from a shift in bond *price* levels. Many of the values in the table are not shown in the bond price graphs displayed in Figures 13-1 through 13-5 and are rarely if ever encountered in most bond investment environments. By concentrating on the capital loss which might be sustained for a

TABLE 13-14
Percentage Bond Price Decline Resulting from 50 Percent Rise in Interest
Rates from Various Yield Levels

Coupon (percent)	Maturity (years)	Percentage decline in price resulting from a 50 percent rise in yield levels from				
		2 to 3 percent	4 to 6 percent	6 to 9 percent	8 to 12 percent	10 to 15 percent
2	30	−19.7	−31.2	−37.8	−40.3	−40.4
2	10	−8.6	−16.0	−22.5	−28.0	−32.7
2	5	−4.6	−8.9	−12.8	−16.5	−19.9
2	1	−0.98	−1.9	−2.8	−3.7	−4.6
4	30	−17.4	−27.7	−33.1	−35.4	−36.1
4	10	−8.0	−14.9	−20.7	−25.7	−29.8
4	5	−4.4	−8.5	−12.3	−15.8	−19.0
4	1	−0.97	−1.9	−2.8	−3.7	−4.6
6	30	−16.2	−25.8	−31.0	−33.4	−34.4
6	10	−7.6	−14.1	−19.5	−24.1	−27.9
6	5	−4.3	−8.2	−11.9	−15.2	−18.3
6	1	−0.97	−1.9	−2.8	−3.7	−4.5
8	30	−15.5	−24.7	−29.8	−32.3	−33.5
8	10	−7.3	−13.4	−18.6	−22.9	−26.5
8	5	−4.2	−8.0	−11.5	−14.7	−17.7
8	1	−0.96	−1.9	−2.8	−3.7	−4.5
10	30	−15.0	−24.0	−29.0	−31.6	−32.9
10	10	−7.0	−12.9	−17.9	−22.1	−25.5
10	5	−4.1	−7.8	−11.2	−14.3	−17.2
10	1	−0.96	−1.9	−2.8	−3.7	−4.5

TABLE 13-15
Summary of Bond Yield and Price Behavior for Fixed Percentage Yield
Increases

Category	Case 1	Case 2	Case 3
Coupon	Fixed	Fixed	If rises
Maturity	Fixed	If lengthens	Fixed
Percentage rise in yields*	Fixed†	Fixed†	Fixed†
Yield-to-maturity level	If rises	Fixed	Fixed
Percentage fall in price	Will rise	Will rise	Will decline

*Expressed as a percentage of the beginning yield level.

†Equivalent to a rising amount of basis points as interest rate levels are allowed to rise.

TABLE 13-16
Basis-Point Change in Yield Resulting from Various Bond Price Changes

Coupon (percent)	Maturity (years)	Basis-point rise in yield to maturity required to cause bond to drop in price from			
		100 to 95	100 to 90	100 to 85	100 to 80
2	30	22.9	47.4	73.6	101.8
2	10	57.0	117.5	181.9	250.6
2	5	108.7	224.1	346.9	478.3
2	1	527.4	1098.4	1719.2	2397.6
4	30	29.8	61.9	96.7	134.6
4	10	63.0	130.1	201.8	278.7
4	5	114.7	236.7	366.8	506.3
4	1	535.3	1115.0	1745.5	2434.6
6	30	37.6	78.4	123.1	172.2
6	10	69.4	143.5	223.0	308.7
6	5	120.9	249.6	387.3	535.2
6	1	543.3	1131.7	1771.8	2471.7
8	30	46.1	96.6	152.2	213.8
8	10	76.1	157.6	245.4	340.3
8	5	127.2	263.0	408.4	564.9
8	1	551.2	1148.4	1798.2	2509.0
10	30	55.3	116.1	183.3	258.3
10	10	83.1	172.4	268.9	373.7
10	5	133.7	276.7	430.1	595.5
10	1	559.2	1165.2	1824.8	2546.4

rise in interest rates, the tables give some indication of the degree of protection afforded by various bonds against rising yield levels. For example, to sustain a fall from 100 to 95, a 2 percent coupon, 30-year bond need only rise by 22.9 basis points (from a 2 percent beginning yield to maturity to a 2.229 percent ending yield to maturity), while a 2 percent coupon, 1-year bond can undergo a rise in interest rates of 527.4 basis points (from a 2 percent beginning yield to maturity to a 7.274 ending yield to maturity).

The particularly strong holding power of short-maturity securities is also shown in the table. For instance, to undergo a price decline from 100 to 85, a 2 percent coupon, 5-year bond can sustain a rise in yield to maturity of 346.9 basis points (from a 2 percent beginning yield to maturity to a 5.469 percent ending yield to maturity), while a 10 percent coupon, 5-year bond can sustain a rise in yield to maturity of 430.1 basis points (from a 10 percent beginning yield to maturity to a 14.301 percent ending yield to maturity). For 1-year bonds, the holding power is even greater: to undergo a price decline from 100 to 85, a 2 percent coupon, 1-year issue can withstand a rise from a 2 percent beginning yield to maturity to a 25.976 ending yield to maturity; a 6 percent coupon, 1-year issue can sustain a rise from a 6 percent beginning yield to maturity to a 30.717 percent ending yield to maturity; and a 10 percent issue can withstand a rise from a 10 percent beginning yield to maturity to a 35.464 percent ending yield to maturity.

Uses and Limitations of Bond Yield and Price Information

The tables and figures in this chapter can be quite helpful in quantifying the variability of bond prices and yields in changing market environments. In addition, they can aid the investor in locating particular areas of bond price volatility in both rising and falling interest rate conditions. If yield changes are expressed in terms of a fixed amount of basis points, bond price volatility tends to increase with *decreasing* yield levels. On the other hand, if yield changes are expressed in terms of a fixed percentage of the beginning yield to maturity, bond price volatility tends to increase with *increasing* yield levels.

The influence of increasing maturity in bond price volatility was shown to be greatest in the range from 0 up to 10 to 12 years. From 10 to 12 years onward, increases in maturity have a continually declining effect on the price volatility of bonds, and after 30 to 40 years incremental gains in maturity add only slightly to the price volatility of bonds. Bonds with a maturity of 1 year and under tend to have relatively strong price resistance to large yield changes, with large shifts in yield levels (amounting to several hundred basis points or more) being necessary to bring about bond price changes of 4 to 5 percent or more.

The influence of the absolute amount of the coupon level was shown to be important in determining bond price volatility. Changes in coupons below the 4 percent level have an especially significant influence on the price volatility of a bond. Above the 4 percent coupon level, changes in the coupon rate have somewhat less impact on the price volatility of a bond.

Several measures have been developed to gauge (1) the yield sensitivity of a bond in response to price level changes and (2) the price sensitivity of a bond in response to yield level changes. For example, investors and dealers in the market for U.S. Treasury and federal agency bonds frequently refer to the changed *yield* value (in basis points) caused by a change of a thirty-second of a (price) point. A recently developed companion measure is the changed *price* value caused by a change of 1 basis point in yield levels. Another measure of the price sensitivity of bonds to yield changes is known as duration. The concept of duration was initially described in detail in 1938 by Frederick R. Macaulay of the National Bureau of Economic Research.

Duration describes the percentage change in the price of a bond of a given maturity, coupon, and beginning yield level resulting from small percentage changes in yield. The duration of a bond is not accurate for large percentage changes in yield, since absolute yield levels influence the percentage change in a bond's price for a given percentage change in yields, particularly when the coupon value is substantially different from the prevailing yield level (that is, when the bond is trading at a considerable distance above or below par). The accuracy of duration in measuring price sensitivity to yield changes also tends to decline with increasing maturities and with downward (more than with upward) movements in interest rates. If the duration of a bond of a certain maturity, coupon, and beginning yield level is 6.75, the bond would decline or rise by 6.75 percent in price for a 100-basis-point rise or fall in yield levels. Duration permits a common comparison of the price sensitivity of bonds with widely varying coupons, maturities, and yields.

A second and not entirely unrelated meaning of duration refers to the amount of time required for the increased or decreased reinvestment income resulting from a rise in yield levels to balance exactly the related decline or rise in the price of a specific fixed-income security. Low reinvestment yields and/or coupon levels increase the amount of time needed to offset a given price change, while high reinvestment yields and/or coupon levels shorten this time span.

Since the analysis in this chapter has been concerned primarily with understanding the mechanics of yield and price relationships for bonds, there has been very little treatment of the practical effects on bond yield and price movements of (1) the movement toward maturity of the bond with the passage of time, (2) the level of coupon income and its reinvestment, (3) specialized investor behavior due to taxes and such bond features as call prices or the value of a bond in reorganization proceedings, (4) fluctuations in the rates of return from a bond due to variations in the length of the holding period, and (5) shifts in the location and shape of the yield curve as interest rates change. Several examples of these effects are presented here.

First, an intermediate-maturity bond may be 2.5 times as sensitive in price to a change in interest rates as a short-maturity issue, but after the passage of several months the intermediate issue (now an even shorter-maturity bond) may become 3.5 times as sensitive in price to a change in interest rates as the short-maturity bond (now an especially short-maturity issue).

Second, a rise in yields causes a decline in the price of a bond but at the same time increases the interest rate at which coupon income can be reinvested. Sufficiently favorable conditions concerning the reinvestment rate, the investor's holding period, the coupon level, and the maturity of the bond may actually provide a realized compound yield (RCY) which exceeds the original yield to maturity of the bond.

Third, high-coupon issues which are subject to call may not rise or fall in price as fully and/or as rapidly as otherwise dictated by yield-to-maturity formulas. On the other hand, because of the different tax treatment of capital gains as compared with coupon income, low-coupon issues which are selling at a deep discount from par in a high-interest-rate environment may trade at different price levels than otherwise specified by yield-to-maturity formulas.

Fourth, because of shifts in the level and the shape of the yield curve, intermediate-term bonds may be more volatile than long-term bonds. This situation tends to arise when the intermediate sector of the bond market undergoes a more substantial basis-point change than does the long-term–maturity sector.

14

The Dynamic Management of Bond Portfolios

Overview

In recent years, certain investors have devoted increasing amounts of attention to the dynamic management of their fixed-income securities holdings. Rather than simply buying a given bond and holding it until maturity, these investors have given active consideration to bond switching (also broadly known as bond swapping), both for offensive reasons (such as the improvement of total income return or the enhancement of capital gains prospects) and for defensive reasons (such as protection against losses due to interest rate increases, credit judgments, or currency depreciation). However, the use of active bond management techniques across a wide spectrum of investors has generally not kept pace with the rise in total fixed-income securities outstanding and the increased trading volume in fixed-income issues.

The wide variations in swapping activity between various groups of investors and between different investors within a given sector of the market can be traced to variations in the following factors, among others: (1) accessibility to and organization of current and historical data which can be used in comparing bonds; (2) expressly stated or traditionally ingrained restrictions against portfolio turnover above a certain level, against the realization of losses or gains, or against investment in specified sectors of the market; (3) transaction costs including commissions, custodial fees, settlement expenses, and any applicable turnover taxes, transfer taxes, withholding taxes, income taxes, or capital gains taxes; (4) the nature and psychology of the ultimate client whose funds are being invested; (5) occasional difficulties in effecting trades of very large or very small size; and (6) widely differing levels of experience in swapping and in the means of effecting swap transactions. The advent of increasingly low-priced and more readily available computing power and data storage capability should permit easier analysis of the diverse terms and types of fixed-income securities which might or might not be substituted for existing positions. Whether or not the investor deems it appropriate to adopt a more active portfolio strategy or considers a given issue egregiously undervalued or overvalued, it can nevertheless be quite beneficial to be aware of the risks, advantages, and means of switching one fixed-income security for another.

This chapter provides an explanation of the motives behind bond swapping and a review of the advantages and disadvantages of such activity. In addition, it describes several tools which can aid the investor in considering and executing a given swap. The mechanics of a bond matrix are discussed, with particular emphasis on its application in the systematic analysis of a specific area of the bond market. Some sample exercises (with answers) which provide guidelines concerning the multiple uses of a bond matrix have been included. In addition, this chapter discusses the effects of several variables on the true value of a bond and/or the expected benefits of a possible swap transaction, including the frequency and form of a bond's coupon payments, the effects of transaction costs on a bond's yield, and the effects of currency changes on the total return from a bond. The chapter concludes with two detailed evaluation worksheets, one for analyzing the needs of an investor in the light of possible swapping activity and the other for analyzing in a comprehensive way the numerous components of the securities involved in a swap.

In this chapter, two specialized sectors of the fixed-income securities universe, the Eurobond market and the Yankee bond market, are frequently used as vehicles of discussion. United States domestic bonds are used in the section which shows examples of specific swap transactions, but it should be pointed out that the Eurobond and Yankee bond markets often provide many examples of interesting swap opportunities, both on issues of the same or similar borrowers and between widely varying sectors of each market.

The Eurobond and Yankee bond sectors are reviewed at some length for several reasons. Eurobonds and Yankee bonds are relatively recent entries upon the fixed-income scene, the former having been inaugurated in the early 1960s and the latter in the mid-1970s. Both these sectors can be encompassed in manageably descriptive form and can be fairly accurately inventoried as to amounts outstanding, coupons, maturities, sinking-fund and call data, and other significant terms. Finally, the Eurobond market, unlike the purely domestic sectors of the fixed-income universe, offers the possibility of investing in a broad range of issues in foreign currencies, in a choice of foreign currency options, or in a composite of foreign currencies. In several cases, there are available bonds of a particular issue which vary substantively only as to currency denomination. Such bonds help to focus the scrutiny of the investor upon the influence of currency devaluations or revaluations on the total return of a bond and thus on its relative attractiveness or unattractiveness as a swap candidate.

Motivations, Advantages, and Disadvantages of Bond Swapping

Bond swapping usually describes the activity of switching from one fixed-income security to another fixed-income security having the same or different coupon, maturity, quality rating, yield level, and other features. Investors usually swap bonds for one of five principal reasons. First, the investor may wish to gain increased current income and/or an increased yield to maturity. This type of swap is often called a "yield pickup swap." Second, the investor may desire to obtain an improved relative price performance in the event of an upward or downward move in interest rates. This kind of swap is also known as a "rate anticipation swap." Third, the investor may want to purchase or sell a security or securities at a historically attractive yield relative to that available on other similar issues. This kind of swap is sometimes referred to as a "substitution swap." Fourth, the investor may wish to purchase or sell a security or securities at a historically attractive yield compared with that available on other groups or types of issues. This type of swap is usually denominated a "sector swap." Fifth and finally, the investor may want to achieve a variety of other investment objectives, such as tax minimization, greater portfolio diversification, or greater portfolio concentration.

There are several reasons why not all investors should attempt bond swapping. Time must be devoted to monitor market trends and the prices of specific issues and then to compare a large number of bonds with one another. Transaction charges and/or other fees may reduce or eliminate entirely the expected benefits of a proposed swap. The ability to identify and act upon the implications of broad trends is at least as crucial as, if not more crucial than, a capacity for the microanalysis involved in substituting one security for a similar issue.

A growing number of competing market participants have computers and other tools at their disposal to assist them in finding overpriced and undervalued securities. It may be difficult for many investors to obtain timely knowledge of historical yield differentials between various types and categories of debt issues. A great deal of information and judgment about market conditions, psychological factors, currency movements, and economic developments is often necessary before swaps can be effectively executed. Finally, a swap transaction can have an effect exactly opposite to that which the investor intended, since in some cases what appears to be a temporarily undervalued security relative to other issues may decline even more in rela-

TABLE 14-1

Variable Factors for Different Types of Swap Transactions

Factor	Yield pickup swap	Rate anticipation swap	Substitution swap	Sector swap
Coupon*	Frequently changes	May change	May change	May change
Maturity	Frequently changes	Frequently changes	May change	May change
Average life	Frequently changes	Frequently changes	May change	May change
Sinking fund	May change	May change	May change	May change
Call provisions	May change	May change	May change	May change
Issuer	May change	May change	May change	Frequently changes
Marketability†	May change	May change	May change	May change
Quality	May change	May change	Rarely changes	May change
Sector‡	May change	May change	May change	Frequently changes
Country	May change	May change	May change	May change
Currency§	May change	May change	May change	May change
Money invested	May change	May change	Usually modest change	May change

*Coupon can change in three ways: (1) absolute amount, (2) fixed rate versus floating rate, and (3) annual, semiannual, or other payment frequency.

†Marketability can be influenced by (1) the issue date, (2) the method and primary locale of syndication, (3) the form (registered or bearer) and denomination of the bond, (4) the place where listed and the primary settlement system, (5) details concerning the issuer, and (6) the total size of the issue and other features of the bond.

‡Broad sectors include (1) government, (2) government agencies, (3) supranational bodies, (4) municipalities, and (5) corporations. Numerous other narrower sectors are often recognized by investors within these broad sectors. For example, within the sector of corporate bonds, investors commonly refer to the industrial sector, the utility sector, and several other sectors.

§Currency option and composite currency unit issues are additional means of varying the currency of the investment.

tive and/or absolute value. This condition may last for extended periods of time.

Investors should also take note of several other important aspects of bond swapping. Swaps may be carried out in connection with the purchase of a new bond issue at the time of its underwriting together with the simultaneous sale of existing securities from the investor's portfolio. When a particular swap has proved successful, an investor may wish to switch back into the original holding (often called a "reverse swap") because of a change in the relationship (1) between the two issues or (2) between the new holding (or the original holding) and the market or (3) for other reasons.

Swap transactions often involve the payment of additional funds (sometimes described as the "payup") or the release of funds (frequently known as the "takeout"). The investor should thus be aware of the possible necessity, depending upon the amounts involved in the swap, of contributing additional money or searching for additional investment outlets. Before initiating a swap transaction, an investor should undertake a broad and complete review of his or her financial situation and objectives as well as of all relevant details of the securities involved in the swap. The worksheets at the end of this chapter should aid the investor in executing this analysis.

Types of Bond Swaps

Table 14-1 lists the relative degree of frequency of change for various features of a bond in the four major types of swap transactions. It should be stressed that the guidelines in the table represent broad generalizations. Coupon, maturity, and perhaps average life tend to be altered rather frequently in a yield pickup swap. Maturity and perhaps average life are generally changed frequently in a rate anticipation swap. By definition, a substitution swap usually involves the replacement of one issue by a very similar bond cousin. On the other hand, a sector swap may bring about a drastic shift in one or all of the major components of a bond's identity, even including its currency of denomination.

The Eurobond Market

The Eurobond market is a primary and secondary marketplace for bonds offered outside the country of the borrower and largely outside the country in whose currency the securities are denominated. Eurobond offerings are generally managed by an international syndicate of investment and/or commercial banks from more than one country. Interest payments on Eurobonds are typically free from all withholding taxes.

From the imposition in mid-1963 of the United States interest equalization tax (one of several factors which spurred the growth of the Eurobond market) until the end of 1978, almost 2600 Eurobond issues (including both public offerings and broadly defined private placements), aggregating more than $94 billion in a variety of currencies, were offered. Table 14-2 shows the total amount of Eurobonds outstanding in selected currencies as of December 31, 1977. Eurobond issues denominated in United States dollars amounted to almost $41 billion of the $64 billion in outstanding Eurobonds listed in the table. Deutsche mark issues totaled almost $18 billion at the end of 1977. The United States dollar equivalent of this sum was considerably augmented by the substantial rise of the Deutsche mark vis-à-vis the dollar during several years in the 1970s.

TABLE 14-2
Total Amount of Eurobonds Outstanding for Selected Currencies, Year-End
1977

Sector	Exchange rate*	United States dollar amount (in millions)
United States dollar issues		$40,795
Deutsche mark issues (DM 34,187 million)	1.9005 DM/$1	17,988
Dutch guilder issues (HF1 5,633 million)	2.0695 HF1/$1	2,722
Canadian dollar issues (C$2,643 million)	0.8535 C$/$1	2,256
	Total	$63,761

*Currency exchange rates as of Oct. 6, 1978, have been used for calculation purposes.

In addition to the Dutch guilder and Canadian dollar issues listed in Table 14-2, lesser amounts of Eurobonds are denominated in Australian dollars, Austrian schillings, Bahraini dinars, British pounds, French francs, Hong Kong dollars, Kuwaiti dinars, Danish kroner, Norwegian kroner, Luxembourg francs, and Saudi Arabian riyals, among others. Mixed-currency issues denominated in European composite units, European currency units, European units of account, and Special Drawing Rights are available.

Governmental entities and corporations in more than 40 countries have issued Eurobonds. An additional sizable category of borrowers includes such multinational authorities and supranational bodies as the Asian Development Bank, the European Economic Community, the European Investment Bank, the Nordic Investment Bank, and the International Bank for Reconstruction and Development (more commonly known as the World Bank).

The complexity and variety of Eurobond markets are underscored by the availability of issues offering the investor the option of receiving interest and principal payments in such currency combinations as sterling–Deutsche marks or Australian dollars–Deutsche marks. The investor can also select from among a variety of Eurobonds which are convertible into the common stock of companies domiciled in France, Hong Kong, Japan, Luxembourg, the Netherlands, Singapore, South Africa, Sweden, Switzerland, the United Kingdom, and the United States. Particularly in the second half of the 1970s, the prefix "Euro-" did not accurately reflect to many investors the growing number of borrowers, investors, and currencies of Middle Eastern, Latin American, and Australasian origin. Using a more comprehensive term, some market participants have begun to call the international external capital markets Xenomarkets, with accompanying Xenocurrencies ("Xeno" derives from the Greek word *xenos,* meaning stranger).

Table 14-3 shows annual Eurobond trading volume as reported by the two major international clearing and settlement systems, Euroclear and Cedel.

Some caveats must be kept in mind concerning the data in this table. The totals are partly inflated by the separate reporting of the purchase and the sale sides of a transaction by different Eurobond dealers. In addition, some primary-issue volume is included in these statistics. Nevertheless, the fact remains that Eurobond turnover as reported by Euroclear and Cedel rose from $16 billion in 1974 to more than $156 billion in 1979.

The Yankee Bond Market

Yankee bonds are Securities and Exchange Commission (SEC)–registered, United States dollar–denominated issues of foreign borrowers which have been syndicated primarily in the American market. The conventional definition of Yankee bonds generally excludes issues of Canadian borrowers, bonds of international organizations of which the United States is a member, and certain (but not all) non-American corporations. The Yankee bond market is thus quite a bit more circumscribed and homogeneous than the Eurobond market.

From the expiration of the United States interest equalization tax (IET) in 1974 to the end of 1978, more than $8 billion worth of Yankee bonds

TABLE 14-3
Total Annual Reported Eurobond Turnover
(Volume in millions)[a]

Year	Euroclear	Cedel
1972	$11,481	$ 5,978[b]
1973	11,092	10,211
1974	8,143	8,067
1975	14,326	13,932
1976	36,965	26,691
1977	65,209[c]	38,556[d]
1978	77,082[e]	39,749[f]
1979	102,080[g]	54,662[b]

[a] Non-United States dollar amounts have been translated into United States dollars at exchange rates prevailing during each year shown.

[b] Total shown is for only 6 months since Cedel began publishing turnover statistics on July 1, 1972.

[c] Of which $9370 million represents turnover in non-United States dollar issues.

[d] Of which $9098 million represents turnover in non-United States dollar issues.

[e] Of which $16,348 million represents turnover in non-United States dollar issues.

[f] Of which $13,611 million represents turnover in non-United States dollar issues.

[g] Of which $18,793 million represents turnover in non-United States dollar issues.

[b] Of which $15,944 million represents turnover in non-United States dollar issues.

were issued in more than 90 bond issues. Many traditional Eurobond investors located outside the United States purchase Yankee bonds because of a familiarity with the borrower, relatively attractive yields, and other advantageous terms of Yankee bond issues, including semiannual coupons as compared with the more usual annual coupons on Eurobond issues. If the bonds are owned by non-United States residents, interest payments are not subject to United States withholding taxes. Yankee bonds are generally larger than Eurobond issues, and most carry ratings from Moody's and Standard & Poor's rating agencies.

Table 14-4 provides a review of the amounts outstanding for most of the Yankee bond issuers (according to the conventional definition) as of July 1, 1978. It should be mentioned that bonds issued in the United States capital market by non-American borrowers prior to the expiration of the IET in 1974 also are not included in the conventional definition of Yankee bonds. From Table 14-4 it can be seen that as of the middle of 1978 France, Australia, and Norway had raised the largest amounts of money, with total Yankee debt outstanding of $1 billion, $975 million, and $850 million respectively.

Partly because of the similarity of issuers in the Eurobond and Yankee bond markets, a number of investors swap back and forth between bonds in these domains. When executing swaps between the Eurobond and Yankee bond markets, it is important to compare yields on a similar basis. This task can be complicated somewhat because most Eurobonds have annual coupons while most Yankee bonds have semiannual coupons. To help investors compare annual and semiannual yields, Table 14-5 presents the yield equivalents of returns computed by assuming semiannual compounding with those computed by assuming annual compounding. Because of the greater frequency of interest compounding, a given semiannual yield equals a higher annual yield. For example, Table 14-5 shows that a semiannual yield of 7 percent equals an annual yield of 7.12 percent.

Use of a Bond Matrix as an Aid in Swapping

Owing to the somewhat uniform structure of the Yankee bond market, it is relatively easy to devise a grid, or matrix, which shows yields to maturity for categories of Yankee bonds. Such a matrix has been computed by using a large number of Yankee bond issues with yields shown as of June 27, 1978. This matrix is presented as Table 14-6.

The matrix permits rapid comparison of yields according to maturity (in vertical columns) and issuer (along the horizontal rows). Similar matrices showing the coupon or another significant feature of a bond in the vertical

TABLE 14-4
Selected Yankee Bond Issues Outstanding, July 1978*

Ratings		Issuer or guarantor	Number of issues	Principal amount (in millions of dollars)	Percent of market
Moody's	Standard & Poor's				
		EUROPEAN SUPRANATIONAL ORGANIZATIONS:			
Aaa	AAA	European Economic Community	2	$ 200	2.9
Aaa	AAA	European Coal and Steel Community	8	775	11.1
Aaa	AAA	European Investment Bank	8	700	10.0
Aaa	AAA	EUROFIMA	1	50	0.7
		Subtotal	19	$1725	24.7
		EUROPEAN COUNTRIES:			
Aaa	AAA	Austria	4	$ 200	2.9
Aa	AAA	Finland	3	200	2.9
Aaa	AAA	France	13	1010	14.4
Aaa	AAA	Norway	8	850	12.1
Aaa	AAA	Sweden	3	325	4.6
Aaa	AAA	United Kingdom	2	350	5.0
		Subtotal	33	$2935	41.9
		OTHER GOVERNMENTS:			
Aaa	AAA	Australia	11	$ 975	13.9
Aaa	AAA	Japan	6	550	7.9
	Not rated	Brazil	2	135	1.9
	Not rated	Mexico	4	235	3.4
Aaa	AAA	New Zealand	1	100	1.4

TABLE 14-4
Selected Yankee Bond Issues Outstanding, July 1978* (Continued)

Ratings		Issuer or guarantor	Number of issues	Principal amount (in millions of dollars)	Percent of market
Moody's	Standard & Poor's				
Aaa	AAA	Venezuela	3	250	3.6
		Subtotal	27	$2245	32.1
		MUNICIPALITIES:			
Aaa	AAA	City of Oslo	1	$ 50	0.7
Aaa	AAA	City of Stockholm	1	50	0.7
		Subtotal	2	$100	1.4
		Grand total	81	$7005	100.0

*Excludes debt issues of Canadian origin, of international organizations of which the United States is a member (such as the International Bank for Reconstruction and Development, the Asian Development Bank, and the Inter-American Development Bank), and of certain non-American corporations such as Imperial Chemical Industries (with two issues totaling $275 million) and British Petroleum (with three issues totaling $300 million).

TABLE 14-5
Yield Equivalents on Bonds with Semiannual Coupons and Annual Coupons

Semiannual yield	Annual yield	Semiannual yield	Annual yield	Semiannual yield	Annual yield
3.00	3.02				
3.25	3.28	7.25	7.38	11.25	11.57
3.50	3.53	7.50	7.64	11.50	11.83
3.75	3.79	7.75	7.90	11.75	12.10
4.00	4.04	8.00	8.16	12.00	12.36
4.25	4.30	8.25	8.42	12.25	12.63
4.50	4.55	8.50	8.68	12.50	12.89
4.75	4.81	8.75	8.94	12.75	13.16
5.00	5.06	9.00	9.20	13.00	13.42
5.25	5.32	9.25	9.46	13.25	13.69
5.50	5.58	9.50	9.73	13.50	13.96
5.75	5.83	9.75	9.99	13.75	14.22
6.00	6.09	10.00	10.25	14.00	14.49
6.25	6.35	10.25	10.51	14.25	14.76
6.50	6.61	10.50	10.78	14.50	15.03
6.75	6.86	10.75	11.04	14.75	15.29
7.00	7.12	11.00	11.30	15.00	15.56

columns could be prepared. The matrix in Table 14-6 also allows the investor to determine possible maturity areas in which purchases might be made as well as those maturity areas in which no Yankee bonds are currently outstanding. For instance, at the time that the matrix in Table 14-6 was prepared, there were no Yankee bonds available with a 1980, 1981, or 1989 final maturity. Similarly, it can be seen at a glance that there was no Latin American debt available with a maturity beyond 1984. The following five sample exercises show how the matrix can be employed practically.

Case 1

An investor owns Commonwealth of Australia bonds of 1984 yielding 8.93 percent. The investor is willing to invest in the bonds of any Yankee bond issuer in order to obtain the highest possible yield while keeping the same maturity. What is the recommended investment, and what is the gross gain (before commissions and other charges) in yield to maturity? *Answer:* Brazilian National Development Bank (BNDE) bonds due in 1984, yielding 9.93 percent, for a 100-basis-point pickup in yield to maturity.

TABLE 14-6
Yields to Maturity of Yankee Bonds

| Years to maturity | 2 | 3 | 4 | 5 | 6 | 7 | 8 | 9 | 10 | 11 | 12 | 13 | 14 | 15 | 16 | 17 | 18 | 19 | 20 |
Issuer / Maturity	80	81	82	83	84	85	86	87	88	89	90	91	92	93	94	95	96	97	98
Supranational bodies:																			
European Economic Community			8.94																
European Coal and Steel Community			8.75	9.07	9.16											9.24		9.55	
European Investment Bank			9.01	8.64	9.15								9.43						9.56
EUROFIMA				8.88															
Scandinavian issuers:																			
Finland				9.31									9.56						
Norway				8.90	8.85														
				8.99	9.07														
Oslo																	9.45		
Stockholm													9.31						
Sweden								9.33											9.74
Norges Kommunal Bank													9.11						9.61
French issuers:																			
BFCE			8.99																
			8.83																
Caisse Nationale des Autoroutes							9.06					9.26						9.54	
Caisse Nationale des Télécommunications		9.03	9.13													9.61			
Électricité de France			9.10			9.32	9.24												

Issuer							
Société Nationale des Chemins de Fer					9.14	9.38	
United Kingdom issuers:							
United Kingdom			8.88			9.39	
Austrian issuers:							
Austria	8.77	8.91		8.83	9.39		
Australian–New Zealand issuers:	8.87						
Australia	8.66	8.71				9.11	9.44
	8.93	9.13				9.40	
	9.21						
	8.76						
New Zealand	8.92	8.88					
	9.04						
	8.50						
Japanese issuers:							
Nippon Telephone and Telegraph			8.96				
Latin American issuers:							
Brazil	9.82						
Mexico	9.86						
Petróleos Mexicanos	9.27						
Venezuela	9.18	9.31					
Brazilian National Development Bank	9.93						

Case 2

An investor owns Kingdom of Norway bonds of 1983 yielding 8.90 percent. The investor desires to earn the maximum possible yield without regard to maturity while staying in a debt issue of a Scandinavian borrower. What is the recommended investment, and what is the gross yield gain? *Answer:* Kingdom of Sweden bonds due in 1998, yielding 9.74 percent, for a gross yield pickup of 84 basis points.

Case 3

The Republic of Finland announces plans to issue bonds with a 1987 maturity. The expected issue price is 100, and the expected coupon is 9.50 percent. Do the bonds appear to be properly priced in relation to other bonds in the matrix? *Answer:* The proposed Republic of Finland bonds do appear to be properly priced, both in relation to the other two Republic of Finland bonds outstanding and in relation to the three bonds also maturing in 1987: Kingdom of Sweden, Electricité de France (EDF), and Nippon Telephone and Telegraph (NTT) bonds.

Case 4

An investor owns Caisse Nationale des Autoroutes (CNA) bonds due in 1997 and yielding 9.54 percent. The investor feels that interest rates will soon be moving higher. The investor would like to remain invested in the French sector of the Yankee bond market but would like to obtain the shortest possible maturity and the highest possible yield on an issue maturing in 1983. What is the recommended investment, and what is the gross yield loss? *Answer:* The Caisse Nationale des Télécommunications (CNT) bonds due in 1983, yielding 9.13 percent and producing a gross yield loss of 41 basis points.

Case 5

An investor owns United Kingdom bonds due in 1988 and yielding 8.88 percent. The investor feels very strongly that interest rates will be declining in the near future. The investor has reached internally set investment limits in the debt of French, Scandinavian, and supranational borrowers, and would like to sell half of the United Kingdom position and diversify into longer-term debt (if possible) of another borrower. What is the recommended investment, and what is the gross yield gain? *Answer:* The Commonwealth of Australia bonds due in 1997, yielding 9.44 percent, for a gross yield pickup of 56 basis points.

Effect of Transaction Costs on Swapping

If the bonds are assumed to be held to maturity, the reduction of the gross yield pickup which is caused by commissions and other charges can be rather substantial. The actual amount of the reduction depends upon the charges as a percentage of the principal value of the bonds, the coupon and prevailing yield levels, and the number of years remaining to maturity. For example, Table 14-7 assumes two different levels of transaction costs whose variance might be due to the nature of the charges, such as commissions, custody fees, taxes, and/or settlement charges which are added to (on the purchase of a bond) or subtracted from (on the sale of a bond) the gross amount involved in a transaction.

TABLE 14-7
Effects of Transaction Costs on Yield to Maturity*

Charge as percentage of principal value	0.165 percent			0.665 percent		
Coupon (percent)	8.00	8.50	9.00	8.00	8.50	9.00
Years to maturity	Reduction in basis points			Reduction in basis points		
1	17.5	17.5	17.6	70.2	70.4	70.7
2	9.1	9.1	9.2	36.5	36.7	36.9
3	6.3	6.3	6.4	25.3	25.5	25.7
4	4.9	4.9	5.0	19.7	19.9	20.1
5	4.1	4.1	4.2	16.3	16.5	16.7
6	3.5	3.6	3.6	14.1	14.3	14.5
7	3.1	3.2	3.2	12.5	12.7	12.9
8	2.8	2.9	2.9	11.4	11.6	11.8
9	2.6	2.7	2.7	10.5	10.7	10.9
10	2.4	2.5	2.5	9.7	10.0	10.2
11	2.3	2.3	2.4	9.2	9.4	9.6
12	2.2	2.2	2.3	8.7	8.9	9.1
13	2.1	2.1	2.2	8.3	8.5	8.7
14	2.0	2.0	2.1	7.9	8.2	8.4
15	1.9	2.0	2.0	7.7	7.9	8.1
16	1.8	1.9	2.0	7.4	7.6	7.9
17	1.8	1.9	1.9	7.2	7.4	7.7
18	1.7	1.8	1.9	7.0	7.2	7.5
19	1.7	1.8	1.8	6.8	7.1	7.3
20	1.6	1.7	1.8	6.7	6.9	7.2

*Or yield to first call, or yield to average life; not current yield.

†Alternatively, to first call or to average life.

The two levels of transaction costs used in Table 14-7 are (1) 0.165 percent of the principal value involved on a given side of a transaction and (2) 0.665 percent of the principal value involved on a given side of a transaction. Each level is used to compute the reduction in realized yields by assuming coupons and prevailing yield levels of 8.00 percent, 8.50 percent, and 9.00 percent. While the investor's transaction costs will often vary from the values listed in Table 14-7, it is useful for the bond investor to take such expenses into account when analyzing the possible benefits and risks inherent in a contemplated bond swap.

As an example of how to use Table 14-7, it is assumed that the investor is subject to the 0.665 percent transaction cost schedule detailed in the table. If this is the case, the gross yield gain of 100 basis points described in case 1 of the Yankee bond matrix discussion would translate into a net yield gain of 71 basis points. This is calculated by subtracting approximately 14.5 basis points (because of transaction costs of 0.665 percent of the gross amount involved in the sale of the Australia bonds) and also by subtracting approximately 14.5 basis points (because of transaction costs on the purchase of the BNDE bonds with the same maturity) from the gross yield pickup of 100 basis points. The arithmetic of this calculation is shown below:

Net yield change = gross yield change − (purchase expenses + sale expenses)

Net yield change = 100 basis points − (14.5 basis points + 14.5 basis points)

Net yield change = 71 basis points

Examples of Swap Transactions

The Yankee bond market having been used for a discussion of the bond matrix and its uses, the United States domestic bond market is drawn upon to provide specific examples of swap transactions. Table 14-8 shows an example of each of the four major types of swap transactions. All prices in the table represent actual bid prices (on bonds being sold) and the offered side of the market (on bonds being purchased). Because of the intentional selection of highest-quality U.S. government, federal agency, and corporate bonds for inclusion in the table, the swap margins are not always very large. The examples are intended primarily to serve as guidelines to the investor in the display and ongoing evaluation of swap transactions. In each swap, the price performance of both the purchased bond and the sold bond has been shown as of a date at least 3 months after the transaction in order to indicate

TABLE 14-8
Examples of Swap Transactions

Type of swap	Date	Action	Description of issue, including coupon and maturity			Price	Current yield	Yield to maturity
Yield pickup swap								
	09/28/79	Sell	U.S. Treasury	6.875	09/30/80	96.438	7.13	10.70
	09/28/79	Buy	U.S. Treasury	8.375	08/31/80	97.844	8.56	10.88
	01/01/80		U.S. Treasury	6.875	09/30/80	96.063	7.16	12.44
	01/01/80		U.S. Treasury	8.375	08/31/80	97.406	8.60	12.47
Rate anticipation swap								
	09/28/79	Sell	U.S. Treasury	8.000	08/15/01*	94.500	8.47	8.55
	09/28/79	Buy	U.S. Treasury	8.000	05/15/82	98.875	8.09	8.36
	01/01/80		U.S. Treasury	8.000	08/15/01*	81.500	9.82	10.12
	01/01/80		U.S. Treasury	8.000	05/15/82	94.250	8.50	10.80
Substitution swap								
	09/28/79	Sell	Southwestern Bell Telephone	8.250	08/01/17	86.375	9.55	9.60
	09/28/79	Buy	Southern Bell T & T	8.250	08/15/16	85.625	9.64	9.69
	01/01/80		Southwestern Bell Telephone	8.250	08/01/17	75.500	10.93	10.99
	01/01/80		Southern Bell T & T	8.250	08/15/16	76.000	10.86	10.92
Sector swap								
	09/29/78	Sell	FNMA	7.900	09/10/86	95.750	8.25	8.65
	09/28/79	Buy	U.S. Treasury	8.000	08/15/86	97.250	8.20	8.48
	01/01/80		FNMA	7.900	09/10/86	86.500	9.13	10.77
	01/01/80		U.S. Treasury	8.000	08/15/86	88.563	9.03	10.43

*First callable in 1996; yield to first call date has been substituted for yield to maturity.

what would have happened to both securities had the swap been executed. Current yields have also been calculated and compared to provide an idea of the costs and benefits of each swap in the short run.

Yield Pickup Swap

On September 28, 1979, the investor sells the U.S. Treasury 6.875 percent note due September 30, 1980, and purchases the U.S. Treasury 8.375 percent note due August 31, 1980. This operation permits a gain of 18 basis points in yield to maturity and 143 basis points in current yield. A payup of 1.406 points ($14.06 per $1000 bond) is also required. As of January 1, 1980, the purchase issue is providing only 3 additional basis points in yield to maturity relative to the sold issue. This margin indicates that the two securities' prices are more closely in line with each other after allowing for differences in coupon and final maturity dates.

Rate Anticipation Swap

On September 28, 1979, the investor feels that interest rates are about to experience a significant rise (in fact, this assumption was later proved correct). The investor decides to decrease the maturity of the securities holdings in the portfolio and, as part of this program, sells the U.S. Treasury 8.00 percent note due August 15, 2001, in favor of purchasing the U.S. Treasury 8.00 percent note due May 15, 1982. This swap results in a decrease of 19 basis points in yield to maturity, a decease of 36 basis points in current yield, and a payup of 4.375 points ($43.75 per $1000 bond).

Three months later, on January 1, 1980, the wisdom of the swap has become more evident. While the sold bond has declined fully 13 points during the intervening period, the purchased bond has declined considerably less: 4.625 points. By shortening maturity 19 years and 3 months, the investor has been able to avoid an incremental loss of 8.375 points ($83.75 per $1000 bond).

Substitution Swap

The investor swaps virtually identical bonds in the substitution swap example shown in Table 14-8. On September 28, 1979, the investor sells a Southwestern Bell Telephone 8.25 percent bond due August 1, 2017, in order to buy a very close substitute, the Southern Bell Telephone 8.25 percent issue due August 15, 2016. This swap produces a pickup of 9 basis points in both yield to maturity and current yield, while allowing a takeout of 0.75 points ($7.50 per $1000 bond). After 3 months, the purchased bond is selling for 0.50 point *more* than the sold bond.

TABLE 14-9
The Effect of Currency Changes on Yield to Maturity

Coupon (percent)	Amount of revaluation (percent)	Years to revaluation	Maturity (years)								
			2	3	4	5	7	10	12	15	20
		1	8.49	7.71	7.32	7.08	6.82	6.62	6.55	6.47	6.40
	5	3		6.00	7.17	6.96	6.73	6.55	6.48	6.42	6.36
		5				6.00	6.64	6.49	6.43	6.37	6.32
		8						6.41	6.36	6.31	6.26
		1	10.89	9.35	8.58	8.12	7.60	7.22	7.07	6.93	6.79
6	10	3		6.00	8.29	7.88	7.42	7.08	6.95	6.82	6.70
		5				6.00	7.26	6.96	6.84	6.73	6.62
		8						6.80	6.71	6.61	6.52
		1	13.22	10.93	9.79	9.12	8.36	7.79	7.58	7.37	7.17
	15	3		6.00	9.37	8.77	8.09	7.59	7.39	7.21	7.03
		5				6.00	7.86	7.41	7.24	7.07	6.91
		8						7.18	7.04	6.90	6.76
		1	9.50	8.82	8.33	8.10	7.84	7.64	7.57	7.50	7.43
	5	3		7.00	8.16	7.96	7.73	7.56	7.50	7.43	7.37
		5				7.00	7.64	7.49	7.43	7.38	7.33
		8						7.40	7.35	7.31	7.26
		1	11.90	10.37	9.61	9.16	8.64	8.26	8.12	7.98	7.85
7	10	3		7.00	9.27	8.88	8.43	8.10	7.97	7.85	7.73
		5				7.00	8.25	7.96	7.85	7.74	7.64
		8						7.78	7.69	7.60	7.52
		1	14.23	11.96	10.84	10.17	9.18	8.86	8.65	8.45	8.25
	15	3		7.00	10.35	9.76	9.10	8.61	8.43	8.25	8.08
		5				7.00	8.83	8.40	8.24	8.09	7.94
		8						8.15	8.01	7.88	7.76
		1	10.50	9.73	9.35	9.12	8.86	8.67	8.60	8.53	8.46
	5	3		8.00	9.15	8.95	8.73	8.57	8.51	8.45	8.39
		5				8.00	8.63	8.49	8.43	8.38	8.33
		8						8.39	8.34	8.30	8.26
		1	12.92	11.39	10.64	10.19	9.68	9.31	9.17	9.03	8.91
8	10	3		8.00	10.26	9.87	9.43	9.12	9.00	8.88	8.77
		5				8.00	9.23	8.95	8.85	8.75	8.66
		8						8.76	8.67	8.59	8.52
		1	15.25	13.00	11.88	11.22	10.48	9.93	9.73	9.53	9.34
	15	3		8.00	11.32	10.75	10.11	9.64	9.46	9.29	9.14
		5				8.00	9.81	9.40	9.25	9.10	8.97

TABLE 14-9
The Effect of Currency Changes on Yield to Maturity *(Continued)*

Cou-pon (per-cent)	Amount of reval-uation (percent)	Years to reval-uation	Maturity (years)								
			2	3	4	5	7	10	12	15	20
		8						9.11	8.99	8.87	8.76
		1	11.51	10.74	10.36	10.13	9.88	9.69	9.62	9.55	9.49
	5	3		9.00	10.14	9.95	9.74	9.58	9.52	9.46	9.41
		5				9.00	9.62	9.48	9.43	9.39	9.34
		8						9.37	9.33	9.30	9.26
		1	13.93	12.42	11.67	11.22	10.72	10.36	10.22	10.09	9.97
9	10	3		9.00	11.24	10.86	10.44	10.13	10.02	9.91	9.81
		5				9.00	10.21	9.95	9.85	9.76	9.67
		8						9.73	9.66	9.58	9.52
		1	16.27	14.03	12.93	12.27	11.54	11.00	10.80	10.61	10.44
	15	3		9.00	12.29	11.74	11.12	10.67	10.50	10.34	10.19
		5				9.00	10.78	10.40	10.25	10.12	9.99
		8						10.08	9.97	9.86	9.76
		1	12.51	11.75	11.38	11.15	10.90	10.71	10.65	10.58	10.52
	5	3		10.00	11.13	10.95	10.74	10.59	10.53	10.48	10.43
		5				10.00	10.61	10.48	10.44	10.39	10.35
		8						10.36	10.33	10.29	10.26
		1	14.94	13.44	12.70	12.26	11.76	11.40	11.27	11.14	11.03
10	10	3		10.00	12.22	11.86	11.45	11.15	11.04	10.93	10.84
		5				10.00	11.19	10.95	10.85	10.77	10.69
		8						10.71	10.64	10.57	10.51
		1	17.28	15.06	13.97	13.32	12.60	12.07	11.88	11.69	11.53
	15	3		10.00	13.27	12.73	12.13	11.69	11.53	11.38	11.24
		5				10.00	11.75	11.39	11.26	11.13	11.01
		8						11.04	10.94	10.84	10.76

Sector Swap

On September 29, 1978, the investor switches from the government agency sector to the U.S. government sector of the bond market. This is accomplished by selling the Federal National Mortgage Association (FNMA) 7.90 percent bond due September 10, 1986, and purchasing in its stead the U.S. Treasury 8 percent note due August 15, 1986. This swap involves a giveup in yield to maturity of 17 basis points and in current yield of 5 basis points. A payup of 1.5 points ($15 per $1000 bond) is also required. After a

TABLE 14-10
Analyzing Investment Objectives

WORKSHEET

Because swapping entails numerous risks as well as rewards, it is necessary to obtain as much information as possible both about the investor and the proposed swap itself before executing a swap transaction. To aid the investor in organizing and obtaining information concerning the ultimate goals of the funds under management, this worksheet contains a list of 30 points which should be reviewed to learn more about the income and capital position of the investor, the investor's safety and quality preferences, the maturity parameters of the investor, the views of the investor concerning interest rate and currency conditions, and other special and technical factors.

I. INCOME AND CAPITAL POSITION FACTORS

1. What is the total amount of money which the investor has to invest?   _____

2. What amounts of money are coming in from existing investments, and when, in the form of interest, dividends, and principal repayments? What known expenses and other commitments will have to be paid out?   _____

3. Is there any regularity to money inflows and outflows?   _____

4. What is the range of variation in money available for investment?   _____

5. What are the investor's current income needs and the minimum yield desired from investments?   _____

6. Does the investor have any special desire to earn capital gains?   _____

7. How are the investor's assets diversified between real assets and financial assets, and what proportion of the latter is invested in credit market instruments?   _____

8. Are the investor's credit market instrument holdings large enough to be subdivided into various categories?   _____

II. SAFETY AND QUALITY FACTORS

1. Does the investor have the financial and emotional capacity to accept losses, whether actually realized or on paper?   _____

2. How sophisticated is the investor? How much time does the investor have to spend on investment matters? How much time will it take for the investor to learn new or complex investment techniques?   _____

TABLE 14-10
Analyzing Investment Objectives *(Continued)*

---

3. Do the investor's quality constraints match the stated yield objectives?   _____

4. Will the investor invest in long-term issues even though this may possibly entail greater capital risks?   _____

5. Do the investor's financial resources, investment temperament, and market outlook permit investing on margin?   _____

6. What forms of hedging are available?   _____

III. MATURITY FACTORS

1. When does the investor desire to have funds returned?   _____

2. Will all or only a part of total investment funds be needed?   _____

3. What are the investor's motives for investing? Is the investment to satisfy known future needs, to generate income, to speculate, or to build up reserves for unexpected needs?   _____

4. Does the investor desire call protection, and if so, how far under the call price can investments be purchased?   _____

IV. MARKET CONDITIONS AND CURRENCY OUTLOOK FACTORS

1. What are the investor's expectations for short- and long-term interest rates over the next 6 months, and why does the investor feel this way?   _____

2. What are the investor's expectations for short- and long-term interest rates over the next 12 months or longer, and why?   _____

3. What are the investor's expectations for currency rates over the next 6 months, and why?   _____

4. What are the investor's expectations for currency rates over the next 12 months, and why?   _____

5. What are the investor's expectations for currency rates over the next 2 to 5 years or longer, and why?   _____

V. SPECIAL AND TECHNICAL FACTORS

1. Does the investor have a special preference for or aversion to certain countries, companies, currencies, or other features of bonds?   _____

TABLE 14-10
Analyzing Investment Objectives *(Continued)*

2. What is the minimum or maximum amount that the investor
will buy or sell?   _____

3. Will the investor invest in securities which are trading above
par? In private placements or other relatively illiquid forms
of investment?   _____

4. When swapping, must the following features be kept generally the same, or can they be varied: coupon, maturity, quality and type of issuer, currency, call protection, sinking fund,
liquidity?   _____

5. From what sources does the investor receive investment information? How much time does the investor spend on investments?   _____

6. How much discretion can the investor exercise in portfolio
management?   _____

7. What is the current and future tax status of the investor? _____

15-month period of generally rising interest rates, the U.S. Treasury issue has
declined in price less rapidly than its federal agency couterpart and thus is
valued 2.063 points higher ($20.63 per $1000 bond).

Effect of Currency Changes on Yields

When considering bond swaps in the international fixed-income securities
markets, it is important to analyze the effect which currency changes can have
on an issue's yield to maturity as expressed in the investor's home currency.
Over a period of time, for internationally oriented investors currency
changes can greatly influence the total return derived from a fixed-income
security. Table 14-9 shows, for coupons of 6 percent, 7 percent, 8 percent,
9 percent, and 10 percent and for currency revaluations in the invested
currency vis-à-vis the investor's home currency of 5 percent, 10 percent, and
15 percent (equivalent to a *devaluation* of the investor's home currency
vis-à-vis the invested currency of 4.76 percent, 9.09 percent, and 13.04
percent respectively), the effect of a currency change which takes place at the
end of the first, third, fifth, or eighth year of the life of the bond investment
on a bond with a maturity of 2, 3, 4, 5, 7, 10, 12, 15, and 20 years.

For example, if a United States dollar–oriented investor purchased a 10-
year-maturity Deutsche mark–denominated bond with a 6 percent coupon

TABLE 14-11
Analyzing Specific Swap Transactions

WORKSHEET

While Table 14-10 examines the needs and objectives of the investor and the resulting investment constraints which may be imposed upon a specific swap transaction, this worksheet contains a list of 25 features of a fixed-income security which should be investigated for both the security to be sold and the security to be purchased in a swap transaction.

Feature	Security to be sold	Security to be purchased	Current differential	Historic differential
1. Coupon[a]	_____	_____	_____	n.a.[b]
2. Price	_____	_____	_____	n.a.[b]
3. Quality	_____	_____	_____	[b]
4. Sinking-fund provisions	_____	_____	_____	n.a.[b]
5. Average life	_____	_____	_____	n.a.[b]
6. Maturity	_____	_____	_____	n.a.[b]
7. Nearest call date and other call provisions	_____	_____	_____	n.a.[b]
8. Call price	_____	_____	_____	n.a.[b]
9. Current yield	_____	_____	_____	_____
10. Yield to average life	_____	_____	_____	_____
11. Yield to first call	_____	_____	_____	_____
12. Yield to maturity (before expenses)[c]	_____	_____	_____	_____
13. Yield to maturity (after expenses)[c]				
14. Size of issue	_____	_____	_____	n.a.[b]
15. Date of offering	_____	_____	_____	n.a.[b]
16. Ownership profile	_____	_____	_____	n.a.[b]
17. Trading liquidity	_____	_____	_____	n.a.[b]
18. Currency	_____	_____	_____	n.a.[b]
19. Other special features[d]	_____	_____	_____	n.a.[b]
20. Form (bearer or registered)	_____	_____	_____	n.a.[b]
21. Denominations	_____	_____	_____	n.a.[b]
22. Listing	_____	_____	_____	n.a.[b]
23. Primary locus of delivery system	_____	_____	_____	n.a.[b]
24. Type of guarantee[e]	_____	_____	_____	n.a.[b]
25. Type of security[f]	_____	_____	_____	n.a.[b]

[a] Should specify whether frequency is annual, semiannual, or other, whether coupon is fixed or floating, and whether coupon rate is subject to change in the future.

[b] Not applicable in most cases.

[c] Expenses can include commissions, custodial fees, and any applicable turnover taxes, transfer taxes, withholding taxes, income taxes, or capital gains taxes.

[d] Including convertibility to common stock or to bonds, accompanying warrants, currency conversion options, private placement features, and maturity extension or contraction options.

[e] Including guarantees by one or more federal, state, or local governments, commercial banks, parent companies, or other bodies.

[f] Including collateral cover, negative pledge clauses, first mortgage, throughput agreements, subordinated status, or unsecured status.

and the Deutsche mark were revalued by 10 percent after the bond had been held for 3 years (and stayed at the revalued parity for the remaining 7 years of the life of the bond), the effective yield to maturity on this investment expressed in dollars would amount to 7.08 percent. This represents a gain of 108 basis points from the original yield of 6 percent.

It is possible to calculate the degree of foreign exchange risk incurred by an investor when swapping from strong-currency bonds (which usually are selling at lower yields than bonds denominated in weaker currencies) into weak-currency bonds (which customarily carry higher yields than stronger-currency issues), or vice versa. Through such a process, the investor can quantify the currency loss which could be withstood on a weaker-currency, high-yielding bond to make it an attractive investment compared with a stronger-currency issue with a low yield. Such currency exchange rates are often referred to as *breakeven exchange rates*. Strauss, Turnbull & Co.[1] has published a series of such analyses under the title *Points of No Return in International Bond Markets*.

The swap evaluation form shown in Table 14-11 can be of particular assistance in dissecting and examining the distinctive characteristics which affect the value of a bond. This is especially important when one security has a yield to maturity which is substantially out of line with that of an apparently similar security. With the aid of Table 14-11, it is possible to verify whether the bonds really are virtual substitutes or whether the issues are actually quite different with regard to such not-so-obvious features as average life, call provisions, size of issue, and type of guarantee and security behind the bonds. Very often, divergences in these elements may be the true cause of different prices for superficially similar issues.

[1]Moongate Place, London EC2R 6HR, England.

15

The Development and Implementation of Fixed-Income Investment Strategy

Overview

One of the most important elements in the investment process is the organization and implementation of portfolio strategy. Over a period of years, many factors underlie the successful execution of portfolio strategy. They include but are not limited to (1) an awareness of broad market trends at several different levels of complexity, (2) a sense of historical perspective, (3) an ability to recognize what constitutes the true value of a particular security or sector of the market, and (4) skill in the timing of specific portfolio maneuvers. This chapter brings together concepts, data, and techniques covered earlier in this book. The main objective of this review is to enunciate the principal details in the development of an investment strategy for a fixed-income securities portfolio in light of existing and expected market conditions in force at a given point in time.

The chapter begins with a system for classifying the major groups of marketable fixed-income securities in chart form, and it ends with a system for grouping specific securities in a format that allows a rapid comparison of different issues. In between this macroanalysis and microanalysis, a series of important diagrams present a number of guidelines which can be used in (1) evaluating individual securities in view of the investor's own goals and requirements, (2) judging the condition and likely direction of the fixed-income securities markets, and (3) implementing a chosen investment strategy for the portfolio. The relationship between each of these three phases of the investment process and their position within this chapter are set forth in Table 15-1. In each of the figures and tables listed in Table 15-1, concrete examples have been drawn from the period at the close of the 1970s. Each figure or table has been designed so that it can be updated by the investor and adapted for use in current market conditions.

PHASE	DESCRIPTION OF FIGURE OR TABLE IN THIS CHAPTER	NUMBER
	DIMENSIONING OF MARKETABLE FIXED-INCOME SECURITIES UNIVERSE	FIGURE 15-1
INVESTOR AND SECURITY EVALUATION PHASE	FACTORS (ABOUT THE INVESTOR) WHICH INFLUENCE THE CHOICE OF A SPECIFIC FIXED-INCOME SECURITY	TABLE 15-2
	FACTORS (ABOUT THE ISSUE) WHICH INFLUENCE THE VALUE OF A SPECIFIC FIXED-INCOME SECURITY	TABLE 15-3
ANALYSIS OF MARKET TRENDS PHASE	FACTORS (ABOUT THE MARKET) WHICH INFLUENCE OVERALL YIELD LEVELS AND/OR SECTORAL YIELD LEVELS	TABLE 15-4
	LISTING AND WEIGHTING OF ARGUMENTS IN CURRENT INTEREST RATE DEBATE	TABLE 15-5
PORTFOLIO STRATEGY EXECUTION PHASE	ALTERNATIVE PORTFOLIO MATURITY MIXES UNDER VARIOUS INTEREST RATE SCENARIOS	TABLE 15-6
	REVIEW AND SELECTION OF SPECIFIC FIXED-INCOME SECURITIES	TABLE 15-7

TABLE 15-1

Investor and Security Evaluation Phase

Before commencing the detailed scrutiny of one's own investment needs and resources and an examination of the components of bond value, it can be fruitful to review bond investments from two broad viewpoints. First, in the light of recent and distant history, it should be decided whether fixed-income securities appear to be a good investment at a given moment in time. Second, the amounts of fixed-income securities of various types should be compared with the size of the economy and with each other to indicate trends in liquidity, solvency, and possible excessive debt formation. The latter form of analysis can be particularly useful when performed over several time periods.

Through the past two centuries or more, bonds have generally been a good investment under some or all of the following conditions: (1) when interest rates have been stable or declining, (2) when the general price level has been stable or falling, (3) when contracts have been honored, and (4) when creditors have been in a preferential position to debtors. The attractiveness of bonds has been further enhanced when coupon income can be profitably reinvested without being spent or paid out in taxes.

In contrast to these conditions, bonds had to cope with the following developments during the past few decades: (1) with some major cyclical reversals, interest rates generally exhibited secularly rising trends in the post-World War II period; (2) after periods of relative stability in the 1950s and early 1960s, the general price level rose more rapidly in the 1970s, meaning that the bond investor received interest and principal payments in currency with significantly diminished purchasing power; (3) although most bond-related contracts and indentures were honored, a number were stretched or even broken; and (4) many debtors, particularly those who used their borrowed funds to purchase assets which appreciated in price, often found themselves in a preferential position to creditors.

If the investor assigns zero (or very remote) probability to the chance of chronic inflation developing into hyperinflation (which destroys virtually all nonindexed domestic bond values in a country experiencing hyperinflation), the bond investment process revolves importantly around (1) anticipating and profiting from cyclical upturns in bond prices (declines in interest rates) and/or (2) maintaining a very safe, short-term, and flexible investment posture while waiting for bullish secular conditions favoring bonds to reassert themselves. It is extremely important to realize that at times the long-term forces affecting bonds may be moving counter to the short-term influences on bond commitments.

Figure 15-1 contains a schematic listing of the total amount of fixed-income assets outstanding as of late 1978. The footnotes are an integral part of the figure, providing a list of the sources of the data so that the investor can update this information at regular intervals. Worth noting are the great variety and the enormous aggregate amounts of possible fixed-income invest-

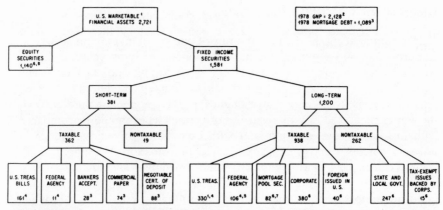

FIGURE 15-1   United States financial assets outstanding (amounts in billions of dollars).

MEMORANDUM

Category	Estimated amount as of year-end 1978
Municipal Bond Funds[9]	$16.0 billion
Closed End Bond Funds[9]	$2.2 billion
Money Market Funds[9]	$10.0 billion
Money Market Certificates[10]	$63.0 billion
Total	$91.2 billion

FOOTNOTES

[1]Excludes Nonmarketable Securities such as (totals as of October 1978): U.S. Savings Bonds ($80.1 billion); Nonmarketable U.S. Treasury obligations in the Investment Series ($2.2 billion); the Depositary Series ($8 million); the Foreign Government Series ($24.0 billion); the Government Account Series ($152.7 billion); and other Nonmarketable Treasury Issues ($24.7 billion). Source: *U.S. Treasury Bulletin.*

[2]Source: *Business Conditions Digest,* U.S. Department of Commerce.

[3]Estimated as of August 1978 (as of second quarter of 1978 for mortgage debt). Source: *Federal Reserve Bulletin.*

[4]As of October 1978; Source: *U.S. Treasury Bulletin.*

[5]Includes $7.1 billion in "on-budget" Federal Agency Securities and $99.2 billion in "off-budget" Federal Agency Securities.

[6]Estimated as of October 1978; Source: *Flow of Funds Accounts,* Board of Governors of the Federal Reserve System.

[7]Includes pass-through and/or guaranteed securities of the Government National Mortgage Association, the Federal Home Loan Mortgage Corporation, and the the Farmers Home Administration.

[8]Includes convertible and nonconvertible common and preferred stock.

[9]Asset holdings of these funds are included in the various categories shown in the table above.

[10]Not included anywhere in the table above since these certificates are considered to be nonmarketable securities.

ments. Thirteen different families of fixed-income securities, totaling $1,581 billion, are shown in Figure 15-1. This sum compares with the 1978 United States gross national product of $2,128 billion, total 1978 mortgage debt outstanding of $1,089 billion, and total market value of equity securities outstanding of $1,140 billion.

Approximately 3 times as much long-term marketable debt as short-term marketable debt is outstanding. Treasury bills ($161 billion), negotiable certificates of deposit ($88 billion), and commercial paper ($74 billion) are the three largest groups of short-term fixed-income securities. In the long-term category, the three largest types of marketable debt are corporate bonds ($380 billion), U.S. Treasury bonds ($330 billion), and state and local government obligations ($247 billion).

In the memorandum section at the bottom of Figure 15-1, four fixed-income–related investments (of appeal primarily to the household sector) are listed. It is important to recognize that the total investments of municipal bond funds, closed-end bond funds, and money market funds are included in the amounts of debt outstanding as shown in the respective groups of securities listed in the figure, while money market certificates (which are nonmarketable securities) are not shown. Money market certificates, issued by thrift institutions and paying 0.25 percent over the rate on 6-month Treasury bills, reached $63 billion in outstandings by December 1978 even though they had been inaugurated only in June 1978.

In determining which of these families of securities and which specific family members are appropriate investments, several considerations must be kept in mind. First and most important are the personal characteristics of the investor. A given bond recommendation may not be appropriate for all investors because of varying tax considerations, liquidity requirements, and other parameters. Table 15-2 reviews many of the most important features which influence the choice of a specific fixed-income security. Although these features do not carry equal weight for every investor, they are often inter-related. They include (1) the investor's state, local, and federal tax status, (2) the amounts of money available for investment, (3) the investor's financial condition, (4) the investor's current and future income needs, (5) the investor's liquidity requirements, (6) the investor's investment horizon, (7) the investor's investment objectives, (8) the investor's investment temperament, (9) the ownership of the capital being invested, and (10) the investor's own cyclical and secular investment outlook. General comments on each of these points are spelled out in some detail in the right-hand section of Table 15-2.

After surveying the important aspects of the investor's investment situation, it is useful to examine some of the characteristics of a bond which determine its intrinsic worth. In this way, a bond's diacritical features can be matched with the investor's special requirements. Table 15-3 contains an overview of the factors which influence the value of a specific fixed-income

TABLE 15-2
Features Influencing the Choice of a Specific Fixed-Income
Security *(Continued)*

Feature	General comments
1. State, local, and federal tax status: High bracket Medium bracket Low bracket Exempt from taxes Future tax status	High tax brackets may lead to *(a)* an emphasis on tax-exempt securities, *(b)* a preference for lower-taxed capital gains, *(c)* investments which defer income, and *(d)* strategies which shelter income through offsetting losses and other means. Low tax brackets or tax-exempt status permit greater investment flexibility in the taxable sectors of the fixed-income securities brackets.
2. Amounts available for investment: $1,000 to $10,000 $10,000 to $100,000 $100,000 to $1 million $1 million to $10 million Over $10 million	Small amounts of investable funds usually cannot be invested in those fixed income securities with high minimum requirements; such sums may be placed with an intermediary (such as a money market fund) to achieve diversification and professional management. Very large or very small amounts invested in any one issue may incur extra charges or price concessions when buying or selling securities.
3. Financial condition: Form and amount of net worth Amount and nature of known obligations Regularity and amount of income flows Size and nature of reserves	Investors with a large absolute net worth, predictable and relatively well-covered obligations, sizable and regular income flows, and adequate, liquid reserves can usually afford more diverse and/or less conventional patterns of investment than investors with a small absolute net worth, unpredictable and less well-covered obligations, small and irregular income flows, and inadequate, illiquid reserves.
4. Current and future income needs: Low income needs now; high later Low income needs now; low later High income needs now; low later High income needs now; high later	Investors with low income needs may consider low-coupon fixed-income securities while high income needs may dictate high-coupon issues. Future income needs may influence the maturity decision, since the investor may desire to lock in or to postpone the receipt of interest and/or principal payments.

Feature	General comments

5. Liquidity needs:
  Low needs for
  liquidity
  High needs for
  liquidity
  Future liquidity needs
	Low liquidity needs permit investments in specialized issues or nonmarketable securities such as private placements. High liquidity needs imply that investments should be concentrated in highly marketable, easily traded securities.

6. Investment horizon:
  1 year or less
  Between 1 and 5
  years
  Between 5 and 20
  years
  Over 20 years
	While it is not necessary to tailor the maturities and liquidity of fixed-income securities investments to one's investment horizon, the length of time before principal is needed can influence the maturity selection. A short investment horizon may cause investments in shorter-maturity issues than a long investment horizon, but the reverse may not be the case.

7. Investment objectives:
  Capital preservation in
  real or nominal terms
  High total
  compounded return
  Capital gains
  High current income
	The investor's objectives may direct funds into more or less volatile bonds. Volatility is influenced by coupon, maturity, and prevailing yield levels.

8. Investment
  temperament:
  Aversions to or
  affinities for specific
  securities
  Sophistication; time
  spent on investments
  Orientation toward
  hedging decisions
  Orientation toward
  speculative forms of
  investments including
  margin
  Legal, accounting, and
  other constraints
	Under their own volition or influenced by outside constraints, some investors prefer to (or not to) invest in bonds of certain maturities, quality ratings, issuers, prices above or below par, coupons, sinking fund and call features, and trading liquidity. In general, lesser investment sophistication and small amounts of time spent on the portfolio may dictate a more conservative spectrum of investments, whereas greater investment sophistication and large amounts of time spent on the portfolio may allow more speculative investments and investment techniques.

TABLE 15-2
Features Influencing the Choice of a Specific Fixed-Income
Security *(Continued)*

Feature	General comments

9. Investment constituency:
  Personal capital
  Family capital
  Corporation, trust, nonprofit organization
  Fund holders
  Depositary contributors
  Contractual contributors
	Different styles of investing may be carried out for one's own personal capital compared with capital managed for the benefit of others. The beneficiaries' needs, psychology, and relationship to the investor must be taken into account in security selection.

10. Cyclical and secular investment outlook:
  Short-term interest rates
  Long-term interest rates
  Inflation
  Yield differentials between market sectors
  Currency exchange rates
  Expectations for alternative investment media
	Rising inflation rates, interest rates, and yield differentials between market sectors may limit or eliminate the real returns offered by specific fixed-income securities. On the other hand, falling interest rates, inflation rates, and yield differentials between market sectors may enhance the real returns offered by specific fixed-income securities. Fluctuating currency rates can also augment or vitiate investment returns offered by investing in issues denominated in foreign currencies.

security. In the table it can be seen that the value of a fixed-income security derives in large part from its (1) coupon, (2) maturity, (3) market price, (4) quality, (5) security or backing, (6) sinking-fund and call features, (7) method of yield calculation, (8) liquidity, (9) operational and technical details, and (10) any other special features related to the security. These 10 features are also often interrelated, and additional general comments have been provided in the right-hand section of Table 15-3. The table can be useful as a checklist in evaluating fixed-income securities investments.

Analysis-of-Market-Trends Phase

One of the most important, if not the most important, details in fixed-income securities investing is the trend of interest rates. It is crucial to reflect upon

TABLE 15-3
Features Influencing the Value of a Specific Fixed-Income
Security

Features	General comments
1. Coupon: 　Absolute level of 　coupon 　Fixed or floating rate 　Frequency of coupon 　payment	A high-coupon security provides greater current income and less volatility than a low-coupon security in response to a change in interest rates. If adjustable frequently enough and if pegged to market interest rates, floating-rate issues can provide price protection in periods of rising interest rates but fewer capital gain opportunities and lower income in periods of declining rates. For ease of comparison, issues' coupon income should be converted to semiannual equivalents.
2. Maturity: 　Final maturity 　Extendable and 　contractable maturity 　options	A long-maturity issue is generally more volatile than a short-maturity security in response to a change in interest rates. The investor should determine at whose option a maturity might be lengthened or shortened.
3. Market price: 　Discount to par 　Premium over par 　Near par 　Relationship to call 　price 　Technical price history	Bonds selling at a premium over par tend to be less volatile in response to a change in interest rates than bonds selling at a discount to par. Discount bonds may be somewhat less subject to being called than bonds selling well over their call price. The technical chart of a bond's price history may provide useful information concerning the price performance of the bond in previous interest rate cycles.
4. Quality: 　Actual ratings 　Status within rating 　category 　Likelihood of rating 　change	High-quality bonds generally yield less than low-quality issues, although the yield differential can vary between two quality rating categories. Stronger or weaker credits within a given rating classification can sell at lower or higher yields respectively than the average for all bonds in that rating category. An upward or downward rating change which is generally unanticipated can cause a significant increase or decrease respectively in an issue's price.

TABLE 15-3
Features Influencing the Value of a Specific Fixed-Income Security *(Continued)*

Features	General comments

5. Security:
    Form of backing and
    collateralization
    Degree of guarantee
    Status within debt
    structure
    Other indenture terms
	Although not widely scrutinized in periods of broad economic expansion, the form of backing, degree of guarantee, and seniority within an issuer's debt structure of an issue can vastly affect its value under certain financial conditions. Generally speaking, the higher and more liquid the degree of security behind an issue, the better its price should perform under circumstances of credit uncertainty.

6. Sinking-fund and call
   features:
    Sinking-fund terms
    Call date and call
    prices
    Refundability
    Weighted average life
	A sinking fund can enhance the value of a bond by reducing the total outstanding and the weighted average life of the debt of the issuer and by providing buying support for the bond if the securities are trading below the sinking-fund call price. Bonds which are or will shortly become callable may be limited in their price appreciation potential if they are trading substantially above their call price. Bonds which are not refundable with the proceeds of lower-cost borrowings may be more valuable than similar issues without such a prohibition.

7. Yield:
    Current yield
    Yield to maturity
    Coupon reinvestment
    rate
    Yield to first call
    Yield to weighted
    average life
    Method of yield
    computation
	When a bond's sinking-fund and/or call features so dictate, it is useful to compute a yield to first call and a yield to weighted average life. The method of yield calculation is important, as is the assumed reinvestment rate of coupon income. The longer the maturity, the higher the coupon, and the higher the prevailing yield level, the greater the amount of the total yield to maturity which is represented by the reinvestment of the coupon income.

the likely course of yield levels both for the credit markets as a whole and for the specific sectors in which the investor plans to place funds. Table 15-4 lists many of the highly interconnected factors which influence overall yield levels and/or sectoral yield levels. Detailed general comments are contained in the right-hand section of the table, which examines the influence of (1) economic conditions, (2) the outlook for inflation or deflation in prices, (3) monetary policy, (4) fiscal policy, (5) the supply of funds, (6) the demand for funds, (7) yields available on alternative investments, (8) timing and

Features	General comments
8. Liquidity: Amount of issue outstanding Date and form of offering Ownership profile Legal investment qualifications Issuer acceptance	A small bond issue or an issue which is concentrated among a small group of public investors may be difficult to buy or sell. Securities which are of broadly and favorably recognized issuers and/or are approved as legal investments by certain groups of institutions may have enhanced marketability.
9. Operational details: Form Denomination Minimum purchase size Listing Settlement terms	Unusual denominations, minimum purchase sizes, forms, or settlement terms for a bond may impair its ease of transferability and thus its value.
10. Special features: Convertibility Other accompanying securities Currency	Convertible bonds usually have lower coupons than otherwise similar securities of the same issue. Accompanying warrants or other securities may also permit a lower coupon. Bonds denominated in foreign currencies carry an added risk of currency devaluation vis-à-vis the investor's domestic currency.

recurrent events, (9) investor psychology, and, not to be omitted from the investor's planning process, (10) unanticipated events.

Developing a bond investment strategy immediately brings the investor into contact with the conflicting arguments over the course of interest rates and bond prices during the 12 to 18 months immediately following the planned investment decision. Using the calendar year 1979 as an example, the details of many of the prevailing arguments (as of January 1979) in favor of lower interest rates or of higher interest rates are summarized in Table 15-5. As of January 1979, the consensus opinion of most bond market participants favored a peak in interest rates late in the second quarter of 1979. Forecasters in the declining-interest-rate camp expected such a pattern to evolve because of (1) a slowing economy, (2) declining borrowing demands, (3) high investor cash levels, and (4) easier monetary policies, which would supposedly be able to be pursued in light of the first three developments.

TABLE 15-4
Features Influencing Overall Yield Levels and/or Sectoral Yield Levels *(Continued)*

Features	General comments

1. Economic conditions:
   Consumer sector
   Business sector
   Government sector
   Net exports
	The growth rate of the economy can directly and indirectly influence yields by causing changes in the supply and demand for funds and in the price level. In turn, the path of the economy is determined by the performance of its various sectors. Consumer spending is influenced by consumer real wage rates and real aftertax income, employment and confidence levels, consumer borrowing and savings rates, and consumers' net worth positions. Business spending is influenced by consumer spending, capacity constraints, inventory levels, regulatory directives, cash flow totals, and financial conditions. Federal, state, and local government spending is influenced by tax receipts and by appropriations made in light of the needs and objectives of the population. Net exports are influenced by relative growth rates of the domestic and international economies, currency changes, and relative inflation rates.

2. Price level changes:
   Supply conditions
   Demand conditions
   Monetary conditions
   Anticipatory forces
   International conditions
	Price inflation or deflation can influence yield levels by raising or lowering the level which investors demand as a return on their funds. Price levels are determined by the interaction of supply and demand forces. Climatic conditions, monetary conditions and policies, the actions of cartels, and governmental programs which stimulate or retard the demand for or supply of goods and services can thus influence price levels, as can labor conditions and energy costs, productivity gains, profit goals, capacity utilization rates, anticipatory and/or psychological forces, and foreign demand, supply, and price conditions.

3. Monetary policy:
   Economic and financial conditions
   Fiscal policy
   Political considerations
   Monetary velocity
   International and currency conditions
	Monetary policy influences yield levels by altering credit conditions and through the direct effects of the Federal Reserve Board on commercial banks' reserve levels and required reserves, on the discount rate, and on the government securities markets through the Federal Open Market Committee. Monetary policy is influenced by economic and financial conditions, fiscal policy, political considerations (to some degree), the income velocity of money, and international and currency considerations.

Features	General comments

4. Fiscal policy:
   Taxation rates and
   receipts
   Spending levels
	State, local, and federal fiscal policies can influence yields by altering tax rates, by stimulating certain sectors of the economy as a result of spending programs and through the way in which government deficits are financed.

5. Supply of funds:
   Supplying sectors
   Flows to supplying
   sectors
	The supply of funds to the various sectors of the financial credit and capital markets directly affects the amount of money available for investment in newly issued and currently outstanding credit market instruments. It is important to be aware of forces acting on the major groups of investors, including households, businesses, state and local governments, foreign entities, the United States government, the Federal Reserve System, federally sponsored agencies and mortgage pools, commercial banks, credit unions, savings and loan associations, mutual savings banks, life insurance companies, property-casualty and other insurance companies, private pension funds, state and local government employee retirement funds, investment companies, finance companies, REITs, and security brokers and dealers.

6. Demand for funds:
   Borrowing sectors
   Flows to borrowing
   sectors
   Costs of alternative
   sources of capital
   Funds arbitrage
   opportunities
	The borrowing demands of various sectors of the economy directly affect the amount of money being sought from investors. It is also important to be aware of forces acting on the major seekers of funds, including the United States government, federal agencies, state and local governments, corporate and foreign entities, and mortgage borrowers. Other vehicles through which funds are raised include consumer credit, bank loans, private short-term paper, and other credit market instruments. The costs of alternative sources of capital and funds arbitrage opportunities can also influence borrowing demands.

TABLE 15-4
Features Influencing Overall Yield Levels and/or Sectoral Yield Levels
(Continued)

Features	General comments
7. Yields on alternative investments: Short term versus long term Quality ratings and sectoral yield spreads Other domestic portfolio or direct investment media International instruments	The rate of return which can be earned on competing investment outlets can influence general or sectoral yield levels. The maturity, quality rating, or issuing sector of a credit market instrument, as well as yields on other domestic or international investment media can determine its relative ability to attract investment funds.
8. Timing and recurrent events: Economic and price level history Leads and lags Anticipatory actions Seasonal and other recurrent events	Yields can be influenced by the position in the economic cycle, the previous behavior of investors in anticipating future developments, the historical leads and lags between economic changes, changes in the inflation-deflation rate, and yield level changes as well as seasonal events (such as tax payment dates) or other recurrent events (such as local or national elections).
9. Investor psychology: Underlying causes of change Duration of change	Investor psychology can influence yields even when fundamental circumstances remain unchanged. Examples include the relatively improved performance of railroad debt securities and the relative underperformance of tax-exempt airport revenue bonds during the oil embargo of late 1973 and early 1974. Investor psychology may be influenced by the degree to which future or existing commitments can be offset by hedging activities.
10. Unanticipated events: Political Domestic International	Unanticipated events can have a profound influence on yields. Past examples include the bankruptcy of a major borrower, natural phenomena, military action or peace treaties, governmental controls, or an abrupt change in a country's government or governmental policies.

TABLE 15-5
Summary of Principal Arguments in the 1979 Interest Rate Debate (*Continued*)

I. Arguments favoring an earlier peak in and/or lower interest rates in 1979	II. Arguments favoring a later peak in and/or higher interest rates in 1979
A. *Slowing economy.* Led by a slowdown in consumer spending (due to high debt levels, declines in real hourly wage rates, and lower consumer confidence ratings), sluggish to recessionary economic conditions were expected to prevail in 1979.	A. *Continuing economic strength and inflation.* Paced by continued strength in personal income, industrial output, and housing activity as well as a pickup in economic growth abroad, the United States economy was expected to slow somewhat but not enter a recessionary phase of any significance during calendar year 1979. For the first time in the economic history of the previous few decades, United States consumers were responding to higher inflation rates not by increasing their level of savings but by borrowing more in order to purchase tangible assets which had exhibited price appreciation. In addition, increased energy costs and wage settlements were expected to keep upward pressure on inflation rates throughout a good part of the year and during the immediately following years.
B. *Declining borrowing demands.* As the economy slowed down and moved into a moderate recession in 1979, private-sector credit demands were projected to lessen, permitting larger flows of funds to financial intermediaries and then into fixed-income issues.	B. *High borrowing relative to funds supplied.* With large borrowing by corporations (due to lower internal cash flow and higher outlays for plant, equipment, and working-capital outlays), as well as by the U.S. Treasury and federal agency sectors, higher interest rates were thought to be necessary to entice the household sector to supply residual credit needs in view of a reduced supply of funds from state and local governments, the foreign sector, and thrift institutions.

409

TABLE 15-5
Summary of Principal Arguments in the 1979 Interest Rate Debate (*Continued*)

I. Arguments favoring an earlier peak in and/or lower interest rates in 1979	II. Arguments favoring a later peak in and/or higher interest rates in 1979
C. Easier monetary policy: In part because of a slowdown in the growth rate of the monetary aggregates during the preceding 12 months (during the preceding 20 months on an inflation-adjusted basis) and in part because of a stabilization or a rise in the foreign exchange value of the United States dollar, the Federal Reserve was expected to be able to relax its credit restraint policies.	*C. Insulation from financial discipline.* Higher interest rates were deemed necessary to reduce credit demands significantly because of the safety valves which numerous sectors of the economy had evolved to insulate themselves from the credit-reducing effects of high interest rates. Such safety valves included the following: (1) In the consumer sector, it had become possible to obtain longer maturities and lower down-payment terms on home mortgages and automobile loans. (2) Many areas of the financial sector had been able to obtain relief from lending at former usury-law interest rate ceilings and to offset or avoid possible disintermediation through the issuance of money market certificates, through the sale of mortgages, mortgage pass-through issues, and/or mortgage-backed securities, and through the raising of funds from new sources such as commercial paper and the Eurocurrency markets.
D. High investor cash levels. It was thought that the commitment of high levels of investor cash (estimated cash reserves of pension funds as of the beginning of 1979 amounted to 18 percent of total assets, versus 14 percent at the beginning of 1978 and 7 percent at the beginning of 1977) to fixed-income securities at the first sign of more favorable market conditions would hasten a rise in fixed-income securities prices and a decline in yield levels.	*D. Investor cynicism about institutionalized inflation.* With inflation and interest rates remaining high on a secular basis even after the worst cyclical recession in postwar history (in 1974–1975), investors had become skeptical about the ability and the willingness of governmental bodies and monetary authorities to fight inflation. Such cynicism also derived from cost-of-living adjustments in many contracts, indexation of social security benefits and many other transfer payments, and an apparent lack of widespread support for paying the *cost* of wringing out inflation (even though there seemed to be broad opposition to banishing the aftertax *effects* of inflation).

I. Arguments favoring an earlier peak in and/or lower interest rates in 1979	II. Arguments favoring a later peak in and/or higher interest rates in 1979

E. Need for currency defense. With no dramatic improvement expected to occur in the first half of 1979 in the balances of trade and payments of the United States, its inflation rate, and its energy situation, it was felt that the Federal Reserve would be forced to keep interest rates high in order to encourage inflows into the United States dollar (or at least to discourage dollar outflows).

F. Credit policy was deemed to have been easy, not tight. After adjustment for inflation and taxes, borrowers had not had to suffer much, while investors and fixed-rate lenders had generally earned negative returns in the period immediately preceding 1979. When the prime rate reached 12 percent in 1974, credit was quite scarce and some borrowers were priced out of the market; with the prime rate at 11.75 percent in January 1979, capital still appeared to be relatively available with few vocalized complaints from borrowers.

TABLE 15-5
Summary of Principal Arguments in the 1979 Interest Rate Debate (*Continued*)

I. Arguments favoring an earlier peak in and/or lower interest rates in 1979	II. Arguments favoring a later peak in and/or higher interest rates in 1979
G. Global buildup in money supply. On a worldwide basis, monetary growth had accelerated during the previous 2 years. With some degree of lag time, such growth was projected to translate into higher inflation and interest rates in the major industrial nations.	
H. Interest rate decline usually after onset of economic downturn. Short-term interest rates had usually reached their peak 6 to 15 months after the onset of the previous three recessions, and taxable long-term interest rates peaked 10 months after the beginning of the most recent recession. Even if a recession were to begin in the first half of 1979, some analysts projected that interest rates would not begin to turn down until late 1979 or early 1980.	

The market participants who believed that interest rates would climb to higher-than-expected levels in 1979 felt this way because of (1) continuing strength in the economy and persistent inflation, (2) high borrowing demands relative to funds supplied, (3) the increasing insulation of the economic system from financial discipline, (4) a greater degree of investor cynicism about institutionalized inflation in the United States, (5) the need to maintain high interest rates to defend the international value of the dollar, (6) signs that true credit restraint had not yet been deeply felt in the financial markets, (7) the rise in the growth rate of global monetary aggregates during the preceding 2 years, and (8) the fact that the timing of interest rate declines in earlier market cycles had usually followed the beginning of an economic downturn by a period of several months or more.

As 1979 unfolded, certain of the factors listed in support of the declining-interest-rate case and in support of the rising-interest-rate case carried greater weight than other factors. In such instances, the investor's judgment assumes a major role in the selection and timing of security transactions. It can be an extremely useful discipline (and a valuable learning tool, after the fact) to organize and write down the reasons why market participants expect interest rates to move upward or downward. The investor may wish to do so in a summary format similar to the one shown for 1979 in Table 15-5.

Portfolio Strategy Execution Phase

Table 15-6 provides guidelines for translating the investor's expected interest rate scenario into specific portfolio strategy maneuvers. For the sake of variety and for instructional purposes, four different interest rate scenarios have been included. Each of the strategies and the percentage breakdowns of the fixed-income securities portfolios shown in the table assume that a sizable sum of new capital has recently been received for deployment as the investor deems appropriate, with emphasis on the interest rate outlook for the 12 to 18 months in the immediately following future. To emphasize the application of this table (but not necessarily these scenarios) over a period of years, the "current year" refers not to the time at which this chapter was written but, instead, to the 12 months immediately succeeding the time of the investor's forecast of alternative interest rate scenarios.

Structurally, Table 15-6 could be further modified by such transformations as (1) showing, at selected points in the future, various percentage breakdowns of a fixed-income securities portfolio according to such parameters as quality rating or coupon and/or (2) including many other possible interest rate scenarios. To give some insight into the translation of a specific viewpoint on interest rates into portfolio strategy, the following paragraphs describe in some detail one possible response to the first two of the four scenarios listed in the table.

TABLE 15-6
Four Possible Scenarios for Interest Rates *(Continued)*

Expected interest rate scenario	Portfolio strategy response	Percentage breakdown of a fixed-income securities portfolio			
		Maturity range	Early in current year (per-cent)	Middle of cur-rent year (per-cent)	Late in current year (per-cent)
Upward, then downward move. Both short-term and long-term interest rates move up to a peak around the middle of the current year and then move downward for the rest of the current year and well into the following year.	From an initial heavy weighting in short maturities, funds are commit-ted to longer maturities as inter-est rates approach and pass their cycli-cal zenith. By the end of the current year, a substantial majority of the portfolio is invested in longer-maturity issues.	Under 1 year	50	20	10
		1–5 years	20	20	10
		5–20 years	20	30	30
		Over 20 years	10	30	50
Continued upward move. Both short-term and long-term interest rates keep rising with some in-terruptions through-out the current year and well into the fol-lowing year.	The portfolio is kept invested in high-return short and intermediate maturities for the greater part of the current year, with some locking in of high long-term yields toward the end of the year.	Under 1 year	90	80	70
		1–5 years	10	20	10
		5–20 years	0	0	10
		Over 20 years	0	0	10

TABLE 15-6
Four Possible Scenarios for Interest Rates *(Continued)*

Expected interest rate scenario	Portfolio strategy response	Percentage breakdown of a fixed-income securities portfolio			
		Maturity range	Early in current year (percent)	Middle of current year (percent)	Late in current year (percent)
Remain at current levels. Both short-term and long-term interest rates remain around present levels during the current year and well into the following year.	Flexibility is maintained, with a large part of the portfolio kept in shorter maturities awaiting some indication of future interest rate trends. A small part of the portfolio is placed in longer maturities to lock in high yields.	Under 1 year	50	50	50
		1–5 years	30	30	20
		5–20 years	20	20	20
		Over 20 years	0	0	10
Early downward move. Both short-term and long-term interest rates begin moving down early in the current year and continue downward for the remainder of the current year and well into the following year.	Funds are rapidly deployed into longer maturities, with additional amounts invested in this area as the year progresses. By the end of the current year a very large percentage of the portfolio has been moved into longer maturities to take advantage of capital gain opportunities.	Under 1 year	20	10	10
		1–5 years	10	10	0
		5–20 years	20	20	20
		Over 20 years	50	60	70

The first scenario forecasts an upward move in interest rates followed by an interest rate decline. The portfolio strategy response involves the movement of funds from short-term to longer-term maturities as interest rates move up to and pass their cyclical peak. For example, early in the current year, 50 percent of the portfolio is invested in fixed-income securities of under 1-year maturity, 20 percent of the portfolio is placed in the 1- to 5-year-maturity range, 20 percent is invested in the 5- to 20-year-maturity sector, and only 10 percent is invested in bonds of over 20 years' maturity. Around the middle of the current year, more of the short-term funds are placed into intermediate- and longer-maturity issues. By the end of the current year, only 10 percent of the portfolio is kept invested in securities of under 1-year maturity, while 50 percent of the portfolio is placed in long-term bonds to lock in high yields and to enjoy the possibility of capital gains as interest rates continue to decline.

A different interest rate scenario is listed second in Table 15-6. Interest rates are projected to rise, with some brief reversals, during most of the current year. Such a scenario calls for the portfolio to be kept invested in high-return short and intermediate maturities for the greater part of the current year. Toward the end of the current year, if interest rates appear to be nearing a cyclical peak, some funds might be committed to longer maturities. Early in the current year, the portfolio is kept 90 percent invested in maturities of under 1 year, and this percentage is gradually reduced over the course of the current year to 70 percent by the latter part of the current year, when 10 percent of the portfolio is invested in securities in the 1- to 5-year-maturity range, 10 percent is placed in the 5- to 20-year-maturity sector, and 10 percent is committed to bonds having maturities of over 20 years.

In performing an analysis of the type outlined in Table 15-6, it is important to be aware of and allow for the risks of the investor's forecast turning out to vary significantly from the actual future course of events. For example, there are several risks if the first scenario in Table 15-6 is incorrect and the second scenario is correct. First, by placing investments in longer-maturity issues, the investor may forgo short-term current yields which are high relative to long-term current yields. Second, if the interest rate structure continues to move upward, the investor will experience larger capital losses on long-term issues than would be suffered on short-term securities. Finally, when interest rates begin to decline, the magnitude of the decline may not be so great. Under the first scenario shown in Table 15-6, long-term interest rates might in fact rise in the first half of the current year, but they might also return at the end of the current year only to levels which prevailed at the start of the current year, and not lower. If this is the case, the hoped-for capital gains would provide a relatively meager reward to an investor who extended the maturity of the fixed-income portfolio.

On the other hand, there are risks if the second scenario is wrong and the first scenario is correct. First, by keeping such a large percentage of funds in the short-term–maturity range, these investments may be reinvested upon maturity at lower yields if interest rates move downward. Second, the investor gives up the opportunity for capital gains if interest rates move downward (substantial capital gains may be missed if the interest rate decline is significant and if a substantial portion of the portfolio is invested in long-term maturities). Third, should short-term interest rates drop sharply and long-term interest rates exhibit a more modest decline, the performance of short-term investments (consisting of high interest payments) may be outweighed by the total return (in the form of interest payments plus capital gains) generated by long-term bonds. Similar analyses of the risks of being wrong can be outlined for the third and fourth interest rate scenarios of Table 15-6 as well as for any other interest rate scenarios which the investor may construct.

To show how projected maturity breakdowns of the portfolio can be integrated with the choice of specific issues, Table 15-7 has been prepared to list representative examples of fixed-income investments, divided into the same four maturity categories shown in Table 15-6: under 1 year, 1 to 5 years, 5 to 20 years, and over 20 years. The scope of Table 15-7 is quite broad. It encompasses 51 possible fixed-income–related investments in the U.S. government, federal agency, municipal, corporate, Yankee, Canadian, Eurobond, and foreign bond sectors as well as short-term money market instruments such as certificates of deposit and bankers' acceptances. In addition, interest rate futures on several financial instruments have been included. All yields shown are as of the beginning of 1979 and are not representative of actual yields after that point in time or of yields which could have been realized for very large or very small transactions.

While most of the issues listed in Table 15-7 are denominated and payable in United States dollars, some are not. In the Eurobond row of the table, the European Investment Bank 7.25 percent issue due in 1984 is denominated in Japanese yen. In the foreign bond row of the table, the Algemene Bank Nederland 10.00 percent issue due on December 1, 1979, is denominated in Dutch guilders, the Swiss Confederation 5.00 percent bond due in 1987 is denominated in Swiss francs, the Republic of France 7.00 percent issue maturing in 1988 is denominated in French francs, and the United Kingdom 3.50 percent war loan bond of perpetual maturity is denominated in pounds sterling.

The highest- and the lowest-priced bond issues shown in Table 15-7 are both for foreign bonds. The United Kingdom war loan issue was trading at 29⅝ percent of par value, and the Republic of France 7.00 percent bond due in 1988 was trading at a price near 400 percent of par value. The high price of the latter issue is explained by the fact that interest and principal payments on this particular security are indexed to the gold bullion price in Paris for

TABLE 15-7

Representative List of Fixed-Income Investments

Maturity Sector	Under 1 year Issue	Yield to maturity[a]	1 to 5 years Issue	Yield to maturity[a]	5 to 20 years Issue	Yield to maturity[a]	Over 20 years Issue	Yield to maturity[a]
United States government	U.S. Treasury bills due 6/28/79	10.03	U.S. Treasury notes 9.875—12/31/80	9.95	U.S. Treasury notes 8.00—8/15/86	9.18	U.S. Treasury bonds 8.25—5/15/05[b]	8.92
	U.S. Treasury bills due 12/11/79	10.51	U.S. Treasury notes 9.375—12/31/82	9.40	U.S. Treasury bonds 8.625—11/15/93	9.06	U.S. Treasury bonds 8.75—11/15/08[c]	8.96
Federal agency	FNMA 9.80—6/11/79	10.19	World Bank 8.00—7/1/81	10.02	Banks for Cooperatives 7.75—1/2/86	9.41	Interamerican Development Bank 9.00—2/15/01	9.52
	Federal Farm Credit 10.80—10/1/79	10.86	Federal Home Loan Banks 9.00—2/25/83	9.50	GNMA pass throughs 9.00[d]	10.10	Washington Metropolitan Transit Authority 8.15—7/1/14	10.10
Municipal	State of New York TRANs 5.25—3/30/79[e]	6.10	Rhode Island Housing and Mortgage Finance BANs 6.00—10/1/80[f]	6.80	Municipal Assistance Corp. 10.25—2/1/93	9.10	Port Authority of New York and New Jersey 8.20—7/15/11	7.23
	State of Tennessee BANs 5.00—8/9/79[f]	6.30	State of California 5.50—4/1/84	5.50	State of Illinois 5.00—11/1/97	6.40	Washington (State) Public Power 6.50—7/1/20	6.90
Corporate	Citibank negotiable certificates of deposit 11.50—7/2/79	11.56	E.I. du Pont 8.00—11/15/81	10.00	Deere & Co. 7.90—3/1/87	9.50	Procter & Gamble 7.00—5/15/02	8.70
	Philip Morris commercial paper due 7/2/79	11.36	Ford Motor credit 8.375—4/1/82	9.95	Williams Companies 9.40—3/15/96	9.95	Teledyne 10—6/1/04	10.81
	North Carolina National Bank bankers' acceptance due 4/24/79	11.31	Sohio/BP pipeline 8.625—2/1/83	9.85	J. P. Morgan 4.75—11/1/98[g]	7.67	Ohio Bell Telephone 9.00—11/1/18	9.38
Yankee and Canadian	Electricité de France commercial paper due 9/28/79	12.14	Commonwealth of Australia 8.75—12/15/83	9.66	Nippon Telephone & Telegraph 8.125—5/1/87	9.54	Government of Canada 9.25—10/15/98[h]	9.47
Eurobond	Bank of America Euro-certificate of deposit 11.875—9/28/79	11.88	European Investment Bank 7.25—5/1/84[i]	5.83	Tenneco International 7.75—5/15/87	9.57	Very few liquid issues available in this maturity range	

TABLE 15-7
Representative List of Fixed-Income Investments

Maturity Sector	Under 1 year		1 to 5 years		5 to 20 years		Over 20 years	
	Issue	Yield to maturity[a]	Issue	Yield to maturity[a]	Issue	Yield to maturity[a]	Issue	Yield to maturity[a]
Foreign	Algemene Bank Nederland 10.00—12/1/79[j]	9.30	Swiss Confederation 5.00—3/1/87[k,l]	3.20	Republic of France . . .[m] 7.00—1988[l,m]	. . .[m]	Government of United Kingdom war loan 3.50[l,n]	. . .[n]
Interest rate futures	CBT 90-day commercial paper December 1979 futures[o]	11.18	CME 1-year Treasury bill December 1979 futures[o]	9.84	CBT 8% GNMA certificate December 1979 futures	8.90	CBT 8% long-term U.S. Treasury bond December 1979 futures	8.90

[a] Except where otherwise noted, all yields to maturity are as of Jan. 1, 1979, and are expressed on a semiannual yield equivalent basis.

[b] Callable beginning in 2000.

[c] Callable beginning in 2003.

[d] GNMA pass-through securities (calculated on 30-year maturity mortgages with an average life of 8 years) and issues of international agencies of which the United States is a member are included in the federal agency category.

[e] TRAN = tax and revenue anticipation note; all tax-exempt securities yields are stated on a gross yield basis.

[f] BAN = bond anticipation note.

[g] Convertible into J. P. Morgan common stock at $80 per share.

[h] Because of a scarcity of Canadian and Yankee bond issues with maturities greater than 20 years, a Canadian issue maturing in 1998 has been included in the over-20-years maturity category even though its maturity is less than 20 years.

[i] Interest and principal payments on the European Investment Bank 7.25—5/1/84 bond are denominated in Japanese yen.

[j] Interest and principal payments on the Algemene Bank Nederland 10.00—12/1/79 are denominated in Dutch guilders.

[k] Interest and principal payments on the Swiss Confederation 5.00—3/1/87 are denominated in Swiss francs. Competent legal counsel should be consulted concerning possible restrictions on the purchase of Swiss securities by non-Swiss citizens residing outside Switzerland.

[l] Withholding taxes may be imposed on interest payments by the issuer's country. In many cases, such taxes can be credited against United States taxes. Professional tax counsel should be consulted for further advice.

[m] Interest and principal payments on the Republic of France 7.0—1988 issue are denominated in French francs and are indexed to the Paris gold bullion price as long as the value of the French franc is not defined in terms of gold (gold exchange standard).

[n] Interest payments on and the principal value of the Government of the United Kingdom war loan are denominated in pounds sterling. At a recent price of 29 3/8, the yield on the 3 1/2% war loan bonds equals 11.8 percent.

[o] CBT = Chicago Board of Trade; CME = Chicago Mercantile Exchange.

as long as the value of the French franc is not defined in terms of gold. It should be mentioned that the issues listed in Table 15-7 are not by any means intended to be recommendations; they have been assembled in this format to demonstrate one method which the investor might use at regular intervals to compare yields on the wide variety of issues in various sectors of the fixed-income securities markets.

In the execution of any fixed-income strategy, it is vitally necessary to maintain a flexible investment posture and to keep close watch over the portfolio. Particularly at major cyclical inflection points, yields, especially short-term yields, can change quickly. Most often during recent years, the fixed-income securities market environment has not permitted a dogmatic buy-and-hold approach to investing. For a large number of investors, an understanding of the interplay of forces acting on fixed-income securities prices has produced advantageous investment results. Setting strategy is an integral part of such a process.

16

Sources of Further Information

Overview

In recent years, there has been a proliferation of statistical and qualitative information on the functions, investors, and techniques of the bond and money markets. This chapter reviews a variety of these periodicals, books, articles, and other sources of information, emphasizing those which are accessible and practical in approach. In many cases, sources which themselves bring together data from a variety of other publications have been selected.

The information sources presented here have been broadly grouped by chapter within the major sections of this book: (1) Introduction to the Bond and Money Markets, (2) Forces Affecting the Bond and Money Markets, (3) Participants in the Bond and Money Markets, and (4) Investing in the Bond and Money Markets. However, many of the information sources overlap several topical areas. For example, the *Treasury Bulletin* and the Federal Reserve Board's *Flow of Funds Accounts* have each been assigned to a single group of sources, but both publications have wide applicability to a large number of chapters and themes throughout the book. It is recommended that the investor read thoroughly the entire list of sources when seeking information on a specific subject.

The investor is also encouraged to draw upon the facilities of a local business library in locating and reviewing sources. Many of the references listed here include the mailing address of the entity mentioned. When applicable, it is often worthwhile to write to the publisher and request sample materials and a price schedule (a number of the sources listed here will provide information free of charge). In general, any expenses incurred to purchase books, periodicals, or other sources designed to improve investment performance are tax-deductible. If the investor has questions in this area, competent tax counsel or the Internal Revenue Service (IRS) should be consulted.

General Sources

One of the single most thorough and thought-provoking sources of information on domestic and international financial markets is the *Annual Report* of the Bank for International Settlements, P.O. Box 262, 4001 Basel, Switzerland. In remarkably clear and concise form, this report provides an excellent survey of economic developments, money, credit, and capital market conditions, gold and other international reserve positions, the Eurocurrency and Eurocapital markets, and the balances of trade and payments for each of the major economies of the world. The Organization for Economic Cooperation and Development (OECD), through the OECD Publications Center, Suite 1207, 1750 Pennsylvania Ave. N.W., Washington, D.C. 20006, produces a number of periodicals dealing with international and domestic economic trends, financial market developments, and other important economic statistics. A full list of these periodicals and annual subscription rates can be obtained by writing to the OECD Publications Center.

The *Catalog of Publications,* published by the World Bank, 1818 H St. N.W., Washington, D.C. 20433, lists free publications and publications for sale in 17 principal topic areas, including analytical methods, economic and social data, employment and income, and finance and debt. Sources of titles in the *Catalog of Publications* include the International Bank for Reconstruction and Development (World Bank) and its affiliated or associated institutions, including the International Development Association (IDA), the International Finance Corporation (IFC), the Economic Development Institute (EDI), and the International Centre for Settlement of Investment Disputes (ICSID).

The Complete Bond Book, by David M. Darst (McGraw-Hill Book Company, 1975), contains a review of the principal features of all types of fixed-income securities. In addition, it surveys the major internal and external factors influencing investment selection, the yield on a particular security, and the overall level of interest rates. Information is also provided on the tools needed for active bond portfolio management, including yield curve analysis and basic bond-swapping techniques. *The Financial Handbook,* edited by Jules I. Bogen (The Ronald Press Company, 1964), furnishes very helpful background information on commercial banks and other lending institutions, savings banks and savings associations, and pension funds and profit sharing plans, as well as many key mechanical and organizational aspects of the securities and participants in the domestic and international capital markets.

Around August of each year, the *Institutional Investor* magazine, 488 Madison Ave., New York, New York 10022, publishes a ranking of the 300 largest investment institutions, with a breakdown of the total assets under management by equities, fixed-income securities, and cash and equivalents. This listing includes bank trust departments, investment-counseling firms, public and private pension funds, insurance and reinsurance companies, mutual fund and investment management companies, foundations, and securities brokerage and investment banking firms that also manage money. The *Financial Analysts Journal,* 1633 Broadway, New York, New York 10019, contains many well-illustrated, wide-ranging articles of interest to the investor in fixed-income securities. Both the strategic and the tactical aspects of bond investing are treated in a thorough and professional manner.

Another invaluable and highly recommended aid to fixed-income investors is *The Money Manager,* published weekly by the Bond Buyer, 1 State St. Plaza, New York, New York 10004. In addition to frequent articles on the economy, interest rate developments, and investment techniques, *The Money Manager* provides regular features on the mortgage market, tax-exempt securities, the corporate and international bond markets, U.S. government and federal agency securities, and financial futures. A more specialized source is the *Newsletter* of the Salomon Brothers Center for the Study of Financial Institutions, published by the New York University Graduate School of Business Administration, 90 Trinity Pl., New York, New York 10006. The *Newsletter* contains a wealth of information on (1) conferences and seminars, (2) sponsored research under way, (3) research projects and proposals in preparation, and (4) monographs and working papers devoted to topics in finance, economics, investing, and capital markets. Most of the publications listed in the *Newsletter* can be ordered at a nominal charge.

Introduction to the Bond and Money Markets

Perspective on Debt Markets

A History of Interest Rates, by Sidney Homer (Rutgers University Press, 1977), is essential reading for the investor who wants to gain a long-term perspective on fixed-income securities investing. With the aid of many tables, graphs, and interesting insights, the author traces the origins and development of the principal credit markets of the world. He is at his strongest in relating political and social trends to the mainstream of interest rate history, from ancient Greece and Rome through medieval Florence, Venice, and Genoa to medieval Antwerp and Lyon, whence to the Dutch Republic and England, and finally to the Western Europe and North America of modern times.

The *Annual Report* and the *Quarterly Review* of the Federal Reserve Bank of New York, 33 Liberty St., New York, New York 10045, often contain articles which assist the investor in gaining perspective about all aspects of the fixed-income securities markets. In addition, similar material is contained in the annual reports and quarterly or monthly reviews of the other 11 Federal Reserve District Banks, whose addresses can be obtained by writing to the Public Information Department of the Federal Reserve Bank of New York. *Economic Perspectives,* published by the Federal Reserve Bank of Chicago, contains a very useful and complete chronology of economic events during each previous year. In the December 1975 and April 1976 issues of *Business Review* (now called *Voice*), published by the Federal Reserve Bank of Dallas, two well-written articles describe the evolution of money, banking, and capital markets in the first 200 years of United States history.

Several very helpful documents which provide long-term perspective on the bond and money markets are available from the Publications Services Section, Division of Administrative Services, Board of Governors of the Federal Reserve System, Washington, D.C. 20551. They include *Banking and Monetary Statistics, 1914–1941* and *Banking and Monetary Statistics, 1941–1970, Annual Statistical Report, 1970–1975,* the *Federal Reserve Monthly Chart Book,* the *Historical Chart Book* (published annually), and *Capital Market Developments* (published weekly). A list of the numerous interesting Federal Reserve staff economic studies, pamphlets, and reprints can be obtained by writing to the Publications Services Section of the Federal Reserve.

Manias, Panics, and Crashes, by Charles P. Kindleberger (Basic Books, Inc., 1978), is an important contribution to the literature of economic history. While the book could have provided more analysis of the true causes of financial breakdowns, it is an instructive and enjoyable account of the market forces and personalities involved in numerous major financial crises in the post-Renaissance period. *How the World Works,* by Jude Wanniski (Basic Books, Inc., 1978), is a wide-ranging discourse on many contemporary economic issues. The provocative nature of many of the points and conclusions in the book will cause the reader to rethink many time-honored financial concepts. *The Great American Bond Market,* by Sidney Homer (Dow Jones-Irwin, Inc., 1978), contains 27 speeches delivered by the author on the bond market and bond investment techniques between 1961 and 1977. Some excellent historical insights, as well as trenchant commentary on the effects of inflation and politics on the bond market and bond investment strategy, are included in the book.

The Analysis of Debt Statistics

The *Bank Credit Analyst,* published monthly by Monetary Research Ltd., Butterfield Building, Front St., Hamilton, Bermuda, provides a thorough overview of the domestic and international monetary and credit conditions affecting the prices of debt and equity securities, currencies, and gold. The organization of this publication is extremely practical, the writing is logical and lucid, and the publication often contains special articles or analytical features which examine in depth a specific sector of the capital markets or which introduce specific techniques and concepts for the analysis of aggregate debt and equity trends.

The *Federal Reserve Bulletin,* published monthly, is available from the Publications Services Section, Division of Administrative Services, Board of Governors of the Federal Reserve System, Washington, D.C. 20551. It contains a great deal of useful information in a clear format on monetary and credit aggregates, interest rates, Federal Reserve policy instruments, commercial bank assets and liabilities, short-term financial markets, federal fiscal and financing operations, long-term securities markets and corporate financing, mortgage financing, consumer installment credit, flows of funds in United States credit markets, and international transactions, including short-term and long-term liabilities to and claims on foreigners, foreign official accounts, and numerous other foreign data.

Around June of each year, the Bond Buyer, 1 State St. Plaza, New York, New York 10004, publishes a comprehensive series of statistics on the tax-exempt bond markets, including the total volume of state and municipal borrowing in the aggregate and by type of issue, the trend of tax-exempt interest rates, total debt outstanding by state and by level of government, election results on bond issues, statutory interest rate ceilings of state and local bonds, per capita state and local tax burdens, and numerous other important data and ratios. The publication is called *Statistics on State and Local Government Finance,* and it also contains several large tables with important information on taxable as well as tax-exempt debt going back to 1929. One of these tables is reproduced in Chapter 3 of this book, as Table 3-2.

Moody's Investors Service, Inc., 99 Church St., New York, New York 10007, publishes a series of voluminous but often indispensable manuals, each of which is devoted to one or two broad sectors of the capital market (such as banks and finance, industrials, municipals and governments, public utilities, and transportation). They contain an enormous amount of aggregate data and other information on debt securities in the special features section of each manual. Two of the largest commercial banks in New York publish highly readable periodicals which frequently contain articles devoted to trends in debt markets. The Citibank Economics Department, 399 Park Ave., New York, New York 10022, produces the *Monthly Economic Letter,* and

Morgan Guaranty Trust Company of New York, 23 Wall St., New York, New York 10015, issues the *Morgan Guaranty Survey.*

Forces Affecting the Bond and Money Markets

The History and Mechanics of Price Level Changes

Business Conditions Digest, published monthly by the U.S. Department of Commerce, Bureau of Economic Analysis (BEA), and available from the Superintendent of Documents, Government Printing Office, Washington, D.C. 20402, contains charts and data on cyclical indicators which have been singled out as leaders, coinciders, or laggers based on their general conformity to cyclical movements in aggregate economic activity. These indicators often prove useful in forecasting, measuring, and interpreting short-term fluctuations in aggregate economic activity. In addition, the *Business Conditions Digest* provides much useful data on (1) selected components of the national income and product accounts, (2) wages, prices, and productivity, (3) the labor force, employment, and unemployment, (4) federal, state, and local government activities, (5) United States international transactions, and (6) selected economic comparisons with major foreign countries.

The Federal Reserve Bank of Richmond has published a very helpful study of the design of price indices called *Measuring Price Changes.* Written by William E. Wallace and William E. Cullison, this booklet discusses both the conceptual and the statistical problems involved in creating price indices, with particular emphasis on the Laspeyres and Paasche methods as applied to the consumer price index, the producer price index, and the GNP deflator. The booklet also has an extensive list of references on the mechanics of price level changes. *Forty Centuries of Wage and Price Controls,* by Robert L. Schuettinger and Eamonn F. Butler (Heritage Foundation, 1979), provides much interesting background on governmental attempts to control wages and prices. The Bureau of Labor Statistics (BLS), 200 Constitution Avenue N.W., Washington, D.C. 20210, publishes a number of monthly reports, bulletins, handbooks, and pamphlets on the consumer price index, the producer price index, and other topics relating to wages, productivity, and employment. A listing of available publications, as well as selected regular press releases on the price indices prepared by the Bureau, can be obtained by writing to the BLS in Washington.

National Economic Trends, prepared by the Federal Reserve Bank of St. Louis, P.O. Box 442, St. Louis, Missouri 63166, contains many useful graphs and rate-of-change data covering total employment, the unemployment rate, the consumer price index, the producer price index (both for industrial commodities and for farm products, processed foods, and feeds), industrial production, personal income, retail sales, productivity, compensation and labor costs, personal consumption and the gross national product (both in current and in constant dollars), the GNP price deflator, gross private domestic investment, government purchases of goods and services, disposable personal income, and corporate profits.

The Causes and Effects of Inflation and Deflation

Many popular books and academic texts on economics contain chapters on the origins of inflation and, to a much lesser degree, on the origins of deflation. Very few current practical books are in print on the effects of inflation and particularly on the effects of deflation. *Corporate Bond Quality and Investor Experience,* by W. Braddock Hickman (Princeton University Press, 1958), is the classic study of the behavior of bond prices on all corporate debt securities issued between January 1900 and January 1944. Although not an exciting book for the average investor to read, this work reveals some extremely significant findings about the cyclical and secular performance of corporate bonds across the full spectrum of quality rating classifications. Most interesting are the conclusions concerning the realized return over a lengthy time frame from low-grade bonds compared with high-grade bonds, viewed from the perspective of the holding period of the investor.

The *Monthly Review* of the Federal Reserve Bank of St. Louis, P.O. Box 442, St. Louis, Missouri 63166, often contains stimulating articles on the subjects of inflation and deflation. In 1959 E. W. Axe & Co., Inc., 400 Benedict Ave., Tarrytown, New York, published a most interesting booklet entitled *Inflation and the Investor.* This booklet contains an extremely detailed summary of the effects of inflation and deflation on the prices of stocks, bonds, and commodities. *Business Week* of May 22, 1978, contained a lengthy special report, "The Great Inflation Machine." This is an excellent analysis of many of the principal reasons for the high underlying rate of inflation in the United States during the 1970s.

A most interesting perspective on inflation and deflation during long periods of history is provided in *The Reigning Error: The Crisis of World Inflation,* by William Rees-Mogg (Hamish Hamilton Press, London, 1975). An excellent and detailed account of the German hyperinflation of 1920 to 1923 and its effects on various classes of investments can be found in *The Economics of Inflation,* by Constantino Bresciani-Turroni (Augustus M. Kelley, Publishers, 1937 and 1968). The stabilization of the currency in Germany after the hyperinflation is described in *The Stabilization of the Mark,* by Hjalmar Schacht (originally published in 1927; reissued in 1978 by Arno Press). *How to Cope with the Developing Financial Crisis,* by Ashby Bladen (McGraw-Hill Book Company, 1980) provides a review of the reasons for the vast expansion of debt in the United States and other countries during the 1960s and the 1970s. The book is particularly clear in its presentation of the effects of inflation on the financial system.

Financial Intermediation in the Credit and Capital Markets

Among the most powerful tools for analyzing the investment behavior of capital market participants are the Flow of Funds Accounts developed and expanded by the Flow of Funds Section, Division of Research and Statistics, Board of Governors of the Federal Reserve System, Washington, D.C. 20551. From the Flow of Funds Section, the investor can obtain (1) *Introduction to Flow of Funds* (published in February 1975), which describes the concept and organization of the Flow of Funds Accounts; (2) *Flow of Funds Accounts, 1945–1972* (published in August 1973); (3) *Flow of Funds Accounts, 1946–1975* (published in December 1976); and (4) annual data for the preceding 10 years and current quarterly data, seasonally adjusted and unadjusted, on total funds flows and assets and liabilities (published around the middle of the second month following the quarter reported). Revisions of previously released annual data are usually reported together with the second-quarter issue of each year's series.

The Federal Reserve Bank of Richmond has issued and periodically revised a very useful publication called *Nonbank Financial Institutions.* Discussion is devoted to the origins, operations, and objectives of nine different groups of nonbank financial institutions. *Credit and Capital Markets,* published annually (usually in late February) by the Economics Division of Bankers Trust Company, P.O. Box 318, Church St. Station, New York, New York 10015, provides much useful historical and projective information about the sources and uses of short- and long-term funds within the major sectors of the economy. In addition, it contains comments about the outlook for interest rates and credit conditions during the coming year. For a very long-term overview of the major suppliers and users of capital in the United States since the turn of the century, the investor is directed to *Financial Intermediaries in the American Economy since 1900,* by Raymond U. Goldsmith (Princeton University Press, 1958).

In a lively, penetrating, and interesting format, the *Institutional Investor,* 488 Madison Ave., New York, New York 10022, reviews many of the current issues facing various types of investing institutions. It is a valuable chronicle of present and future trends in the investment industry, not only from the investor's point of view, but also from that of securities brokerage and investment banking firms as well. *Institutional Investing,* by Charles D. Ellis (Dow Jones-Irwin, Inc., 1971), describes the decision-making processes utilized in the management of mutual funds, pension funds, trust funds, and endowments, with particular emphasis on the organizational, analytical, and policy-setting aspects of the subject. Although the examples in the book are derived from the era of the 1960s and the very early 1970s, many of its observations have held true over a long time frame.

Macroanalysis of Credit Market Instruments

In this book, the principal line of analysis of credit market instruments focuses on their chief holders and distribution patterns (a *macro* analysis) rather than examining the specific features and terms of each type of instrument (a *micro* analysis). The sources enumerated here have been selected with this approach in mind. *Studies in the National Balance Sheet of the United States,* by Raymond U. Goldsmith, Robert E. Lipsey, and Morris Mendelson (Princeton University Press, 1963), provides year-end totals for most major investor sectors and credit market instruments (with some differences from the classifications utilized in the Federal Reserve Flow of Funds Accounts) for the period from 1900 through 1958. For the period prior to the mid-1940s, no other source provides similar data, which are extremely useful to analysts wishing to trace the development of the capital markets in the United States during the first half of the twentieth century.

The Report and the Staff Studies (Parts 1 and 2) of the *Joint Treasury–Federal Reserve Study of the U.S. Government Securities Market* (Publications Services, Division of Administrative Services, Board of Governors of the Federal Reserve System, Washington, D.C. 20551), published in stages in 1969, 1970, and 1971, contain much informative material on the investors in and the market for governmental securities of all types and maturities. Especially interesting is Part 1 of the Staff Studies, which discusses the activities of the Federal Reserve account, of government securities dealers, and of institutional investors in governmental issues.

The Government Securities Market, by Ira O. Scott, Jr. (McGraw-Hill Book Company, 1965), is particularly effective in describing the day-to-day activities of many principal investors in governmental issues. Although the character, size, and major investor groups in the U.S. government and federal agency securities markets have altered greatly since the mid-1960s, this compact treatise is noteworthy for its methodology, organization, and blend of practicality with theory. The arrangement and contents of the bibliography are impressive. *The Money Market: Myth, Reality and Practice,* by Marcia Stigum (Dow Jones-Irwin, Inc., 1978), reviews most of the instruments traded in the domestic and Eurodollar money markets. The book is the result of interviews with more than 200 money market participants and contains much practical information on how brokers, dealers, and investors view and use the market for money market instruments.

Participants in the Bond and Money Markets

The Investment Behavior of Households, the Business Sector, Governmental Bodies, and International Entities

Some excellent sources of information on the activities of bank trust departments are their published annual reports. Two bank trust departments which consistently publish informative reports of their investment performance and other data of interest to investors are Citibank, N.A., 399 Park Ave., New York, New York 10022, and the Trust and Investment Division of Morgan Guaranty Trust Company, 9 West 57th St., New York, New York 10019. *Trusts and Estates* magazine, published by Communication Channels, Inc., 461 Eighth Avenue, New York, New York 10001, contains a plethora of articles about the management and administration of personal trusts. Two useful sources of information on the activities and aggregate assets of foundations are the Council on Foundations, 1828 L St. N.W., Washington, D.C. 20036, and the Foundation Center, 888 Seventh Ave., New York, New York 10019. The latter organization prepares numerous detailed publications on foundations, including the *National Data Book* and *The Foundation Directory.*

The Investment Counsel Association of America, 127 East 59th St., New York, New York 10022, regularly publishes a directory of the names, addresses, and telephone numbers of its member investment-counseling firms, together with a listing of the names of the firms' partners or principals and associates. Information on these firms can be obtained by writing to them directly or by checking their Securities and Exchange Commission (SEC) file (if registered with the SEC).

Source Securities, 70 Pine St., New York, New York 10005, has compiled from SEC computer tapes a most useful listing, by state and foreign country, of the more than 4000 investment advisers registered with the SEC. By following the instructions listed in the introduction to the directory, it is possible to obtain an adviser's SEC file, which includes the names, educational and professional background, and prior business experience, but not the performance record, of the principals of any registered investment advisory or money management firm.

Statistics of Income, published by the IRS and distributed by the Superintendent of Documents, Government Printing Office, Washington, D.C. 20402, contains much data on the financial status and investments of the business sector. Numerous other texts on managerial finance describe the investment limitations and practices of businesses. Among the best of these books are *Principles of Financial Management,* by Ward S. Curran (McGraw-Hill Book Company, 1970); *Basic Business Finance,* by Pearson Hunt, Charles M. Williams, and Gordon Donaldson (Richard D. Irwin, Inc., 1966); *Financial*

Management and Policy, by James C. Van Horne (Prentice-Hall, Inc., 1974); *Managerial Finance,* by J. Fred Weston and Eugene F. Brigham (Holt, Rinehart and Winston, Inc., 1972); *Financial Management,* by Robert W. Johnson (Allyn and Bacon, Inc., 1971); and *Business Finance: Theory and Management,* by Stephen H. Archer and Charles A. D'Ambrosio (The Macmillan Company, 1972).

A helpful source of information on closed-end investment companies is the Association of Publicly Traded Investment Funds, 666 Fifth Ave., New York, New York 10019. At regular intervals this association publishes a brochure listing all member funds, their current investment assets, and their investment objectives. Another thorough overview of closed-end investment funds is *The Investor's Guide to Closed-End Funds: The Herzfeld Hedge,* by Thomas J. Herzfeld (McGraw-Hill Book Company, 1980).

The *Treasury Bulletin,* published monthly by the U.S. Treasury Department and made available for sale by the Superintendent of Documents, Government Printing Office, Washington, D.C. 20402, contains abundant data on federal fiscal operations, the financial accounts of the U.S. Treasury, the quantity of coin and currency in circulation, federal financing operations, the ownership of Treasury and government-sponsored agency securities, the international financial position of the United States, and capital flows into and out of the country. Also useful is the *Annual Report of the Secretary of the Treasury,* available each year from the Government Printing Office. *Governmental Finances,* compiled by the U.S. Bureau of the Census and distributed by the Government Printing Office, encompasses a great deal of statistical information on the finances and investments of the general funds of state and local governments.

Some excellent sources of information on the investment activities of federally sponsored credit agencies and mortgage pools are the annual reports, brochures, and other literature which they make available to investors. These publications can be obtained by writing to (1) the Federal Home Loan Bank Board, 1700 G St. N.W., Washington, D.C. 20552; (2) the Fiscal Agency for the Farm Credit Banks (which manages many of the financing programs for the Banks for Cooperatives, the Federal Intermediate Credit Banks, and the Federal Land Banks), 90 William St., New York, New York 10038; (3) the Federal National Mortgage Association, 3900 Wisconsin Avenue N.W., Washington, D.C. 20016; (4) the Government National Mortgage Association, 451 Seventh St. S.W., Washington, D.C. 20410; and (5) the Federal Home Loan Mortgage Corporation, 1700 G St. N.W., Washington, D.C. 20006.

For a detailed discussion of the investment practices of the Federal Reserve System, with particular emphasis on how its portfolio and open-market operations influence bank reserves and securities prices, it is worthwhile to consult *Open Market Operations,* by Paul Meek (Federal Reserve Bank of New

York, 1973), and *Modern Money Mechanics: A Workbook on Deposits, Currency, and Bank Reserves,* by Dorothy M. Nichols (Federal Reserve Bank of Chicago, 1975), both of which are extremely clear in explanations and practical examples. In addition, the *Quarterly Review* (usually the spring issue) of the Federal Reserve Bank of New York, 33 Liberty St., New York, New York 10045, generally contains a detailed study of the open-market operations conducted within the framework of the monetary policies practiced during the previous year. A thorough treatment of the holdings of and transactions in U.S. Treasury and federal agency securities by the Federal Reserve System is contained in the April 1978 issue of the Federal Reserve Bank of Kansas City's *Economic Review.*

Three major New York–based commercial banks publish excellent monthly reviews of international economic and capital markets conditions. *World Financial Markets* is published by Morgan Guaranty Trust Company of New York, 23 Wall St., New York, New York 10015; *International Finance* is produced by the Economic Research Division, Chase Manhattan Bank, N.A., 1 Chase Manhattan Plaza, New York, New York 10005; and *International Economic Letter* is published by Citibank, N.A., 399 Park Ave., New York, New York 10022.

The International Monetary Fund (IMF), 19th and H Sts. N.W., Washington, D.C. 20431, compiles a most useful publication, *International Financial Statistics.* For each IMF member country, this very detailed reference work provides monthly data (and a yearly supplement) on central bank reserves, gross national product, interest rates, exports and imports, and many other financial and demographic statistics. The *Annual Report* of the IMF is also an extremely interesting review of the international financial scene. The *International Letter,* published by the Federal Reserve Bank of Chicago, Public Information Center, P.O. Box 834, Chicago, Illinois 60690, contains quite a bit of timely information on international investment and capital flows both to and from the United States.

The Investment Behavior of Commercial Banks and Thrift Institutions

Each year the Federal Deposit Insurance Corporation (FDIC), 550 Seventeenth St. N.W., Washington, D.C. 20429, publishes *Assets and Liabilities,* which reports data for commercial banks and mutual savings banks. This publication furnishes a plentiful series of aggregate year-end information on total loans, securities positions, cash holdings, deposits, equity capital, and selected income and expense data of commercial banks grouped by insurance status, class of bank, state, size of bank, and Federal Reserve district. Similar statistics are provided for nondeposit trust companies and mutual savings banks. Spring and fall call report data on commercial banks, nondeposit trust companies, and mutual savings banks are available upon written request to the Bank Statistics and Financial Analysis Section, Division of Management Systems and Economic Analysis, at the FDIC.

Investment Portfolio Management in the Commercial Bank, by Roger A. Lyon (Rutgers University Press, 1960), and *The Management of Bank Funds,* by Roland I. Robinson (McGraw-Hill Book Company, 1962), although somewhat dated, contain much useful intelligence on the factors influencing the investment policies of commercial banks. *The Bankers' Handbook,* edited by William H. Baughn and Charls E. Walker (Dow Jones-Irwin, Inc., 1966), includes 87 chapters on the banking industry, with detailed treatment of such topics as the financial management of a bank, investments and securities markets, credit policy and administration, international banking, and bank regulation and supervision. The Association of Reserve City Bankers, 135 South LaSalle St., Chicago, Illinois 60603, has published a series of more than 20 monographs on commercial banking. The monographs, many of which are devoted to the investment practices of commercial banks, are detailed and quite practical in orientation.

Two extremely valuable sources of information and commentary are produced annually by associations which group together the two major categories of thrift institutions. The *Savings and Loan Fact Book,* published by the United States League of Savings Associations, 111 E. Wacker Drive, Chicago, Illinois 60601, contains important descriptions of and data about the function, structure, and environment of savings and loan associations. The activities, financial structure, and organization of mutual savings banks are thoroughly profiled in the *National Fact Book of Mutual Savings Banking,* produced by the National Association of Mutual Savings Banks, 200 Park Ave., New York, New York 10017.

The National Credit Union Administration (NCUA), 2025 M St. N.W., Washington, D.C. 20456, produces monthly reports on the assets and liabilities of credit unions. In addition, NCUA can make available detailed information on the goals and operations of credit unions in the United States.

The Investment Behavior of Insurance Companies and Pension Funds

One of the most detailed and authoritative sources of information on the life insurance industry is the *Life Insurance Fact Book.* It is published annually by the American Council of Life Insurance, 1850 K St. N.W., Washington, D.C. 20006, and it includes data and commentary on life insurance ownership, benefit payments, assets and investments, and a multitude of related topics. The annual editions of *Best's Fire and Casualty Aggregates and*

Averages, published by Alfred M. Best Company, Inc., Oldwick, New Jersey 08858, are the major source of data on the financial condition, ratings, underwriting experience, and investments of the property-casualty insurance companies.

Investment Policies of Life Insurance Companies, by Lawrence D. Jones (Division of Research, Graduate School of Business Administration, Harvard University, 1968), is a monumental study of the process by which life insurance companies make their portfolio selections. The book not only describes the basic investment objectives of life insurance companies and the legal and tax considerations which condition their investment practices, it explores the most important determinants of their investment decisions. Special emphasis is given to the role played by expectations of future investment opportunities, interest rate levels, and investable cash inflows. Another helpful source of information on the worldwide life and non-life insurance industry is *Experiodica,* published by Swiss Reinsurance Company, Mythenquai 50, 8022 Zurich, Switzerland.

Information on the aggregate investments of state and local government employee retirement systems is contained in *Governmental Finances,* published by the U.S. Census Bureau and distributed by the Superintendent of Documents, Government Printing Office, Washington, D.C. 20402. Private pension funds' investment holdings are detailed in the *Statistical Bulletin* of the SEC, also distributed by the Government Printing Office.

Each year, *Institutional Investor* magazine, 488 Madison Ave., New York, New York 10022, publishes a *Pensions Directory,* profiling the size, location, persons responsible for asset management supervision, and internal or external managers of the 350 largest corporate pension funds, the 50 state pension funds, and the 35 largest county and municipal pension funds. In addition, the directory contains a list of pension consultants and the services offered by each. Two very informative magazines on developments in the pension field are *Pensions and Investments,* published by Crain Communications, 740 Rush St., Chicago, Illinois 60611, and *Pension World,* published by Communication Channels, Inc., 461 Eighth Ave., New York, New York 10001.

The Investment Behavior of Finance Companies, Real Estate Investment Trusts, Open-End Investment Companies, Money Market Funds, and Security Brokers and Dealers

The Board of Governors of the Federal Reserve System, Washington, D.C. 20551, publishes a quinquennial census, supplemented by monthly surveys, of the investment position of finance companies. Quarterly data on the financial condition of the REIT industry is available from the National Association of Real Estate Investment Trusts, 1101 Seventeenth St. N.W., Washington, D.C. 20036.

Each year, the Investment Company Institute, 1775 K St. N.W., Washington, D.C. 20006, produces the extremely interesting and detailed *Mutual Fund Fact Book.* This book describes the growth, development, management, regulation, taxation, and asset structure of the mutual fund industry. The Public Information Department of the Investment Company Institute also publishes *Mutual Fund News,* a regular overview of important developments affecting mutual funds. Much information on money market funds is contained in the *Mutual Fund Fact Book.* For more data and descriptive material on these funds, a highly respected source is *Donoghue's Money Fund Report,* P.O. Box 450, Holliston, Massachusetts 07160.

The Association of Publicly Traded Investment Funds, Information Bureau, 666 Fifth Ave., New York, New York 10019, publishes a brochure listing all member funds, their current investment assets, and their investment objectives. A similar brochure covering all types of no-load funds is available from the No-Load Mutual Fund Association, Inc., Valley Forge, Pennsylvania 19481. Around the third quarter of each year, *Forbes* magazine, 60 Fifth Ave., New York, New York 10011, produces an annual survey of the investment company industry. This survey shows the investment results and total assets of virtually all of the major investment companies in the United States.

Investment Companies, published yearly by Arthur Wiesenberger & Company, 61 Broadway, New York, New York 10006, reviews the historical investment performance, strategic goals, and management details of most mutual funds. The annual reports of the leading security brokers and dealers provide a large amount of useful information (including the total size of their securities position holdings, in the financial review section of their annual reports) on the asset structure and major developments affecting the securities industry. Two other good weekly sources of information on the industry are *Securities Week,* published by McGraw-Hill, Inc., 1221 Avenue of the Americas, New York, New York 10020, and the *Wall Street Letter,* produced by Institutional Investor Systems, Inc., 488 Madison Ave., New York, New York 10022. The *Annual Report* of the SEC, Washington, D.C. 20549, contains important data and commentary on the activities of security brokers and dealers.

The *Joint Treasury–Federal Reserve Study of the U.S. Government Securities Market* and accompanying Staff Studies, Parts 1 and 2 (mentioned previously in the sources section on "Macroanalysis of Credit Market Instruments"), contain a very comprehensive review of the activities and attitudes of security brokers and dealers in their investment and market-making functions in debt securities.

Investing in the Bond and Money Markets

Yield and Price Relationships for Fixed-Income Securities;
Graphical Analysis of Bond Yields and Prices

One of the best ways to plumb the subtleties of yield and price relationships for various types of fixed-income securities is to peruse several of the yield books published by the Financial Publishing Company, 28 Brookline St., Boston, Massachusetts 02215. Upon request, this company will provide a catalog of available publications for all types of bonds, mortgage securities, and other fixed-income instruments. In addition to a wide range of yield tables and charts, the Financial Publishing Company has a team of consultants in financial mathematics who have developed numerous creative and efficient solutions to problems in specialized areas of the bond world, including currency considerations, bond prepayment and extension options, and other price calculations.

An extremely penetrating analysis of many of the practical and mathematical fine points of bond yields and prices is contained in *Inside the Yield Book,* by Sidney Homer and Martin L. Liebowitz (Prentice-Hall, Inc., and the New York Institute of Finance, 1972). This book delves deeply yet creatively into some of the most fundamental and some of the most sophisticated aspects of interest, bond yield and price calculations, and swaps. Martin L. Liebowitz extended several of these concepts to a high degree of refinement in a series of articles which appeared in the spring 1975 issue of *The Journal of Portfolio Management* and in *The Money Manager* magazine of July 25, 1977, August 1, 1977, and November 7, 14, and 21, 1977.

Moody's Bond Survey, published weekly by Moody's Investors Service, Inc., 99 Church St., New York, New York 10007, contains an exceptionally useful section which provides commentary and very legible charts on yield spreads between various types and categories of fixed-income securities. Another detailed source of information on yield spreads is *A Perspective on Yields,* published by the Chicago Board of Trade, LaSalle at Jackson, Chicago, Illinois 60604. This unusually helpful booklet has more than 35 charts which compare various yield series with one another and with other indices such as the adjusted moving average of change in the consumer price index.

The Dynamic Management of Bond Portfolios; The
Development and Implementation of Fixed-Income Investment
Strategy

The Journal of Portfolio Management, published quarterly by Institutional Investor Systems, Inc., 488 Madison Ave., New York, New York 10022, contains many useful and pragmatic articles devoted to the management of fixed-income and equity funds. One of the best and most complete sources of information on historical yield relationships is *An Analytical Record of Yields and Yield Spreads,* published by Salomon Brothers, 1 New York Plaza, New York, New York 10004. This invaluable aid to the prospective bond swapper probes and subjects an extremely wide variety of securities and interest rates to comparative scrutiny. A number of clear charts depicting many yields and yield relationships are available on separate loose sheets.

Inter-Bond Services Ltd., London, England, produces a very useful and complete monthly booklet, *AIBD Quotations and Yields,* which contains prices, yields, and a host of other details on Eurobond issues. These data, also published in the *Financial Times* newspaper at the close of each month, are based on quotations obtained on the last business day of each month from market-maker members of the Association of International Bond Dealers (AIBD), which was founded in 1969 and which by 1980 comprised more than 450 institutions in some 27 countries.

Several publications furnish regular and cogent analyses of current conditions in the Eurobond markets. The Monday issues of the *Financial Times, The Wall Street Journal,* and the *International Herald Tribune* contain lucid reviews of market developments and other insightful information. Periodicals covering developments in the Eurobond and Yankee bond financial markets include *Euromoney,* the *FT Euromarket Letter,* the *International Insider,* and the *Agefi International Bondletter and Eurocurrency Financial Review.* The *Financial Times* and the *International Herald Tribune* also publish regular in-depth surveys of the Eurobond markets which are included as supplementary sections in these two newspapers.

Two excellent sources of monthly information on all types of domestic bond yields, prices, ratings, sinking-fund and call terms, interest payment dates, and other information are the *Bond Guide,* published by Standard & Poor's, 345 Hudson St., New York, New York 10014, and *Moody's Bond Record,* compiled by Moody's Investors Service, Inc., 99 Church St., New York, New York 10007. Moody's also produces the *International Bond Review,* which contains rating information, commentary, call notices, and other information on Canadian and Yankee bonds and Eurobonds, as well as certain related short-term instruments.

One of the most comprehensive and up-to-date sources of statistical information on currency movements is *Pick's Currency Yearbook,* published annually. It contains a review and appraisal of more than 100 major currencies and accessory units, 40 minor moneys, and gold bullion and coin prices. Resident and nonresident transferability regulations and domestic currency restrictions are also discussed. Some of the clearest charts on the development of currency exchange rates, as well as on the value of bonds and stocks denominated in various currencies, are produced by Bank Julius Baer & Co. Ltd., Bahnhofstrasse 36, 8001 Zurich, Switzerland. Strauss, Turnbull & Co.,

Moorgate Pl., London EC2R 6HR, England, has published a thought-provoking and helpful series of studies called *Points of No Return in International Bond Markets,* which quantify the investment risks and rewards derived from possible future interest rate levels and currency exchange rates.

The Federal Reserve Bank of St. Louis, P.O. Box 442, St. Louis, Missouri 63166, publishes a series of charts called *U.S. Financial Data.* This publication can be quite helpful in summarizing current market conditions as background for the development and implementation of investment strategy. It contains charts showing the recent development of the adjusted monetary base (consisting of member bank reserves at the Federal Reserve Banks, currency held by the public and in the vaults of commercial banks, and an adjustment for reserve requirement ratio changes); total adjusted Federal Reserve credit; the money stock plus net time deposits (commonly known as M_2); total demand deposits plus currency and coin held by the nonbank public (commonly known as M_1); net time deposits at all commercial banks; certificates of deposit of large commercial banks; business and commercial loans of large commercial banks; and the currency component and the demand deposit component of the money stock. *U.S. Financial Data* also shows recent yield levels on 90-day certificates of deposit, prime 4- to 6-month commercial paper, prime bankers' acceptances, corporate Aaa bonds, federal funds, 3-month Treasury bills, 6-month Treasury bills, 1-year Treasury bills, 3- to 5-year Treasury securities, and long-term Treasury securities. Reviewing such data and charts is an essential part of the preparation process for setting fixed-income investment strategy.

The Theory and Practice of Bond Portfolio Strategy, edited by Peter L. Bernstein (Institutional Investor Systems, Inc., 1977), provides much modern and practical material on both the environment for bond management and the techniques of bond investing. *The Investment Manager's Handbook* (Dow Jones-Irwin, Inc., 1980) contains numerous articles submitted by over 40 practitioners in several interesting segments of the institutional investment arena.

Index